D1561279

Men's Gender Role Conflict

Men's Gender Role Conflict

PSYCHOLOGICAL COSTS, CONSEQUENCES, AND AN AGENDA FOR CHANGE

JAMES M. O'NEIL

American Psychological Association

Washington, DC

Published by
American Psychological Association
750 First Street, NE
Washington, DC 20002
www.apa.org

To order
APA Order Department
P.O. Box 92984
Washington, DC 20090-2984
Tel: (800) 374-2721; Direct: (202) 336-5510
Fax: (202) 336-5502; TDD/TTY: (202) 336-6123
Online: www.apa.org/pubs/books
E-mail: order@apa.org

In the U.K., Europe, Africa, and the Middle East, copies may be ordered from
American Psychological Association
3 Henrietta Street
Covent Garden, London
WC2E 8LU England

Typeset in Goudy by Circle Graphics, Inc., Columbia, MD

Printer: Edwards Brothers Malloy, Ann Arbor, MI
Cover Designer: Minker Design, Sarasota, FL

The opinions and statements published are the responsibility of the authors, and such opinions and statements do not necessarily represent the policies of the American Psychological Association.

Library of Congress Cataloging-in-Publication Data

O'Neil, James M.
   Men's gender role conflict : psychological costs, consequences, and an agenda for change / by James M. O'Neil.
      pages cm
   Includes bibliographical references and index.
   ISBN 978-1-4338-1818-9 — ISBN 1-4338-1818-3   1. Men—Psychology. 2. Masculinity. 3. Sex role. I. Title.
   BF692.5.O5966 2015
   155.3'32—dc23
                                      2014013551

British Library Cataloguing-in-Publication Data
A CIP record is available from the British Library.

Printed in the United States of America
First Edition

http://dx.doi.org/10.1037/14501-000

I dedicate this book to my son, Kirill James O'Neil, and all men and women who actively commit themselves to deconstructing restrictive gender roles in hopes of creating a more humane society free from sexism and other oppressions.

CONTENTS

ACKNOWLEDGMENTS

With a research program that spans four decades, I have many people to thank. I mention here those individuals who have been the most critical in developing the gender role conflict (GRC) research program. A perusal of the References section is the best way to acknowledge everyone, but there are a few who deserve special mention.

My mentors played a huge role in my development and shaped my desire to contribute to research and the clinical practice of psychology. Thomas M. Magoon, John Holland, and Larry Wrightsman were instrumental in helping me develop my confidence to do research and make a contribution to the field. Tom taught me about innovation and introduced me to the field of counseling psychology and how to use the scientific method to make change. He showed me by his example how to make a difference in people's lives using psychology. John supported me when I was working on his Self-Directed Search and wrote a promotion letter in which he said that I "should spend more time developing my own ideas." That one sentence encouraged me to create knowledge, something I had never seriously considered doing. Larry spent time with me and told me that my GRC ideas would have a "short shelf life" unless I measured them. He taught me how to measure GRC. Without his support and generosity, there would not have been a GRC research program. These men lived positive masculinity long before it became popular, and for their many gifts I am very thankful. There were other mentors, some I met briefly and others only through their writings or personal presence. Pierre Teilhard de Chardin, Mahatma Gandhi, Daniel Berrigan, Matthew Fox, Robert F. Kennedy, and the Jesuits taught me about social justice, non-violence, and the importance of activism as part of one's spiritual journey.

In the early days of my career there were only a handful of students and colleagues who believed in what I was doing. Glenn Good, when he was at the University of Missouri (he is now at the University of Florida) was a prime mover for the GRC research, and together we cosponsored, for 17 consecutive years, a symposium at the Annual Conventions of the American Psychological Association (APA) that focused specifically on GRC research. Our teamwork with those convention programs, Glenn's research expertise, and his personal support were critical in developing GRC research in the 1980s and 1990s. Jim Mahalik at Boston College also did seminal research on GRC in the 1990s and, along with Clara Hill (University of Maryland), stimulated a special section on GRC in the *Journal of Counseling Psychology*. This made GRC nationally visible, and so Jim and Clara were instrumental in promoting GRC research when there was still inertia around men's issues nationally. Jim has now developed his own scale, the highly respected Conformity to Masculine Norms Inventory.

There are so many people to thank who have made contributions that it is difficult to single out individuals. Chris Blazina (Tennessee State University) and Stewart Pisecco (University of Houston) did the innovative work in developing the Gender Role Conflict Scale for Adolescents, and Stephen Wester and Lindsey Danforth (University of Wisconsin–Milwaukee) and David Vogel (Iowa State University) did all the empiricism on the Gender Role Conflict Scale Short Form. With colleagues, Jay Kim developed the Korean version of the Gender Role Conflict Scale, and Chunju Zhang and colleagues created the Chinese Gender Role Conflict Scale Short Form. These very talented researchers expanded the utility of the GRC construct and extended it to more diverse groups.

A number of colleagues believed that GRC had therapeutic utility and published articles about the importance of using GRC in therapy. They include Gary Brooks (Baylor University), Sam Cochran (University of Iowa), Fred Rabinowitz (University of Redlands), Matt Englar-Carlson (California State University, Fullerton), Mark Stevens (California State University, Northridge), Mark Kiselica (College of New Jersey), and Louise Silverstein (Yeshiva University). There have been others who developed research programs or a series of important studies on GRC that built momentum in the field. They include Jonathan Schwartz, Stephen Wester, Ryon McDermott,

David Vogel, Matt Breiding, Jim Mahalik, Aaron Rochlen, Jay Wade, Jesse Steinfeldt, Dawn Syzmanski, Glenn Good, Puncky and Mary Heppner, Michael Addis, Jim Rogers, Bob Rando, Ann Fischer, Will Liu, Marty Heesacker, Ron Levant, Aaron Blashill, Joel Wong, David Tokar, and Jay Kim, to name a few. In the early days, there were colleagues who gave me support to keep pursuing what GRC might imply, including Chris Kilmartin, Murray Scher, Puncky Heppner, and David Braverman, and they still provide support and guidance. All my colleagues in the Society for the Psychological Study of Men and Masculinity (Division 51 of APA) have been very supportive of my ideas, and there are more than 50 additional colleagues who should be thanked, if space allowed.

Writing this book was a challenge, and at times I was uncertain about how to proceed with the conceptualizations. Numerous colleagues came to my rescue with their advice and guidance: Marty Heesacker, Stephen Snowden, Chris Liang, Jay Wade, Chris Kilmartin, Stephen Wester, David Vogel, Andrew Smiler, Matt Breiding, Will Liu, Charles Field, and David Becker. Each of them, in their own way, gave collegial support and advice and corrected some of my loose thinking on critical topics. In addition, Robyn Denke, my graduate assistant for 2013–2014, provided a scholarly critique on every chapter, and her advice really made a difference in the closing months when there were still conceptual gaps in numerous chapters.

I was blessed with many skilled people who helped me with the technical aspects of writing this book: Sara Renzulli, Adrian Paulsen, Jo Ann Easton, Lainie Hiller, Maxine Marcy, Christine Dimock, Kathy Savadel, Ann Butler, Ron Teeter, and Lisa Ferraro Parmelee. Each made important contributions to the final product.

The University of Connecticut has been very supportive of my research over the years, specifically the Department of Educational Psychology in the Neag School of Education. Sally Reis, Joe Renzulli, and Preston Britner at the University of Connecticut have been especially helpful with my work and career. The Research Foundation of the University of Connecticut awarded me two grants to write aspects of this book. I also want to thank my 90-year-old mother, Kay O'Neil Kurtz, who sent me off on a positive life trajectory by her constant care, support, sacrifice, and hard work. My family—Marina O'Neil, Kirill O'Neil, and Tanya Cherbotaeva—have been supportive of me and tolerated the many hours away to write this book. I would also like to thank Maureen Adams and David Becker, editors at APA Books, for their expert guidance and advice about how to make this book useful to others. I hope it stimulates more involvement in the psychology of men and that men's GRC is replaced with more positive and healthy conceptualization masculinity over the coming decades.

Men's Gender Role Conflict

INTRODUCTION

In 1981, I was reading an issue of *Professional Psychology* in my kitchen in Lawrence, Kansas, when I came across an article called "The Prevention of Sexism" (Albee, 1981). It got my attention because the author was a man writing about sexism. The provocative article was a call to action for psychologists to confront sexism as delusional and dangerous, even a form of psychopathology. Although I did not know at the time that the author, George Albee, was a famous psychologist and past president of the American Psychological Association, I did know that his article was a significant state-ment about the psychology of men because he argued that sexism affects both men and women and that both can be victims.

I was so moved by the article that I called Albee in Vermont to con-gratulate him on being the first male psychologist I knew of to publish a journal article on the prevention of sexism. Our conversation was brief, but he received my praise graciously. That call was a breakthrough moment in

http://dx.doi.org/10.1037/14501-001

my career. Albee had a way of getting people to think divergently and to reconsider established truths. His article would become a primary reading for the gender role journey workshop I conducted every summer from 1984 to 2006 (O'Neil, 1996; O'Neil & Roberts Carroll, 1988). Students' reactions to the article were emotional and mixed because they were jarred by the in-your-face truths about the causes and consequences of sexism.

For psychologists, Albee's call to action was the throwing down of a gauntlet. "Will psychology have the courage to face and challenge the religious and economic causes of sexism?" Albee demanded of the field (p. 26). He soon made clear that he was calling individual practitioners to account as well: "The middle-class professional must continuously decide whether she or he is a defender of the established social-economic order or whether she or he must become an advocate for the victims of that order" (p. 26). Also, he warned, taking up the challenge would not be without risks:

> Professionals who see and describe sexism as an exploitative and de-humanizing system are in danger of being made visible and labeled as radical or rebels with emotional problems. We need to support each other in these matters, or we will be picked off one by one! (pp. 26–27)

I knew this feeling of "being picked off" as I experienced the increasing negative reactions to my work on men's issues coming from "the system" in the late 1970s (see Chapter 2, this volume). My concern was outweighed, however, by the urge to create concepts that might explain how sexism affects both men and women. I had already begun when my encounter with Albee's article and his ideas became central to developing the gender role conflict (GRC) paradigm. Now, more than 35 years later, a summary of the GRC research program is needed. In this book, with Albee's challenge still ringing in my ears, I summarize what we know about men's GRC and what we should do next.

The psychology of men has been an upstream battle over the past three decades, and my impatience with the slow evolution of knowledge and research has been expressed in public meetings. I am not sure professionals in the field of the psychology of men have delivered very well on Albee's call; certainly we could have done more. So, rather than continuing to just rant and rave, this book is my attempt to do something concrete to move the discipline along. I have collected all the GRC studies ($N = 350$) for over 35 years from more than 500 colleagues who have done the research. In many ways, these researchers deserve the credit for how the GRC paradigm has grown, and this book is a chance to showcase their work collectively in one place. When you focus on a single construct for 35 years, you have insights to share, and you hope that they stimulate comment, critique, and better constructs. This is one of the ways that the field of the psychology of men can move forward.

In this book, I make a call to action for greater involvement by psychologists and other human services providers in developing the psychology of men. Even though much has happened in this area over the past two decades, this call to action is needed because there still are very few theoretical paradigms about men's gender role socialization, and the research studies that are conducted often are not very useful to practicing psychologists with clients. On the positive side, research findings now exist on the serious consequences of restrictive gender roles for men. These findings need to be more widely disseminated if they are going to make any differences in people's lives. The GRC research program is one of the only theoretically based and empirically focused areas of study in the psychology of men. What I provide in this book is a summary of studies and implications of the GRC data for therapy, preventive programming, helping diverse groups of men, and eradicating oppression that will be valuable for practicing therapists, psychoeducators, and research psychologists who are committed to advancing the psychology of men and gender.

I wrote this book for researchers, practicing therapists, and other human services providers, especially graduate students who are looking for place to make a difference in people's lives through their careers. Professionals in the field of student affairs and professors who teach the psychology of women or men may find this book quite useful (O'Neil & Renzulli, 2013a, 2013b). The primary goal of the book is to expand the reader's contextual understanding of GRC in research, clinical practice, and psychoeducational programming. There now exist new conceptual models linking GRC to psychosocial development, diversity and social justice, contextual research, therapeutic assessment and interventions, and psychoeducational programming. Not everyone will agree with all the points made in this book and alternative perspectives are needed if my call to action is to be more than just words. My hope is that the book is a catalyst for new concepts that stimulates dialogue and expands the theory, research, and practice in the psychology of men.

I

AN OVERVIEW OF GENDER ROLE CONFLICT AND ITS HISTORY

1

A CALL TO ACTION TO EXPAND THE PSYCHOLOGY OF MEN

All truth passes through three stages. First, it is ridiculed. Second, it is violently opposed. Third, it is accepted as being self-evident.
—Arthur Schopenhauer

In February 1972, Edmund Muskie, front-runner for the Democratic presidential nomination, appeared to shed tears as he responded to attacks on his wife in the press—an incident still remembered as contributing to the subsequent collapse of Muskie's campaign because many perceived his reaction as that of a weak and less than rational man who was unfit to lead the nation. Forty years later, Barack Obama expressed tears of gratitude to his staff for helping him win the 2012 election. This and subsequent occasions when Obama openly wept were televised repeatedly on national television, and no one, including the media, accused him of being weak or out of control. Indeed, some saw his emotionality as a sign of strength. "Before you take issue with the president's tears," wrote Monica Potts (2012) in *The American Prospect*, shortly after his anguished response to the massacre of schoolchildren and their teachers in Newtown, Connecticut, "remember that Obama's empathy is always what made him seem most presidential."

http://dx.doi.org/10.1037/14501-002
Men's Gender Role Conflict: Psychological Costs, Consequences, and an Agenda for Change, by J. M. O'Neil
Copyright © 2015 by the American Psychological Association. All rights reserved.

A paradigm shift is occurring in America with regard to our definition of masculinity, the most visible sign of which is the men who are active, engaging fathers with their sons and daughters (Pleck, 2010). As the incidents recounted above vividly demonstrate, something significant is also happening with how U.S. society perceives male emotions. More than ever before, men are being allowed to be vulnerable, emotional human beings. This transition is hopeful and important, but painfully slow. This book represents a call to action for practitioners, researchers, professors, and all human services providers to accelerate this process and help men overcome *gender role conflict* (GRC), a psychological state in which socialized gender roles have negative consequences for oneself or others. GRC occurs when rigid, sexist, or restrictive gender roles lead to personal restrictions, devaluation, or violation of others or oneself (O'Neil, 2008b). The ultimate outcome of this kind of conflict is the loss of the human potential of the person experiencing the conflict or someone else.

The greatest obstacle to overcoming GRC is a failure to see men as full human beings. In psychology, men have been studied not as gendered human beings but as generic persons based on stereotypes (Kimmel, 2011; Smiler, 2006). The study of men as gendered human beings is a relatively new phenomenon in psychology. A major goal of this book is to explain how men have been affected by restrictive gender roles and how GRC is a serious mental health problem that deserves the full attention of psychologists and other human services professionals.

So common is the problem of discounting men's full humanity that it has, to a large extent, gone unidentified. In any first encounter, men are usually perceived in terms of stereotypes of masculinity based on a preconceived ideal body type and other criteria of biological maleness. The second impression of a man is usually based on how well he conforms to masculine stereotypes, norms, and standards. If one moves past the first two impressions, the man can be experienced as a full human person, with all the positive (and negative) qualities and vulnerable possibilities of any human being living in a complex world. This experience does happen, but it occurs mainly in selective situations, such as funerals, births, religious experiences, and other events in which life is the primary focus and stereotypes do not matter.

Unfortunately, stereotyping and then objectifying men are what people do. The sexist stereotypes by which men have been narrowly defined have slowly but consistently deadened the male spirit. Indeed, the human qualities of both sexes have been diminished by patriarchal stereotypes as the capitalist U.S. society has striven to make profits, shape public opinion, and control people's behavior, resulting in a dehumanization that lies at the root of the widespread violence and despair that plagues many technologically advanced societies (Fox, 1988). This book reveals its cost by presenting restrictive gender roles as a psychological problem for both men and women.

Why write an entire book on men's GRC? The simple answer is that a considerable amount of empirical evidence indicates that GRC is significantly related to serious psychological problems for both men and women. In this book, I present this evidence and discuss its implications for psychologists and other human services providers. I also make the case that GRC and its related concepts provide a critical context in which to understand men and empower them to live and love more humanly.

This book is needed because men's lives are not understood by either sex. Confusion about gender roles has prevailed for a very long time. Sigmund Freud's famous question "What do women want?" suggests he was perplexed about how masculinity and femininity were played out in men's and women's lives. Freud's full statement was in fact, "The great question that has never been answered and which I have not yet been able to answer despite my thirty years of research into the feminine soul, is 'what does a woman want?'" (see http://www.notable-quotes.com/f/freud_sigmund.html). Was Freud experiencing GRC when he posed this question? Nobody knows for sure, but some of his ideas certainly located women in a negative and subordinate position. What is ironic is that Freud never asked, "What do men want?" Perhaps he was concerned about raising other questions about masculine vulnerabilities or opening the floodgates of inquiry about the psychology of men, something he strongly resisted (see Connell, 1994). Freud was not alone in his resistance; it characterized the formative years of psychoanalytic thought. Connell provided an excellent analysis of the gender role dynamics between Freud and his early followers (Connell, 1994, 2005), with whom he had numerous conflicts over conceptions of masculinity and femininity (Connell, 1994). Masculinity drove both the discussion and the dissent among Freud and Carl Jung, Alfred Adler, and the early pioneers in psychological thought.

The best example of early resistance to discussing men's issues was the reaction to a series of lectures given by Adler before the Psychoanalytic Society in Vienna in 1911 on the patriarchal values that cause problems for men and women. He presented his theory of masculine protest, one of the first about masculinity as a psychological construct. E. Jones (1958, cited by Connell, 2005) documented the tension and anger that arose between Freud and Adler about such conceptualizations of masculinity, which contributed to a permanent split between the two analysts, and Colby (1951) provided a complete analysis of the unpleasant exchanges on the subject between the two.

Sixteen years later, Adler published his book *Understanding Human Nature* (1927), which made a strong case for feminism and the importance of masculine protest to understanding neurosis and ordinary people's problems in living. A careful reading of this book shows how masculinity issues threatened the psychoanalytic status quo. Unfortunately, Adler's critical theory of masculine protest was subordinated over time to the concept of striving for superiority (Connell, 1994) and thus was never fully developed. One wonders whether Adler was worn down by the patriarchal forces that rejected his brilliant feminist analysis. Ideas about men's gender roles were mostly abandoned and given only cursory attention by theorists until five decades later, in the 1980s (Connell, 1995). The philosopher Arthur Schopenhauer captured the past and present difficulties by acknowledging how patriarchal structures produce GRC when he said, as quoted at the outset of this chapter, "All truth passes through three stages. First, it is ridiculed. Second, it is violently opposed. Third, it is accepted as being self-evident." Unfortunately, as most feminists know, and as Adler may have anticipated, it has been very hard to move into the third phase of truth, to acknowledge how restrictive gender roles are harmful to both men and women.

Over 100 years ago, the psychology of men threatened the status quo, and that threat continues to be felt today because the psychology of men is complex and controversial and stimulates personal and political issues for both men and women. The neglect of men's lives as a topic in the psychological sciences has been costly in terms of human suffering. As I discuss in this book, GRC has been correlated with serious problems with men's emotional health, conflicts with women, violence, and dysfunctional interpersonal relationships. Indeed, a more relevant question than Freud's "What do women want?" is, "How do restrictive gender roles and fears about femininity drive men to prove their masculinity and develop rigid gender role attitudes and behaviors that are psychologically dysfunctional?"

Proving your masculinity (Kimmel, 2011; Vandello & Bosson, 2013; Vandello, Bosson, Cohen, Burnaford, & Weaver, 2008) has been a consistent theme in the literature, but how to define masculinity in human terms that are positive and healthy has a very short history. My goal in this book is to explain how restrictive gender roles are dangerous to one's psychological and physical health using the GRC construct by presenting, unlike Alder, research that documents this fact.

I want to make clear that my GRC analysis in this book is not about blaming men or contributing to the internalized oppression that many men feel because of sexism. My goal is the opposite: to expose GRC so that men can become responsible for their problems and consequently liberate themselves from restrictive gender roles. Furthermore, this book has nothing to do with the men's rights propaganda that has blamed women and feminists for men's problems. If anything, I seek to correct such distortions and promote a pro-feminist, gay-affirmative, and positive masculinity perspective.

THE PERSONAL AND POLITICAL DIMENSIONS OF
DECONSTRUCTING MASCULINE GENDER ROLES

Convincing professionals in the field of mainstream psychology to study men has been difficult because, until the 1980s, patriarchal values dominated psychological theory and research. White males were the normative referent group for research and psychological knowledge during the first eight decades of American psychology. Consequently, the psychology of men is frequently associated with biased studies, sexism, male dominance, the devaluation of women, and research and theories narrowly defined by sex differences rather than men's real-life experiences. As I show in this book, the new psychology of men is not about these sexist aspects of scientific study.

One explanation of why the psychology of men has been slow to develop is that the issues are both controversial and intensely personal and political. The primary way to understand sexism and GRC is by deconstructing traditional gender roles, a process that has been championed by women feminists in psychology and other disciplines (Enns, 2004; Enns & Williams, 2013). Deconstructing gender roles means telling the truth about sexist assumptions and stereotypes that distort what it means to be fully human, confronting the lies about the rewards of highly sex-typed attitudes and behaviors, and identifying and correcting the myths that men and women are more different than alike (O'Neil & Renzulli, 2013a). It involves the critical analysis of destructive gender role stereotypes and the evaluation of unverified sex differences that underlie sexism for both men and women as well as examining research evidence about sex differences while resisting the temptation to settle for simple answers to complex human problems—for instance, the superficial "Mars and Venus" explanations of men's and women's relationships (e.g., Gray, 1993).

Furthermore, the deconstruction of traditional gender roles can reveal the personal, social, and political realities of personal oppression, discrimination, and social injustice. Reaching this deeper level requires that one analyze how race, class, ethnicity, religion, and sexual orientation affect psychological functioning and that one make an effort to acknowledge the effects on people's lives of personal and institutional forms of sexism, racism, classism, heterosexism, ethnocentrism, or any other kind of discrimination. The deconstruction process raises significant questions about how gender roles relate to sex discrimination, emasculation, homophobia, homonegativity, poverty, sexual assault, harassment, emotional abuse, and societal violence. In the course of this deconstruction process, one must recognize and confront the status quo's investment in sexism by coming to understand how the dominant cultures oppress vulnerable groups, including women, people of color, sexual minorities, immigrants, and even White men. Also to be acknowledged are the economics of oppression, which are understood by explaining that profits are made when agents of destructive capitalism use stereotypes to foster injustices and discrimination.

On a personal level, the deconstruction of gender roles can challenge ethnic, familial, religious, or cultural mores related to masculinity and femininity, which can threaten personal identities, violate family values, and even invalidate established worldviews. In this context, the personal becomes political very quickly, and polarization and strong emotions can arise. On a societal level, the oppressiveness of the status quo becomes very visible and obvious when these issues are illuminated. In short, the assessment of patriarchal structures is unsettling and can destroy the illusion that everything is okay in men's and women's lives. It compels us to admit that men are troubled and that the entire social system is vulnerable and unstable. Activists who expose these realities threaten dominant power brokers who profit from the inequities. They also threaten regular people whose lives are based on traditional gender roles.

Given the complexity and volatility of the issues, many people find the deconstruction of gender roles overwhelming and thus retreat from the realities and inevitable problems it exposes. Over the past several decades, even activists have tired with the struggle as opposition to and support for feminism have ebbed and flowed. In this book, I try not to sidestep these critical issues but to connect them to GRC and to men's and women's gender role journeys (O'Neil & Egan, 1992a, 1992b; O'Neil, Helms, Gable, David, & Wrightsman, 1986).

Although vulnerabilities and insecurities do arise from the deconstruction of gender roles, eventually a single truth emerges: Outdated, stereotypical, and restrictive gender roles do not provide the foundation for equality between the sexes; instead, they provide the basis for sexism and other forms of oppression that cause violence and social injustices. As all mental health professionals know, social injustice causes poverty and serious psychological problems for men, women, and children and is therefore a critical issue for psychologists and other caring professionals to address.

WHERE THE PSYCHOLOGY OF MEN HAS BEEN AND HOW IT EVOLVED

A paradigm shift in the psychology of men is unlikely to occur unless mental health professionals attain some clarity about where we have been as a discipline and our current status. The following brief history of the psychology of men provides a context in which to understand how the recognition and study of GRC have developed over the decades.

The feminist movement of the 1970s was the primary stimulus for the men's liberation movement that ultimately evolved into men's studies and the psychology of men. Feminist psychologists exposed the myths of stereotypical gender roles and criticized biased research on sex differences. As women feminists challenged sexist beliefs and attitudes and traditional gender roles, male feminists began to ask questions about the hazards of being male (Goldberg, 1977). Before 1974, only a few scholarly articles on men's gender roles had been published; most of the literature was in the form of popular paperbacks written by the leaders of the men's liberation movement. From 1974 to 1977, however, six seminal books were published that gave men's liberation national prominence (for more details, see O'Neil, 2012b). These books were special because they challenged patriarchal values, something that had not occurred since Adler's feminist manifesto of the 1920s.

Scholarly models to explain the psychological issues concerning masculinity were slower in coming; in the late 1970s and early 1980s, there were none. The one notable exception was Joseph Pleck's (1981) book *The Myth of Masculinity*, in which he critically evaluated the biased sex role identity model and proposed a new *gender role strain model*, which hypothesized that restrictive gender roles could be psychologically dysfunctional for both men and women. The book was a major contribution to the field, but it left a great many questions about men unanswered, for example, why were men so unhappy and seeking liberation in the men's movements? Why did men have so many problems with women in intimate and work relationships? Why did men communicate differently than women and not express many feelings? Why did men work so much and die earlier than women? Why did men avoid domestic work and fathering roles? Why were men violent? Why did men molest children, fear homosexuals, and become addicted or sexually dysfunctional? Why did men harass, rape, and batter women? How could we get men to change? Clearly, much would be at stake in any effort to answer these questions about restrictive gender roles in men's lives.

The next significant event to promote the psychology of men and the GRC construct came nearly a decade after the publication of *The Myth of Masculinity*, with a gathering of 50 psychologists at the 1990 convention of the American Psychological Association (APA) in Boston to discuss the possibility of creating a specific division of APA that would focus on the psychology of men. From this meeting, a steering committee began the process of applying for divisional status in APA. Five years later, in 1995, the Society for the Psychological Study of Men and Masculinity (SPSMM; 2012) was unanimously approved by APA. This new division gave the psychology of men a permanent home from which to become a part of mainstream psychology. Another 5 years later, with the creation of the journal *Psychology of Men & Masculinity*, the psychological study of men became part of the social sciences. By 2014, more than 350 empirical studies had been published in *Psychology of Men & Masculinity*, and the psychology of men was formally recognized as a discipline in psychology.

WHERE ARE WE NOW: WHAT'S NOT KNOWN

Today, 18 years after the official birth of the formal study of the psychology of men, the slow pace of development of the discipline has prompted my call to action in this book. After all this time, what do we know about men's lives? The part played by sexism and restrictive gender roles in serious mental health issues for men is still not understood very well, and many of the questions raised in the 1980s—critical questions about how gender roles contribute to men's problems and significant societal problems—remain unanswered. For example, how do men's socialized gender roles contribute to what may be America's most pressing problem: men's violence toward women, children, and other men? Analyses of the epidemic of violence in America, most recently brought to the forefront of public awareness by frequent school shootings, rarely address men's socialized gender roles as a factor. This suggests that either psychologists have not made a convincing case for "violent masculinity," or the public is in denial about this explanation. Also, although restrictive gender roles have been implicated in men's suicide, depression, anxiety, substance abuse, and interpersonal dysfunction (O'Neil, 2008c), the ways in which sexism and male privilege (or lack thereof) contribute to these problems has not been fully addressed. Moreover, only a few statements exist in the psychology of men on how oppression (in the forms of, e.g., racism, classism, and heterosexism) affects men's gender roles and their psychological functioning (Kimmel, 1994; Liang, Rivera, Nathwani, Dang, & Douroux, 2010; Liang, Salcedo, & Miller, 2011; Liu, 2002a).

Also unknown is how well men's psychological problems fit conventional diagnostic criteria in the therapy room (Robertson, 2012; Rochlen & Hoyer, 2005). Men's depression, for example, is still not fully understood or defined in gendered ways that enable clinicians to make effective interventions. Is it manifested in the same ways as women's depression, or is it more masked? The lack of an answer is not surprising given that the first psychology books on men's depression were published in 1999 and 2000 (Cochran & Rabinowitz, 2000; Lynch & Kilmartin, 1999). It is remarkable that psychologists did not acknowledge male depression as an area of scholarly inquiry for the first 80 years of psychology.

The deficiencies in applied men's psychology go further. Very little attention has been given to sexist biases against boys and men in therapy, for instance; and although male mental health issues have been addressed, the ways in which sexism contributes to them has gone unspecified. In addition, how to help troubled boys and men who are experiencing gender role transitions is unknown, and few clinical paradigms are available to assess men during psychotherapy. Why men tend to avoid counseling services altogether is still unclear, and little research has examined male clients who have effectively used them. According to Cochran (2005), "The psychology of men as a distinct practice and research area has yet to generate controlled studies demonstrating differential effectiveness of specific treatments with men" (p. 650).

Also to be considered is the fact that, if treatment is to be effective, men's lives need to be understood in context (Addis, Mansfield, & Syzdek, 2010; K. Jones & Heesacker, 2012)—specifically, in a multicultural context that assesses diversity and the role of oppression in men's lives. Although multicultural guidelines for conducting therapy have been specified, they have not included issues related to men and masculinity (Liu, 2005), for reasons that are not clear. Might there be worry that including men in the multicultural criteria would return the discipline to the biased psychology of the past? More likely, the problem is that a coherent, multicultural approach to understand men's diversity does not exist because the ways in which race, class, ethnicity, nationality, age, religion, and sexual orientation affect male socialization have not been fully discussed. In Chapter 6, I discuss in more detail these important multicultural issues.

The lack of focus on the multicultural aspects of masculinity brings to mind the male terrorists who carried out the September 11, 2001, attacks on the World Trade Center and the Pentagon. Few Americans can forget where they were during the traumatic days that immediately followed that horrific event, and even now, more than a decade later, the United States as a society still has not entirely recovered. One obstacle to our healing is that the public still lacks knowledge on who the attackers were and, more to the point, why they attacked. Although much has been written about the 9/11 terrorists, little is known about how their masculinity ideologies and their religious and cultural belief systems contributed to their decision to commit mass murder. One speculative question we may ask is whether they were influenced by GRC. One need only consider the lingering perception of the terrorists in some parts of the world as courageous male martyrs and heroes to connect them to psychological issues related to men, masculinity, and GRC.

DO MEN AND BOYS REALLY HAVE PROBLEMS? THE STATISTICAL DOCUMENTATION

Over the past 15 years, boys' lives have been in the national spotlight, with numerous publications generating heated debates about their current status. According to William Pollack's (1998b) book, *Real Boys: Rescuing*

Our Sons From the Myths of Boyhood, boys are in trouble, whereas the title of Peg Tyre's (2006) *Newsweek* magazine cover story warns of "The Boy Crisis." On the other side are David Von Drehle's (2007) *Time* magazine cover story, "The Myth About Boys," which says the "boy crisis" is blown out of proportion, and Christina Hoff Sommers's (2000) book, *The War Against Boys: How Feminism Is Harming Our Young Men*, which concludes that no such crisis exists. Hoff Sommers attacked the research of William Pollack and Carol Gilligan, two of the most influential feminist scholars on both boys' and girls' development, arguing that their findings do not justify their alarm about the dire state of boys' lives.

Through such opposing views, boys' psychological health has become part of the cultural clashes in America, and feminism and scientific rigor have been the battleground. My response to the debate is to present in this book research and documentation about boys'—and, by obvious extension, men's—problems. Two questions are relevant. First, is there evidence that boys and men have problems? Second, if so, are these problems related to masculine gender roles?

Statistical analyses dispel any denial that men and boys have problems and any superficial illusions that all is well with them. In Exhibit 1.1, I list the problems that have been documented. A careful reading of Exhibit 1.1 raises some provocative issues that provide a context for every chapter of this book.

These statistics, as sobering as they are, represent only reported problems and therefore underestimate the true state of men's and boys' lives. The critical question is whether socialized gender roles contribute directly to their psychological problems and, if they do, how? Experts over the past 30 years have theorized that they do (Courtenay, 2011; David & Brannon, 1976; Goldberg, 1977; Kilmartin, 2010; O'Neil, 1981a, 2008c, 2012b; Pleck, 1981; Pleck & Sawyer, 1974; Pollack, 1998b; Robertson, 2012), but only recently has any empirical evidence been presented (Levant & Richmond, 2007; O'Neil, 2008c). The chapters in this book provide theoretical rationales and empirical evidence showing that restrictive gender roles are significantly related to the problems in Exhibit 1.1.

SOME EVIDENCE ABOUT MEN'S PROBLEMS, MASCULINITY IDEOLOGY, AND GENDER ROLE CONFLICT

A brief review of the research on masculinity ideology and GRC sets the stage for the body of this book. According to a definition as drawn from the literature, *masculinity ideology* describes how men are socialized to masculine stereotypes. It has been operationalized by the concepts of masculine norms and roles (Levant et al., 1992; E. H. Thompson & Pleck, 1986) and masculine conformity and nonconformity (Mahalik, Locke, et al., 2003).

EXHIBIT 1.1
Statistical Documentation of Men's and Boys' Problems

- 93% of sentenced prisoners are male (Carson & Sabol, 2012).
- 9.2% of male deaths are caused by suicide for males ages 10–14, 16.2% for males ages 15–19, 16% for males ages 20–24, and 14.7% for males ages 25–34 (Centers for Disease Control and Prevention, 2009).
- 94% of school shootings between 1979 and 2011were committed by males (Klein, 2012).
- 8.2% of boys in Grades 9–12 have carried a gun to school, 40% have been in a physical fight, 18% have been bullied, and almost 10% have been threatened or injured with a weapon (Eaton et al., 2012).
- 10% of all men report depression, and 14% report anxiety (Schiller, Lucas, & Peregoy, 2012).
- 23% of males report binge drinking (Centers for Disease Control and Prevention, 2012).
- 30% of men have lifetime prevalence rates for alcohol and drug dependence (Robin & Reiger, 1991).
- 85% of school violence is perpetrated by boys (Media Education Foundation, 1999).
- 80% of high school boys have reported being bullied (U.S. Census Bureau, 2005).
- 12% of high school boys have reported being threatened or injured with a weapon on school property (Centers for Disease Control and Prevention, 2007).
- 12% of males ages 18–24 are high school dropouts (U.S. Census Bureau, 2005).
- 16% of school-age boys have been diagnosed with attention-deficit/hyperactivity disorder (Centers for Disease Control and Prevention, 2005).
- 19% of men did not have a usual place to obtain health care in 2011 (Schiller et al., 2012).
- 41% of men are overweight (Schiller et al., 2012).
- 75% of people who die from heart attacks are men (American Heart Association, 1994).
- 66% of children receiving special education services are boys (Wagner, Marder, & Blackorby, 2002), and boys are 3 times more likely to be enrolled in a special education class than girls (U.S. Census Bureau, 2005).
- 8.5% of males dropped out of school in 2010 (U.S. Department of Education, 2011).
- 15% of boys received regular medication in 2011 (Bloom, Cohen, & Freeman, 2012).
- 15.3% of men serving in active duty in the U.S. armed services have committed suicide (Armed Forces Health Surveillance Center, 2012).

Masculinity ideology represents the primary values and standards that define, restrict, and negatively affect boys' and men's lives (Levant et al., 1992; Mahalik, Locke, et al., 2003; Pleck, 1995; Pleck, Sonenstein, & Ku, 1993; E. H. Thompson & Pleck, 1995). It refers "to beliefs about the importance of men adhering to culturally defined standards for male behavior" (Pleck, 1995, p. 19) and involves "the individual's endorsement and internalization of cultural belief systems about masculinity and male gender, rooted in the structural relationships between the sexes" (Pleck, 1995, p. 19). Masculinity ideologies can be dysfunctional because restrictive gender roles can have negative consequences for men, causing them to be dysfunctional in their interpersonal relationships. The negative outcomes of adhering to or deviating from culturally defined and restrictive masculinity ideologies result in GRC and strain (O'Neil, 2008c; Pleck, 1995), whereas internalizing rigid masculinity ideologies can produce distorted gender role schemas (Mahalik, 1999a; O'Neil & Nadeau, 1999; see also Chapter 5, this volume) and GRC that are potentially damaging to men and others.

As indicated above, the critical question is, "What evidence exists to relate masculinity ideology and GRC to men's psychological and interpersonal problems, as enumerated in Exhibit 1.1?" This question is answered in Table 1.1, which comprises a literature review of published studies that have assessed whether masculinity ideology and GRC are correlated with negative psychological outcomes for men and boys. The review includes empirical studies that use one or more of the following five published measures: (a) the Masculine Role Norms Scale (E. H. Thompson & Pleck, 1986), (b) the Male Role Norms Inventory (Levant et al., 1992), the Conformity to Masculine Norms Inventory (Mahalik, Locke, et al., 2003), the Masculine Gender Role Stress Scale (Eisler, 1995), and the Gender Role Conflict Scale (GRCS; O'Neil et al., 1986).

The goal of this literature review is to develop an overall summary of the significant empirical relationships between masculinity scales and men's

TABLE 1.1
Masculinity Ideology and Gender Role Conflict Subscales Correlated
With Men's Problems

Masculine Role Norms Scale[a] Subscales: Status Norms, Toughness Norms, Anti-Femininity Norms	
Reference sources	Psychological problems correlated with subscales
Kilianski (2003)	Negative attitudes lesbians, hostile sexism, negative attitudes toward women
E. H. Thompson & Pleck (1986)	Opposition to the Equal Rights Amendment, preference for a virgin wife
Abreu et al. (2000)	Lack of ethnic belonging
Pleck et al. (1993)	Suspension from school, drinking and use of drugs, being picked up by police, coercive sex
Locke et al. (2005)	Increased sexual risk
Blazina et al. (2007)	Loneliness, separation–individuation problems
Wilkinson (2004)	Restricted affectionate behavior between men, fear of appearing feminine, anti-gay attitudes
Jakupcak et al. (2005)	Overt hostility and aggression
Good, Heppner, et al. (1995)	Adversarial sexual beliefs, rape myths, psychological violence

TABLE 1.1
Masculinity Ideology and Gender Role Conflict Subscales Correlated
With Men's Problems   *(Continued)*

Conformity to Masculine Norms Inventory[b]
Subscales: Winning, Emotional Control, Risk Taking, Violence,
Power Over Women, Dominance, Playboy, Self-Reliance, Primacy of Work,
Disdain for Homosexuals, Pursuit of Status, Total Conformity

Reference sources	Psychological problems correlated with subscales
Mahalik, Locke, et al. (2003)	Social dominance, aggression, muscularity
Mahalik, Lagan, & Morrison (2006)	Unhealthy alcohol use, neglecting preventive skin care, health screenings, not seeking help with emotional difficulties, not going to health care appointments, getting into physical fights, difficulty managing anger, taking risks, risky behavior with automobiles and with sexual practices
Liu & Iwamoto (2007)	Substance use, marijuana use, binge drinking
Mahalik & Rochlen (2006)	Unhealthy responses to depression
Mahalik, Levi-Minzi, & Walker (2007)	Health risks, few health promotion behaviors
Smiler (2006)	Sexism
Mahalik, Burns, & Syzdek (2007)	Lack of health promotion behaviors
Kimmel & Mahalik (2005)	Internalized homophobia, unhealthy masculine body ideal, distress
Burns & Mahalik (2006)	Poor sexual functioning
Mahalik, Pierre, & Wan (2006)	Racial identity, Pre-Encounter phase, lower self-esteem, psychological distress
Good et al. (2006)	Negative attitudes about help seeking
Cohn & Zeichner (2006)	Laboratory shocks given during competition

Male Role Norms Inventory[c]
Subscales: Avoidance of Femininity, Fear and Hatred of
Homosexuals, Self-Reliance, Aggression, Achievement/Status,
Non-Relational Attitudes Toward Sex, Restrictive Emotionality

Reference sources	Psychological problems correlated with subscales
Levant et al. (2003)	Alexithymia
Wade & Brittan-Powell (2001)	Negative attitudes about racial identity and women's equality, positive attitudes toward condoning the sexual harassment of women
Liu (2002a)	Racial group marginalization, ethnocentrism,
Berger et al. (2005)	Negative attitudes toward help seeking

(continues)

TABLE 1.1
Masculinity Ideology and Gender Role Conflict Subscales Correlated With Men's Problems *(Continued)*

Masculine Gender Role Stress Scale[d]
Subscales: Physical Inadequacy, Emotional Inexpressiveness,
Subordination to Women, Intellectual Inferiority, Performance Failure

Reference sources	Psychological problems correlated with subscales
Cosenzo et al. (2004)	Increases in systolic blood pressure, impaired cognitive performance
Moore & Stuart (2004)	Higher state anger, negative intent attributions, verbal aggressions
Eisler et al. (2000)	Greater negative intent; greater irritation, anger, jealousy, and aggression
Eisler et al. (1987)	Anger, increases in anxiety, poorer health habits
Lash et al. (1990)	Greater systolic blood pressure
McCreary & Sadava (1995)	Lower work satisfaction
Franchina et al. (2001)	Negative attributions and negative affect, verbal aggression
Jakupcak et al. (2006)	Alexithymia, lack of social support
Jakupcak et al. (2005)	Overt hostility and aggression
Mahalik et al. (2005)	Controlling behaviors, fearful attachment

Gender Role Conflict Scale[e]
Subscales: Success, Power and Competition; Restrictive Emotionality; Restrictive
Affectionate Behavior Between Men; Conflict Between Work and Family Relations

Reference sources	Psychological problems correlated with subscales
Blazina & Watkins (1996), Cournoyer & Mahalik (1995), Fragoso & Kashubeck (2000), Good et al. (1996), Good & Mintz (1990), Good & Wood (1995), Hayashi (1999), Magovcevic & Addis (2005), Mahalik & Cournoyer (2000), Sharpe & Heppner (1991), D. S. Shepard (2002), Simonsen et al. (2000)	Depression
Blazina & Watkins (1996), Cournoyer & Mahalik (1995), Fragoso & Kashubeck (2000), Good et al. (1996), Good et al. (2004), Hayashi (1999), J. A. Hayes & Mahalik (2000), Sharpe & Heppner (1991), Theodore & Lloyd (2000)	Anxiety and stress
Berko (1994), Cournoyer (1994), Hayashi (1999), J. Kim et al. (2006), Mahalik et al. (2001), Sharpe & Heppner (1991)	Low self-esteem

TABLE 1.1

Masculinity Ideology and Gender Role Conflict Subscales Correlated
With Men's Problems   *(Continued)*

Blazina & Watkins (1996), Korcuska & Thombs (2003), Monk & Ricciardelli (2003)	Alcohol and substance abuse
Breiding (2004), Campbell & Snow (1992), Rochlen & Mahalik (2004), Sharpe et al. (1995)	Low marital satisfaction, adjustment, and happiness
Cournoyer & Mahalik (1995), Fischer & Good (1997), Good et al. (1995), Sharpe et al. (1995), Sharpe & Heppner (1991), Theodore & Lloyd (2000)	Lack of intimacy
Cohn & Zeichner (2006), Glomb & Espelage (2005), Kassing et al. (2005), Kearney et al. (2004), Rando et al. (1998), Schwartz et al. (2005), Senn et al. (2000)	Abusive behaviors and coercion, hostile sexism, hostility toward women, rape myth acceptance, positive attitudes toward and tolerance for sexual harassment, self-reported violence and aggression
Blazina & Marks (2001), Blazina & Watkins (1996), Good et al. (2006), Good et al. (1989), Good & Wood (1995), Lane & Addis (2005), Robertson & Fitzgerald (1992), Simonsen et al. (2000), Wisch et al. (1995)	Negative attitudes toward help seeking

Note. From *Oxford Handbook of Counseling Psychology* (pp. 375–408), by E. Altmaier & J. Hansen (Eds.), 2012, New York, NY: Oxford University Press. Copyright 2012 by Oxford University Press. Adapted with permission.
[a]From E. H. Thompson & Pleck, 1986. [b]From Mahalik, Locke, et al., 2003. [c]From Levant et al., 1992.
[d]From Eisler, 1995. [e]From O'Neil, Helms, Gable, David, & Wrightsman, 1986.

and boys' problems by determining whether the studies statistically correlate men's psychological and interpersonal problems with each scale; this is the first such summary to do so. Significant statistical relationships are defined as any correlational tests at the $p < .05$ level between any scale (or any of its subscales) and a psychological or interpersonal variable. Given the complexity of reporting the subscales, only overall relationships between each scale and dependent measures are reported in the table.

Table 1.1 contains a summary of the 93 studies reviewed for the five masculinity scales. The author(s) and the name of the scale are given first, followed by the names of the subscales. For each scale, the dependent variables that significantly correlate with men's psychological and interpersonal processes are enumerated. References to the studies summarized in Table 1.1 are available from the author upon request and many of them are listed at the end of the book.

The summary of the masculinity ideology and GRC scales in Table 1.1 (Masculine Role Norms Scale, Male Role Norms Inventory, Conformity to Masculine Norms Inventory, Masculine Gender Role Stress Scale, and the GRCS) indicates that attitudes about masculinity have been statistically correlated with a wide variety of psychological and interpersonal problems in more than 90 studies. More than 90 dependent variables related to men's problems have been significantly correlated with masculinity ideology, norms, and conformity, GRC, and stress.

Overall, the results of the studies reviewed in Table 1.1 provide a convincing case that masculinity ideology and GRC have significant relationships to psychological and interpersonal problems for both boys and men. The results across many studies point to significant relationships between masculinity ideology and negative psychological attitudes toward women and gay men, violent attitudes toward women, dangerous risk taking in regard to sex and health issues, substance use and abuse, psychological stress and strain, negative attitudes toward help seeking, delinquent behavior, low self-esteem, hostility and aggression, higher blood pressure levels, depression, anxiety, and marital and family problems.

These findings shed light on the statistical data on male problem areas listed in Exhibit 1.1, which document the high incidence among men and boys of substance abuse, depression, anxiety, learning problems, threats, bullying, and violence. Returning to the earlier question of whether men's problems are related to socialized gender roles, the answer, based on the correlational data, is an absolute yes.

DENIAL ABOUT MEN'S PROBLEMS: A SIGNIFICANT BARRIER

Both Exhibit 1.1 and Table 1.1 provide convincing evidence that boys and men have psychological problems and that empirical research documents a relationship between these problems and masculinity ideology and GRC. Almost everyone knows that males have problems, but society as a whole has been slow to acknowledge this fact. The evidence in Exhibit 1.1 and Table 1.2 can influence a paradigm shift with regard to how men and masculinity are perceived, but strong unconscious defenses can interfere with taking the data seriously.

For men's lives to improve, the misinformation and dubious assumptions that reinforce denial about boys' and men's problems need to be exposed. The best-known example of denial is the "boys will be boys" assumption. This misconception implies that boys' problems are normal and insignificant, usually only short term, remediated as the boy matures, and do not affect adulthood. The "boys will be boys" denial is superficial because it does not consider the etiology of boys' problems from the perspective of restrictive gender roles, and it ignores the sociocultural impacts of sexism on boys' lives. Worse, it does not capture the deeper and unidentified sources of boys' conflict. Even among boys who appear normal, underneath the defensive masks of many are turmoil and trouble, and many do carry their unidentified adolescent problems into adulthood.

This denial is reinforced by the belief that boys' behavior is mostly influenced by innate and hormonal factors during puberty and that therefore not much can be done. This deduction deserves scrutiny because it represents an essentialist perspective on gender roles based on either natural law or religious, ethnic, or family values. Biology does affect boyhood during puberty and should be part of any discussion about boys' lives, but it should not detract from the consideration of how socialized gender roles shape attitudes and behaviors. Essentialists argue against interfering with biological imperatives driving male behavior, but rarely do they consider how socialized gender roles shape boys' behavior (Kenrick, 1987).

Another false assumption is that knowledge about gender roles could negatively affect boys' gender role identity and promote homosexuality. Many times these worries, often harbored by parents and teachers, represent homophobic reactions and interact with limited information about how restrictive gender roles affect sexism in boys' lives. Even assuming that the acquisition of any information can influence sexual orientation, information about masculine gender roles in particular does not focus on sexual orientation issues or support the feminization of boys. In fact, education about GRC facilitates a boy's positive views of what it means to be a man in terms of healthy character development, life skills, and the full realization of one's potential (O'Neil & Lujan, 2009b).

In short, to deny men's problems is to minimize them and invalidate male experience and struggles. Such a denial creates an attitude that permits men's problems to be normalized, accepted, and largely ignored. In this book, I challenge this attitude and break through any denial about what is at stake using theory, research, and arguments for expanding and deepening the psychology of men.

THE PLAN OF THE BOOK

The overall purpose of this book is to promote activism to help boys and men with their GRC. It is designed to summarize, in one place, past and previous GRC theory, research, and service options, as well as new ideas and research that can be useful to that end.

Contextualism is the driving dimension in this book, and it is my hope that, through the discussion of more elaborate GRC contexts, the complexity of men's lives can be better understood. Previous GRC conceptualizations have been limited, and the chapters in this book discuss many new contexts of GRC that can broaden the psychology of men in significant ways.

The book has seven overall contextual domains: (a) macro–societal–sociopolitical; (b) developmental–psychosocial; (c) empirical research; (d) multicultural–diversity; (e) gender-related concepts; (f) applied, therapeutic, and clinical; and (g) applied, preventive, and psychoeducational. The contextual thrust of the book is actualized by more than a dozen conceptual models that organize the contexts in heuristic ways. Furthermore, more than 40 theoretical assumptions or hypotheses about men are stated across the seven contextual domains. In addition, the contexts have utility for therapists and educators in that more than 10 practical tools or interventions are described that facilitate the assessment of men and boys during therapy or psychoeducational programs.

One of most significant contexts is a macrosocietal and sociopolitical perspective on GRC that conceptualizes oppression and social injustices as a result of patriarchal norms and masculine gender roles. This book is about men and women who are oppressed by restrictive gender roles. Oppressed people are individuals who are devalued, restricted, and violated because they have deviated from expected gender roles or because of their sex, sexual orientation, race, class, ethnicity, national origin, or any other characteristic. Many times the oppressed are those who are not part of the status quo, which in the United States is defined as being White, male, heterosexual, middle class, Eurocentric, and American. Even individuals who fit the above majority criteria can be oppressed by sexism and patriarchal values because with discrimination there are the psychological costs for both the victim and the oppressor. The dominant majority reaps benefits from oppressive systems, but few people are spared from patriarchal abuses and violence in our capitalist society.

In addition, in this book, I present a psychosocial, developmental context of GRC that promotes the study of how masculinity affects growth and development over the life cycle. Contextual ways of assessing GRC, approaches to therapy, and psychoeducational programming are new contexts that make the book useful to practitioners and activists in the psychology of men. The new contextual research paradigm expands the GRC research agenda to answer questions about how GRC is activated by situational contingencies in the environment. Furthermore, more elaborate contexts are discussed that explain how GRC relates to gender role transitions, distorted gender roles schemas, and masculinity ideology. Finally, healthy and positive masculinity is a new context that supports reducing and preventing GRC in men's lives.

Part I of this book contains this chapter and continues with Chapter 2, in which I provide a historical context of the GRC research program, describing how it started and has developed over the past three decades. Details of my personal experiences, political dynamics, and significant developments convey a sense of the driving forces and the difficulties that have inhibited the GRC research program over the years.

Part II comprises three chapters in which I present the theoretical and empirical foundations of GRC. Chapter 3 encompasses the conceptual definitions, concepts, and models of GRC; I discuss its complexity from macro-societal, functional, and microcontextual perspectives and offer details of new conceptual paradigms to facilitate the next wave of knowledge about men's GRC. In Chapter 4, I discuss how to measure GRC and describe the phases of the gender role journey (O'Neil, Egan, Owen, & Murry, 1993). I review the initial development of the GRCS (O'Neil et al., 1986) and its later adaptation for adolescents (Blazina, Pisecco, & O'Neil, 2005) and discuss the newer short form of the GRCS (Wester, Vogel, O'Neil, & Danforth, 2012). The adaptation of the GRCS for women, and the Gender Role Journey Measure (O'Neil et al., 1993), also are described. The emphasis in this chapter is on the psychometric properties of the instruments and evidence of their reliability and validity. In Chapter 5, I offer a new developmental context on GRC across the life span, based on psychosocial theory (B. Newman & Newman, 2015) and the gender role journey paradigm (O'Neil & Egan, 1992a, 1992b; O'Neil et al., 1993) that includes gender role transitions and learning distorted gender role schemas.

The three chapters of Part III summarize empirical research on men and boys. These chapters represent a summary of the empirical evidence about GRC from more than 335 studies, and the calls to action are justified using this database. In Chapter 6, I review the multicultural and diversity studies on GRC for men of different ages, races, ethnicities, classes, sexual orientations, and nationalities, and other special groups. I provide an analysis of the studies I review, and I present a multicultural psychology of men model that relates men's oppression to masculinity ideology, GRC, internalized oppression, and psychological problems. In Chapter 7, I analyze the research from 1984 to 2014, including more than 300 empirical studies that have used the GRCS over the past 30 years, and I discuss how GRC has been correlated with 90 different dependent variables and 27 major categories of men's personal and interpersonal functioning. I outline in Chapter 8 four research paradigms that can guide future research on GRC, with emphasis on contextualizing GRC and creating more moderator and mediator studies to capture its complexity in a variety of real-life contexts. This chapter is a response to critics' questions regarding what can be done next with the empirical validation of men's GRC.

In Part IV, I present the practical applications of GRC in therapy and in preventive programming. These contexts demonstrate how GRC theory and research can be used as part of the call to action. In Chapter 9, I present an assessment paradigm for men's therapy using a nine-cell diagnostic schema supported by the GRC research reviewed in Chapters 6 and 7. In Chapter 10, I discuss the first full explanation of how GRC can be used by clinicians. Gender Role Journey Therapy is presented in the context of deepening (Rabinowitz & Cochran, 2002) and transtheoretical approaches (Brooks, 2010; Prochaska & Norcross, 2001). For the first time, past GRC research and current theory are used to establish a process for conducting therapy with men. Using the diagnostic schema in Chapter 9 and the description of gender role journey therapy in Chapter 10, I present a case study of one of my current clients in Chapter 11. This represents the first full description of how to apply GRC theory to an actual therapy client.

In the last two chapters of Part IV, I summarize more practical topics related to the call to action. In Chapter 12, I discuss a theoretical and empirical justification for providing psychoeducational programming for boys and men, and in Chapter 13, I present a service delivery system and describe three evaluated interventions that used GRC concepts with boys, men, and women. The service delivery model and interventions were designed to help practitioners apply GRC concepts in psychoeducational settings outside therapy sessions.

The final chapter, 14, includes further personal and professional insights on GRC from a societal perspective, and I summarize the 40 assumptions and 90 contexts developed in the book. I discuss what should be done next with 22 action plans and the contexts described in the book and extend to readers a personal invitation to get involved.

2

MY PERSONAL GENDER ROLE JOURNEY WITH THE GENDER ROLE CONFLICT RESEARCH PROGRAM

Men adopt self-destructive and alienating male roles, not because men are evil or stupid, but because a sexist society confers real power on those who conform to male supremacist values.

—Harry Brod, 2013

My study of men began with my first professional position as a professor and psychologist in the University Counseling Center at the University of Kansas. Fresh out of graduate school in 1975 at age 27, I had clinical and teaching responsibilities and a tenure-track position that meant developing a research program and publishing. My interest in restrictive gender roles and oppression as a mental health problem began in my undergraduate and graduate school education. As an undergraduate at Le Moyne College, I learned from the Jesuits that injustices in society require an active response from spiritually evolved persons. As a graduate student in the University of Maryland's Counseling and Student Personnel Program, my mentors were activists who researched racism and restrictive gender roles and how they presented critical mental health issues.

During this time, women feminists asked significant questions about men's problems, abuse, and violence. I listened and wanted to be part of the

http://dx.doi.org/10.1037/14501-003
Men's Gender Role Conflict: Psychological Costs, Consequences, and an Agenda for Change, by J. M. O'Neil

dialogue on these important issues. Some radical feminists who were separatists dismissed me without any dialogue. The separatist feminists were making statements like "All men are oppressors," "All men rape," and "All men should be blamed for the pervasive sexism against women in American society." In those days, the verbal attacks on men (i.e., male bashing) were less subtle than they are today. Naturally, those statements got everyone's attention and led to much polarization. The radical feminists' anger, rage, and very relevant questions certainly got my attention and increased my commitment to feminism and both women's and men's issues.

The more moderate feminists thought it might be important to study men. They, too, asked important questions, but I had few answers to the issues they raised. I wanted to understand how sexism could produce such intense anger toward me, other men, and the patriarchal system in general. Those were lonely days for me, not only for these political reasons but also because there was little support for my interest in men's issues. Furthermore, I was starting my own gender role journey (O'Neil & Egan, 1992a; O'Neil, Egan, Owen, & Murry, 1993) and discovering my own pain from my sexist socialization.

I had colleagues scattered across the University of Kansas campus who were interested in gender roles, but I found that it was graduate students who were a source of support and stimulation. The students would listen and helped create a scholarly environment for the study of men. Sitting there in my counseling center office in 1978, I remember pondering the many questions feminists were asking about men's violence, sex discrimination, harassment in the workplace, and men's abusive power and control at work and in family relationships. I knew there must be a reason why men were sexist and that it was more complex than reducing all men to innate misogynistic oppressors. I reasoned that there must be something in the capitalist or family system that contributes to men's sexism against women. Part of my problem was that I had no conception of how patriarchy worked and how sexism was a political reality in my own life. What really bothered me was that I could not answer the reasonable questions that feminists were asking about men's problems.

From that time on, men's gender role conflict (GRC) became a major part of my professional life and my primary research program. I wanted to develop a theory and research program that explained how sexism and gender roles interact to produce oppression for both sexes. During those early days, I felt that both sexes were victims of sexism. Women as victims of sexism could be easily documented, but men as victims was harder to document and harder still to conceptualize. The GRC construct was one way to theorize about sexism against men. Those heated discussions with feminists in the 1970s were the primary stimuli for creating research on men's GRC.

THE LITERATURE REVIEW AND REACTIONS
TO MY STUDY OF MEN

I thought some explanation for men's problems could be found in the psychology journals, and so I obtained a grant from the University of Kansas to research the literature on men and masculinity. In 1977, I began my review, hoping to create some conceptualizations that might respond to the questions feminists were asking. I wanted to explain why men were violent, interpersonally rigid, sexist, homophobic, unemotional, and unhappy with themselves and others.

When I started the research on men, some of my male colleagues had some questions and concerns. They wondered about my topic and about me. On some level, they recognized that the topic was about them, and they found that unsettling. Some colleagues thought I was gay because I was studying men. One day, I stared down unconscious homophobia when a colleague said in a sarcastic, high-pitched, girly voice, "We heard you're REALLY into men these days." The sexual innuendo certainly got my attention. Finding my research on men suspect was one thing, but challenging my heterosexual identity—well, that brought the dynamics to a new level of conflict and threat. Also, there were a couple of gay men on campus who were interested in getting to know me better, and so I had to manage my responses to them. Having people think that I was gay was a new experience and prompted an examination of my own homophobia and heterosexism. I remember thinking at the time that studying men was taking me places that I never knew existed in my life.

Some women feminists thought my motivation to study men was to justify men's problems and violence. In reality, I was trying to do just the opposite: explain how men's restrictive gender roles contribute to violent, abusive, and controlling behaviors in relationships. These were difficult days in my gender role journey (O'Neil & Egan, 1992a; O'Neil et al., 1993). My own hyped-up emotions and the confrontational interpersonal dynamics surrounding my scholarship convinced me that studying men's lives was going to be a challenging but a provocative opportunity for my personal and professional growth. Sometimes I was anxious, but mostly I was excited, enthused, and energized.

MY GENDER ROLE JOURNEY

My 4-month-long literature review was disappointing because I found very little information on men in books and the professional journals. Most of the literature was in the popular paperbacks spawned by the men's liberation movement. Moreover, as I reviewed the literature on men, I had to face my own psychological issues with sexism, including my relationship with my father and my interactions with both men and women. These emotional issues interfered with my writing as I variously experienced confusion, loss, anger, and periodic depression. There were numerous times that I stopped writing completely because I had to process the flood of repressed emotions from the past.

Part of the process was coming to terms with the feeling that I did not really like men that much. Disliking my own gender prompted much soul searching, and then a transformative insight crystallized. I recognized that my dislike of other men really represented what I disliked about myself and my father. Slowly, with this one insight, I began to feel less anger toward and more compassion for men. At the same time, I generated more compassion for myself and my father. I recognized that my problems and my father's limitations both related to our sexist gender role socialization. After reaching that insight, my feelings toward my father and other men changed. I learned that my compassion for men had the capacity to mediate my anger and liberate me from my sexist past. These profound insights helped me see how my gender role journey could be liberating and healing. After this gender role transition (see Chapter 5, this volume), I began to connect with men I respected and wanted to emulate. Some were men whom I had never met (Mahatma Gandhi, Robert Kennedy, Teilhard de Chardin, the courageous Martin Luther King), some were men whom I had met only briefly (Daniel and Philip Berrigan, George Albee), and some were men in my personal and professional life (Tom Magoon, Delbert Shenkel, Larry Wrightsman, Puncky Heppner, Murray Scher, Joe Pleck, Brooks Collison, and Gary White). These men gave me hope and evidence that the radical separatists were "off" in describing all men as innate oppressors and misogynists. The list of men and women whom I admired got longer over the years as I met more male colleagues who were feminists and committed to the psychology of men and women. Many of these colleagues' works are cited throughout this book.

CONCEPTUAL DILEMMAS AND CONFUSION

In 1981, Joseph Pleck's breakthrough book *The Myth of Masculinity* was published, and this single text became the theoretical foundation for the GRC construct. Pleck described a new model of sex role strain with 10 new propositions about gender roles.

Even with this useful publication, there were many theoretical dilemmas to work out in creating the GRC construct. I got lost in the literature because most of the gender role studies were related to women and there were no integrative reviews about men. Most of the literature on the psychology of women focused on sex differences and androgyny without any mention of men's gender roles. I was discouraged to not find information about men in the literature, and I wondered why this area had been neglected. On the basis of what I found in the literature, I still did not have concrete answers to the feminists' questions, and I did not know what to do next.

EARLY REACTION TO THE GENDER ROLE CONFLICT CONSTRUCT: LATE 1970s AND EARLY 1980s

Pleck's (1981) sex role strain model was the only theoretically rich conceptualization to expand our knowledge about men, and therefore I decided to explore the psychological implications of sex role strain. Pleck's analysis did not specify what the specific socialization outcomes were for boys and men, and therefore the GRC construct became the theoretically defined result of sex role strain. I reached two other conclusions from the literature search: (a) that sexism negatively affects both sexes and (b) that GRC was a significant mental health issue for both men and women (O'Neil, 1981a, 1981b, 1982). After integrating the literature to reach these conclusions, I wanted to create a model that explained why men were sexist, dysfunctional, unhappy, violent, and conflicted because of their socialized gender roles and answer the following question: "Are men victims of sexism?"

In 1979, at the American College Personnel Association convention in Los Angeles, I gave my first professional presentation on GRC; it was entitled "The Male Sex Role and the Negative Consequences of the Masculine Socialization Process: Implications for Counselors and Counseling Psychologists" (O'Neil, 1979). I remember being nervous about my paper because I had decided to present my work on the GRC and share my vulnerable feelings publicly, which certainly went counter to the patriarchal male role. Yet I felt that the concepts would be more valid if they were owned and personalized. The response to my vulnerability was positive, and I felt a new kind of strength and energy.

In 1980, I organized a symposium on men at the annual American Psychological Association (APA) convention in Montreal, Quebec, Canada, one of the first symposia on men in psychology. In the middle of presenting my first GRC model there was a sudden, unsolicited rush to the front of the room by dozens in the audience to get my paper. We were all stunned by this spontaneous burst of energy. I left the convention convinced that this topic moves people in special ways.

The outcomes of my literature searches were three published articles (O'Neil, 1981a, 1981b, 1982), the development of the Gender Role Conflict Scale (GRCS; O'Neil, Helms, Gable, David, & Wrightsman, 1986), and the beginnings of the GRC research program that is summarized elsewhere (see http://jimoneil.uconn.edu). One article published in *The Counseling Psychologist* had an elaborate conceptual model and listed 18 psychological conflicts and 26 effects of men's rigid and sexist gender role socialization. One year later, *Playboy* published a sarcastic critique of the listing of the 18 conflicts and 26 effects with the mocking title: "So You Think You've Got Problems, Fella." The brief article read like this:

> Changes in sex roles seem to be a growing cause of stress among men. *Sexuality Today* recently published a list of common conflicts prepared by James M. O'Neil, a University of Kansas psychologist. Just in case you think you have nothing to worry about, here is a partial list of O'Neil's selections: fear of femininity, fear of emasculation, fear of vulnerability, fear of failure, homophobia, limited sensuality, restrictive and affection-ate behavior between men, treating women as inferior and as sex objects, low self-esteem, work stress and strain, restrictive emotionality, restrictive communication patterns, obsession with success and achievement, socialized power needs that restrict self and others, socialized competitiveness that restricts self and others, socialized dominance needs that restrict self and others. We recommend that you clip this list, carefully fold it and keep it in your wallet for the next time someone asks you what is bugging you.

I was initially irritated that 3 years of my work on men was reduced to a joke and a denial of men's gender role problems. This reaction had deeper meaning than a simple repudiation of my scholarship. This devaluation of my work was more evidence that GRC was threatening to the status quo; therefore, I concluded that it was important and should be pursued vigorously.

To simplify the long list of men's problems, I created a conceptual model that captured as many of these conflicts as possible (O'Neil, 1981a, 1982). The model implied that men's gender role socialization and the values of the "masculine mystique" are all related to the fear of femininity. The six patterns of GRC, hypothesized to relate to the fear of femininity and men's gender role socialization, include (a) restrictive emotionality; (b) health care problems; (c) obsession with achievement and success; (d) restrictive and affectionate behavior; (e) socialized control, power, and competition issues; and (f) homophobia. These six patterns are hypothesized to result from both personal and institutionalized sexism and were part of my early attempt to operationally define men's GRC.

THE MENTOR: LARRY WRIGHTSMAN
MAKES THE REAL DIFFERENCE

Around the same time, I was sharing my work with Dr. Lawrence (Larry) Wrightsman, an eminent social psychologist at the University of Kansas. He liked the models I was developing, and he surprised me when he said "they could have far-reaching impact like the androgyny models and measures like the Bem Sex Role Inventory (BSRI) and Personal Attributes Questionnaire (PAQ)." I was receiving critical feedback about my ideas from everyone, and so Wrightsman's supportive comments were like buoys for me. His confirmation and support were critical to my ongoing process. This one man's support of my ideas made all the difference in regard to the development and ultimate success of the GRC research program. As one might expect, I am very grateful to Larry for changing my career and life with his generous help and support.

Like all good mentors, Larry challenged me. He said the ideas were important but that "they would have minimal impact," meaning a "short shelf life," without empiricism on the six patterns of GRC" (personal communication, May 26, 1981). Specifically, he challenged me to develop an empirical measure of the six patterns of GRC. I was becoming a decent clinician and an effective professor, but I had no real experience developing a psychological scale. After some resistance on my part, I decided to learn about more test construction and, with some colleagues, developed the GRCS. I knew from my clients and from my own life that men experienced GRC, but in the psychological sciences, empirical data and scientific tests are needed to promote one's theoretical constructs. With another grant from the university and the gracious help of Nancy Betz at Ohio State University, the GRCS was developed and psychometrically tested. We analyzed the data, and four patterns of GRC emerged from the factor analyses and the reliability tests. We submitted the article to the journal *Sex Roles*, and it was published in 1986 (O'Neil et al., 1986).

THE MID- AND LATE 1980s: EXPOSING GENDER ROLE
CONFLICT AT NATIONAL CONVENTIONS

During the 1980s, I gave 18 presentations on the GRC model at 12 different conventions to recruit others to use the GRCS and gather feedback on the construct. From 1984 to 1990, only five dissertations used the scale, and just one article that used it—Good, Dell, and Mintz's (1989) landmark study on help seeking—was published in the literature. I remember wondering why men's problems were not of interest to professionals in the mainstream counseling and psychology professions. I concluded that the time was not right and this upstream battle was occurring because no discipline existed to promote the psychology of men.

THE 1990s AND BEYOND

The 1990s were a time when GRC began to receive more attention and critiques. Betz and Fitzgerald (1993) described the extant GRC research as influential in explaining the restrictiveness of men's gender roles but cited numerous limitations to the GRCS and the overall research on the psychology of men. On the basis of this critique, I teamed up with Dr. Glenn Good at the University of Missouri–Columbia, and we conducted a symposium at the annual APA conventions for 17 consecutive years, from 1991 to 2008. Those 17 years of symposia allowed for the presentation of more than 79 empirical studies by 70 colleagues or their students.

I raised questions about men as victims of sexism in 1991 at an APA symposium in San Francisco in front of 100 psychologists (O'Neil, 1991). One of the discussants, a prominent feminist, told the audience that my allegation of "men as victims of sexism" was polarizing and that I should back off. I hadn't actually said that men are victims of sexism but instead had strongly suggested that it was a meaningful question to be discussed if there were to exist a feminist psychology of men. Moreover, backing off from a meaningful question is something I rarely do, and I repeated that it was a necessary and legitimate question. Much of the opposition to the idea of men as victims of sexism was based on the politics of gender roles in those early days when the psychology of men was forming. Now, 25 years later, the idea of men as victims of sexism has evolved into the concept of gender role trauma strain (O'Neil, 2008c; Pleck, 1995) that is developing in the psychology of men. There is a growing recognition that sexism can be victimizing and traumatic not just for girls and women but also for boys and men.

In 1995, the first major summary of GRC studies was provided in Ron Levant's and William Pollack's book *A New Psychology of Men* (O'Neil, Good, & Holmes, 1995) and, thanks to Jim Mahalik at Boston College and Clara Hill at the University of Maryland, a special section of the *Journal of Counseling Psychology* was devoted to men's GRC in 1995 (Tracey, 1995). The GRC research web page (http://web.uconn.edu/joneil/) was created in 1998 and summarized the 100 studies that have provided researchers with a quick but comprehensive way of understanding the GRC paradigm. In 1999, GRC theory was used to conceptualize men's violence against women with an elaborate model and 15 assumptions (O'Neil & Nadeau, 1999). In 2005, an adolescent version of the GRCS was published (Blazina, Pisecco, & O'Neil, 2005), and in 2012, a short form of the GRCS was created (Wester, Vogel, O'Neil, & Danforth, 2012). These new scales gave the GRC research study more comprehensiveness and utility (see Chapter 4, this volume). From 1995 to 2005, the number of GRC empirical studies increased significantly, from 65 to more than 230. In 2008, a summary of the 233 studies was published as a special issue of *The Counseling Psychologist* (O'Neil, 2008c; see also Chapter 7, this volume). Currently, there are over 350 studies on men's GRC.

GIVING CREDIT WHERE CREDIT IS DESERVED

I do take credit for developing the GRC research program over the years, but the real credit goes to the hundreds of researchers and their mentors who actually did the research. In Table 2.1, I list the many colleagues and friends who have significantly contributed over time to the GRC research program. The list is long, and I hope I have not missed anyone who made significant and long-term contributions. The References section of this book also identifies many others who have significantly contributed to the GRC research program. Table 2.1 and the References demonstrate one of my strong professional beliefs: Individual achievement and success is usually not a solo activity but occurs through the efforts of many others who contribute to our projects. The colleagues mentioned throughout this book deserve full recognition for their many contributions to the GRC research program over the past 30 years.

What did I learn from my gender role journey that I can pass on to future researchers? First, women feminists taught me that good intentions do not make you credible; instead, your actions and advocacy are what count. Second, research can significantly challenge the status quo and your colleagues: If you are doing anything important, there will be negative reactions, resistance, and threat. In addition, conducting research can promote your personal growth and connect you to exciting people who share your goals, mission, and vision. Furthermore, researching a new topic brings confusion and ambiguity, and persistence is required so that the new concepts can be operationalized. When there is no resolution conceptually, create your own ideas and be ready to measure and defend them. I also have learned that telling your truth and being personally vulnerable are credible professional roles that can activate both confrontational and supportive forces; therefore, be ready for all kinds of reactions to your work. Developing theory-based psychological models from the literature can be exciting, and when your research is published, colleagues pay attention. Also, mentors really matter and can change your life, as in my own case when I worked with Larry Wrightsman. I also have learned that patience, effort, and national networking are required to develop a research program. Finally, I have learned to always give credit to those who deserve it (see Table 2.1). Regardless of what we achieve, it is usually not just about our personal accomplishment but due to the efforts of many others who have given their time, effort, and special contribution to our cause.

TABLE 2.1

Researchers and Colleagues Who Made Considerable Contributions
to the Gender Role Conflict Research Program

Name	Institution
Glenn Good	University of Florida
Jim Mahalik	Boston College
Chris Blazina	Tennessee State University
Gary Brooks	Baylor University
Stewart Pisecco	University of Houston
Matt Breiding	Centers for Disease Control and Prevention
David Smith	University of Notre Dame
Will Liu	University of Iowa
Ron Levant	University of Akron
Aaron Rochlen	University of Texas
Jay Wade	Fordham University
Paul (Puncky) Heppner	University of Missouri–Columbia
Mary Heppner	University of Missouri–Columbia
Ryon McDermott	University of Houston
Bonnie Moradi	University of Florida
Phil Amato	Salem State University
Dawn Syzmanski	University of Tennessee
Jon Schwartz	University of New Mexico
John Robertson	Renewal Center, Lawrence, KS
Don McCreary	York University
David Tokar	University of Akron
Jim Rogers	University of Akron
Robert Rando	Wrights State University
Jay Kim	Seoul, South Korea
Chris Kilmartin	Mary Washington University
Cisco Sánchez	University of Wisconsin, Milwaukee
Ann Fischer	Southern Illinois University
Matt Englar-Carlson	California State University at Fullerton
Joe Pleck	University of Illinois
Robert Carter	Columbia University
Sam Cochran	University of Iowa
Fred Rabinowitz	University of Redlands
Will Courtenay	Independent Practice, Berkeley, CA
Marty Heesacker	University of Florida
Andy Horne	University of Georgia
Murray Scher	Private Practice, Greensboro, TN
Jesse Steinfeldt	Indiana University
David Vogel	Iowa State University
Joel Wong	Indiana University
Michael Addis	Clark University
Carolyn Enns	Cornell College
Aaron Blashill	Harvard University
Michele Harway	Antioch University
Roberta Nutt	University of Houston
Mark Kiselica	The College of New Jersey
Holly Sweet	MIT
Louise Silverstein	Yeshiva University

II

THE THEORETICAL FOUNDATIONS OF GENDER ROLE CONFLICT

3

NEW CONTEXTUAL PARADIGMS FOR GENDER ROLE CONFLICT THEORY, RESEARCH, AND PRACTICE

I once told one of my health care providers that I was writing a book on men's gender roles, and he immediately responded, "The whole book could be reduced to just one page: Men get the remote control and women get everything else that they want." I asked him to repeat that statement a couple of times because I could not understand what he meant. Maybe he thought men's issues are primarily control and power struggles between men and women. The meaning of his one-liner was ambiguous, but the comment reflected a reductionist and simplistic view of the complex problems men have with their gender roles.

This brief exchange demonstrated an unspoken reality to me: Today's gender roles produce ambivalence, confusion, annoyance, and conflict for many people. Reducing gender roles to simplistic conclusions is a way to cope and avoid emotional turmoil, an attempt to find security in one's identity amid contradiction and paradox. A transitional vacuum currently exists in which

http://dx.doi.org/10.1037/14501-004

old world stereotypes about sex and gender roles are incompatible with the mandated equality between the sexes and an acceptance that humans can be gendered and express their sexuality in many different ways. Our capacity to accept new definitions of masculinity and femininity is evolving, but painfully slowly, and therefore complexity, conflict, and confusion still exist.

In this chapter, I discuss the complexity of gender role conflict (GRC) by moving beyond the history I discussed in Chapter 2. Here, I address the past definitions and the early theoretical concepts of GRC (O'Neil, 1981a, 1981b, 1982, 1990, 2008c; O'Neil, Good, & Holmes, 1995; O'Neil, Helms, Gable, David, & Wrightsman, 1986). I follow the presentation of these concepts with a discussion of past criticism of the GRC paradigm and the Gender Role Conflict Scale (GRCS; O'Neil et al., 1986) and argue for more contextualization of GRC to continue to move the paradigm forward. Next, I present two new contextual models that explain the complexity of men's experiences with GRC. One model is contextually descriptive and the other focuses on understanding men's behaviors in functional, microcontextual, and situational dimensions. Fourteen assumptions about GRC are enumerated at the end of the chapter to provide contexts for the major themes of this book.

PAST DEFINITIONS OF GENDER ROLE CONFLICT

The definition of GRC has evolved from a series of theoretical and research papers produced over the past 35 years (O'Neil, 1981a, 1981b, 1982, 1990, 2008c; O'Neil et al., 1986, 1995; O'Neil & Egan, 1993; O'Neil & Nadeau, 1999). GRC is defined as a psychological state in which socialized gender roles have negative consequences for the person or others. It occurs when rigid, sexist, or restrictive gender roles result in personal restriction, devaluation, or violation of others or oneself (O'Neil, 2008c). The ultimate outcome of this kind of conflict is the restriction of the human potential of the person experiencing it or a restriction of another person's potential. GRC has been operationally defined by four psychological domains, three situational contexts, and three personal and interpersonal experiences. These represent the complexity of GRC in people's lives, and I describe them in the following sections.

The Four Psychological Domains of Gender Role Conflict

The four psychological domains of GRC imply problems that occur at four overlapping and complex levels—(a) cognitive, (b) emotional (affective),

(c) behavioral, and (d) unconscious—and are caused by restrictive gender roles learned in sexist and patriarchal societies.

- The *cognitive* aspect of GRC pertains to thoughts and questions about gender roles, the understanding of which varies on the basis of the developmental level of the man. Dualistic thinkers experience gender roles differently than men with more cognitive complexity. Thinking that one does not meet expected masculine norms or cannot compete in society can cause discrepancy strain (Pleck, 1995).
- The *emotional/affective* domain includes how a man feels about gender roles, including the degree of comfort or conflict he experiences living out his gender role identity. Negative emotions can lead to dysfunction, strain, and GRC (O'Neil, 2008c).
- *Behavioral* aspects of GRC include ways men respond to and interact with others and themselves that produce negative intra- and interpersonal outcomes. Discrimination against men that is based on sexist assumptions are examples of how GRC can be expressed behaviorally.
- *Unconscious* GRC encompasses thoughts, feelings, and behaviors related to conflicts with gender roles that are beyond our awareness. Early psychoanalytical theorists—such as Freud, Jung, Adler, and Horney—who discussed unconscious conflict with gender roles were, in many ways, referring to GRC.

The Four Situational Contexts of Gender Role Conflict

GRC previously was conceptualized as occurring in four situational contexts (or categories) that gave the construct a simple explanation and form. These contexts were defined as (a) GRC *within the man* (intrapersonal), (b) GRC *expressed toward others* (interpersonal), (c) GRC *experienced from others* (also interpersonal), and (d) GRC *during gender role transitions*.

GRC in an intrapersonal context is a man's experience of negative emotions and thoughts when experiencing gender role devaluations, restrictions, and violations. I discuss these private—and many times unconscious—dynamics in more detail below. GRC expressed toward others occurs when the man's gender role problems cause him to devalue, restrict, or violate someone else, for example, telling sexist jokes or committing sexual harassment. GRC from others occurs when someone devalues, restricts, or violates another person who deviates from or conforms to masculinity ideology and norms. Finally, GRC can occur during gender role transitions that are part of psychosocial development; this is discussed fully in Chapter 5.

Gender Role Conflict: Gender Role Devaluations, Restrictions, and Violations

The first of the three personal and interpersonal experiences mentioned above is *gender role devaluation*. Such devaluations are negative critiques of oneself or others when conforming to, deviating from, or violating stereotypical gender role norms of masculinity ideology. They result in a lessening of status, stature, and self-esteem, possibly leading to shame, fear, and anger that may be turned inward and in turn cause depression and isolation. Men can devalue themselves, be devalued by others, or devalue someone else.

When a man cannot achieve the expected masculine norms dictated by masculinity ideologies, he may devalue and blame himself. Self-devaluations may, for example, occur when a man fails to meet his expectations for success at work; when he cannot provide for his family; or when he cannot be an effective father or spouse because of work overload, stress, and exhaustion. Other devaluations may occur as the result of lost career dreams, unemployment, traumas, divorce, and decreased sexual stamina.

Devaluations from others—in particular, competitors, parents, or family members—can be especially painful and can trigger defensiveness, withdrawal, and sometimes even violence. Examples of being devalued by others include being bullied or subjected to emasculating remarks that imply the man is a loser, a failure, or somehow inadequate. Men may devalue others when they do not meet, or when they deviate from, expected masculine and feminine norms. Gay men and heterosexual women can be targets of devaluations because they deviate from the stereotypes of, respectively, masculinity and femininity. Gender role devaluations can be salient activators of men's emotional and interpersonal problems.

The second of the three personal and interpersonal experiences is *gender role restriction*, which implies that GRC confines oneself or others to stereotypical and restrictive norms of masculinity ideology and expected gender roles. Gender role restrictions also result in attempts to control people's behavior, limit their potential, and decrease human freedom. They occur when masculine and feminine norms prohibit flexibility in work situations and negatively affect family and interpersonal relationships. Such restrictions narrow options and deny people's needs, and they can result in manipulation and abuses of power. The costs of restricting oneself or others include feelings of loss, guilt, anger, and powerlessness. As with devaluation, men can restrict themselves, be restricted by others, or restrict someone else. Men's restriction of their own emotions, self-disclosure, and overall communication limits behavioral flexibility and adaptability to life's unpredictable events. They may, for instance, restrict themselves by devoting their primary energies to work at the expense of their family and parenting roles, which may reduce intimacy, cause work overload, and leave little room for relaxation and a healthy lifestyle. Rigid gender role norms may be forced on others by demanding they conform to one's own masculinity or femininity ideology, sometimes subjecting them to excessive control, manipulations, criticism, and even emotional abuse.

Gender role violations represent the most severe kind of GRC. They occur when people harm themselves or others or are harmed by others because of destructive gender role norms of masculinity ideology. To be *violated* means to be victimized and abused, resulting in emotional and physical pain, and sometimes gender role trauma strain, which can in turn result in severe negative outcomes in terms of psychological functioning. Men violate themselves by subjecting themselves to overwork, excessive stress, dangerous risks, and substance abuse to dull painful emotions and life events. Unexpressed emotions such as fear, anger, and shame can be internalized, which can cause chronic depression, self-hatred, isolation, serious health problems and, in some cases, suicide. Gender role violations of others include discriminatory behavior toward women, sexual harassment, homophobic and antigay attitudes, emotional abuse, and even sexual and physical assault, all of which stem from stereotypical attitudes about gender roles. Men are violated by others through physical violence, molestations, unfair custody decisions, unjust corporate downsizing, and exposure to dangerous work settings that cause serious injuries. Although men's violations of others are commonly reported in the media, how gender roles contribute to these incidents is rarely explained.

In sum, gender role devaluations, restrictions, and violations are the personal and interpersonal experience of GRC and are critical to understanding how men become conflicted with their gender roles. I discuss the experiences of GRC further in Chapter 6 in regard to diversity; in Chapter 9 in regard to assessment; and in Chapters 10 and 11, which are devoted to men's therapy. In the next section, I operationalize definitions of GRC using past conceptual models.

PAST THEORETICAL AND CONCEPTUAL PARADIGMS OF GENDER ROLE CONFLICT

In this section, I summarize the GRC model and its key components and introduce a second element of GRC: the gender role journey paradigm.

Early Gender Role Conflict Model

Figure 3.1 shows the primary theoretical model that has previously been used to summarize the premises of men's GRC and to explain how to measure it using the GRCS (O'Neil, 1981a, 1990, 2008c; O'Neil et al., 1995).

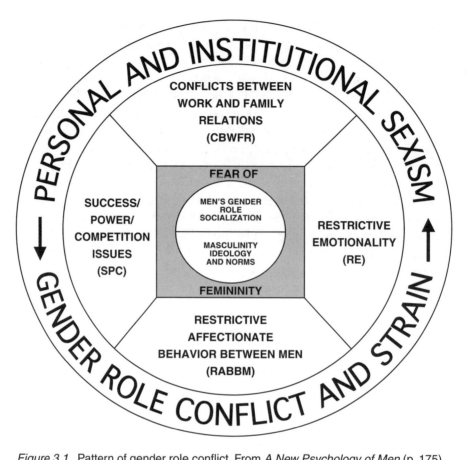

Figure 3.1. Pattern of gender role conflict. From *A New Psychology of Men* (p. 175), by R.F. Levant and W.S. Pollack (Eds.), 1995, New York, NY: Perseus Books. Copyright 1995 by R.F. Levant and W.S. Pollack. Reprinted with permission.

The model provides a summary of the conceptual ideas of GRC developed over the past 30 years.

At the center of Figure 3.1 are men's gender role socialization and masculinity ideology and norms. The latter are primary values and standards that define, restrict, and negatively affect boys' and men's lives. Reviews of the masculinity ideology studies (Levant & Richmond, 2007; O'Neil, 2010; O'Neil & Crapser, 2011) indicate that restrictive ways of thinking about masculine norms are significantly correlated with men's psychological problems, interpersonal conflicts, and GRC. Two such reviews found more than 70 psychological problems for men correlated with masculinity ideology (O'Neil, 2010, 2012b), and some of the research on this topic is reported in Chapter 1 of this volume.

Figure 3.1 shows men's gender role socialization and the masculinity ideology and norms as conceptually related to men's fear of femininity (FOF), which is central to understanding men's GRC (O'Neil, 2008c; O'Neil et al., 1986). FOF encompasses negative thoughts and emotions associated with stereotypical feminine values, attitudes, and behaviors and are learned in early childhood when gender role identity is being shaped by parents, peers, and societal values. Men's conscious and unconscious fears of femininity have been discussed in the theoretical literature for many years (Blazina, 1997, 2003; Boehm, 1930; Freud, 1937; Horney, 1967; Jung, 1953, 1954; Kierski & Blazina, 2009; Levinson, Darrow, Klein, Levinson, & McKee, 1978; Norton, 1997) and play a critical role in men's gender role socialization.

Moving outward from the center of the figure, one sees that men's fears about appearing feminine are theoretically linked to four patterns of GRC. These patterns, which reflect ways in which men experience negative consequences because of restrictive gender roles, have been empirically studied using the GRCS in more than 350 studies, many of which are described in Chapter 7. The pattern referred to in the figure as *Success/Power/Competition* refers to personal attitudes about success pursued through competition and power. *Restrictive Emotionality* is defined as having restrictions and fears about expressing one's feelings, as well as in finding words to express basic emotions. *Restrictive Affectionate Behavior Between Men* represents restrictions in expressing one's feelings and thoughts with other men and difficulty in touching them, and *Conflicts Between Work and Family Relations* reflects the experience of restrictions in balancing work, school, and family relations, resulting in health problems, overwork, stress, and a lack of leisure and relaxation.

Finally, the outer boundary of Figure 3.1 depicts personal and institutional sexism and GRC and strain as interrelated realities that shape men's lives. This part of the model implies that sexist structures in society and men's gender role socialization are directly related to men's GRC and psychological problems. As I discussed in both Chapters 1 and 2, GRC is a political issue as well as an area in which psychological and interpersonal problems can arise.

The Gender Role Journey Paradigm

Another central concept in the GRC research program is the gender role journey. The gender role journey is a metaphor and framework that helps people examine how their gender role socialization, GRC, and sexism have affected their lives (O'Neil & Egan, 1992a). The journey involves doing a retrospective analysis of early family experiences with gender roles, making an assessment of one's present situation with sexism, and making decisions about how to act in the future. The overall purpose of the process is to evaluate how gender roles and sexism have affected one's life personally, professionally, and politically and use this knowledge to improve one's life and society.

In Exhibit 3.1, I describe three phases of the gender role journey, which EX 1 imply change and transitions with gender roles: (a) acceptance of traditional roles; (b) gender role ambivalence, confusion, anger, and fear; and (c) personal and professional activism (O'Neil et al., 1993). The gender role journey

---

EXHIBIT 3.1
Phases of the Gender Role Journey

Acceptance of Traditional Gender Role Attitudes and Beliefs

In this phase of the gender role journey, people endorse traditional gender role stereotypes of masculinity and femininity. There are male and female roles based on biological imperatives or some other essentialist value system. Men should be in charge at work and in the home, and women should be the primary providers of child care. Men should be strong and not show weakness, and women should be more passive and not assertive. In this phase, there is limited awareness of how sexism can hurt people, a belief that feminists have caused problems between men and women, and no interest in doing anything about sexism and discrimination.

Gender Role Ambivalence, Confusion, Anger, and Fear

In this phase of the gender role journey, people are confused about gender role stereotypes and have some fear about the journey. There is vacillation between accepting the stereotypes and recognizing how they negatively restrict people in relationships. There is fear about questioning or changing gender role stereotypes, and people need help with the process. This phase is characterized by anger about sexism, but people are not clear why this emotion exists and do not know what to do about it. There may be limited outlets for anger. The more people express their anger about sexism, the more conflict they have. Some people in this stage have intense anger because they know that they and others have been victims of sexism and restrictive gender role socialization. Anger is pivotal in moving a person from a dysfunctional to a functional phase of the journey. Some people believe that staying angry or getting stuck in one's anger is counterproductive. Some conclude that the stereotypes are insufficient to build a human identity. Only when anger becomes great is there willingness to take risks of challenging the status quo.

Personal and Professional Activism

Activism means changing oneself by integrating the anger and by making commitments to reduce sexism in one's own life. This begins when talking does not work and action is perceived to be a better course to pursue. In this phase, people attempt to live a life free from restrictive gender role stereotypes and feel an inner strength and power that are based on rejecting restrictive gender roles and sexism. Their anger, pain, and emotions are used to reduce sexism and raise other people's consciousness through teaching and other activist agendas. There is the strong belief that they are responsible for reducing sexism and that something can be done to prevent it through activism. Increased self-communication is required to remain in the activism stage. There is greater compassion for the self and for other people's gender role journeys.

---

also involves identifying gender role transitions as they occur in life and reexamining gender role schemas (O'Neil & Egan, 1992b; O'Neil & Fishman, 1992; O'Neil, Fishman, & Kinsella-Shaw, 1987). The Gender Role Journey Measure (GRJM; O'Neil, Egan, Owen, & Murry, 1993) was created to help both men and women determine the phases of the gender role journey with which they identify. Part of the journey is the process of coming to understand how GRC develops in the family and how it is the result of other socialization experiences in society. Full theoretical descriptions of these phases can be found in earlier studies (O'Neil et al., 1993; O'Neil & Egan, 1992a; O'Neil & Roberts Carroll, 1988) and are discussed more fully in Chapters 4 and 10 of this volume.

PAST CRITICISM OF THE GENDER ROLE CONFLICT PARADIGM AND THE GENDER ROLE CONFLICT SCALE

Over the years, much critique has shaped the GRC paradigm (O'Neil, 2008a, 2008c) and produced revisions and adaptations of the GRCS (Blazina, Pisecco, & O'Neil, 2005; Wester, Vogel, O'Neil, & Danforth, 2012). I have tried to graciously accept the feedback without becoming stressed, but I do remember frantically making an appointment with Dr. Julian Rotter, the famous personality psychologist at the University of Connecticut, to ask his advice about a researcher's claim that the GRCS was invalid because it correlated significantly with measures of social desirability. Rotter, a veteran test developer (he was the creator of the Internal–External Locus of Control Scale; Rotter, 1966) calmed me down and pointed out that the correlations would need to be much higher than .12 to matter much.

What have the critics said about the GRCS? The following are some of the key criticisms. First, the research program has failed to assess GRC longitudinally by identifying developmental tasks and contextual demands that interface with men's socialization (Enns, 2000; Heppner, 1995; Smiler, 2004). Another limitation of the research program has been the lack of research on how GRC affects others and how it is experienced when coming from others (Rochlen & Mahalik, 2004). Questions have been raised about whether Conflict Between Work and Family Relations is really a pattern of GRC unique to men (Good et al., 1995). The similarities and differences between men's and women's GRC have been discussed as unexplored areas of research (Enns, 2000; Zamarripa, Wampold, & Gregory, 2003). The GRCS also has been criticized as not fully measuring conflict (Betz & Fitzgerald, 1993), but the research completed and item analyses have documented that the scale does indeed measure men's conflict with their gender roles (O'Neil, 2008c). The most in-depth analysis of the GRCS and the GRCS for Adolescents (Blazina, Pisecco, & O'Neil, 2005) was by Beaglaoich, Sarma, and Morrison (2013). They criticized the initial development of the GRCS in 1980 and questioned the relevancy of the scales for cross-cultural samples. Most of their criticisms are valid because the scale development standards of the 1970s were used to create the GRCS, not the current criteria for scale development. Beaglaoich et al.'s criticism is critical to researchers developing GRC scales in the future. In addition, some critics have alleged that the GRCS measures a limited of behavioral domains and does not assess important areas such as men's sexuality, performance, homophobia, and health issues (E. H. Thompson & Pleck, 1995). The critics are correct about the limited number of behavioral domains, and therefore the call to action should include further scale development.

Another criticism is that GRC theory is disconnected from the larger societal and political systems (Enns, 2000). How the larger social system endorses gender as a set of power relations that affect social policies and produce discrimination that restrict humans' behavioral options has not yet been addressed (Enns, 2008; Wester, 2008a, 2008b). Enns (2008) discussed this issue when she wrote that the social system perspective of GRC "has received only limited attention to date but seems important for understanding the diversity of masculine GRC and for guiding explorations of power and abuse (e.g., violence against women)" (p. 447). GRC was hypothesized in its earliest formulations as related to institutional sexism and power structures (O'Neil, 1981a, 1981b, 1982; O'Neil & Egan, 1993), but this issue has remained unclarified over the years. The earlier GRC model did depict institutional sexism as a part of GRC (see Figure 3.1), but the observation that GRC has been disconnected from societal and political systems is accurate. More complex models are needed to explain how GRC is experienced at the macrosocietal level and in sociopolitical contexts (Enns, 2000; Good, Heppner, DeBord, & Fischer, 2004; Tokar, Fischer, Schaub, & Moradi, 2000).

Furthermore, some scholars have argued that men's GRC has not been *contextualized*, meaning that situational and real-life contingencies that affect men's lives have been neglected in the theory and research (Addis, Mansfield, & Syzdek, 2010; K. Jones & Heesacker, 2012; O'Neil, 2008c; Smiler, 2004). The critics argue that GRC theory is trait based and does not address states of men's experience. This criticism is off the mark somewhat because GRC theory has always been discussed in a situational context and measured that way. Sixteen items of the Gender Role Conflict Scale—II (GRCS–II) measure situations of GRC in which the respondent reports degrees of conflict and comfort in gender conflict situations (O'Neil et al., 1986). Although this scale has been seldom used because of reliability issues with one of the subscales, its existence confirms that GRC has been conceptualized as a situational construct.

The critics are mostly correct that research has failed to assess GRC in a situational context, although seven studies have found situational dynamics relate to men's GRC (Breiding, 2004; Breiding, Windle, & Smith, 2008; Cohn, Seibert, & Ziechner, 2009; Cohn & Zeichner, 2006; Cohn, Zeichner, & Seibert, 2008; K. Jones & Heesacker, 2012; Windle & Smith, 2009). Overall, the GRC model of the 1980s (see Figure 3.1) does not address the causal questions of how, why, and when a man becomes conflicted with his gender roles. Furthermore, the previous GRC contexts (intrapersonal, interpersonal, and therapeutic) have limited explanatory power; more comprehensive domains need to be defined.

Altogether, the critiques support the development of new GRC models that are more complex and comprehensive and that advance research and clinical practice. The ideas published in the 1980s (O'Neil, 1981a, 1981b, 1982) are still relevant, but the previous models do not provide a coherent, heuristic, or action-oriented framework to help frame an understanding of men's development over the life span or explain how men's problems develop from restrictive gender roles and are experienced situationally in real time.

CALL TO ACTION: CONTEXTUAL PARADIGMS OF MEN'S GENDER ROLE CONFLICT

Not only has GRC been theoretically limited but also the psychology of men has lacked operational concepts to explain men's lives. Without a more expansive conceptual foundation, the discipline cannot fully pursue needed research and make clinical advances that can help men. Still missing are explanations of the complexity of men's lives at both the macrosocietal and microcontextual levels—that is, how both patriarchal values and actual GRC situations play out in men's lives.

Both developmental and social psychologists have indicated that the study of gender roles needs to be contextual (Eckes & Trautner, 2000; Smiler, 2004; Trautner & Eckes, 2000) because gender roles are influenced by many personal, societal, racial, cultural, political, religious, and situational contingencies (Addis et al., 2010; Deaux & Majors, 1987; C. A. B. Johnston & Morrison, 2007; K. Jones & Heesacker, 2012). According to Smiler (2004), "Future researchers must begin to examine the influence of contextual factors [on gender roles], including verification of the assumptions of the invariance of an individual's masculine behavior across settings" (p. 25). The overall consensus is that contextualism can help explain the complexity of gender roles, but how to study contextualized gender roles is still in the early stages of development.

DIFFERENT KINDS OF CONTEXTUALISM

One of the difficulties with studying contextualized gender roles is that definitions of *contextualism* are both general and specific and emanate from different approaches to science. The three most prominent definitions identified in the literature are (a) developmental contextualism (Lerner, 2001), (b) descriptive contextualism, and (c) functional contextualism (Biglan & Hayes, 1996; S. C. Hayes, 1993; S. C. Hayes, Hayes, Reese, & Sarbin, 1993).

Developmental contextualism focuses on creating knowledge about human growth that captures the complexity of psychosocial development. Lerner (2001) defined developmental contextualism as the integration of "actions of people in and on the world," and "the actions of the world on people, that shape the quality of human behavioral and psychological functioning" (p. 85). Human experience is shaped by many factors operating in concert with one another (Ford & Lerner, 1992; Lerner, 1992). A contextual analysis focuses on people's real-life situations and the dynamic interaction between individuals and the environment in which they live. Information is obtained by assessing this interplay. Contextualism is concerned with how ecological factors dynamically operate to shape experience and how biological, cultural, psychological, interpersonal, spiritual, political, and social contexts affect behavior. Lerner's developmental contextualism is highly relevant to understanding the developmental aspects of masculinity.

S. C. Hayes (1993) indicated that contextualistic theories can be differentiated by their analytic goals into two categories: (a) descriptive contextualism and (b) functional contextualism. *Descriptive contextualism*'s primary goal is to understand the complexity and richness of a whole event through an appreciation of its participants and features. Knowledge is specific, personal, and spatiotemporally restricted and focuses on the individual in context. Descriptive contextualism has been categorized as a social constructionist way of understanding behavior and therefore relevant to psychology of men's theory and research.

The primary goal of *functional contextualism* is the prediction and influencing of events using empirically based concepts and rules. Functional contextualists frameworks "seek the development of an organized system of empirically based concepts and rules that allow behavioral phenomena to be predicted and influenced with precision, scope, and depth" (Biglan & Hayes, 1996, pp. 50–51). Functional contexualists are driven by behavioral principles and seek to understand behavior in specific settings during real time, accounting for situational cues and environmental stimuli. Researchers in the psychology of men have been advocating that research on men be conceptualized from a functional contextual perspective (Addis et al., 2010; K. Jones & Heesacker, 2012).

CRITICISM OF PAST ATTEMPTS TO
CONTEXTUALIZE GENDER ROLE CONFLICT

In the *Counseling Psychologist*'s 25-year summary of GRC research (O'Neil, 2008c), seven contextual domains, 18 contextual hypotheses, and two contextual research paradigms were proposed to guide future research focused on moderation and mediation studies. Even with these contextual developments, Addis et al. (2010) and K. Jones and Heesacker (2012) have argued for even more precise assessment of men's behavior from a microcontextual or gendered social learning perspective. Addis et al. proposed the gendered social learning research approach that promotes a contextual and contingent-based, cue-oriented agenda for studying how gender-relevant cues elicit male behavior. A second contextual approach is what K. Jones and Heesacker called the study of "microcontexts" of men's issues, that is, sets of cues, norms, and outcome expectations associated with a temporally limited environment. The term *microcontexts* is used to distinguish "brief experiences from the broader contextual factors associated with people's cultural and subcultural experiences" (K. Jones & Heesacker, 2012, p. 295). Both of these perspectives, combined with the past theories of contextual research (Deaux & Majors, 1987; Ford & Lerner, 1992; S. C. Hayes, 1993; S. C. Hayes et al., 1993), are important in developing more comprehensive knowledge about men and masculinity.

Addis et al. (2010) criticized GRC and the way masculinity is currently being conceptualized and empirically measured. They argued that current research in the psychology of men limits scientific rigor and does not promote social action. Given that this book is a call to action, their critique is especially relevant. They indicated that all the previous measures of masculinity ideology and GRC are not designed to be sensitive to contextual influences of social learning.

Addis et al. (2010) argued that gendered social learning is the future of research in the psychology of men and that human activity is best understood by considering the historical and current context in which it operates. They claimed that what should be studied are the "settings in which gender activity occurs, and the consequences of the gendered activity, positive, negative, distal, and proximal" (p. 78).

Addis et al.'s (2010) criticism is that the past GRC correlational research does not explain how to influence a man's behavior in one way or another. They indicated that very few studies have manipulated independent variables and answered such questions as "how men learn about gender, why men learn about gender, how to influence what men learn about gender, how to use what men learn about gender to develop health enhancing interventions, etc." (p. 80). They argued for social learning research that focuses on *situated learning*, meaning particular actions that are followed by particular consequences in specific contexts. They claimed that men and women learn to enact gendered repertoires of behaving to achieve social means or ends. From this perspective, gender consists of layers of situated and contested social practices.

Addis et al. (2010) further argued that the measures used in the study of the psychology of men, including the GRCS, are exclusively trait based and therefore have limited utility in assessing the situational dynamics of gendered behavior. In my opinion, this assertion goes too far in discounting the GRCS and GRC theory as irrelevant to gendered social learning research. From the earliest development of GRC theory, the situational aspects of GRC have been theorized, and the GRCS–II), although not developed fully, measures GRC in 16 situational contexts. Furthermore, the GRCS may appear to be exclusively trait based but, as reported earlier, it has been operationalized in research in the situational contexts for which Addis et al. (2010) argued (see Breiding, 2004; Breiding et al., 2008; Cohn et al., 2008; K. Jones & Heesacker, 2012).

K. Jones and Heesacker (2012) built on Addis et al.'s (2010) critique with their microcontextual analysis of gender roles and GRC. They provided a useful differentiation between overall context and microcontexts. Overall, *context* is defined as an individual subculture or wider culture in which different men find themselves (e.g., regional masculinity or African American masculinity). As mentioned earlier, they offered the concept of microcontexts, which they defined as brief experiences from the broader contextual factors associated with people's cultural and subcultural experiences. Specifically, they defined microcontexts as the set of cues, norms, outcomes, and expectations associated with a temporally limited environment that define how gender manifests and is transformed in time. Situation-specific factors may elicit, reinforce, or normalize a particular set of behaviors related to gender. They argued that men should be studied in context and suggested concepts like gender context dependency and microcontextual dependency as foundations for such research. Furthermore, they argued that GRC is not a static construct but is responsive to proximal cues in an array of contexts (Deaux & Majors, 1987). In their first microcontextual study, they documented that GRC can vary as a function of immediate context (K. Jones & Heesacker, 2012).

K. Jones and Heesacker (2012) also contended that men's negotiation of multiple conceptions, enactments, and situational contingencies related to gender have received little attention. They recommended that researchers study gendered behavior that responds flexibly to contextual cues in one's environment. Like Addis et al. (2010), they conceived of gender and masculinity as gendered repertoires rather than fixed states or traits. They used the concept of *behavioral repertoires* to understand gendered behavior that responds to contextual cues in one's environments to facilitate comprehension of how changes in men's environments may lead to changes in men's behavior. They argued that men experience varying degrees of pressure to adhere to traditional gender roles or deviate from them and research should capture this variation if we are to understand the complexity of men's lives. They also advocated for socially contingent (Addis et al., 2010) and socially constructed (Connell & Messerschmidt, 2005) notions of gender roles that represent men's everyday lives. In a critique of the early GRC research models (O'Neil, 2008c), they indicated that "the term *context* has been perhaps been defined too narrowly thus far to refer only to factors that may moderate or mediate the impact of GRC on various outcomes for men" (p. 294). They offered a broader aspect of contextualism that focuses on situations that influence GRC. They advocated for studying situation-specific factors such as gender contextual dependency and microcontextual dependency. From their perspective, microcontextual research can help clinicians understand the fluidity of gender as they help men in therapy.

RESPONSE TO THE CONTEXTUAL CRITICISM

On the basis of the criticisms just described, what would be goals for any new contextual models of GRC that could expand the psychology of men? Theoretically, the contextual goal is to generate more descriptive gender role concepts that can ultimately be translated to research and clinical practice. This goal is important because the psychology of men has very few defined concepts and even fewer that have empirical support. Second, I agree with K. Jones and Heesacker's (2012) and Addis et al.'s (2010) critiques of the past contextual research on the psychology of men. Therefore, the next goal is to expand gendered social learning and microcontextual research that is critical to understanding men's growth and development (Addis et al., 2010; K. Jones & Heesacker, 2012). This kind of research could document how men learn restricted gender roles, experience GRC in specific situations, and under what conditions and with what negative and positive consequences and outcomes. New contextual models could also promote a better understanding of how positive healthy masculinity is achieved developmentally from childhood throughout the life cycle (Lerner, 2001). More expansive contextual analyses could also help therapists and psychoeducators conceptualize more effective, evidence-based interventions with men (see Chapters 9–13, this volume).

On the basis of these criticisms and the need for more expansive theory on the psychology of men, I have proposed contextual models that are developmental, descriptive, and functional. First, a descriptive and developmental contextual model establishes more concepts to understand men as individuals in the context of GRC and masculinity ideology. The descriptive contextual model depicts the psychosocial–developmental, macrosocietal, and gender role–related contexts in men's lives.

The second model addresses the microcontextual and social learning perspectives of how men's actions in environments and their gendered interactions with others cause GRC and other psychological problems (Addis et al., 2010; K. Jones & Heesacker, 2012). This model is designed to promote increased knowledge about the situational aspects of men's GRC in real time (Addis et al., 2010; K. Jones & Heesacker, 2012).

DESCRIPTIVE CONTEXTUAL MODEL OF MEN'S GENDER ROLE SOCIALIZATION AND GENDER ROLE CONFLICT

Figure 3.2 depicts a new descriptive model that expands the contextual understanding of gender roles and GRC. The new contextual model has three separate but related parts: (a) psychosocial developmental contexts, (b) macrosocietal contexts, and (c) gender-related contexts. The purpose of this model is to convey descriptive (generalized) contexts to understand men and their GRC. First, on the left and at the bottom of the figure are the life stages, psychosocial developmental contexts, and gender role transformation and growth through healthy positive masculinity. Second, the bold black triangle in the middle of the figure, with the three boxes at the corners, is the macrosocietal context. This context includes three components: (a) patriarchy, hegemonic masculinity, sexism, and stereotypes, as organizers of society; (b) personal and institutional oppression from discrimination that creates social injustice; and (c) stereotypes and differential socialization of boys and girls to sexist masculinity and femininity ideologies. Finally, the gender-related contexts are all concepts inside the bold triangle, shown as two trapezoids. The gender-related context focuses on gender role identity and the patterns of GRC. The gender role identity context is shaped by situational, biological, unconscious, familial, multicultural, racial, and ethnic contingencies; restrictive and sexist masculinity and femininity ideologies; FOF; and distorted gender role schemas. In the second trapezoid, the patterns of GRC, as the negative outcomes of sexism and other oppression, are discussed in the context of defensiveness; gender role devaluations, restrictions, and violations; and male vulnerability. Both the macrosocietal and gender-related contexts point directly to the rectangle at the bottom of the figure, which shows men's psychological and interpersonal problems, internalized oppression, and violence.

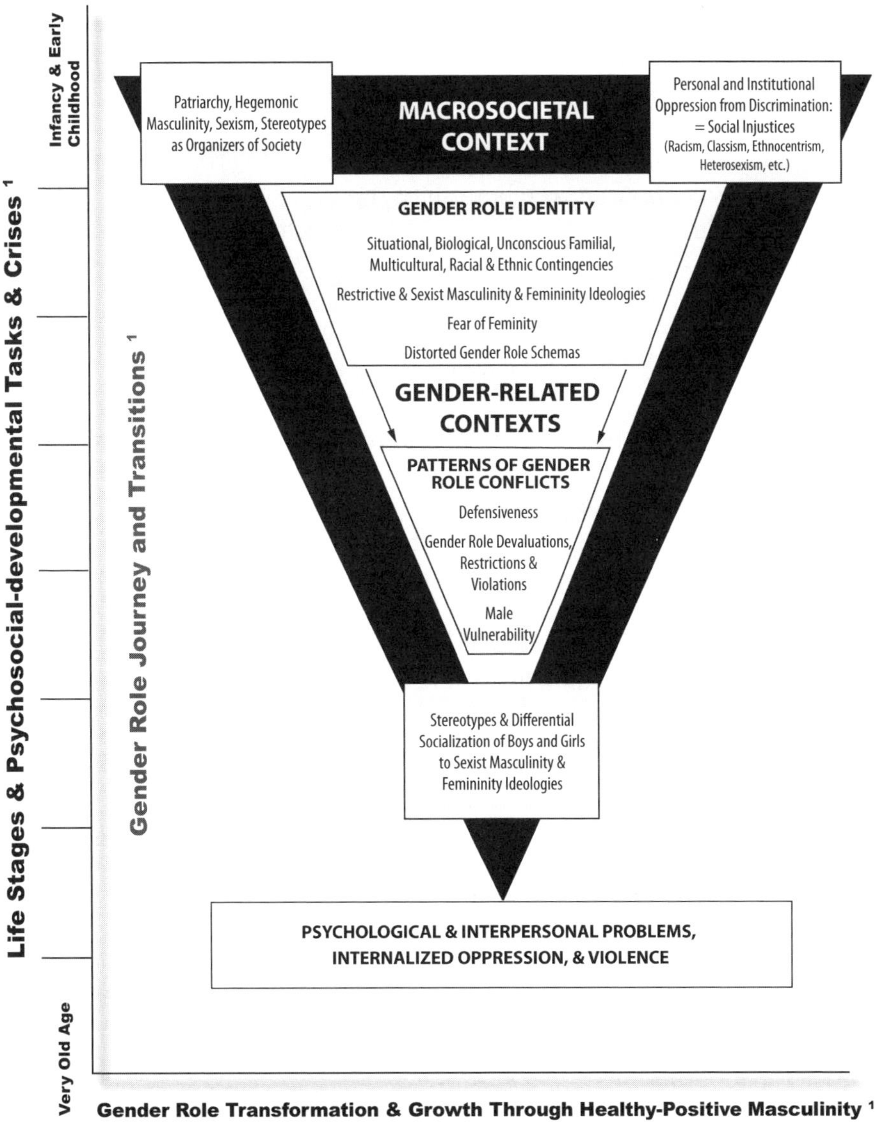
Infancy & Early Childhood
Life Stages & Psychosocial-developmental Tasks & Crises [1]
Very Old Age
Gender Role Journey and Transitions [1]
Patriarchy, Hegemonic Masculinity, Sexism, Stereotypes as Organizers of Society
MACROSOCIETAL CONTEXT
Personal and Institutional Oppression from Discrimination: = Social Injustices (Racism, Classism, Ethnocentrism, Heterosexism, etc.)
GENDER ROLE IDENTITY
Situational, Biological, Unconscious Familial, Multicultural, Racial & Ethnic Contingencies
Restrictive & Sexist Masculinity & Femininity Ideologies
Fear of Feminity
Distorted Gender Role Schemas
GENDER-RELATED CONTEXTS
PATTERNS OF GENDER ROLE CONFLICTS
Defensiveness
Gender Role Devaluations, Restrictions & Violations
Male Vulnerability
Stereotypes & Differential Socialization of Boys and Girls to Sexist Masculinity & Femininity Ideologies
PSYCHOLOGICAL & INTERPERSONAL PROBLEMS, INTERNALIZED OPPRESSION, & VIOLENCE
Gender Role Transformation & Growth Through Healthy-Positive Masculinity [1]

[1] Psychosocial Developmental Contexts

Figure 3.2. Descriptive contextual model of men's gender role socialization, gender role conflict, and psychological and interpersonal problems.

All developmental stages and psychosocial processes on the left side of Figure 3.2 are affected by the contexts within the bold triangle, resulting in possible psychological and interpersonal problems. In other words, gender-related conflicts that cause psychological problems can occur any time throughout the life cycle, from early childhood to very old age. The directionality of the pointed bold triangle does not imply that problems are experienced only at the very old age end of the life cycle. GRC can occur at any time in one's life; the same is true for the gender role transformation and growth processes shown at the bottom of the figure. Each of these descriptive contexts include expanded conceptual knowledge about men and are defined below.

PSYCHOSOCIAL DEVELOPMENTAL CONTEXTS

The *psychosocial developmental contexts* are defined as the overarching structures of gender role socialization and include life stages, developmental tasks, psychosocial crises, the gender role journey and transitions, and gender role transformations that promote healthy, positive development. I describe these psychosocial and developmental contexts more fully in Chapter 5 but briefly summarize them here.

Life stages are defined as developmental periods that have a specific structure, from infancy and early childhood to very old age. GRC occurs across the life span and specifically during the mastery of developmental tasks in each pertinent period. Psychosocial crises occur during each stage of development; these involve a normal set of stressors and coping strategies associated with exerting psychological effort to adjust to the conditions of a new level of maturity and growth (B. Newman & Newman, 2015). Many of the psychosocial crises can result in activating GRC as men develop their gender role identity.

The gender role journey described earlier in this chapter reflects an additional context of men's lives. As defined earlier in the chapter, the gender role journey is a metaphor to help people examine how their gender role socialization and sexism have affected their lives by providing a framework for evaluating thoughts, feelings, and behaviors about gender roles, sexism, and GRC (O'Neil & Egan, 1992a). This journey parallels the life stages and is moderated and mediated by psychosocial–developmental tasks and crises.

The second developmental context is the gender role transformation from sexist socialization to healthy and positive masculinity shown at the bottom of Figure 3.2. A definition of healthy and positive masculinity is when psychosocial growth with the developmental tasks and psychosocial crises are resolved in positive ways. One of the primary goals of the psychology of men is to promote transformations from sexism, other oppression, and GRC to healthy, positive masculinity. Four properties of the transformative process are (a) changes in psychological defenses, (b) facing and dealing with false assumptions about gender roles, (c) increases in internal dialogues with the self, and (d) internal psychological warfare. In Chapter 5, I elaborate further on each of these transformative properties and imply that problems with GRC and sexism can be resolved in positive ways.

MACROSOCIETAL CONTEXTS

The *macrosocietal context* is defined as the social, political, economic, and religious systems based on patriarchy that shape both men and women's gender role socialization. This macrosocietal context has evolved over the centuries and is based on patriarchal values that have produced hegemonic masculinity, sexism, and restricted stereotypes. This means that the macrosocietal context is fully integrated into the economic, political, religious, ethnic, and familial structures of most societies. Feminists have exposed the personal and institutional oppression that emanate from the macrosocietal context, but many people have a limited awareness of how macrosocietal factors negatively shape their lives. How the oppression operates and the actual dynamics of this oppression are invisible to many to men and women.

The macrosocietal contexts are shown at the corners of the bold black triangle in Figure 3.2 and consist of (a) patriarchy, hegemonic masculinity, sexism, and stereotypes as organizers of society; (b) personal and institutional oppression from discrimination equaling social injustice (racism, classism, ethnocentrism, and heterosexism); and (c) stereotypes and differential socialization of boys and girls to sexist masculinity and femininity ideologies. As depicted in the figure, these three sets of contexts are directly related to one another. They represent the political, social, and interpersonal etiology of GRC and sexism in people's lives that contribute to psychological and interpersonal problems, conflicts, and violence. I discuss each of these three contexts in the sections that follow.

PATRIARCHY, HEGEMONIC MASCULINITY, AND SEXISM

In the upper left triangle of Figure 3.2 are listed patriarchy, hegemonic masculinity, sexism, and stereotypes as organizers of society. Organizers of society are those structures on which governments, religions, and economic systems are established to maintain order and to promote ideologies that support the human life. *Patriarchy* is the rule and domination of men over women and children in every aspect of life and culture. It is expressed though the economic oppression and overt discrimination of women in careers, religion, politics, families, and civic life. Men pay a price for patriarchy given that there are costs for the oppression of others. Patriarchy also damages men when they are pitted against each other in unhealthy competition. For example, with capitalism there are usually winners and losers and, for many men, losing is emasculating.

Hegemonic masculinity is the normative ideal of masculinity to which men are supposed to aspire; qualities that define it include aggressiveness, strength, drive, ambition, and self-reliance. Hegemonic masculinity is also a set of practices that permit men's dominance over women (Connell, 1995; Connell & Messerschmidt, 2005) through gender practices that legitimatize patriarchal values and guarantee the dominant position of some men over others and the subordination of women. Patriarchy, hegemonic masculinity, and sexism are critical contexts that explain the causes and negative aspects of GRC.

Sexism maintains the patriarchal and hegemonic status quo by promoting power differences between men and women as natural and necessary, but these differences result in injustices and, according to Albee (1981), psychopathology. Simply put, patriarchy and sexism are incongruent with democratic processes because they violate fundamental concepts of equality and human freedom.

Stereotypes—rigid, inflexible ways of perceiving a particular group of people (in this case, males and females)—work in conjunction with sexism to violate equality and individuality.

Personal and Institutional Oppression
From Discrimination: Social Injustice

Racism, classism, ethnocentrism, heterosexism, and other types of oppression that cause discrimination and social injustice are shown in the upper right triangle of Figure 3.2. Patriarchal values and stereotypes contribute to and maintain discrimination and oppression. Feminists and multiculturalists recognize the oppressiveness of macrosocietal context, but this context is unknown to many people.

The societal oppression and discrimination against both men and women make masculinity ideology and GRC a political and social justice issue. From a GRC perspective, personal and societal oppression occur because of men's abuses of power, destructive competition, homophobia, and interpersonal violence that maintain privilege and power over others. These oppressive dynamics are reinforced by other contexts, such as the prohibition of expressing emotions; fears about and devaluations of femininity; and the obsessive need to win, be in control, and not lose power. In addition, societal oppression results from inequities in the distribution of needed human resources for safety, security, and survival. Many times these inequities are also caused by oppression that is directly tied to masculinity ideologies and GRC. Under these conditions, vulnerable groups (women, members of racial and ethnic minority groups, immigrants) experience poverty and barely subsist at the edges of society. Furthermore, oppressed individuals are marginalized and stigmatized; they experience gender role devaluations, restrictions, and violations both by individual people and the dominant culture. The personal pain of oppressed individuals is visible in U.S. society, but patriarchal masculinity has not been fully factored into an explanation of the injustices. Oppressors are often oblivious to their injustices, but they cause serious mental health problems for both themselves and those whom they oppress. The critical issue here is how racism, classism, ethnocentrism, heterosexism, ageism, and all other forms of oppression are directly related to patriarchal, masculine structures and GRC that oppresses men, women, and children (see Chapter 6, this volume). This implies that sexism and GRC constitute not just a personal issue but one that emanates from the oppressive ways that societies are structured and the distribution, use, and abuse of power and resources.

Stereotypes and Differential Socialization of Boys and Girls to Sexist Masculinity and Femininity Ideologies

The third macrosocietal component, depicted in the triangle at the bottom of Figure 3.2, is the differential socialization of boys and girls to sexist stereotypes and restrictive masculinity and femininity ideologies. One of ways that patriarchal oppression continues is through the institutionalized practices of socializing boys and girls to sexist stereotypes of masculinity and femininity rather than human values that sustain life and foster psychosocial development. These stereotypes emanate from the macrosocietal contexts that promote the differential socialization of boys and girls in most family systems. This socialization is based on the values of the patriarchal system that subordinates, exaggerates, and devalues femininity and elevates and distorts masculinity in negative ways. This produces different gender role socialization practices that shape restrictive attitudes and behaviors about the appropriate gender roles for each sex and represents the beginning of GRC and power conflicts between the sexes. Furthermore, the overvaluation of masculinity combined with the devaluation of femininity promotes different power bases for each sex, with males having more power than females. Parents and educators who endorse restrictive and stereotyped gender roles with children are the primary enforcers of stereotypes that shape gender role identities that can later be vulnerable to restrictive behavioral repertoires. These repertoires can cause GRC and subsequent emotional and psychological problems. Research has documented that boys and girls are differentially treated by parents, with boys given more encouragement for instrumental activities and girls given more encouragement to be expressive but not to be assertive or to set goals (Block, 1984). This family socialization and how the stereotypes play out in schools are precursors of GRC and potential psychosocial problems later in life.

Patriarchy and hegemonic masculinity, personal and institutional oppression/injustices, and the differential and sexist socialization of boys and girls based on restrictive stereotypes are reciprocal (i.e., they interact with each other) and result in GRC. This reciprocity results in serious psychological problems of women, diverse racial and ethnic groups, and members of sexual minority groups.

GENDER-RELATED CONTEXTS: GENDER ROLE IDENTITY AND PATTERNS OF GENDER ROLE CONFLICT

Gender-related contexts are the third perspective and are shown in the center of Figure 3.2 inside the black triangle. Macrosocietal realities influence people's gender role experiences and contribute to GRC. The relationships among the gender-related contexts are not depicted in the figure, but all of them contribute to interpersonal and psychological problems, internalized oppression, and violence, as shown in the box at the tip of the black triangle at the bottom of the figure. Each context, which was briefly defined earlier in the chapter, is defined in more detail below.

GENDER ROLE IDENTITY CONTEXT

Breaking with a purely social constructionist view, gender role identity is shown in Figure 3.2 as a dominant context. It is defined as the total conception of one's roles, values, functions, expectations, and belief system and includes everything a person does to communicate his or her masculine and feminine dimensions. Gender role identity is both conscious and unconscious, begins at a very early age, develops slowly but continuously, and is directly affected by the oppressiveness of macrosocietal contexts as it affects a person's life. Gender role identity was a controversial topic with the early founders of psychology, including Freud, Jung, Adler, Horney, and others (see Chapter 1). Developing a healthy gender role identity requires awareness of oppression and the capacity to deconstruct gender roles across the life span.

Gender role identity is central to understanding men's GRC and opportunities for gender role transformations and the creation of healthy, positive masculinity.

Situational, Biological, Unconscious, Familial, Multicultural, Racial, and Ethnic Contingencies

A multiplicity of contexts affects gender role identity and how GRC, and therefore many different indices, needs to be identified and studied. Situational, biological, unconscious, familial, multicultural, racial, and ethnic contexts contribute to and activate GRC and experiences with gender roles in both positive and negative ways. All of these contexts affect the development and reevaluation of one's gender role identity. Moreover, they can be predictors of GRC regardless of whether they are time-limited situations, demographic categories, oppressive institutional structures, family values and mores, acts of violence, or sexist situations. Many of these contexts are described in more detail in Chapters 6 and 8.

Restrictive and Sexist Masculinity and Femininity Ideologies

Restrictive and sexist masculinity and femininity ideologies, norms, and conformity both predict and cause GRC. Restrictive and sexist masculinity and feminine ideologies are learned from the macrosocietal context and in families, schools, and peer groups. Masculinity ideology is a cofactor of GRC that describes how men are socialized to masculine stereotypes and has been operationalized by the concepts of masculine norms and roles (Levant et al., 1992; E. H. Thompson & Pleck, 1986) and masculine conformity and nonconformity (Mahalik, Locke, et al., 2003). Masculinity ideology represents the primary values and standards that define, restrict, and negatively affect boys' and men's lives (Levant et al., 1992; Mahalik, Locke, et al., 2003; Pleck, 1995; Pleck, Sonenstein, & Ku, 1993; E. H. Thompson & Pleck, 1995). *Masculinity ideology* refers "to beliefs about the importance of men adhering to culturally defined standards for male behavior" (Pleck, 1995, p. 19) and involves "the individual's endorsement and internalization of cultural belief systems about masculinity and male gender, rooted in the structural relationships between the sexes" (Pleck, 1995, p. 19). Masculinity ideology is a primary way that boys and men live out macrosocietal influences, but these patriarchal and sexist values can have negative consequences in interpersonal relationships. The negative outcomes of adhering to or deviating from culturally defined and restrictive masculinity ideologies can result in GRC through the internalization of rigid masculinity ideologies that produce distorted gender role schemas and patterns of GRC that are potentially damaging to men and others (Mahalik, 1999a; O'Neil, 2008c; O'Neil & Nadeau, 1999; Pleck, 1995). The research on how masculinity ideology predicts psychological problems for boys and men was discussed more fully in Chapter 1.

Fear of Femininity

FOF, as discussed earlier in the chapter, occurs because of the patriarchal values of the macrosocietal contexts and the transmission of archetypes over the centuries (Jung, 1953). It is both conscious or unconscious, and it affects how gender role identity and GRC are experienced. Such fears have been discussed in the theoretical literature for many years (Blazina, 1997, 2003; Boehm, 1930; David & Brannon, 1976; Freud, 1937; Horney, 1967; Jung, 1953; Kierski & Blazina, 2009; Levinson et al., 1978; Norton, 1997), and they are frequently described as comprising antifemininity or a "no sissy stuff" attitude. FOF develops in men before, during, and after experiencing GRC. Boys learn to avoid most stereotypical feminine qualities in response to both peers' and parents' displeasure at their deviation from masculine norms. The rejection and repression of the feminine parts of their personalities from an early age can produce a lifelong aversion to any quality perceived as feminine, a constant striving for the ways to be masculine, a male image that prohibits open expression of feelings and feminine characteristics, and an emotional and physical distance among men because of feared homosexuality. The unconscious aspect of FOF and its relationship to GRC are critical issues in understanding men's gender role socialization and masculinity problems.

Distorted Gender Role Schemas

Gender role schemas are cultural definitions of maleness and female-ness that organize and guide an individual's perception of masculinity and femininity on the basis of sex and expected gender roles. These schemas become part of a person's self-concept and are used to evaluate one's personal adequacy to live up to the male or female stereotypes. Distorted gender role schemas comprise exaggerated thoughts and feelings about the role of masculinity and femininity in a man's life that occur when he experiences intense pressure to meet stereotypical notions of masculinity, resulting in fears and anxieties about not measuring up to traditional gender role expectations.

Distorted gender role schemas as contexts result from the influence of the macrosocietal level that promotes restrictive masculinity ideologies, fears about femininity, and other situational contexts that contribute to GRC. Distorted gender role schemas are important to redefine because they are both cognitive and affective and can negatively influence psychosocial development and maintain patterns of GRC (see Chapter 5).

PATTERNS OF GENDER ROLE CONFLICT CONTEXT

As discussed earlier in this chapter, the patterns-of-GRC contexts include defensiveness; gender role devaluations, restrictions, and violations; and male vulnerability. All of these contexts point toward the bottom tip of the large bold triangle in Figure 3.2: psychological and interpersonal problems, internalized oppression, and violence.

Patterns of GRC—Success/Power/Competition, Restrictive Emotionality, Restrictive Affectionate Behavior Between Men, and Conflict Between Work and Family Relations—were described earlier in this chapter. The 350 studies on these patterns are reviewed in Chapter 6 and 7 and represent the most evidence-based part of the model. These patterns are outcomes of both the macrosocietal context and what men internalize in their gender role identity. The patterns of GRC result from learning restrictive and sexist masculinity and femininity ideologies that produce distorted gender role schemas. In Chapters 9 through 13, I discuss how to resolve these patterns during therapy and when implementing psychoeducation programs.

Defensiveness

Masculine defenses are activated to help men cope with GRC and avoid dealing with it. Defenses as contexts for understanding GRC are relevant because both conscious and unconscious thoughts, feelings, attitudes, and behaviors are activated to mediate negative emotions when fears develop about not meeting expected gender role norms. Second, defenses are needed to protect one's gender role identity when threatened. Defensive strategies serve a number of psychological functions, including defending men against losses of power and control in interpersonal relationships; protecting men from labeling, experiencing, or expressing strong emotions in interpersonal exchanges; and defending men against threats to their heterosexuality, fears about their own homosexual inclinations, and the homosexual orientation of others. The psychological outcomes of defensiveness include personal restriction and rigidities in thought and behavior, psychosocial delays, restriction of others, emotional distortions, overreactions, cognitive blind spots, and increased potential for self-destruction or abuse of others. How to find portals (i.e., openings) that mediate men's defenses is a critical issue for any man to change his sexist gender role socialization.

Gender Role Devaluations, Restrictions, and Violations

Gender role restrictions, devaluations, and violations as the personal experiences of GRC negatively affect men's interpersonal, career, and family lives as well as their health (O'Neil, 1981a, 1981b, 1982, 1990, 2008c; O'Neil & Egan, 1993; O'Neil et al., 1995; O'Neil & Nadeau, 1999). These three experiences were defined earlier in the chapter and had previously been the missing contexts to help understand men's GRC and the negative consequences of violating or deviating from restrictive masculinity ideologies and norms. In Chapters 6 and 7, I report research on these contexts, and in Chapters 9 through 11, I discuss the use of these contexts in therapy.

Masculine Vulnerability

The patterns involved in GRC produce vulnerability that ultimately causes psychological and interpersonal problems and conflicts, internalized oppression, and violence. Unresolved GRC results in observed vulnerability or hidden feelings of weakness, fragility, and psychological symptoms that become part of the man's gender role identity and sense of self. *Vulnerability* is an emotional and cognitive state in which a person feels weak, insecure, frail, inferior, exposed, unprotected, worthless, and shameful. Everyone experiences fragility as part of the human experience, in particular, during transitions, crises, illnesses, and traumas. Vulnerability can develop when one is striving to meet or failing to meet gender role norms of masculinity ideology. For men, the emotional and cognitive state of masculine vulnerability results in the feeling that one is emasculated, weak, inferior, unmanly, worthless, ashamed, and/or feminine. Vulnerability is sometimes masked as defensiveness to avoid being seen as weak or to decrease the chance of being humiliated, shamed, or personally attacked. Other outcomes of vulnerability include depression, anxiety, personal rigidity, low self-esteem, inadequate empathy for others, and violence toward others. Sources of vulnerability include institutional and personal oppression and discrimination (racism, classism, ethnocentrism, heterosexism, and ageism); poverty; unemployment; being addicted, hopeless, or ill; feeling like one has no purpose, confidence, or positive identity; being bullied; and physical, psychological, or sexual victimization. In Chapter 6, I offer examples of vulnerable men and research on them.

Psychological and Interpersonal Problems, Internalized Oppression, and Violence

The combined effects of the psychosocial–developmental perspective, the macrosocietal context, and gender-related contexts result in psychological and interpersonal problems, and sometimes *internalized oppression*, the process whereby a person in an oppressed group accepts and lives out the inaccurate stereotypes applied to that group, thereby experiencing significant psychological problems and wounds. In this way, the person uses the methods of the oppressor in their negative evaluation of themselves and others. All of the gender-related indices listed in the middle of Figure 3.2 culminate and point to psychological and interpersonal problems, internalized oppression, and violence. The way these problems occur is very idiosyncratic.

Summary of the Descriptive Contextual Model

Figure 3.2 provides many concepts to help one understand men's problems in a broad, descriptive contextual sense; it represents a substantial expansion of earlier GRC theory and makes new conceptual connections not made before. The model provides a theoretical foundation for forthcoming chapters on developmental aspects of masculinity (Chapter 5), diverse men (Chapter 6), contextual research (Chapter 8), clinical practice (Chapters 9–11), and psychoeducational programming for men (Chapters 12 and 13). Figure 3.2 provides an expanded number of descriptive contexts in which to think about men's lives in developmental, macrosocietal, and gender-related ways. The contexts have potential for stimulating future GRC research, but other concepts in the psychology of men could be substituted in the figure, and therefore the model is only one way to explain men's problems from restrictive gender roles. Researchers and theoreticians are encouraged to add (or substitute) their own concepts to the theoretical formulations in Figure 3.2 to broaden the contextual understanding of men's GRC and healthy, positive masculinity.

The new model in Figure 3.2 raises numerous theoretical and empirical questions to be pursued in the future. For example, what are the developmental and psychosocial contexts of gender roles across the life span that promote developmental growth or GRC for boys and men (see Chapter 5, this volume)? How do situational, biological, unconscious, familial, multicultural, and racial/ethnic contingencies affect gender role development over the life span? Furthermore, does GRC differ across races, classes, cultures, and nationalities? If so, are the differences associated with variations in racial/ethnic, class, and cultural values related to gender roles (see Chapter 6)? For example, how, exactly, does GRC relate to racial and sexual identity, family, cultural and religious values, racism, ethnocentrism, and acculturation for immigrants (see Chapter 6)? In addition, the political aspects of masculinity and GRC are articulated in a more direct way in this new model. How do different political systems—for example, capitalism, socialism, and tribal governance—affect men and their masculinity? In the political and economic realms, does oppression cause GRC, or vice versa, or both? How do patriarchy and hegemonic masculinity relate to GRC and societal discrimination against men and women? Is there evidence that masculinity issues and

GRC cause internalized oppression? Furthermore, how do ethnic and family values contribute to different degrees of GRC for men in different countries (see Chapter 6, this volume)? Finally, what therapeutic interventions can help men change and move toward more positive healthy masculinity (see Chapters 11–13)? Researchers and practitioners can use the descriptive concepts in Figure 3.2 to conceptualize future research and implement new interventions with men.

As noted earlier in this chapter, the new model does not directly address men's actions in environments, microcontextual issues, and the immediate experiences in men's lives. Not physically depicted in Figure 3.2 are the microcontextual cues, norms, and outcomes, expectations associated with temporally limited environments (K. Jones & Heesacker, 2012) and the social learning of gender (Addis et al., 2010). In the next section, I address the criticism from contextual experts (Addis et al., 2010; K. Jones & Heesacker, 2012) of my previous attempts to contextualize (O'Neil, 2008c) GRC theory.

A FUNCTIONAL AND MICROCONTEXTUAL MODEL OF MEN'S GENDER ROLE CONFLICT

The critical issue of how, when, and why GRC occurs (O'Neil, 2008c) stimulates several contextual questions that could broaden the study of the psychology of men. Can GRC be activated by microcontexts that are time limited and stimulated by situational cues unique to certain circumstances and expectations (K. Jones & Heesacker, 2012)? How does GRC relate to the "experiential tensions that occur between the situational variability of masculinity and the need for cross-situational consistency" (C. A. B. Johnston & Morrison, 2007, p. 662)? How do men learn about gender and express it in situational contexts (Addis et al., 2010)? Is there evidence that masculinity issues and GRC cause internalized oppression, and what interventions can help men develop more positive healthy masculinity? Finally, how can the psychology of men promote social change through research, teaching, and activism (Addis et al., 2010; O'Neil & Renzulli, 2013a, 2013b)? These contextual and situational issues are crucial ones that must be pursued.

For me, the most challenging part of writing this book was conceptualizing a new contextual model that responds to the previous criticism of GRC (Addis et al., 2010; K. Jones & Heesacker, 2012). My own call to action was stopped (or stalled) numerous times because little information exists on how a functional, microcontextual model should be conceptualized. Operant and behavioral terminology has been used to justify new models, including gender-relevant environmental cues, situational contingencies and enactments, discriminative stimuli in situations, past gendered social learning, settings of the gender activity, and expected gender role repertoire (see Addis et al., 2010; K. Jones & Heesacker, 2012). These terms are relevant to any contextual analyses, but no heuristic synthesis has occurred that supports the functional and microcontextual study of men's behavior and their situational dynamics.

The development of a new model was particularly challenging because I am knowledgeable about applied behavioral analysis, social learning, and functional contextualism, but I am not an expert or an authority. To compensate for this, I consulted others and reviewed papers that might provide clues on how to facilitate a paradigm shift in how research on men is done. Ambiguity and confusion arose as I created more than a dozen drafts of possible models of functional and microcontextual aspects of the psychology of men.

The critical question is this: What kind of model can organize contextual and situational processes to capture the complexity of GRC in real time as men live their lives? No answer currently exists to this question in regard to the psychology of men. Previously in my career, when a model was needed but nonexistent, I was ambivalent about creating a new one because it usually involves thinking outside the box and venturing into uncharted territory. I was unclear about where to start and what body of knowledge to study. Moreover, I knew that the creative process is a venture into the unknown; sometimes you find the gestalt, and sometimes it is elusive. Many times you generate more questions than answers, which is uncomfortable. I decided to push past my discomfort and create a preliminary model for others to consider, correct, and build on.

A PRELIMINARY MODEL OF FUNCTIONAL AND MICROCONTEXTUAL ASPECTS OF MEN'S GENDER ROLE CONFLICT

I found an information-processing model that captures some of the key elements of assessing men's actual behaviors and interactions (Crick & Dodge, 1994).[1] I have altered and simplified the model to serve as an initial template for understanding situational and microcontextual aspects of men's actions and behaviors. For full details and more in-depth accounts of the information-processing theory, see Crick and Dodge (1994).

Crick and Dodge's (1994) model depicts a social information-processing mechanism in children's social adjustment, and I adapt it here to understand men's GRC. The model also depicts behavior as having a past "database" that includes memory store, acquired rules, social schemas, and social knowledge.

---

[1] I am grateful to Marty Heesacker and Steven Snowden for helping me locate the Crick and Dodge (1994) model and their advice on model development and microcontextual aspects of masculinity.

Their model depicts, in a circular fashion, six behavioral processes that can be adapted to understand men's behavior and interactions: (a) encoding of cues, (b) interpretation of cues, (c) clarification of cues, (d) response access or construction, (e) response decision, and (f) behavioral enactment.

Figure 3.3 depicts an adaptation of Crick and Dodge's (1994) information-processing conceptualization by integrating their concepts with their descriptive contexts depicted in Figure 3.2. Crick and Dodge's information-processing perspective is multifaceted and complex compared to my simple adaptation. Nonetheless, the processes described provide a preliminary example of functional and microcontextual analyses and, with more work, could be operationalized in research. On the left of the figure are the descriptive contexts described earlier in the chapter (psychosocial–developmental, gender role journey phases and transitions, macrosocietal, and gender related). The small arrows imply that the descriptive context directly affects the entire information processing described in the rest of the figure. Furthermore, the model shows the positive and negative outcomes leading back to the databases and the descriptive antecedent contexts in a circular way (see longer arrows). This implies that the consequences of gender-related situations contribute to the ongoing shaping of the person and the larger macrosocietal system in a circular way.

The descriptive contexts are shown as influencing a man's database, shown in the second rectangle on the left in Figure 3.3. This means that

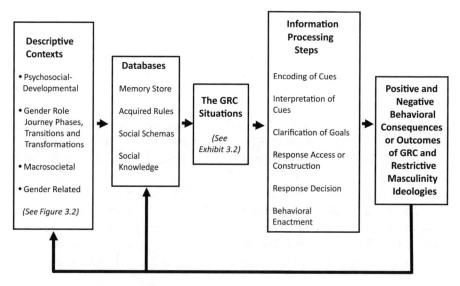

Figure 3.3. Descriptive, functional, and microcontextual model of men's gender role conflict.

psychosocial developmental aspects of gender roles, the macrosocietal dimensions, and the gender-related dynamics all become internalized psychologically in the man's mind. Crick and Dodge (1994) defined this information as comprising databases that include memories, acquired rules, social schemas, and social knowledge. Each of these databases has direct implications for the internalization of masculine gender roles and the development of male gender role identity (see Figure 3.2). Furthermore, the database categories all relate to the internalization of gender role norms and conflicts (masculinity ideologies and GRC) that are relevant to understanding men's processes and behavior in situations.

I now discuss each of the databases using constructs from the psychology of men. The first database is *memory store*. Boys and men have many conscious and unconscious memories associated with gender roles that begin during infancy and span the life cycle. These memories are part of the overall latent memory structure related to gender roles. Memories and past experiences with gender roles during the gender role journey and during psychosocial growth are central to understanding men's immediate reactions to GRC in immediate situations. The second database involves the *acquired rules* of expected and socially sanctioned gender roles that represent sexist, restrictive stereotypes and norms of masculinity ideology learned in patriarchal and sexist societies (i.e., the macrosocietal context). These rules are part of how GRC develops in families, in schools, and with peers. These rules can also be conceptualized as learned norms and behaviors of positive and healthy masculinity. Third, from the memory and rules, social *schemas* (cognitive structures) develop to help men interpret internal and external gender role cues in any social situation. In Chapter 5, I define these structures as normal gender role schemas and distorted gender role schemas that are part of psychosocial development. Fourth and last is *social knowledge*: the structure of schemas and scripts that boys and men use to organize and interpret information so they can process future cues. In this way, every gender-related situation guides possible behavioral options in the future.

Crick and Dodge (1994) summarized the databases in information processing with four summary statements. These statements are altered in my contextual analysis of men's internal processing and interactions and include the following:

- Gender role experiences create latent mental structures that are stored and carried forward over time in memory in the form of gender-related knowledge (i.e., masculinity ideology and GRC).
- These mental structures constitute the database in processing gender-related situations and social cues.
- Immediate processing of cues directly influences gender and social behavior.

- The boy or man mentally internalizes thoughts and feelings about the gender roles, social behavior, and outcomes by storing them in memory, where they become part of gender identity and knowledge that influence future actions.

GRC and restricted masculinity ideology can be part of these dynamics of information processing. These psychological processes add significant contexts to understanding the complexity of men's internal processes that result in specific behavior in a variety of situations.

Next, in the middle of Figure 3.3 are shown "the GRC situations," which include any event or interaction that stimulates GRC or other gender-related dynamics. All of the database processes described above directly point to gender-related situations. Examples of both positive and negative gender-related situations are listed in Exhibit 3.2. These situations activate a man's memory, gender role rules, schemas, and gender-related knowledge as part of the actual informational processing. As described below, these gender-related situations can be operationalized by real life scenarios that create situational dynamics that can be tested with contextual research.

Next, Crick and Dodge (1994) hypothesized six information-processing steps that add significantly to explaining men's internal processing of gender related situations and GRC: (a) encoding of cues, (b) interpretation of cues, (c) clarification of goals, (d) response access or construction, (e) response decision, and (f) behavioral enactment (see Figure 3.3).

During *encoding and interpreting of gender-related cues*, the man selectively attends to both situational and internal cues and interprets them. The man's response is based on his long-term mental memory of past situational cues related to gender roles and GRC, his assessment of the causal analysis of the event, and an appraisal of whether the goal has or was met. Furthermore, the processing includes inferences about what others think of him in the situation (i.e., possible affirmation or gender role devaluation); for example, is the evaluation affirming (strong and powerful) or negative in that it does not meet the masculine norms (i.e., ineffective, weak, a wimp)? Also, the motivation of others involved is assessed in the context of the man's past experiences from previous gender-related exchanges in similar situations. Finally, there is an evaluation of outcome expectations and self-efficacy predictions as it relates to peers. The man may reflect, "Can I pull this off, and what will others think of me as man if I can't?" Both self-evaluations and evaluations by others related to masculinity issues are considered or unconsciously operate. Furthermore, the man processes what he wants to happen, wonders what his options are, and reflects on how to evaluate positive or negative outcomes and how others will do the same. All of these processes are affected by information stored in the memory: the database context mentioned earlier and the situational cues of the moment.

EXHIBIT 3.2
Gender-Related Situations

Examples of Negative Functional and Microcontextual Situations
  Experiencing negative attachment and bonding
  Being unable to control impulses and emotions
  Being picked last for sports teams
  Being called "gay" by one's peer group
  Failing at an adolescent task
  Academic failure
  Having a traumatic experience
  Not making the team
  Being reprimanded at age 3 years for cross-dressing
  Crying in front of peers
  Experiencing discrimination and oppression
  Being bullied
  Being rejected by one's peer group
  Overconforming, or not conforming, to traditional gender roles
  Having a negative attitude toward help seeking
  Sexual dysfunction
  Being cut off in traffic
  Experiencing a power play at work
  Infertility
  Losing one's job or being unemployed
  Experiencing spousal conflict or criticism
  Being devalued as a man (emasculated)
  Experiencing a loss of an intimate relationship
  Conforming to restrictive gender role (macho)
  Becoming disabled

Examples of Positive Functional and Microcontextual Situations
  Having a supportive and nonsexist home environment
  Mastering developmental tasks and psychosocial crises
  Observing and experiencing men's empathy
  Experiencing effective parenting
  Having a good relationship with one's father and mother
  Having supportive mentors
  Achieving success in sports or some other activity
  Demonstrating academic achievement
  Developing emotional intelligence
  Creating effective peer relationships
  Developing a positive male peer group
  Learning respect for girls and women
  Developing equitable, nonexploitative relationships
  Making a congruent career choice
  Developing a nonsexist parenting philosophy
  Demonstrating success as a provider
  Being an effective father
  Being able to manage loss and emotional pain
  Having a positive attitude toward aging and death

After all this processing, a *clarified goal* or desired outcome is mentally selected, many times on the basis of an arousal state that is connected to the desired outcome. This arousal state could be related to the FOF or negative emotions from past or present GRC. Next, during the *response access or construction step*, the man generates possible responses to the situation from memory of previous experiences or creates a response (i.e., the *response decision*; see Figure 3.3) if it is a novel situation. In the response decision step, the man evaluates the possible responses and selects the most positive one based on masculine outcome expectations, his self-efficacy, and the appropriateness of the response. In evaluating the responses and choosing one (i.e., *behavioral enactment*), restrictive gender roles can narrow the behavioral options and possibilities. In this last step, the chosen response is implemented and the behavioral outcome and consequences are observed. These consequences become part of the person's cumulative database and influence the descriptive contexts, mainly the macrosocietal ones (see the long arrows connecting outcomes with the databases and descriptive contexts). These six processing steps convey many new contexts to understand men's GRC in actual situations.

On the far right side of Figure 3.3 are the behavioral consequences or outcomes of GRC and restrictive masculinity ideologies. The behavioral consequences could be positive (affirming) or negative and emotionally stressful. An example of a positive outcome would be affirmation by others when a man deviates from the masculine stereotypes in the service of others. A negative outcome is when a man is emasculated and ridiculed for demonstrating "feminine" qualities in a social exchange. These positive and negative consequences become part of the man's database of memory, rules, schemas, and social knowledge and contribute to the macrosocietal contexts as shown by the long arrow spanning the bottom of Figure 3.3.

SUMMARY OF THE FUNCTIONAL AND MICROCONTEXTUAL MODEL OF MEN'S GENDER ROLE CONFLICT

The concepts depicted in Figure 3.3 are designed to be a simple template for conceptualizing male behavior in situational contexts and have possibilities for generating research that is pragmatic and focused on the gendered social learning and microcontextual events. The template is not a full and comprehensive model of the gendered social learning and microcontextual analysis, but it does provide an example from an information-processing perspective of what could be developed in the future. The model is a beginning step toward exploring functional and microcontextual approaches to men's behavior. Future researchers and theoreticians can develop this area in more detail.

The relationships depicted in Figure 3.3 represent a more focused contextualism than the concepts in Figure 3.2 and promote a more progressive understanding of men in contexts and their actual experiences with gender roles in real life. Moreover, the descriptive contexts and the situational contexts (in this case, information-processing steps) need to be considered simultaneously. As shown in Figure 3.3, the descriptive, functional contexts (on the left side of the figure), the databases, and the behavioral consequences and outcomes (in the center and left side of the figure) are all theoretically related. The descriptive and functional contexts directly affect the entire information-processing dynamics and behavioral outcomes. In addition, the behavioral consequences and outcomes of the processing steps continuously contribute to the descriptive contexts (see long arrows in Figure 3.3). For example, negative outcomes of sexist interactions and GRC become part of macrosocietal stereotypes that affect values about psychosocial development and are the spawning ground for gender-related problems (i.e., GRC).

The agenda for the future is how to operationalize this kind of model with research. This is the future work of applied behavior analysts, functional contextualists, and others who can apply their research expertise to study men's behaviors and interactions. My contribution to this new empirical agenda is found in Chapter 8, in which I discuss the contextual issues portrayed in Figures 3.2 and 3.3 with regard to new research models and hypotheses.

The models illustrated in Figures 3.2 and 3.3 comprise only one way to make sense of the complexity of men's lives and think about how sexism results in negative outcomes for men, women, and children. Other models that capture what has been missed, or that take other perspectives, are certainly needed. This quest for better contextual theory and conceptual understanding of men's lives is a high priority in any future elucidations of the psychology of men.

NEW THEORETICAL ASSUMPTIONS ABOUT MEN'S GENDER ROLE CONFLICT

The new contextual models respond to the past critiques by expanding the definition of GRC in more comprehensive ways to include greater societal, developmental, situational, and gender-related contexts. Both Figure 3.2 and Figure 3.3 imply that society is organized and based on patriarchal values that foster stereotypes and sexist ways of thinking that cause psychological problems. The new contextual paradigms provide a theoretical foundation for the rest of the chapters in this book. A summary of theoretical assumptions in Figures 3.1 through 3.3 provides a conceptual lens for each chapter and supports the call to action I discuss throughout the book.

In Exhibit 3.3, 14 theoretical assumptions that represent a summary of the expanded GRC theory are enumerated. The assumptions represent

EXHIBIT 3.3
New Theoretical Assumptions About Men's Gender Role Conflict Based on Figures 3.2 and 3.3

1. Descriptive contexts in men's lives can be identified that explain GRC and possibilities for growth to healthy, positive masculinity.
2. Gender role development, transitions, and transformations are experienced while mastering the developmental tasks and psychosocial crises over the life span.
3. Journeying with gender roles over the life span and managing gender role transitions are parts of seeking positive and healthy masculinity.
4. Macrosocietal contexts negatively restrict male gender role socialization and include patriarchy, sexism, restrictive stereotypes, oppression and social injustices, and the differential socialization of boys and girls to sexist masculinity and femininity ideologies.
5. Gender role identity is negatively and positively affected by the macrosocietal contexts.
6. Situational, biological, unconscious, familial, multicultural, and racial/ethnic contingencies shape gender role identity in both positive and negative ways.
7. Three gender-related contexts that negatively affect men's gender role identity are (a) restrictive and sexist masculinity and femininity ideologies, (b) the fear of femininity, and (c) distorted gender role schemas.
8. The effects of a restrictive gender role identity produce patterns of GRC, defensiveness, and gender role devaluations, restrictions, and violations.
9. GRC, defensiveness, and the gender role devaluations, restrictions, and violations promote male vulnerability.
10. The negative results of the macrosocietal and gender-related contexts are internalized oppression, psychological and interpersonal problems, violence, and social injustice.
11. The microcontextual, functional, and situational contexts of men's lives need to be studied so that both the positive and negative outcomes and consequences of male gender role socialization and GRC can be documented.
12. Microcontextual, functional, and situational contexts of men's lives can be understood with further conceptualization and work by applied behavioral scientists.
13. Therapeutic and psychoeducational interventions can be developed to help men and boys heal from their GRC and their gender-related problems.
14. A call to action is needed to advance the psychology of men in theoretical, research, and psychological service domains.

an expanded way of thinking about GRC across the life cycle and are connected to personal and institutional oppression at the macrosocietal level. The assumptions also support assessing men's attitudes and behavior in situations using microcontextual and gender social learning perspectives.

The 14 assumptions in Exhibit 3.3 are directly related to each chapter in the book. Assumptions 1 and 2 convey that masculine contexts can be positive, negative, and developmental for men across the life cycle. I address these contexts in Chapters 1, 5, 6, and 7. These contexts also include men's gender role journeys reflected in Assumption 3 and are discussed in Chapters 2, 5, 10, and 11. Assumptions 4 and 5 convey the perils of the macrosocietal dimensions of sexist and patriarchal societies; I elaborate on this in Chapter 6. The many demographic, multicultural, and situational contingences that shape male identity in both positive and negative ways are captured with Assumption 6 and addressed in Chapters 6 through 8. Assumption 7 addresses nine gender-related contexts that negatively shape male identity and are discussed in all chapters. Assumption 8 establishes the negative effects of GRC, specifically gender role devaluations, restrictions, and violations, and are addressed fully in Chapters 6 through 7 and 9 through 11. Assumption 9 suggests that male vulnerability emanates from gender role devaluations, restrictions, and violations, GRC, and defensiveness, which are discussed in Chapter 6, 9, and 11. Assumption 10 hypothesizes that the macrosocietal system and the gender-related contexts cause internalized oppression, psychological and interpersonal problems, and violence. I discuss these critical mental health issues in Chapters 1, 6, 7, and 9. Assumptions 11 and 12 focus on a research agenda for GRC that I have discussed in this chapter, and I extend it in Chapte 8. Assumption 13 establishes that therapeutic services can be developed to help men, and in Chapters 10 through 13, I provide a rationale and data-based examples for these services. Finally, Assumption 14 encourages a call to action in the psychology of men that is discussed throughout the book but most fully in Chapters 1 and 14. Overall, these assumptions provide an advanced organizer for the rest of the book.

4

SCALE DEVELOPMENT AND MEASUREMENT IN THE GENDER ROLE CONFLICT RESEARCH PROGRAM

Measure what can be measured, and make measurable what cannot be measured.

—Galileo Galilei

My research team at the University of Kansas began the psychometric development of the various versions of the Gender Role Conflict Scale (GRCS; O'Neil, Helms, Gable, David, & Wrightsman, 1986) in the fall of 1980. Little conceptual information existed on men's problems with gender roles when we began our conceptualizing and item generation. No operational definitions of *gender role conflict* (GRC) existed, and only one journal article had suggested that sex role strain had negative consequences (Garnets & Pleck, 1979). The task at hand was to define the GRC construct globally and to hypothesize GRC patterns that could be measured on the basis of the men's liberation literature. Like this chapter's opening quote from Galileo, we were attempting to measure a construct that had not been defined or measured before. After much thought, we created the operational definition of GRC; it emphasized negative consequences from restricted gender roles that resulted in the restriction, devaluation, or violation of the self or

http://dx.doi.org/10.1037/14501-005
Men's Gender Role Conflict: Psychological Costs, Consequences, and an Agenda for Change, by J. M. O'Neil

others. All the GRCS items were linked theoretically to this definition and the fear of femininity.

In this chapter, I describe the different versions of the GRCS. The GRCS was first published in the journal *Sex Roles*, and it was followed by adaptations for use with adolescents (GRSC–A; Blazina, Pisecco, & O'Neil, 2005); women (Borthick, 1997; Borthick, Knox, Taylor, & Dietrich, 1997); Korean men (J. Kim, Hwong, & Ryu, 2003); and, most recently, Chinese men (Zhang, Blashill, et al., 2014). On the basis of psychometric criticism of the GRCS (Norwalk, Vandiver, White, & Englar-Carlson, 2011; J. R. Rogers, Abbey-Hines, & Rando, 1997), a short form of the GRCS also was developed (GRCS–SF; Wester, Vogel, O'Neil, & Danforth, 2012). Practical GRC checklists (O'Neil, 1988b, 1988c) were developed to assess GRC in therapy, classes, and workshop settings (O'Neil, 1996; O'Neil & Roberts Carroll, 1988; Robertson, 2006).

Full psychometric details about the GRCS can be found on the GRC Research Program web page: http://web.uconn.edu/joneil/; in this chapter, I provide only basic information about the reliability and validity of the scale. I first provide a brief summary of the evolution of GRCS-focused studies and describe the different kinds of studies. Next, I present basic information on the psychometric properties of the GRCS and the GRCS–SF. I then describe the GRCS–A and discuss the GRCS's adaptation for women and its adaptation to checklist formats for use in therapy and workshops. Finally, I describe the Gender Role Journey Measure (GRJM; O'Neil, Egan, Owen, & Murry, 1993) as a scale to help people resolve GRC and understand gender role transitions.

NUMBER OF STUDIES AND DEMOGRAPHICS OF THE GENDER ROLE CONFLICT SCALE

There has been a considerable increase in the number of published articles, dissertations, and other GRC studies over the past few decades. During the 1980s and early 1990s there were fewer than 30 studies, but by the end of that decade there were 90, and by 2005 more than 200 studies had been completed. Over the past 8 years (2006–2014), another 80 studies have been completed. I discuss these studies in more detail in Chapter 7.

Currently, more than 350 separate studies have used the GRCS, and 181 (56%) of these studies have been published as articles in the psychology literature in 46 different journals. The GRCS has been used in 235 doctoral dissertations, and more than 180 GRC studies have been presented at the Annual Convention of the American Psychological Association from 1982 through 2011. Outside the United States, 73 studies have been completed at 51 institutions in 32 countries, including 10 in Australia; nine in South

Korea; seven in Canada; five each in Germany, Great Britain, and Ireland; two each in Indonesia, Japan, Philippines, and Hong Kong; and one each in Iran, Iraq, Egypt, China, Hungary, Colombia, Portugal, Taiwan, Poland, Spain, Lithuania, Russia, Tasmania, Costa Rica, Sweden, South Africa, Croatia, Turkey, Singapore, Thailand, and Malta. The GRCS has been translated into 20 different languages.

A majority of the GRC studies have examined White, heterosexual college students, but in the last 8 years researchers have begun to focus more on diverse samples. Thirty-one studies have focused on adult men over 30, 26 studies have examined African American men, 10 studies have looked at Mexican American men, six studies have focused on Asian American men, and 28 studies have examined gay men. Seventeen studies have assessed age differences in GRC from boyhood to retirement age. Eight studies have looked at adolescent boys (using the GRCS–A), and three studies have examined retired men's GRC (Graham & Romans, 2003; W. G. Hill & Donatelle, 2004; Lontz, 2000). The GRC Research Program web page mentioned above summarizes all the GRC studies completed in 24 informational files for researchers.

THE GENDER ROLE CONFLICT SCALE

The GRCS was developed through item generation and reduction, content analysis of items, factor analysis, and tests of reliability with a sample of college men ($N = 586$). First, 85 items were generated to assess the hypothesized six patterns of GRC (O'Neil, 1981b, 1982). All items were responded to using a Likert scale that ranged from *strongly disagree* (1) to *strongly agree* (6), with higher scores indicating a greater degree of conflict regarding the GRC factors. Principal-components and common-factor analysis, with both orthogonal and oblique rotations, were used to determine the best simple structure of the observed factors for the items (O'Neil et al., 1986). To be retained, items were required to have a factor loading of 0.30 or greater, to not cross-load on other factors, and to have a standard deviation of at least 1.00 on a 6-point scale. The factor analysis resulted in a 37-item scale with four factors rather than the six original factors that explained 36% of the variance.

The names of the four factors are (a) Success/Power/Competition (SPC; 13 items, e.g., "I worry about failing and how it affects my doing well as a man"), (b) Restrictive Emotionality (RE; 10 items, e.g., "I have difficulty expressing my tender feelings"), (c) Restrictive Affectionate Behavior Between Men (RABBM; eight items, e.g., "Affection with other men makes me tense"), and (d) Conflict Between Work and Family Relations (CBWFR; six items; e.g., "My work or school often disrupts other parts of my life: home, health, or leisure"). Assessments of the scales' reliabilities revealed that internal consistency scores using Cronbach's alpha ranged from .75 to .85. Four-week test–retest reliabilities ($N = 17$) ranged from .72 to .86 for each factor. Subscale scores are calculated by adding the subscale items and dividing this by the number of items in that subscale. Some researchers have used the total GRCS score by adding all the GRCS items and dividing that number by 37.

SPC describes personal attitudes about success pursued through competition and power. RE is defined as having restrictions and fears about expressing one's feelings as well as restrictions in finding words to express basic emotions. RABBM represents restrictions in expressing one's feelings and thoughts with other men and difficulty touching other men, and CBWFR reflects experiencing restrictions in balancing work, school, and family relations that result in health problems, overwork, stress, and a lack of leisure and relaxation.

As I discussed in Chapter 3, the GRCS items are theoretically related to the psychological domains, personal experiences, and situational contexts in the following ways (O'Neil, 1990; O'Neil, Good, & Holmes, 1995). Sixty-two percent of the items assess men's personal experience of GRC. Eighteen items assess gender role restrictions, and five items assess gender role devaluations and violations. All the items but one assess GRC within the man, and 78% of the items are couched in an interpersonal context. Only four items assess GRC caused by others, and only one assesses GRC expressed toward others. There is a good mix of items across the cognitive, affective, and behavioral domains of GRC. The GRCS has 11 cognitive items, 15 affective items, and 20 behavioral items. Six items overlap in the affective–behavioral domain. No items that tap unconscious processes are part of the GRCS.

The Gender Role Conflict Scale II (GRCS–II; O'Neil et al., 1986) was also developed to measure GRC in 16 situations. The factor analysis yielded four factors (Success/Power/Competition [SPC]; Homophobia, Lack of Emotional Responses, and Public Embarrassment From Gender Role Deviance), but one of the factors has low internal consistencies, and therefore the GRCS–II was never developed further. The GRCS–II is important, though, because it conceptualized GRC as occurring in a situational context, and the initial evidence overall supported this alternative way of understanding GRC.

WHAT DOES THE GENDER ROLE CONFLICT
SCALE REALLY MEASURE?

Three of four GRCS factors (RE, RABBM, and CBWFR) have direct relationships to the operational definitions of GRC. The GRCS is a measure of men's gender role restrictions with RE, RABBM, and CBWFR. To a much lesser extent, the GRCS measures devaluations and violations, but only with five items. SPC is a masculinity ideology/norms factor that more indirectly assesses GRC by measuring personal attitudes about success pursued through competition and power. The GRCS items assess GRC primarily within the man (i.e. intrapersonally) and in an interpersonal context. The GRCS has an equal mix of items relating to men's thoughts, feelings, and behaviors that result in negative psychological outcomes.

The relationship between Pleck's (1995) three strain subtypes and GRCS is critical to explain. Discrepancy and trauma strain are not testable with the GRCS. Researchers have implied that GRCS measures discrepancy strain (Levant, 1996; Pleck, 1995), but the GRCS items are incongruent with this kind of assessment. Furthermore, GRC is probably traumatic for some boys and men, but the GRCS does not assess trauma strain as defined by Pleck. However, the GRCS does measure Pleck's dysfunction strain. The hypothesis that prescribed gender roles (masculinity ideology) are psychologically dysfunctional and lead to personal and interpersonal conflict can be tested with the GRCS. The four factors of the GRCS measure prescribed aspects of men's gender roles that are potentially dysfunctional for men, women, and families. The empirical question is whether research documents that GRC significantly relates to men's psychological problems and dysfunctions.

EMPIRICAL STUDY OF THE GENDER ROLE CONFLICT SCALE

The GRCS has been subjected to considerable empirical scrutiny, including of its internal consistency reliabilities, test–retest reliability, potential social desirability response bias, and convergent and divergent validity; however, more work, with more diverse samples, is needed.

Reliability, Validity, and Psychometric Properties

Many researchers have studied the factor structure of the GRCS. Twenty-four factor analyses have been completed on the GRCS to document its factorial validity. Overall, factor analyses of the GRCS with American college students have shown the scale to have construct validity (Englar-Carlson & Vandiver, 2002; Good et al., 1995; Kratzner, 2003; Moradi, Tokar, Schaub, Jome, & Serna, 2000; Norwalk et al., 2011; O'Neil et al., 1986; J. R. Rogers et al., 1997). The factor intercorrelations are moderate, with intercorrelations ranging from .35 to .68 (Moradi et al., 2000), implying that the factors are related to each other but also are separate entities.

Researchers have suggested using confirmatory factor analysis (CFA) to strengthen the GRC model conceptually and give greater support to the subscales (Betz & Fitzgerald, 1993). Eleven studies have used CFAs in verifying the four-factor structure (Englar-Carlson & Vandiver, 2002; Faria, 2000; Good et al., 1995; Herdman, Choi, Fuqua, & Newman, 2012; J. Hernandez, Sánchez, & Liu, 2006; Kratzner, 2003; Moradi et al., 2000; Norwalk et al., 2011; J. R. Rogers et al., 1997; Wester, Pionke, & Vogel, 2005; Zhang, Blashill, et al., 2014). There has been some controversy with how the CFAs have been interpreted. For example, J. R. Rogers and his colleagues found support for Good et al.'s (1995) four-factor model but questioned whether their CFA met the conventional criteria for acceptable model fit data. They recommended that certain items be rewritten or dropped to make the GRCS more pure and to improve the goodness-of-fit indices. A third group of researchers questioned both Good et al.'s and J. R. Rogers et al.'s (1997) results, indicating that these studies did not consider how the value of fit indexes were influenced by indicator-per-factor (p/f) ratios (Moradi et al., 2000). Moradi et al. (2000) used rationally and randomly derived parceling procedures. Strong support was found for the structural validity of the GRCS, and the researchers concluded that the original four-factor model could be used with confidence. Overall, these important CFAs support the four-factor model as initially hypothesized (O'Neil et al., 1986).

Another criticism of the GRCS has been the lack of factorial validity studies on diverse samples from various racial/ethnic and socioeconomic groups as well as men who are gay, physically challenged, or from other countries (Good et al., 1995; Heppner, 1995; Moradi et al., 2000). Heppner (1995) critiqued the GRCS and argued that "additional examination of the factor structure across diverse samples and cultures offers a great deal of potential for increasing the understanding of the universality of GRC as well as for stimulating theory development about human nature in general" (p. 21). Furthermore, researchers have recommended testing the structural validity of the GRCS on underresearched samples such as African Americans, Latinos, gay men, and bisexual men (Moradi et al., 2000).

Since the time these critiques were levied, the GRCS has been factor analyzed using diverse samples of men living in the United States and all over the world. The GRCS has been factor analyzed for samples of Hispanic, African American, and Asian American men (Pytluk & Casas, 1998); gay men (Herdman et al., 2012; Simonsen, Blazina, & Watkins, 2000; Wester et al., 2005); lesbians (Herdman et al., 2012); airline pilots (Chamberlin, 1993); women (Borthick, 1997; Borthick et al., 1997); adult men (Lontz, 2000), Chinese heterosexual and homosexual men (Zhang, Blashill, et al., 2014); and adolescent boys (Blazina et al., 2005). Furthermore, the GRCS has been factor analyzed with men from Australia, Portugal, Korea, Japan, Spain, Sweden, Germany, China, Canada, Turkey, and Indonesia (Bjerke & Skyllingstad, 2002; Chartier, Graff, & Arnold, 1986; Faria, 2000; Gulder, 1999; Hayashi, 1999; J. Kim et al., 2003; Lease, Ciftci, Demir, & Boyraz, 2009; Nauly, 2002;

Theodore, 1998). With all of these diverse samples, researchers have found a factor structure similar to that of the initial study of men's GRC (O'Neil et al., 1986). The variance explained in these factor analyses across the studies ranges between 32% and 52%. In a few of these studies, less-than-perfect replication of the factor structure was found but only minor differences were reported. In all cases, the researchers reported that the psychometric qualities of the GRCS were acceptable for use with their samples. Five studies of diverse men have used CFA. Three studies were conducted with gay men (J. Hernandez et al., 2006; Wester et al., 2005; Zhang, Blashill, et al., 2014), one focused on Portuguese men (Faria, 2000), and one assessed African American men (Norwalk et al., 2011). Additional CFAs on the GRCS, with diverse samples, are needed.

Internal Consistency Reliabilities

Ten studies have completed internal consistency analyses on diverse men (Chamberlin, 1993; Chartier et al., 1986; Cournoyer, 1994; Good, Dell, & Mintz, 1989; Good et al., 1995; M. M. Hayes, 1985; Horhoruw, 1991; Kaplan, 1992; E. J. Kim, 1990; Mendelson, 1988). The results indicated that for the SPC factor, alphas ranged from .83 to .89, with an average of .86; for RE, alphas ranged from .81 to .91, with an average of .84; for RABBM, alphas ranged from .82 to .88, with an average of .84; and for CBWFR, alphas ranged from .73 to .87, with an average of .80. For seven studies with a GRCS total score, alphas ranged from .75 to .90, with an average of .88. The range of reliabilities for the four factors has been .71 to .91 for men from Korea, Germany, Canada, Taiwan, and Sweden, as well as for American men who are gay, African American, Asian American, or Hispanic.

Test–Retest Evidence and Social Desirability

Test–retest reliabilities were assessed in two studies over a 1-month period (Faria, 2000; O'Neil et al., 1986). In both studies, reliabilities ranged between .72 and .86 across the four factors, indicating that the GRCS is stable over this time period. Social desirability tendencies of the GRCS have been low and practically insignificant (Fischer & Good, 1997; Good et al., 1995; Kang, 2001; Mendelson, 1988; Senn, Desmarais, Verberg, & Wood, 2000).

Convergent and Divergent Validity

The convergent validity of the GRCS has been examined using the following popular masculinity measures: the Masculine Gender Role Stress Scale (Eisler, Skidmore, & Ward, 1987), the Brannon Masculinity Scale (Brannon

& Juni, 1984), the Masculine Role Norms Scale (E. H. Thompson & Pleck, 1986), Male Role Norms Inventory (Levant et al., 1992), the Conformity to Masculine Norms Inventory (CMNI; Mahalik, Locke, et al., 2003), and the Reference Group Identity Dependence Scale (RGIDS; Wade & Gelso, 1998). All of these measures have been significantly correlated with the GRCS, with median rs ranging between .32 and .49. In another analysis (O'Neil & Denke, in press), correlations between the GRCS and four masculinity ideology measures across 20 studies ranged from .20 to .45. These significant correlations suggest that the GRCS is related to these masculinity scales, but the low to moderate correlations suggest that the GRCS measures a different construct. The divergent validity of the GRCS has been studied by correlating the GRCS with measures of sex role egalitarianism and homophobia. Three of the four GRCS factors (SPC, RE, and RABBM) correlated negatively with sex role egalitarianism (Englar-Carlson & Vandiver, 2002), and three studies have found that either SPC, RE, or RABBM significantly correlated with homophobia (Kassing, Beesley, & Frey, 2005; Tokar & Jome, 1998; D. F. Walker, Tokar, & Fischer, 2000).

ADAPTATIONS OF THE GENDER ROLE CONFLICT
SCALE FOR PRACTICAL USES

The GRCS has been used in therapy with men (O'Neil, 1996; Robertson, 2006; see also Chapter 11, this volume) and during psychoeducational workshops (Braverman, O'Neil, & Owen, 1992; O'Neil, 1996; O'Neil & Roberts Carroll, 1988). More experimentation and research on using the scale with clients and workshops is needed. The GRCS has also been adapted for specific use with clients and others. One adaptation is a simple checklist of the patterns of GRC (the GRC Checklist; O'Neil, 1988c) and the other is the Devaluations, Restrictions, and Violations Worksheet (O'Neil 1988b; see also Chapter 11, this volume). Each of these adaptations is a quick and direct way to obtain information about a man's or boy's GRC that can be used therapeutically.

SUMMARY OF RESEARCH ON THE
GENDER ROLE CONFLICT SCALE

Research results indicate that the GRCS has good construct validity on the basis of many factor analyses and tests of reliability and validity from varied samples. On the basis of the correlational data, the GRCS appears to have convergent validity with commonly used masculinity measures and discriminant validity with sex role egalitarianism and homophobia. The validity data indicate that the GRCS assesses a construct that is distinct from other masculinity measures and relates to measures of masculinity ideology (Pleck, 1995), masculine norms (Mahalik, Locke, et al., 2003), gender role stress (Eisler, 1995), and reference group identity (Wade & Gelso, 1998).

CURRENT CRITICISM AND CHALLENGES
TO THE GRC RESEARCH PROGRAM

In this section, I summarize the previous criticism of the GRC Research Program. Some of the criticism can be answered directly, and some requires future research and scholarly exchange. The challenges to the GRC Research Program can be grouped into three categories: (a) programmatic critiques; (b) the GRCS as a measure of conflict; and (c) Beaglaoich, Sarma, and Morrison's (2013) critique.

Critics have identified important limitations to the overall GRC Research Program. First, some researchers have argued that third variables explaining GRC's relationship to psychological problems have gone unidentified (Good, Heppner, DeBord, & Fischer, 2004). Furthermore, some have recommended that more complex models be devised to explain how GRC is experienced (Enns, 2000; Heppner & Heppner, 2008; Tokar, Fischer, Schaub, & Moradi, 2000). Moderator and mediator studies have been suggested so that how GRC affects psychological maladjustment can be more precisely determined (Heppner, 1995). In addition, the GRC Research Program has been criticized for failing to assess GRC longitudinally and not identifying developmental tasks and contextual demands that interface with men's gender role socialization (Enns, 2000; Heppner, 1995). Researchers have also noted that GRC's impact on others has been studied infrequently (Rochlen & Mahalik, 2004) and that the similarities and differences between men's and women's GRC have gone unexplored (Enns, 2000; Zamarripa, Wampold, & Gregory, 2003). Finally, the GRCS has been criticized for measuring only limited behavioral domains and not assessing areas such as sexuality, performance, homophobia, and health issues (E. H. Thompson & Pleck, 1995). All these criticisms have merit and support the development of a more complex GRC research model that is contextual (see Chapter 8).

Another area of critique is whether the GRCS truly measures conflict (Betz & Fitzgerald, 1993). Researchers have also questioned whether the GRCS implies conflict rather than states it directly. These critics are probably correct in arguing that some of the GRCS items could have been written to more directly assess conflict. Betz and Fitzgerald's (1993) criticism is appropriate for the SPC factor. The majority of the SPC items do not directly assess men's GRC. Only two of 13 SPC items use conflict terminology, and only two items reflect gender role devaluations. SPC is therefore defined as a masculine norms/ideology factor that more indirectly assesses GRC by measuring personal attitudes about success pursued through competition and power. This definition is also supported by previous empirical research indicating that SPC is correlated with masculinity ideology (D. F. Walker et al., 2000). Future researchers should acknowledge that the SPC factor assesses masculinity ideology/norms and is a more indirect assessment of GRC.

However, the items of the three other GRCS factors (RE, RABBM, and CBWFR) use conflict-related terminology and convey the negative consequences of men's gender roles. Twenty-six of the GRCS items (70%) use words that are directly connected to conflict, such as *difficulty*, *discomfort*, and *worry*. All of the items for RE and CBWFR use conflict-related terms, as do 75% of the RABBM items. Furthermore, 62% of the items assess gender role devaluations, restrictions, or violations as operationally defined areas of conflict, and two studies have provided empirical support that the GRCS is a measure of men's conflict using dream analysis and real and ideal levels of GRC (Liu, Rochlen, & Mohr, 2005; Rochlen & Hoyer, 2005). Evidence that the GRCS factors are related to conflict is apparent from the many studies in this review that indicate GRC is significantly related to anxiety, depression, low self-esteem, violence, and other interpersonal problems.

How well do the GRCS items assess gender role devaluations, restrictions, and violations across the four factors using the operational definitions? In other words, do the items imply gender role devaluations, restrictions, and violations? Twenty-three (62%) of the items can be categorized as assessing potential devaluations, restrictions, or violations. For RE and CBWFR, 100% of the items had one or more of these dimensions, and for RABBM 63% of items fit into one of these categories. SPC had only two items (15%) that could be categorized as devaluations, restrictions, or violations. From this analysis, SPC is not a full measure of men's personal experience of GRC. The SPC items measure attitudes and values related to success, competition, and control rather than any direct experience of GRC. An assessment of the 23 items that did reflect devaluations, restrictions, or violations indicate an interesting trend: Eighteen of the 23 items were related to gender role restrictions, with the other five being split between gender role devaluations and restrictions.

The most in-depth and critical analyses of the GRCS and the GRCS–A have been by Beaglaoich (2013) and Beaglaoich et al. (2013). I provide here a summary of their critique in shortened form, but this analysis is important to guide future development of the GRCS. Building on my previous critiques of the GRCS, their analysis included a scale-by-scale and item-by-item examination of the GRCS as well as criticism of how the measure was developed without assessing the relevance of items to respondents. The criticisms included the following:

- the lack of information relating to the development of scale items;
- the fact that not all items measure conflict;
- the observation that elements of devaluation, restriction, and violation are missing from some scale items;
- limited assessment of GRC toward others;
- the absence of face or content validity of the scale;
- mismatches between items and the response format; and
- conceptual issues relating to what each factor is measuring (e.g., SPC as a measure of masculine ideology.

Beaglaoich et al. concluded that additional GRCSs should be developed to address the critical points made in their analysis.

A RESPONSE TO THE CRITIQUES: THE GENDER ROLE CONFLICT SCALE—SHORT FORM

The areas of criticism that have been addressed relate to three main categories: (a) questions about whether certain items elicit different responses based on race (Norwalk et al., 2011), (b) questions about whether certain GRCS items really measure conflict (Betz & Fitzgerald, 1993; E. H. Thompson & Pleck, 1995), and (c) the need to improve or delete certain questions to meet conventional criteria for acceptable model fit with the data (J. R. Rogers et al., 1997). On the basis of the previous critiques of the GRCS, a revised, short version of the GRCS was created: the GRCS–SF (Wester et al., 2012). The main goal of this revision was twofold: to (a) reduce the factorial variance across diverse groups and (b) examine the distribution of items measuring conflict across the four subscales. A third goal was to develop a shorter, more cultural applicable measure of GRCS and to test several of the specific items identified by Norwalk et al. (2011) as problematic.

Exploratory factor analyses and CFAs were implemented with numerous multicultural samples of men to revise and shorten the GRCS. Across the samples, items that had factor loadings less than 0.60 were deleted, resulting in the elimination of 21 items. Four items from each of the four subscales were retained based on loadings that were less than .60. With regard to reliability, the revised RE and CBWFR subscales returned coefficient alphas of .77, and the revised RABBM and SPC subscales returned coefficient alphas of .78 and .80, respectively. The 16 items retained at this step in the process all seemed to adequately address the operational definitions of GRC. An examination of the items was conducted to confirm whether the items identified by Norwalk et al. (2011) as contributing to factorial variance between Caucasian and

African American respondents had been included or excluded by the new analyses. The item reduction eliminated all but three of the items Norwalk et al. had questioned as contributing to factor invariance based on race. The CFA indicated that the four-factor model using the GRCS–SF provided a good fit for the data, and a correlational analysis between the GRCS–SF and the original GRCS found that all subscales correlated with each other as expected, with minimal overlap in variability.

THE GENDER ROLE CONFLICT SCALE—ADOLESCENTS

Very few masculinity measures have been developed for adolescent boys, and therefore an adaptation of the GRCS for adolescents, the GRCS–A, was created (Blazina, Pisecco, O'Neil, 2005). After reviewing the items of the original GRCS (O'Neil et al., 1986), an adaptation of the original GRCS was made that was developmentally appropriate for adolescent boys yet theoretically consistent with the items' original construct. More specifically, the items of the GRCS–A were reworded to shift the focus from sexual to personal relationships. For example, an item discussing emotions during sex was altered to sharing feelings in relationships. Second, school activities were included as a possible source of conflict for adolescents (e.g., "My career, job, or school effects the quality of my leisure or family life") and a source of success, power, or competition (e.g., "Getting to the top of my class is important to me"). Finally, all items were reviewed and revised to lower the required reading level for the new measure.

Boys ages 13 to 18 years took the GRCS–A. To examine the structure of the GRCS–A, data were factor analyzed using an oblique rotation solution. Scree test and eigenvalues (> 1.0) were used to choose the number of factors to be rotated. Items were included on the final version of the GRCS–A if they loaded significantly (> 0.30) on a given factor and lower than 0.30 on the other factors.

Using these procedures and inclusion criteria, the factor analysis resulted in four factors that accounted for 40.9% of the total variance. Cross-loaded items and those that did not load were deleted from the instrument, which resulted in a measure consisting of 29 items. Of the original 37 items, one failed to significantly load on any single factor, and seven significantly loaded on more than one factor. This left the final version with a total of 29 items. The first factor accounted for 20.4% of the total variance, and the seven items that loaded on this factor measured the construct Restricted Affection Between Men (e.g., "Hugging other men is difficult for me"). The second factor accounted for 9.4% of the total variance, and the nine items that loaded on this factor measured the construct Restricted Emotionality (e.g., "It's hard for me to talk about me feelings with others"). The third factor accounted for 6.6% of the total variance, and the seven items that loaded on this factor measured the construct Conflict Between Work, School, and Family (e.g., "My work or school often disrupts other parts of my life [home, health, leisure]"). The fourth factor accounted for 4.5% of the total variance, and the six items that loaded on this factor measured the construct Need for Success and Achievement (e.g., "I strive to be more successful than others").

The four factors yielded internal consistency coefficients that ranged from .70 (Need for Success and Achievement) to .82 (Restricted Affection Between Men). Test–retest reliability coefficients (over 2 weeks) for each of the subscales were as follows: Need for Success and Achievement (.95); Restricted Emotionality (.87); Restricted Affection Between Men (.83); and Conflict Between Work, School, and Family (.60). Convergent validity evidence between the GRCS–A and the adult version indicated that the correlations between each scale's subscales ranged from .78 to .88.

GENDER ROLE CONFLICT SCALE—FEMALES

Women's GRC as a psychological construct is undefined in psychology, and currently no theoretically derived measure of women's conflicts with their gender roles exists. Women also have socialized conflicts with gender roles because of sexism, and these problem areas can be assessed. Even though the GRCS was created for men, the measure was modified to use with women (Borthick et al., 1997). This was done by changing the pronouns for each item. A female sample ($n = 462$) were given the revised scale, and all items except one loaded on the appropriate factor that explained 38% of the total variance. Factor analysis of the GRCS—Females indicated that the scale items loaded in a way similar to the men's version. Internal consistency reliabilities for each factor were as follows: .84 for SPC, .86 for RE, .83 for RABBM, and .81 for CBWFR.

GENDER ROLE JOURNEY MEASURE

The Gender Role Journey Measure (GRJM) was developed to help men and women resolve their GRC and facilitate their gender role transitions (O'Neil et al., 1993). The five phases of the gender role journey were theorized in the late 1980s and early 1990s, and empirical research validated three distinct phases of the journey. As I discuss in more detail in Chapter 13, the gender role journey concept has been the theoretical foundation for the Gender Role Journey Workshop (O'Neil, 1996; O'Neil

& Egan, 1992a, 1992b; O'Neil & Roberts Carroll, 1988). The five phases of the gender role journey were hypothesized to be (a) acceptance of traditional gender roles, (b) ambivalence, (c) anger, (d) activism, and (e) celebrating and integrating gender roles. These phases were defined as individuals' experience with their gender roles cognitively, affectively, and behaviorally. Forty-six items were generated that captured aspects of the five phases, and various statistical analyses were performed to finalize the scale.

Psychometric evaluation of the GRJM was completed through factor analysis and reliability estimation. Exploratory principal factor analysis (i.e., a common factor analysis) was completed on the 46-item GRJM. The goal of this analysis was to investigate the latent structure of the factors for the items. All items with factor loadings less than 0.35 were excluded from consideration. Also, no item was allowed to cross-load on any other factor in the construction of the scale. Internal consistency estimates for each factor score were calculated using Cronbach's alpha. In addition, 2-week test–retest reliabilities for each factor score were calculated on a subset of the sample.

Exploratory principal factor analyses were completed on subsamples of females ($n = 563$) and males ($n = 315$) to assess whether the factor structure was different for men and women. The oblique rotation (direct quartimin, with $\delta = 0$) yielded the most satisfactory interpretation. The results indicated an invariant factor structure across genders. Therefore, the data were combined in an overall factor analysis for the entire sample. This principal factor analysis, with an oblique rotation, yielded three meaningful factors. All retained items for the three meaningful factors were items that had loadings greater than 0.35 and did not load on any other items. Thirty-four of the 46 original items were related to one of the three factors. The factors were (a) Acceptance of Traditional Gender Roles (10 items); (b) Gender Role Ambivalence, Confusion, Anger, and Fear (11 items); and (c) Personal–Professional Activism (13 items).

A few studies have used the GRJM. Research has shown that an educational intervention can change students' phase of the gender role journey (Gertner, 1994) and sex differences on the subscales were found in one study (O'Neil et al., 1993). Different phases of the gender role journey have been significantly correlated with men's GRC, hypermasculinity, hostility toward women, sexually aggressive experiences, and likelihood of forcing sex (Kaplan, 1992; Kaplan, O'Neil, & Owen, 1993). For adult women, the different phases of the gender role journey have been significantly correlated with positive and negative affect, depression, religious well-being, and emotional distress (Mock, 1995). The Gender Role Ambivalence, Confusion, Anger and Fear subscale has been found to be a significant predictor of escalating strategies and negative attributions (McDermott, Schwartz, & Trevathan-Minnis, 2012), and other research has found support for the different subscales in terms of various contextual variables (McDermott & Schwartz, 2013). Research has also found that Personal–Professional Activism subscale is a predictor of feminist activism (White, 2006).

CONCLUSION

The GRCS and its various adaptations have been used to document men's and boys'—and even women's—GRC in more than 350 studies and therefore are among the most widely used measures in the psychology of men. The scale has received more scrutiny than any other measure in the psychology of men, and the published critiques have deemed the scale to have good construct validity and reliability across diverse groups of men. The criticisms have improved the scale, specifically, the development of the GRCS–SF, which eliminated items that decreased its validity for men who are members of racial/ethnic minority groups (Wester et al., 2012). The scale has been used with diverse men across many racial/ethnic, age, and sexual orientation categories. It also has been used in many different countries, and although more study is needed, the construct validity for the GRCS is good for men who reside outside the United States. This cross-cultural research suggests that GRC is a construct that has some universality, but much more work is needed to document how GRC is experienced and can be measured in different cultures and countries. The critical comments by Beaglaoich et al. (2013) are highly relevant to the future validation of any new GRCS in other cultures and countries.

5

A DEVELOPMENTAL MODEL OF MASCULINITY: GENDER ROLE TRANSITIONS AND MEN'S PSYCHOSOCIAL GROWTH

Constant development is the law of life, and a man who always tries to maintain his dogmas in order to appear consistent drives himself into a false position.

—Mahatma Gandhi

Developmental perspectives on men do not exist in the psychology of men. This lack of knowledge is significant because how males develop is critical to an accurate understanding of their problems and potential. Although changes in men's gender roles have been generally acknowledged for decades (Heppner, 1995; Levinson, Darrow, Klein, Levinson, & McKee, 1978; Moreland, 1980; Smiler, 2004; Woodford, 2012), the ways in which gender roles affect psychosocial development and the mastery of developmental tasks have not been analyzed. General theories about gender roles exist in social and developmental psychology (Eckes & Trautner, 2000; Trautner & Eckes, 2000), but those theories do not explain the complex transitions men experience. A developmental model of masculinity is needed because research indicates that masculinity ideologies and gender role conflict (GRC) significantly correlate with men's psychological problems over the life span (Levant & Richmond, 2007; O'Neil, 2008b, 2008c). Furthermore, teachers are challenged to help boys developmentally in schools, and clinicians struggle to

http://dx.doi.org/10.1037/14501-006
Men's Gender Role Conflict: Psychological Costs, Consequences, and an Agenda for Change, by J. M. O'Neil

help men who have delayed psychosocial development. Therefore, in this chapter I focus on developing more expansive developmental perspectives on how boys become men.

My goal in this chapter is to present a developmental framework that uses the concepts of GRC and gender role transitions (O'Neil & Egan, 1992a) to explain boys' and men's development. First, I discuss the lack of study on gender role transitions and define them in the context of demonstrating, resolving, reevaluating, or integrating aspects of masculinity ideology. Second, I introduce gender role schemas, including distorted ones, as critical concepts in understanding gender role transitions. Next, to establish a developmental foundation to understand men's lives, I integrate a summary of B. Newman and Newman's (2015) psychosocial theory with gender role constructs. I introduce a conceptual model grounded in psychosocial theory that describes how GRC, masculinity ideology, and gender role transitions relate to developmental tasks and psychosocial crises. Numerous theoretical assumptions about male development over the life cycle are specified to give greater clarity, depth, and utility to men's gender role transitions. I also discuss two inhibitors of gender role transitions: (a) the fear of femininity (FOF) and (b) homophobia. Next, I use the gender role journey and five transformational processes to describe how gender role transitions can be facilitated. The chapter closes with a brief case study of one of my clients who experienced delayed psychosocial development, GRC, and then gender role transitions that allowed him to transform himself.

THE LACK OF RESEARCH ON MEN'S GENDER ROLE TRANSITIONS

Although the field of developmental psychology has provided some useful information on how boys acquire gender roles in early and middle childhood, the specific ways in which gender roles change have been largely unexplored. Specific changes have gone unnoticed and unlabeled, except perhaps for puberty, the best-known male gender role transition. The lack of specific research on how gender roles change is noteworthy, and the reasons why psychologists have not studied how people reevaluate and change their gender roles are unclear. The field of psychology has not provided a conceptual basis for explaining how gender role ideologies develop and change, nor have psychologists completed research on the process. These omissions are ironic because although, as noted, everyone experiences these transitions and alters their views of gender roles, the reasons why they do it remain unknown. Perhaps men and women are so involved in gender role change (or not conscious of it) that attitudinal shifts with masculinity and femininity are difficult to label while they are happening. Even the two best-known gender role changes, puberty and menopause, are not understood well in any emotional or psychological sense. Everyone undergoes changes in the ways they perceive masculinity and femininity over the life cycle. These changes are usually not dramatic shifts, but instead slow, ambiguous reconsiderations of masculinity and femininity. The processes of these gender role transitions can be arduous and taxing because they are so time consuming and important, requiring one to integrate thoughts and feelings, process losses and generate new life concepts, and evaluate and change established gender role ideologies and perspectives on human nature. The real question is, when people do change, why and how do they experience the process, both cognitively and emotionally? In this chapter, I begin to address this question in the context of gender role transitions and GRC.

DEFINING GENDER ROLE TRANSITIONS

Gender role transitions are events in a person's gender role development that produce changes in his or her gender role identity and self-assumptions. Understanding gender role transitions across the life span by journeying with them is one way to understand GRC and develop healthy, positive masculinity. In the midst of gender role transitions, men and women demonstrate, resolve, reevaluate, and integrate new or old conceptions of masculinity and femininity—as West and Zimmerman (1998) put it, they are "doing gender" or "redoing gender." Gender role transitions are hypothesized to relate to mastering developmental tasks, resolving psychosocial crises, and facing dilemmas with maturity. They can produce positive growth or confusion, anxiety, and despair, and the failure to resolve them may stimulate GRC and other emotional problems. Four action-oriented processes can occur during gender role transitions: The person can make a concerted effort to (a) demonstrate, (b) resolve, (c) reevaluate, or (d) integrate (in the case of a man) masculinity ideology issues. I define each of these in the following paragraphs.

The *demonstration* of masculinity ideology ("doing gender") is central to the formation of a functional gender role identity for a man or boy. When a male demonstrates his masculinity, he shows himself and others he is male. He confirms for himself his masculine gender role identity and hopes for affirmation from others. Demonstrating masculinity is accomplished stereotypically by striving for power, control, status, wealth, achievement, affirmation, and success. These strivings are by themselves positive qualities to demonstrate but, taken to an extreme, they could be problematic.

A history of manhood suggests that many of men's problems and their defensiveness relate to feeling compelled to demonstrate, test, and prove their masculinity. According to Kimmel (2005), this single premise of proving one's masculinity has affected contemporary men's lives from the early part of the 19th century until today. He argued that "the quest for manhood—the effort to achieve, to demonstrate, to prove our masculinity—has been one of the formative and persistent experiences in men's lives" (p. 3). This historical analysis is important because proving one's masculinity has powerful psychological significance in explaining men's gender role transitions and conflict.

An important thesis about precarious masculinity and the costs of proving one's masculinity has been the subject of recent discussion (Vandello & Bosson, 2013; Vandello, Bosson, Cohen, Burnaford, & Weaver, 2008). *Precarious masculinity* implies that manhood is an elusive state, one that needs to be earned and, once achieved, is tenuous and can be lost or taken away by others; therefore, it requires public demonstration or proof. Vandello and colleagues (Vandello & Bosson, 2013; Vandello et al., 2008) have connected precarious masculinity to GRC but indicated that the issues are complex and deserve further thought and research. How precarious manhood is a result of demonstrating and proving one's masculinity, and how these issues relate to psychosocial development and gender role transitions, are important topics to explore in the future.

The *resolution* of a masculinity ideology issue occurs when the man brings closure to a significant question about gender roles or his gender role identity. Throughout the life cycle, critical points occur when the question of how to be a man becomes paramount. The issues are complex, and ambiguity usually surrounds what to do or whom to be. Vital questions need to be answered: How do I handle failure or success as a man? How do I relate to women and other men? How do I feel about multiple male sexualities? How do I become a father or loving spouse? Developmental tasks must be worked through, and psychosocial crises resolved, for these questions to be answered and future growth and development to occur.

During the *reevaluation* process, men critically evaluate gender role stereotypes and masculinity ideologies, assessing and redefining their feelings, thoughts, and behaviors about masculinity and femininity. On some level, and to varying degrees, gender roles are deconstructed during these reevaluations. This process calls for much soul searching and raises further questions about the limits of one's masculinity ideology and whether proving one's masculinity is possible—or worth it. As men age, stereotypical feminine values may seem more acceptable than masculine values and not as threatening to their gender role identity.

Finally, *integration* of new gender role values occurs if a man is able to reconcile his previous gender role ideology with new definitions of masculinity and femininity. These integrations are often connected to his developmental growth and the acceptance of new roles and responsibilities. The process requires acknowledging that the old gender role values are no longer functional and that new values are needed if the man is to be fulfilled and capable of facing life's challenges.

The demonstration, resolution, reevaluation, and integration of masculine and feminine values occur during the normal maturation process. The transitional processes can open up internal parts of the man, expand his self-definition, and promote personal exploration and growth. One of the more vital issues is how these four psychological processes occur cognitively and emotionally in conjunction with gender role schemas as men face developmental tasks and challenges in life.

GENDER ROLE SCHEMAS AND DISTORTED GENDER ROLE SCHEMAS

Personal changes to and modifications of gender role values are not completed in a vacuum, and the thoughts and feelings that get demonstrated, resolved, reevaluated, or integrated are a critical issue. Usually, there are cognitive and affective processes operating that facilitate the completion of gender role transitions. The transitions are experienced in the context of certain gender role schemas.

Gender role schemas are cultural definitions of maleness and femaleness that organize and guide an individual's perception of masculinity and femininity based on sex and gender roles. The schema is related to the person's self-concept and is used to evaluate his or her personal adequacy as male or female. The issue of personal adequacy to meet the demands of restrictive gender roles schemas is part of the gender role strain and conflict that both men and women experience. Gender role schemas are considered, and at times struggled with, as boys or men demonstrate, resolve, reevaluate, and integrate masculinity and femininity during gender role transitions.

Many men have learned gender role schemas that are distorted and based on sexist stereotypes. *Distorted gender role schemas* are exaggerated thoughts and feelings about masculinity and femininity as they apply to major life issues. The distortion occurs because of perceived or actual pressure to meet stereotypical notions of masculinity, resulting in fears and anxieties about not measuring up to traditional gender role expectations. These distorted gender role schemas are part of the man's restricted masculinity ideology that produce GRC and what has been conceptualized as precarious masculinity (Vandello et al., 2008; Vandello & Bosson, 2013).

Some gender-related questions that arise in regard to the modification of one's gender role values include the following: With what schemas do men struggle during gender role transitions? What schemas need to demonstrated, resolved, reevaluated, and finally integrated? What schemas get distorted and contribute to GRC? Table 5.1 lists 20 gender role schemas and

TABLE 5.1

Definitions of Gender Role Schemas and Distorted Gender Role Schemas

Gender role schema	Definition	Distorted gender role schema
1. Success	Attaining wealth, favor, or eminence	Success is a measure of my manhood.
2. Achievement	Successful completion and accomplishment brought about by resolve, persistence, and/or endeavor	I have to achieve regularly to feel good as a man.
3. Competence	Having adequate ability, qualities, and a capacity to function in a particular way	I can never fail as a man.
4. Control	Regulating, restraining, and having others or situations under one's command	I have to always be in control to feel secure.
5. Power	Obtaining authority, influence, or ascendancy over others and one's environment	Without my power, I am less of a man.
6. Competition	Striving against others to gain something and establishing one's superiority or skill	I have to always win to feel good.
7. Strength	Having a capacity for endurance physically, emotionally, intellectually, and spiritually	I should never show weakness.
8. Personal worth	Being valued by others and valuing one's self	I have to prove my personal value over and over again.
9. Provider role	Assuming economic responsibility for family	I am less of a man if I cannot take care of my family.
10. Personal communication	Verbal and nonverbal ways of interpersonal exchange	The less said, the better.
11. Women's and men's work roles	Perceptions of appropriate work roles for each sex	Men should work, women should take care of the home/kids.
12. Health care	Recognition of factors that maintain a healthy life	I don't ever have to go to the doctor.
13. Fatherhood	Parental role with sons and daughters	I have the ultimate say in the family.
14. Sexuality	Understanding sexual needs, attitudes, values, and behaviors	Performance is a measure of my manhood.
15. Intimacy	Understanding intimacy needs, attitudes, values, and behaviors	Getting close emotionally is risky and can cost me.
16. Emotionality	Understanding of and ability to express emotions	Emotions are feminine and therefore not for me.
17. Homosexuality	Sex between people of the same sex	Being gay is disordered, morally wrong, and bad for society.
18. Dependence	A need for or reliance on others	I don't need anybody; I can do everything on my own.
19. Vulnerability	Feeling of weakness	Never show any weakness because you will be taken advantage of by someone.
20. Performance	Being able to demonstrate one's skills	If I don't perform every time, I am a loser.

their distortions. These schemas comprise the gender-related themes that boys and men process during gender role transitions and therefore are critical to an understanding of developmental masculinity.

INTEGRATING DEVELOPMENTAL MASCULINITY WITH B. NEWMAN AND NEWMAN'S PSYCHOSOCIAL THEORY

Most of the literature in developmental psychology has focused on how sex- and gender-typed behavior is acquired and learned. Missing theoretically are the psychosocial processes involved as one forms a gender role identity or a masculine self. *Psychosocial theory* was created by Barbara and Phillip Newman. It is based on the work of Erik Erikson and presented in the Newmans' (2015) book *Development Through Life: A Psychosocial Approach*, the purpose of which is to help with the integration of psychosocial development with gender role development. First published 25 years ago and now in its 12th edition, the book is research based and highly organized in describing the transitions and crises that are part of the life cycle. Its assumptions provide a heuristic psychosocial framework for integrating the concepts of GRC and gender role transitions that can be helpful to clinicians and generate more elaborate research on the developmental aspects of gender roles. In this section, I present seven of B. Newman and Newman's psychosocial assumptions as composing a theoretical foundation for describing men's psychosocial growth in the context of gender role transitions.

B. Newman and Newman (2015) suggested first that growth is continuous across the life stages from infancy to very old age, with every person contributing to his or her own development. A similar statement can be made about gender role development. Changes in gender roles occur across the entire life span, with all individuals involved in demonstrating, resolving, reevaluating, and integrating gender as they age. Gender role identity is a change process in which individuals, passively or actively, strive to understand both masculinity and femininity. The process can be a conscious one, but many are unaware of the masculine and feminine ideologies they are embracing and living out.

Second, both biological and environmental factors affect growth. In an extrapolation of this premise, gender role development is a combination of biological and environmental factors that contribute to either the adoption or rejection of restrictive gender role stereotypes as a person develops. Family, school, peers, and the larger society influence gender role identities, and biological changes influence thoughts and feelings as boys and men move through early sex typing, puberty, hormonal changes, and/or loss of sexual stamina and testosterone as they age.

Third, B. Newman and Newman (2015) defined 10 stages of human development, from infancy to old age, each of which characterized by a specific underlying structure (see Figure 5.1). Developmental and social psychologists have likewise theorized that gender roles have stages of development and an underlying structure that changes over the life span (Eccles, 1987; Eckes & Trautner, 2000; Levinson et al., 1978). Conceptions of gender role growth can positively influence development at any stage of life, or they can limit the person through restrictive gender role stereotypes.

Fourth, at each stage of life the person needs to master specific developmental tasks to move on to the next stage of development and psychosocial growth. Developmental task is a set of skills and competencies that contribute to increased mastery over one's environment and that define what is healthy, normal development at each age in a particular society (B. Newman & Newman, 2015). The tasks occur during sensitive periods when an individual is ready to acquire a new ability and reflect gains in physical, cognitive, emotional, social, and/or emotional skills that all affect self-concept. Examples include fantasy play in toddlerhood and the challenges of learning skills and engaging in self-evaluation in middle childhood. Examples in early adolescence include puberty, emotional development, and finding a peer group and, in later adolescence, autonomy from one's parents and choosing a career path. Failure to master these tasks can result in developmental delay as well as emotional and interpersonal turmoil.

Numerous theorists have suggested that gender role development evolves through stages that relate to developmental tasks (Block, 1984; Eccles, 1987; Rebecca, Hefner, & Olenshansky, 1976). Furthermore, these tasks interface with gender role stereotypes, which are learned by men and boys and reinforced by family, peers, and the larger hegemonic society. The struggle to master the tasks, and a failure to do so, can result in turmoil. For example, failure to develop self-esteem, emotional control, autonomy, success in work, effective relationships, and success in school can result in developmental delay and emotional problems such as depression and anxiety. Attempts to, and difficulties in, mastering developmental tasks can also stimulate GRC that is based on rigid masculinity ideologies.

Fifth, the attempt to master a developmental task produces a psychosocial crisis at each stage of development, which needs to be resolved for growth and development to continue. Although the word *crisis* usually has a negative connotation that suggests an extreme situation, it also can imply the tension and conflict produced by cultural pressures and expectations that are necessary elements for development throughout the life span. *Psychosocial crisis* refers to a normal set of stressors and coping strategies associated with exerting psychological effort to adjust to the conditions of a new level of maturity and growth (B. Newman & Newman, 2015). The individual makes the adjustment by

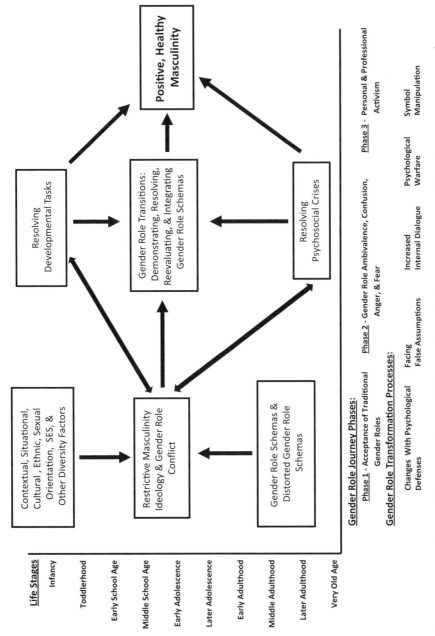

Figure 5.1. Developmental model of masculinity: Psychosocial development across the life span.

integrating the personal needs, skills, and social demands that vary from stage to stage. At the end of the stage, he or she tries to resolve the crisis by translating the societal demands into personal change, producing a state of tension that is experienced in terms of polarities or opposites—for example, trust versus mistrust or autonomy versus shame. Both polar ends foster development, but the tension between them must be reduced for the person to proceed to the next stage and meet new challenges.

The psychosocial crisis in early school age occurs when initiative comes into conflict with guilt, and during middle childhood the challenge is reconciling inferiority and industry. Group identity versus alienation and individual identity versus identity confusion characterize the crises of early and later adolescence, respectively. The associated stress and strain can be related to gender roles and compel the individual to demonstrate, resolve, reevaluate, or integrate new or old definitions of masculinity and femininity into the process of maturing. Many of the psychosocial crises can result in individuals both consciously and unconsciously activating GRC as they raise questions about gender role identity. Some of the crises are directly related to gender roles and occur during gender role transitions when a man or boy has to redefine himself in the context of masculinity and femininity and his new life role or situation.

Sixth, maladaptive coping with psychosocial crises leads to the emergence of core pathologies that guide individual behavior in negative directions, produce emotional distress, and impede further development. Similarly, the inability to work through gender role transitions can produce maladaptive coping and psychological problems (e.g., GRC) that can restrict behavior and stunt psychosocial growth. When important issues with gender roles go unresolved or distorted gender roles schema are played out, GRC can occur with significant psychological costs.

Seventh, B. Newman and Newman (2015) stated that culture and context help shape an individual's growth. Situational, cultural, racial/ethnic, and sexual orientation, as well as socioeconomic factors, all affect growth and development. Again, gender role development is shaped by these same factors that affect the rate and direction of growth and development. Contextual or cultural factors can produce restrictive gender roles that result in the adoption of an exaggerated masculinity ideology to compensate for a failure to resolve developmental tasks and psychosocial crises, which may be interpreted as not meeting masculine expectations for success and competence.

B. Newman and Newman's (2015) assumptions have direct implications for gender role development, and each assumption provides a base from which to theorize about masculine gender role development. In the next section, I present a psychosocial developmental model to expand an understanding of developmental masculinity and a context in which to understand gender role change and conflict.

DEVELOPMENTAL MODEL OF MASCULINITY: PSYCHOSOCIAL DEVELOPMENT ACROSS THE LIFESPAN

Psychosocial theory provides a vantage point from which to theorize about gender role transitions and developmental changes in men and boys. Figure 5.1 depicts a developmental model that integrates gender role transitions and GRC with psychosocial theory (B. Newman & Newman, 2015). The left of the figure shows life stages during which psychosocial gender-related processes are experienced from infancy to very old age. The vertical listing of the stages on the left implies that the gender-related processes can occur at any time during life. At the bottom of the figure are shown the phases of the gender role journey and the gender role transformation processes. The three gender role journey phases are (a) acceptance of traditional gender roles; (b) gender role ambivalence, confusion, anger, and fear; and (c) personal and professional activism. Later in this chapter, I discuss the gender role journey as a metaphor for analyzing one's views about gender roles over the life span through personal transformation. The transformational processes include working with defenses, considering false assumptions, engaging self-dialogue and psychological warfare, and symbol manipulations. The six rectangles in the middle of Figure 5.1 reflect the complexity of GRC from a developmental perspective in the context of the life stages, psychosocial development, and the gender role transformation processes.

First, the model in Figure 5.1 indicates that restrictive masculinity ideology and GRC, shown on the left, are shaped by contextual and situational factors, including cultural, racial/ethnic, socioeconomic status, and sexual orientation indices that ultimately affect psychosocial growth at each life stage. Also affecting restrictive masculinity and GRC are gender role schemas and distorted gender role schemas, also shown at the left of Figure 5.1. As I discussed earlier, gender role schemas and their distortions are part of psychosocial development that can result in fears and anxieties about not measuring up to traditional gender role expectations. Restrictive masculinity ideology is the sum total of all the gender role schemas; distorted gender role schemas; and the contextual, situational, cultural factors that can have a positive or negative effect on the boy or man's life. The interaction of the contextual factors, distorted gender role schemas, masculinity ideologies, and GRC all directly impact developmental tasks and the psychosocial crises (see bidirectional arrows in the middle of Figure 5.1)

The bidirectional (or reciprocal) arrows between restrictive masculinity ideology and GRC and the resolution, respectively, of developmental tasks and psychosocial crises, suggest two hypotheses: that (a) restrictive masculinity ideologies, distorted schemas, contextual factors, and GRC negatively affect the resolution of developmental tasks and psychosocial crises; and (b) the tasks and crises can produce GRC or contribute to restrictive masculinity ideology.

One can see in the middle of Figure 5.1 that the working through of the tasks and crises is accomplished through gender role transitions that come about through the action-oriented processes of demonstrating, reevaluating, performing, and integrating gender role schemas. Finally, as shown toward the right of the figure, the effective resolution of gender role transitions, developmental tasks, and psychosocial crises results in psychological health and maturity: what currently is known as positive, healthy masculinity (Kiselica, 2011; Kiselica & Englar-Carlson, 2010). Previous definitions of healthy masculinity have enumerated male strengths and adaptive and positive aspects of being a man. I extend this definition by describing positive, healthy masculinity as full maturation gained by mastering developmental tasks and resolving the psychosocial tasks and crises across the life cycle. Figure 5.1 provides an overall framework around which to discuss developmental assumptions about psychosocial growth in the context of developmental masculinity.

THEORETICAL ASSUMPTIONS ABOUT DEVELOPMENTAL MASCULINITY: GENDER ROLE CONFLICT, GENDER ROLE TRANSITIONS, AND PSYCHOSOCIAL GROWTH

Theoretical assumptions about how psychosocial theory can be integrated with GRC constructs are enumerated in Exhibit 5.1. A careful reading of these assumptions suggests that gender role transitions occur throughout the life stages as boys and men experience varying degrees of restrictive masculinity ideology and GRC that affect psychosocial development in each developmental period. Numerous contextual and situational factors affect how masculinity ideology and GRC affect psychosocial growth, including mastering developmental tasks. Efforts to master the developmental tasks and resolve psychosocial crises can cause GRC. Furthermore, gender role transitions may be necessary to master the developmental tasks and resolve the psychosocial crises. Mastering developmental tasks and resolving psychosocial crises involves, at least in part, changes in gender role values and self-assumptions. Journeying with one's gender roles is needed to resolve gender role transitions, and this involves demonstrating, resolving, redefining, and integrating gender role schemas related to masculinity and femininity ideologies. Restrictive masculinity ideology and GRC may limit the behavioral and emotional flexibility needed to master developmental tasks and resolve psychosocial crises. Distorted gender role schemas about masculinity and femininity may need to be corrected (redefined) to effectively resolve developmental tasks and the psychosocial crises. FOF and homophobia are major inhibitors of men who are managing gender role transitions, mastering

EXHIBIT 5.1
Theoretical Assumptions About Developmental Masculinity

1. GRC and gender role transitions exist throughout the life cycle.
2. During the different life stages, boys and men have varying degrees of restrictive masculinity ideology and GRC that affect their psychosocial development in that developmental period.
3. Numerous contextual, cultural, and situational factors affect how masculinity ideology and GRC influence psychosocial growth, including mastery of developmental tasks and psychosocial growth.
4. Gender role transitions may be necessary to master the developmental tasks and resolve the psychosocial crises of each life stage.
5. Mastering the developmental tasks and resolving the psychosocial crises can produce changes in a man's gender role values and self-assumptions.
6. Resolving gender role transitions related to developmental tasks and psychosocial crises involves demonstrating, resolving, redefining, and integrating gender role schemas related to masculinity and femininity ideologies.
7. Restrictive masculinity ideology and the patterns of GRC (Success, Power, and Competition; Restrictive Emotionality; Restrictive Affectionate Behavior Between Men; and Conflict Between Work and Family Relations; see Chapter 4) may limit behavioral and emotional flexibility and interfere with the developmental tasks and the resolution of the psychosocial crises (see bidirectional arrows in Figure 5.1).
8. Efforts to master the developmental tasks and resolve psychosocial crises can cause GRC.
9. Distorted gender role schemas about masculinity and femininity may need correction to effectively resolve developmental tasks and the psychosocial crises.
10. Fear of femininity and homophobia can interfere with effectively managing GRC and resolving developmental tasks and psychosocial crises.
11. Optimal development and positive masculinity are achieved when the developmental tasks and psychosocial crises have resolved and there has been full gender role transition, meaning that the changed self-assumptions about gender roles facilitate rather than delay further development.
12. Journeying with one's gender roles can facilitate gender role transitions and includes recognizing the costs of GRC, including gender role devaluations, restrictions, and violations.
13. The transformation process of journeying with gender roles includes changing psychological defenses, facing false assumptions, increasing internal dialogue, managing psychological warfare, and symbol manipulation.
14. Therapists and psychoeducational programmers can use gender role transitions, gender role schemas, and the gender role journey in therapy with men and during preventive interventions.

the developmental tasks, and resolving psychosocial crises. Optimal development and positive masculinity occur when the developmental tasks and psychosocial crises are resolved and there is a positive transition to the next stage of development. Clinicians can use gender role transitions, gender role schemas, and the gender role journey in therapy with men and during psychoeducational interventions (see Chapters 9–13, this volume).

IDENTIFYING GENDER ROLE TRANSITIONS IN THE CONTEXT OF PSYCHOSOCIAL THEORY

In this section, I list many gender role transitions that relate to developmental tasks and psychosocial crises discussed in psychosocial theory. The life stages, developmental tasks, and psychosocial crises proposed by B. Newman and Newman (2015), and specific examples of gender role transitions or tasks related to the transitions, are shown in Table 5.2. In the first column at the left of Table 5.2 are listed the 10 life stages, and in column 2 are listed at least one of Newman and Newman's developmental tasks corresponding to each. The psychosocial crises for the 10 stages are listed in the third column, followed in the fourth column by the gender role transitions that characterize each period of growth and development. If we apply the relationships proposed earlier with the theoretical assumptions and the model shown in Figure 5.1, we can hypothesize that each developmental task and psychosocial crisis involves one or more gender role transitions that are vital to mastering the task and resolving the crisis. In this way, we can see that issues related to masculinity and femininity are directly related to psychosocial growth. In accordance with the definition of *gender role transitions*, each task and crisis involves some aspect of demonstrating, resolving, reevaluating, or integrating masculinity norms and standards. The associations made at each life stage provide a preliminary developmental framework to help understand boys' and men's gender role socialization over the life span in the context of male development and psychosocial growth. GRC results when the psychosocial issues (i.e., the tasks and crises) are delayed or go unresolved.

MAJOR INHIBITORS TO GENDER ROLE TRANSITIONS: FEAR OF FEMININITY AND HOMOPHOBIA

Fear of Femininity

A major inhibitor of gender role transitions is FOF: a strong, negative emotion associated with feminine values, attitudes, and behaviors, which are regarded as inferior, inappropriate, and immature—in short, a devaluation of all that is feminine (O'Neil, 1981a, 1982). Fears of femininity are learned primarily during early childhood socialization, when gender identity is being formed by input from parents, peers, and societal institutions. They are also stimulated in later years by physical maturation, developmental changes, and life events. Jung (1953) believed that difficulties with femininity were archetypal, passed down over the centuries, and usually outside the man's consciousness.

TABLE 5.2

Developmental and Psychosocial Aspects of Gender Role Transitions Over the Life Cycle

Life stage	Developmental tasks	Psychosocial crisis	Gender role transitions
Infancy (birth–2 years)	• Attachment	Trust vs. mistrust	• Bonding with a trusting parent
Toddlerhood (2–4 years)	• Fantasy play	Autonomy vs. shame/ guilt	• Creating gender labels • Doing gender typing
Early school age (4–6 years)	• Gender identification	Initiative vs. guilt	• Recognizing gender constancy, gender role stability • Learning gender role, standards, schemas, stereotyping • Identifying with parents' gender • Having gender preferences • Choosing gender segregation with peers • Acknowledging gender consistency • Demonstrating sex typing during play • Accepting and liking gender self
Middle childhood (6–12 years)	• Learning skills • Self-evaluation	Inferiority vs. industry	• Entering school • Experiencing physical maturation • Identifying with peer group identification • Demonstrating masculine skill • Affirming masculine self • Demonstrating self-efficacy • Affirmation by same-sex playmates • Early male bonding • Facing female peer group norms • Experiencing heterosexual antagonism
Early adolescence (12–18 years)	• Puberty • Emotional development • Finding a peer group	Group identity vs. alienation	• Experiencing puberty • Accepting biological, body, and sexual changes • Making a tentative career choice • Managing emotionality • Managing teen dating relationships • Initiating heterosexual/homosexual relationships

(continues)

TABLE 5.2
Developmental and Psychosocial Aspects of Gender Role Transitions Over the Life Cycle   (Continued)

Life stage	Developmental tasks	Psychosocial crisis	Gender role transitions
Later adolescence (18–22 years)	• Autonomy from parents • Choosing a career path	Individual identity vs. identity confusion	• Gender role identification reevaluation • Gender role constancy reevaluation • Gender role preference reevaluation • Sexual dimensions of gender reevaluation • Gender role standards reevaluation • Managing dependence/independence • Managing work/school effectively
Early adulthood (23–34 years)	• Intimacy–marriage • Childbearing • Early work–career	Intimacy vs. isolation	• Leaving home • Negotiating relationships • Learning control + power sharing • Becoming a father • Demonstrating work success • Fulfilling provider role
Middle adulthood (34–60 years)	• Managing career/home • Maintaining intimate relationships	Generativity vs. stagnation	• Having continued work success and contribution • Maintaining intimacy, or divorce • Maintaining provider role • Experiencing career transitions • Letting go of one's children • Relaxing gender role standards
Later adulthood (60–75 years)	• Accepting one's life • Redirecting energy to new roles	Integrity vs. despair	• Evaluating one's life work • Experiencing a loss of stamina • Redefining self after retirement • Managing health problems
Very old age (75 years–death)	• Coping with physical changes from aging • Dealing with death	Immortality vs. extinction	• Continuing loss of stamina • Managing health problems • Accepting death

Note. The developmental concepts in this table are only examples of developmental tasks, psychosocial crises, and gender role transitions and are not representative of the full range of changes that boys and men experience across the life cycle.

Despite the prominence of the subject in the psychoanalytical discourse of the early 1900s (Connell, 2005), the centrality of femininity in men's lives has been only partially explored in the field of the psychology of men. David and Brannon (1976) proposed the concept of antifemininity, and antifemininity subscales are found on the Male Role Norms Scale (E. H. Thompson & Pleck, 1986) and the Male Role Norms Inventory (Levant et al., 1992). Men's fears about their femininity are a very important part of male development because many of the gender role transitions enumerated in Table 5.2 are associated with struggles, conflicts, and fears about femininity.

For example, while masculinity is being learned or validated, fears of femininity may occur during all of the following gender role transitions included in Table 5.2: learning gender role standards, schemas, and stereotyping; peer group identification; early male bonding; facing female peer group norms; heterosexual antagonism; dealing with homophobia; managing teen relationships; managing emotionality; and initiating heterosexual/homosexual relations. Failures at and worries about these gender role transitions can stimulate fears about femininity and highly sex-typed or hypermasculine behavior.

Some of the gender role transitions require a young boy or man to do two things: (a) integrate feminine losses and give up parts of himself and (b) manage rejections from authorities who represent the feminine, and do so by actually devaluing the feminine in others. These include transitions like heterosexual antagonism, development of masculine gender role standards, same-sex gender role preferences, peer group identification, early male bonding, teenage gender role identification and learning, and first job or work experience. These transitions may produce anger and rage at anything that is feminine. Some gender role transitions are experienced with other boys and men, emphasizing the great importance of a masculine peer group in shaping (through male bonding) fears of femininity.

Other transitions that may require boys or men to come to terms with femininity are those that involve direct contact with the feminine through contact with girls and women. These include transitions such as entering school, interacting with female peer group norms, dating, and initiating heterosexual/homosexual relations. These transitions present a contradiction in that although men may be directly connected to women in positive ways through them, they will sometimes experience fears, conflict, and rage toward these feminine forces. Such fears of femininity may be a source of hostility between the sexes and motivate acts of violence against women. Femininity becomes so threatening and emasculating to some boys and men that they literally try to destroy it in a desperate attempt to deny their own femininity and preserve their masculinity. Being required to alter their perspectives on gender roles and directly face femininity in their lives may be unsettling to their sense of masculinity to the point that they become fearful and anxious about their gender identity. How this kind of FOF might relate to Vandello and Bosson's (2013) conceptualization of precarious manhood could be an important topic to pursue in the future.

The antidote to FOF is to embrace the feminine, and to do so a boy or man has to go deep inside himself and travel symbolically to his internal core. Otherwise, he will believe he can control the feminine force through external manipulation and through attaining forms of success, power, and status he perceives as masculine. Masculinity becomes the primary way to control life rather than participate in it. Many boys and men are unconscious of their need to control the feminine. Trying to control the uncontrollable is a certain path to self-destruction and continual anxiety. The male's alternative is to identify the gender role transitions that trigger fears about the feminine and use them to transform himself into a more fully functioning human being.

Homophobia

Another inhibitor of men's gender role transitions is homophobia—a form of sexism that inhibits men from exploring their femininity and masculinity and completing gender role transitions over the life span—and the presumed relationship between feminine values and homosexuality. Homophobia contributes significantly to distorted gender role schemas and hypermasculine attitudes and behaviors. In the dualistic culture of the United States, femininity and homosexuality and masculinity and heterosexuality have been erroneously linked. If you are male and act feminine, the assumption is that you are not a "real" man. If you are not a man, you are like a woman, and this means you are a homosexual because stereotypically gay men are viewed as feminine. This illogical reasoning is the source of destructive heterosexism and homophobia. As both Addis, Mansfield, and Syzdek (2010) and Kimmel (1994) have pointed out, homophobia is best understood not as a fear of gay men but as the fear of intimacy among men and the possibility of being categorized as an outcast, shamed, or otherwise punished by other men. All of these issues are related to difficulty with making gender role transitions and a successful gender role journey.

THE GENDER ROLE JOURNEY AND GENDER ROLE TRANSFORMATIONAL PROCESSES

My ideas about of how people experience gender role transitions have developed by observing students enrolled in the Gender Role Journey Workshop from 1984 to 2006 (for a more thorough discussion of this workshop, see Chapter 13, this volume). From these observations, I have concluded that resolving gender role transitions can be conceived of as the ongoing process of consciousness raising over the life span and a journey with one's gender roles (O'Neil & Egan, 1992a; O'Neil, Egan, Owen, & Murry, 1993). The gender role journey is a metaphor that can help people understand how they process gender roles and how their socialization, sexism, and adherence to gender role stereotypes may negatively affect their lives personally, professionally, and politically. As I described in Chapter 3, the gender role journey provides a framework for evaluating thoughts, feelings, and behaviors about gender roles, sexism, and GRC by promoting a retrospective analysis of early family experiences with gender roles, an assessment of how sexism is currently experienced, and decision making about how gender roles will shape one's behavior in the future.

As mentioned earlier, the three phases of the gender role journey are listed at the bottom of Figure 5.1: (a) acceptance of traditional gender roles; (b) gender role ambivalence, confusion, anger and fear; and (c) personal and professional activism. Part of the journey is the process of gaining an understanding of how GRC develops in the family and as the result of other socialization experiences, as well as identifying gender role transitions and distorted gender role schemas (O'Neil & Egan, 1992b; O'Neil & Fishman, 1992; O'Neil, Fishman, & Kinsella-Shaw, 1987). More information about the gender role journey can be found in Chapter 3, Chapter 4, and Chapter 10 of this volume.

GENDER ROLE TRANSFORMATIONAL PROCESSES

The critical question central to the gender role transformation process is how to journey with gender roles, resolve gender role transitions, and effectively redefine distorted gender role schemas to enrich one's life. This process is challenging and relates to transformations (see the bottom part of Figure 5.1). Gould (1978, 1980) has defined *transformation* as expanding one's self-definition to produce inner freedom without conflict or anxiety, thereby internalizing a maximum sense of personal security. Likewise, gender role transitions can produce a redefinition of masculinity and femininity, decreased GRC, greater freedom with gender roles, and increased self-confidence. Gould posited numerous properties of the transformation process that are relevant to explaining the internal dynamics of gender role transitions and the gender role journey, including changes in psychological defenses, facing and dealing with false assumptions, increases in internal dialogue with the self, internal psychological warfare. I add symbol manipulation to Gould's properties of transformation, and in the following paragraphs I elaborate further on each of these in the context of men's gender role transitions.

When a person struggles to change his or her fundamental conception of gender roles, the defensive structure of that individual's personality may need to be altered to foster more functional and expansive ways to live. One's past defenses may no longer function fully; new psychological mechanisms may be needed to enhance coping and promote the transformation. Defensive structures vary greatly, but repression, projection, regression, rationalization, and reaction formation are quite common. The essence of most defense mechanisms is the inability to face emotions and feelings and a resultant emotional leveling off or shutdown. Emotions relevant to one's gender role identity can be intellectualized, denied, repressed, and projected in the form of anger and hostility toward others. Therefore, gender role transitions may require a fundamental change in people's psychological defense system and new ways of experiencing deep emotions as part of the gender role journey.

Furthermore, false assumptions or illusions about gender roles may help maintain a defensive posture. Before the transformation occurs, false ideas about gender roles (i.e., distorted gender role schemas) from childhood consciousness usually establish the functional boundaries of self-definition. These functional boundaries are maintained until the false ideas are disconfirmed and disbelieved. For example, beliefs that real men always have to be strong, successful, powerful, unemotional, and in control are gender role illusions that reflect societal stereotypes. These stereotypes are usually internalized at an early age to establish both men's and women's gender role identity. Willingness to challenge these false ideas may depend on obtaining new information, deep emotional awakenings, and political awareness that sexism violates women and men in a capitalist society.

More important, gender role transitions stimulate an internal dialogue in the context of one's new, emerging gender role identity. This internal dialogue may inhibit transformation because the false ideas may produce anxiety about the meaning of change. Usually, the false self-assumptions prohibit the gender role transition process and maintain personal anxiety and GRC. If men can face these false assumptions, they can begin the internal dialogue necessary to deconstruct gender roles and prompt gender role change.

This internal dialogue may bring about psychological warfare between the person and the external world or between the old self and the new, emerging identity. During gender role transitions, "enemies" of the self from sexism and other oppressions are sometimes identified from the intense emotions, especially anger and fear; however, who these enemies are may be unclear. Women, other men, parents, children, and institutional structures may be targeted as the enemy to be attacked or avoided. Men may identify a weakened sense of themselves as the enemy, in terms of their self-imposed restrictions, devaluations, and personal limitations. Identifying "the enemy within" usually produces low self-esteem, anxiety, anger, and defensiveness that can destabilize a person. How to use these emotions (turning negatives into positives) is the therapeutic issue.

Adding to Gould's (1978, 1980) definition of transformation, gender role transitions may require a new symbol and the use of metaphors for change and healing. Instrumental, masculine outcomes, such as success, status, and power, can be replaced with transformative myths, metaphors, symbols, and images. Past interest in mythology (Campbell, 1988; Johnson, 1986) represents an evolving person's desire to use symbolic representation to find greater meaning in life. Johnson (1986) indicated that the "most rewarding mythological experience you can have is to see how it lives in your own psychological structure" (p. x). Myths offer us the truth about ourselves and dispel the hardened illusions on which we have based our lives.

The use of metaphors, images, and symbols gives men and women an opportunity to redefine their gender perspectives. In my gender role journey workshops (O'Neil, 1996; O'Neil & Roberts Carroll, 1988; see also Chapter 13, this volume), I have seen the power of symbols and metaphors in promoting transformation. For example, if the symbols (i.e., stereotypes) of power and control have been rigidly internalized as money, status, authority, and power over others, then a new conceptualization of power and control can be developed. *Power* could be redefined as the symbolic and real activity of empowering others; for example, the symbol of "power over others" becomes transformed to "conscious empowerment of others" through service, leadership, and nurturing support.

Helping people manipulate symbols related to masculinity and femininity requires that one face the illusions of gender role stereotypes. For gender role transitions to occur, the artificiality and illusions of gender role stereotypes need to be assessed through the deconstruction process. For example, one illusion is the value of highly sex-typed behavior and masculine and feminine stereotypes as a basis for healthy self-definition. For an evolving person who is seeking transformation, stereotypes no longer have the same power or utility in coping with life events. The person recognizes that stereotypic masculinity and femininity are not synonymous with health. This recognition represents a significant breakthrough toward a more substantial understanding of gender and human identity. The past gender role stereotypes are exposed as shallow and as not sustaining the person on a deeper, internal level. The illusions of the stereotypes must be explored if real growth is to occur over the life span. This process involves capturing deep emotions about masculinity and femininity and finding new meaning in them.

These five processes can facilitate gender role transitions and the deconstruction of sexist gender roles resulting in transformation and psychosocial growth. In the next section, I provide a brief case study to give an example of a man who experienced psychosocial delay and then growth and development.

CASE STUDY: JACK SMITH

In this section, I describe a case study: that of Jack Smith (a pseudonym), a previous client whose psychosocial delay, difficulties with gender role transitions, and GRC caused significant mental health problems over the course of his life. Jack gave permission for this case to be used before his death, and he told me that if anyone can learn from his life, he would be very pleased. In a previous book chapter, I presented Jack's therapy as a case study (O'Neil, 2006), but I did not describe how his psychosocial development contributed to his GRC. This brief case description shows how Jack's delayed psychosocial development contributed to his GRC and serious emotional and interpersonal problems.

Psychosocial Delay, Gender Role Conflict, and Difficulties With Gender Role Transitions

Jack was a 44-year-old White man who requested career counseling, but his real problem was that he was alone, angry, depressed, and confused by his continuous life problems. He described his family of origin as tense, cold, and emotionally vacant. His absent, alcoholic father and his overcontrolling and dominating mother did not promote Jack's psychosocial development. For Mrs. Smith, having Jack "become a man" was critical given that her husband was weak, ineffective, and powerless. Young Jack observed his mother as a powerful feminine force who emasculated his father. Furthermore, she vented her rage and disappointment at Jack, who became her personal project—" a man in the making." Jack never had a loving bond with either parent, thought no one cared for him, and learned Restrictive Emotionality (RE; see Chapter 4, this volume, for more details on Restrictive Emotionality and other formal components of GRC). Only one emotion was prevalent at home; as Jack put it, "I was numbed by my childhood anger." Jack's performance in school was mixed and far below his high intelligence, and he vacillated between being the teacher's pet and an obnoxious, disruptive, and rebellious boy. He challenged authority figures outside home because his mother could never be challenged at home. He learned to strive for power, to seek control over and dominate others, and to compete (never lose) with others to demonstrate his manhood. These qualities were part of Jack's GRC of Success, Power, and Competition.

Jack left for college with very little personal strength or emotional stability. During his freshman year, his dependency, limited self-confidence, and intense pressure to succeed made it difficult for him to study, and he flunked out. He enrolled at a less difficult college and graduated, got married, had a son, and flunked out of the graduate program he had entered. He had numerous affairs, got divorced, and at age 25 was an angry man on the run. His anger and depression led him to substance abuse, and he had numerous intense, objectifying, and abusive relationships with women whom he dominated and controlled personally and sexually. These relationships mirrored the abusive relationship with mother and his emotionally absent relationship with his father. Over the years, Jack's career development revealed a man running away from himself, having had six different jobs in seven different settings. At age 40, Jack entered therapy with me with much despair, depression, and both career and relationship dissatisfaction. His restrictive masculinity ideology and GRC comprising RE and Success, Power, and Competition, along with self-devaluation, restrictions, and violations, contributed to his low self-esteem, anxiety, depression, and substance abuse.

Psychosocial and Developmental Analysis of Jack's Gender Role Conflict

My overall assessment was that Jack was a victim of sexism because of his sexist gender role socialization that contributed to his psychosocial delay. The RE and many distorted gender role schemas that he learned in his dysfunctional family resulted in numerous personality problems and dysfunctional behaviors that limited his growth and development as a young boy into his adulthood.

As shown in Exhibit 5.1, the developmental tasks of the first five life stages include attachment, fantasy play, gender identification, learning skills, self-evaluation, puberty, emotional development, and finding a peer group. Jack's psychosocial delay with these developmental tasks was progressive from infancy through adolescence into adulthood and interacted with his gender role development, causing serious psychological problems. Jack's gender role socialization in his family and school contributed to a lack of mastery with the following developmental tasks:

- infancy: attachment and bonding;
- early school age: gender identification and self-control;
- middle childhood: positive self-evaluation;
- earlier adolescence: emotional development and control;
- early adolescence: positive peer play;
- adolescence: autonomy from parents;
- early adulthood: congruent career choice;
- early and middle adulthood: intimate relationships;
- middle adulthood: managing a career; and
- middle adulthood: maintaining intimate relationship and embracing new roles as he aged.

Each of these failed developmental tasks interacted with his gender role social-ization and difficulties working through gender role transitions and defining and redefining gender role schemas. Jack also did not resolve many of the psychosocial crises in the first 18 years of his life, including autonomy ver-sus shame/doubt (2–3 years), initiative versus guilt (4–6 years), industry versus inferiority (6–12 years), and having a group identity versus alienation (12–18 years). As his life progressed he also was unable to resolve the psycho-social crises of intimacy versus isolation (24–34 years), and generativity versus stagnation (34–60 years).

On the basis of what Jack had disclosed, he never bonded or attached to either of his parents, and therefore he had trouble trusting others and himself. He never resolved the psychosocial crises of trust versus mistrust; this negatively affected all his intimate and work relationships. Furthermore, not trusting others contributed to his inability to trust himself and develop self-confidence as a man. The lack of bonding affected his ability to identify with either parent and resolve the psychosocial crises in toddlerhood and the early school age struggles of autonomy versus shame/doubt and initiative versus guilt. By age 6 years, he had trouble directing his energy, being alone, and liking himself, and he was negatively dependent on his mother for his sense of self.

Jack's emotional development was restricted by both parents' RE. He did not learn to process emotions in the home (i.e. fear, sadness, loss, shame, joy, love), but he was quite effective in communicating anger, what he believed to be the only legitimate male emotion. In childhood, he never learned self-control because he was totally controlled by his mother's anger and disapproval. Jack's anger and emotional turmoil made it difficult for him to be productive; feelings of inferiority, a lack of confidence, and fears about failure made him insecure and ineffective in school (industry versus inferiority). No young boy can grow psychosocially under these conditions. All of the negative family and gender dynamics resulted in Jack's low self-esteem and his critical devaluations of himself and others. Jack's gender role transition to school was difficult, and his adjustment to learning from teachers was problematic. His peer relationships mirrored the family dynamics, so he had no close friends and was lonely and isolated (group identity vs. alienation). Instead of becoming independent, autonomous, and his own person, he was covertly dependent, resulting in self-doubt and shame. Puberty was a rough period because he had no one to talk to about the significant changes occur-ring in his body and becoming a man. By age 18, he had no clear gender role identity as a person and felt alienated. These psychosocial delays prohibited him from knowing who he was, what he wanted in life, and what careers to pursue. Because of his anger he had no close relationships, producing isolation, loneliness, and an inability to resolve the intimacy-versus-isolation psychosocial crisis.

By adulthood, the best he could do with relationships was to seek out women whom he could control personally and sexually. The interaction of restricted gender roles, GRC, and psychosocial delays produced long-term psychological problems and despair. Jack never was able to give back to others, and at age 40 he feared that his life had been a waste and there was nothing he could do to reverse his life course (generativity vs. stagnation). Jack's transformation and gender role transitions during therapy are summarized elsewhere (O'Neil, 2006), and through therapy he was able to make significant gains in transforming himself.

IMPLICATIONS OF THE DEVELOPMENTAL MODEL OF MASCULINITY

The model presented in this chapter is preliminary and needs more development, but it represents one of the first developmental paradigms to describe how male gender role development interfaces with overall psychosocial development. Very little research has assessed psychosocial development in the context of masculinity ideology and GRC, and therefore this area deserves greater theoretical and empirical attention from scholars in the field of psychology of men. Therapists can use the developmental model and psychosocial concepts when assessing clients, as I illustrate with the case study of Thomas (see Chapter 11, this volume). More theory and research on developmental masculinity are important parts of any call to action because they can improve the lives of boys and men over the life cycle. It is my hope that the model can stimulate further conceptualizations that explain how boys become men by resolving gender role transitions and conflict in a psychosocial context.

III

EMPIRICAL RESEARCH ON GENDER ROLE CONFLICT IN BOYS AND MEN

6

A MULTICULTURAL PSYCHOLOGY OF MEN MODEL: REVIEWING RESEARCH ON DIVERSE MEN'S GENDER ROLE CONFLICT

No one is free if anyone is oppressed.

—Author Unknown

During the celebration of the 50th anniversary of Dr. Martin Luther King Jr.'s "I Have a Dream" speech in 2013, numerous documentaries showed the civil rights protests of the 1960s and the turbulence and violence that occurred. Many of the protests showed African American men carrying signs that said, "I am a Man." Those signs were (and still are) the most vivid example of how masculinity intersects with racism, discrimination, gender role conflict (GRC), and social injustice. King spoke to this issue when he said, "We are tired of our men not finding work, so they can't be men!" (see http://www.americanrhetoric.com/speeches/mlkihaveadream.htm). Discrimination, oppression, and injustice toward men are emasculating; they compromise men's power and cause gender role self-devaluations that lead to anger, loss, depression, apathy, and violence.

I appreciate the helpful review of this chapter by Jay Wade (Fordham University) and Chris Liang (Lehigh University).

http://dx.doi.org/10.1037/14501-007
Men's Gender Role Conflict: Psychological Costs, Consequences, and an Agenda for Change, by J. M. O'Neil

In this chapter, I review research on diverse groups of men and explain how GRC and restrictive masculinity ideology relate to men's psychological problems, discrimination, oppression, and social injustice. My goal is to present a multicultural psychology of men model and review the GRC research related to it. The studies I review connect the macrosocietal level of oppression to men's personal experience of it at the microinterpersonal level. I report evidence that diverse men's GRC relates to psychological problems, discrimination, and internalized oppression. I close the chapter with a perspective on why resistance exists in discussing diversity, multiculturalism, and societal oppression.

DEFINITIONS OF DIVERSITY AND MULTICULTURALISM

The psychology of men supports multiculturalism, as is stated in the mission statement of the Society for the Psychological Study of Men and Masculinity (SPSMM; 2012), but how masculinity ideology and GRC relate to definitions of diversity has not been fully articulated. Contextual definitions of *diversity* and *multiculturalism* are needed to create a multicultural psychology of men that fully captures the variations in how men internalize masculinity ideology. The multiculturalism and diversity perspectives in the field of the psychology of men must be expanded so that the discipline can serve more than heterosexual, White, middle-class American men and boys.

Diversity encompasses differences in culture, background, and experiences among individuals and groups and includes differences in race/ethnicity, national origin, color, gender, sexual orientation, gender identity, age, and physical and cognitive disabilities. Numerous perspectives on diversity provide a broader meaning for the term. For example, endorsing diversity means accepting and respecting all people regardless of their race/ethnicity, gender, gender identity, national origin, sexual orientation, age, religious affiliation, socioeconomic status (SES), disability, and other indexes of difference. Appreciating diversity means more than tolerating differences; it means celebrating the rich dimensions of human uniqueness. Acknowledging diversity means appreciating the interdependence of humanity and respecting cultures that differ from one's own. On the social and political levels, diversity is recognizing that personal, cultural, and institutional discrimination creates privileges for some while creating disadvantages for others. Diversity is best expressed when it is practiced, meaning that it stimulates activism and alliances to eradicate all forms of discrimination. Diversity has been accepted in U.S. society, but intolerance, discrimination, and oppression based on stereotypes and ignorance still exist, resulting in serious psychological problems for many men, women, and children.

Multiculturalism is a belief system that appreciates diversity of cultures and works to help people appreciate their own heritage and those who differ from themselves. Multiculturalists believe that differences between individuals and groups are potential sources of strength and renewal instead of division and strife. Multicultural activities promote the ideals of equality, fairness, and individual freedom; principles that are part of the overall democratic ideology of the United States. Multiculturalism also encourages the exploration of our families of origin and the roots of our racial/ethnic, and religious heritages. This exploration increases personal awareness of our unique lives and encourages greater understanding of people who are different from us. Embracing diversity means engaging others who are different from ourselves rather than ignoring them, distancing them, or pushing them away. By understanding each other's uniqueness, we understand ourselves in deeper ways and recognize that differences are to be celebrated and cherished. Multicultural consciousness emphasizes not only the diversity of human beings but also the common humanity that transcends race, class, nationality, religion, and other demographics that have pitted one group against another for so long.

MULTICULTURAL PSYCHOLOGY OF MEN, DIVERSITY, GENDER ROLE CONFLICT, AND SOCIAL JUSTICE

The multicultural psychology of men explores the commonalities and differences among men across many contextual and situational indexes and explains how GRC, masculinity ideology, and oppression are experienced in the context of race/ethnicity, class, age, sexual orientation, nationality, religious orientation, physical disability, and other indexes of diversity. Furthermore, this discipline explains how sexism, racism, classism, ethnocentrism, heterosexism, ageism, and all forms of oppression interact with patriarchal and masculinity structures. This kind of research exposes discrimination and social injustices that emanate from patriarchal sexism and other oppressions. In this way, the multicultural psychology of men explains how men, women, and children experience the injustices by being devalued, restricted, and violated by patriarchal and masculinity norms and standards. In addition, when the economic and psychological costs of oppression are exposed, these social and political realities expand the psychology of men in very significant ways. In this context, GRC and restrictive masculine norms are political issues because they address multiculturalism, discrimination, oppression, and social injustice simultaneously.

The psychology of men is fully compatible with multicultural and social justice frameworks when patriarchal values, GRC, and masculinity ideology are shown to contribute to societal oppression and discrimination against both sexes. From a multicultural psychology of men perspective, personal and societal oppression occur because of men's abuses of power, destructive competition, and interpersonal violence against women and men in order to maintain privilege and power over others. These oppressive dynamics are reinforced by prohibitions on expressing emotions, fears about and devaluations of femininity, homophobia and heterosexism, and obsessive needs to be in control and not lose power.

These social and political realities are more than abstract truths about the limitations of democracy and the excesses of destructive capitalism in America. These realities have significant human costs in terms of poverty, psychological trauma, and societal violence. The inequities in the distribution of human resources needed for human safety and security are caused by oppression (e.g., sexism, racism, classism, ethnocentrism) and produce vulnerable groups (e.g., women, members of racial/ethnic minority groups, immigrants) who experience poverty and live on the edge of survival. Furthermore, oppressed groups are marginalized and stigmatized and experience gender role devaluations, restrictions, and violations by others and from themselves (O'Neil & Renzulli, 2013a). These devaluations, restrictions, and violations also occur when racial/ethnic, class, and sexual orientation prejudices are directed at individuals in harmful and inhuman ways. The personal pain from sexism, racism, classism, ethnocentrism, and heterosexism is the most visible sign of the oppression. These injustices many times are unconscious to the oppressor but cause most serious mental health problems for both the victims and the victimizers (Sue, 2005).

The social, political, and economic implications of men's diversity form one of the most important areas in the psychology of men, but discrimination, oppression, and social injustices have not received much attention in this study area (O'Neil & Renzulli, 2013a). In the field of the psychology of men, only a few studies on discrimination against men have been published (Liang, Rivera, Nathwani, Dang, & Douroux, 2010; Liang, Salcedo, & Miller, 2011; Liu, 2002a; Liu, Iwamoto, & Chae, 2010; Wade & Rochlen, 2013). Recently, Latino, Asian American, and African American men have been studied in the contexts of gendered and perceived racism (Liang et al., 2011), racialization and discrimination (Liu et al., 2010), and racism and racial identity (Carter, Williams, Juby, & Buckley, 2005; Wade & Rochlen, 2013; Wester, Vogel, Wei, & McLain, 2006). The few studies published on oppressed men are discrepant with the psychology of men's public endorsement of multiculturalism and social justice. The mission statement of SPSMM (2012) indicates that the psychology of men is committed to "the support of groups such as women, gays, lesbians, and people of color that have been uniquely oppressed by gender/class/race systems." Beyond this statement, SPSMM's position on multiculturalism, oppression, and social injustice issues has been vague and underdeveloped.

My own work on diversity and multiculturalism has also been lacking. Societal oppression and GRC were conceptually related in my early work, but the ideas were also vague and underdeveloped (O'Neil, 1981a, 1981b, 1982; O'Neil & Egan, 1993; O'Neil & Nadeau, 1999). GRC and masculinity ideology were conceptually related to personal and institutional sexism, but the relationship to discrimination and oppression was not fully explained. Enns's (2008) critique on this point indicated that "masculine GRC is hypothesized to intersect with institutional sexism and power structures, but this process remains largely unclarified" (p. 447). She also implied that this societal aspect of GRC "has received only limited attention to date but seems important for understanding the diversity of masculine GRC and for guiding explorations of power and abuse (e.g., violence against women)" (p. 447). This means that the relationship between the macrosocietal and personal levels of oppression discussed in Chapter 3 has not been fully developed. On the basis of this critique, in this chapter, I discuss both the macrosocietal and microinterpersonal levels of gender roles and oppression in the context of GRC as well as a new multicultural model of men and masculinity.

CONTEXTUALIZING GENDER ROLE CONFLICT: DIVERSITY, OPPRESSION, AND SOCIAL JUSTICE

GRC and masculinity ideology contribute to social injustice when patriarchal and sexist norms cause societal oppression and discrimination against both men and women. Figure 3.1 depicts a hypothesized reciprocal relationship between (a) patriarchy, hegemonic masculinity, sexism, and stereotypes as organizers of society and (b) personal and institutional forms of oppression (racism, classism, ethnocentrism, and heterosexism) at the macrosocietal level. Furthermore, societal oppression was hypothesized to contribute to boys' and girls' internalization of sexist masculinity and femininity ideologies that produce stereotypes and unequal power bases between the sexes. This macrosocietal perspective established that personal oppression exists when women, members of racial/ethnic minority groups, and emasculated males become victims of patriarchy through various forms of discrimination and injustices. GRC is both an outcome and contributor to this oppression that causes emotional and psychological pain for men, women, and children.

The contextual models discussed in Chapter 3 lack specificity in explaining the complexity of multicultural and diversity issues. How GRC contributes to discrimination, oppression, and social injustices is challenging to capture because no coherent, multicultural approach currently exists in the psychology of men. E. H. Thompson, Pleck, and Ferrera (1992) stated more than 20 years ago that "we are largely unfamiliar with how age, generation, sexual orientation, class, race, and ethnicity differentially structure the form and content of men's lives and the standards of masculinity to which they adhere" (p. 602). More has been written recently on men's diversity and multiculturalism (Wade & Rochlen, 2013), but E. H. Thompson et al.'s statement is still valid. The critical issue now is explaining how societal oppression becomes personal oppression in men's lives and how masculinity ideologies and GRC play a critical role in that process. This issue of oppression is directly relevant not only for marginalized men and men who are members of racial/ethnic minority groups but also for men in general (Liang et al., 2010; Liang, Molenaar, & Heard, in press). Assumptions and conceptual models are needed to explain how GRC and masculinity ideologies relate to multicultural diversity, discrimination, and societal oppression.

SEVEN ASSUMPTIONS ABOUT THE MULTICULTURAL PSYCHOLOGY OF MEN

Seven multicultural and diversity assumptions provide a context for the multicultural studies reviewed in this chapter:

1. The multicultural psychology of men identifies the commonalities and differences between men (i.e., diversity) but also studies the psychological costs of the macrosocietal oppression that emanates from restrictive masculinity ideologies and GRC.
2. Forms of macrosocietal oppression comprise organizers of society and include patriarchy, classism, racism, ageism, heterosexism, and other unjust discrimination that negatively affect men, women, and children.
3. Stereotypes and biases about men cause discrimination, GRC, oppression, and social injustices.
4. A macrosocietal analysis of men's oppression explains how GRC and masculinity ideologies predict, moderate, mediate, and cause psychological problems, discrimination, and social injustices in men's and women's lives.
5. Many different masculinity ideologies and identities exist based on racial/ethnic, age, nationality, religious, sexual orientation, and other situational indexes of diversity that differentially predict, moderate, mediate, and cause GRC.
6. At the microinterpersonal level, contextual, situational, and multicultural factors (i.e., race, sex, ethnicity, class, culture, reli-

gion, sexual orientation, nationality, acculturation, age, and other diversity indexes) are related to men's restrictive masculinity ideologies; GRC; and gender role devaluations, restrictions, and violations.

7. Men experience vulnerability, societal discrimination, internalized oppression, psychological/emotional problems, and violence as a result of gender role devaluations, restrictions, and violations and other forms of dehumanization.

Overall, these assumptions imply that the multicultural study of men involves analyzing how diversity indexes shape many different male ideologies and identities. Furthermore, the costs of patriarchy, GRC, stereotypes, and biases about men emanating from the larger macrosocietal system cause internalized oppression; psychological problems; and gender role devaluations, restrictions, and violations. These assumptions support the development of a multicultural psychology of men model that can promote further conceptualizing and research on men's diversity.

A MULTICULTURAL MODEL OF THE PSYCHOLOGY OF MEN

Based on the seven assumptions just listed, a multicultural psychology of men model is shown in Figure 6.1 that connects the macrosocietal and microinterpersonal dimensions of men's lives. As I discussed in Chapter 3, the *macrosocietal context* is defined as the social, political, economic, and religious systems based on patriarchy that shape both men and women's gender role socialization. In Figure 6.1, the numbers positioned close to each arrow convey a correlational relationship between the different macrosocietal and microinterpersonal factors. Later in the chapter, I operationalize these numbered lines in terms of specific research questions related to racial/ethnic minority men's GRC and the factors that moderate and mediate their experiences as men.

The outer triangle in Figure 6.1, which represents the macrosocietal level of analysis, connects patriarchy, sexism, and other oppressions as organizers of society, with stereotypes and biases about men, with discrimination and social injustice (see the double-headed arrows numbered 1–3). The outer triangle represents the sociopolitical aspects of diversity and multiculturalism and provides a context in which to understand how multicultural factors, restrictive masculinity ideologies, and GRC cause emotional and psychological problems and internalized oppression.

The microinterpersonal level of analysis is shown inside the macrosocietal dimensions described above. The microinterpersonal dimensions reflect the emotional–psychological experiences with contextual, multicultural,

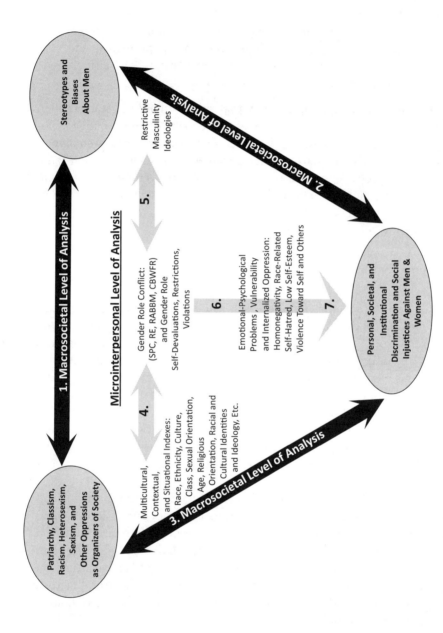

Figure 6.1. A multicultural model of the psychology of men. SPC = Success, Power, and Control; RE = Restrictive Emotionality; RABBM = Restrictive Affectionate Behavior Between Men; CBWFR = Conflict Between Work and Family Relations.

and gender role issues that are shaped by the macrosocietal dynamics. Many times, this connection is unknown or unclear to individual men and women, but it is fully operative in negative ways that affect people's lives. In the top middle part of Figure 6.1, the microinterpersonal level, are shown the GRC patterns: Success, Power, and Competition (SPC); Restrictive Emotionality (RE); Restrictive Affectionate Behavior Between Men (RABBM); and Conflict Between Work and Family (CBWFR), as well as the personal experiences of GRC in terms of gender role devaluations, restrictions, and violations. On the far left of the figure the multicultural, contextual, and situational indexes include race/ethnicity, culture, class, sexual orientation, age, religious orientation, and cultural identities and ideologies, and other diversity factors. The bidirectional arrows show that these diversity indices and GRC relate to each other (Point 4). Furthermore, the right side of the figure shows restrictive and sexist masculinity and femininity ideology and the GRC patterns and gender role devaluations, restrictions, and violations relating to each other (Point 5).

Multicultural, contextual, and situational indexes; the GRC patterns; and masculinity ideology are hypothesized to relate emotional and psychological problems and vulnerability for men, resulting in emotional–psychological problems, vulnerability, internalized oppression (Point 6). In other words, studying the multicultural psychology of men involves not only documenting the commonalities and differences between men (i.e., diversity) but also assessing the psychological costs of endorsing restrictive masculinity ideologies that cause personal, societal, and institutional discrimination and injustices against men and women (Point 7).

Diversity and the multicultural psychology of men are studied to better understand the relationships shown in Figure 6.1. The critical question is whether any empirical research exists to document the relationships in Figure 6.1. For example, is there any evidence that the contextual, situational, and multicultural indexes of diversity predict, moderate, or mediate GRC and masculinity ideology, resulting in negative psychological outcomes and oppression for diverse men and others in their lives? The literature I review in the next section includes studies related to the assumptions discussed earlier and the concepts depicted in Figure 6.1.

RESEARCH REVIEW OF GENDER ROLE CONFLICT DIVERSITY STUDIES IN FOUR CATEGORIES

The term *diversity* is defined broadly in this review to include demographic, contextual, situational, and multicultural indexes because the study of men is complex and needs to be contextualized in more useful ways than in the past (Addis, Mansfield, & Syzdek, 2010; K. Jones & Heesacker, 2012). Table 6.1

TABLE 6.1
Categories and Frequency of Diversity Studies

Diversity category	Number of studies
Contextual, demographic, and multicultural	
African American	26
Hispanic/Latino men	10
Asian American men	6
Gay men	28
Transgendered persons	1
Women	11
Age differences and stage of life	14
Boys	8
Retired men	3
Class and socioeconomic status	1
International men	
Australia	10
Canada	7
Great Britain	4
Germany	5
South Korea	9
Ireland	5
Japan	2
Indonesia	2
Philippines	2
Hong Kong (China)	2
China, Taiwan, Hungary, Poland, Russia, Sweden, Malta, South Africa, Iraq, Egypt, Columbia, Tasmania, Lithuania, Croatia, Portugal, Iran, Turkey, Costa Rica, Puerto Rico, Singapore, Thailand	1
Situational indexes of vulnerable men	
Homeless men	2
Oppressed men who experienced or perceived discrimination	3
Prisoners	1
Unemployed men	1
Self-destructive and suicidal men	2
Victims: sexual, emotional, cancer, injury	4
Men with low self-esteem	19
Abusive and violent men	22
Situational: Vulnerable Men in Work Roles	
Police officers	4
Firefighters	1
Combat veterans	2

lists the frequencies of GRC studies in the following four diversity categories: (a) contextual, demographic, and multicultural indexes; (b) nationality indexes and international studies; (c) situational indexes of vulnerable men; and (d) situational indexes of men in vulnerable work roles. The studies assessed many different variables using a variety of measures with diverse samples of men. The contextual, demographic, and multicultural indexes include ten areas of research: (a) African American men, (b) Hispanic/ Latino men, (c) Asian American men, (d) gay men, (e) transgendered persons, (f) women, (g) age difference and stage of life, (h) boys, (i) retired men, and (j) class and SES. The second category is nationality and international men. The 74 international studies are from 25 different countries, with 34% of the studies conducted in English-speaking countries outside the United States. The third category is indexes of vulnerable men, including men who have been oppressed or discriminated against, as well men who are homeless, in prison, unemployed, and self-destructive. This includes men who have low self-esteem, are abusive and violent toward others, or have been victims themselves. The fourth diversity category is a situational category of men in vulnerable work roles (police, firefighters, and combat veterans). The number of diversity studies is increasing, but sweeping generalizations are unwarranted because of the limited number of studies in each diversity group.

All studies reviewed used the Gender Role Conflict Scale (GRCS; O'Neil, Helms, Gable, David, & Wrightsman, 1986) and assessed the four GRC factors of SPC, RE, RABBM, and CBWFR. Each category of diversity in Table 6.1 is reviewed next and followed by a summary of how the empirical research relates to the seven assumptions above and the conceptual relationships in Figure 6.1. The review of the literature is sequenced by reporting the four diversity categories as they are listed in Table 6.1.

Contextual, Demographic, and Multicultural Categories

The contextual, demographic, and multicultural categories are numerous and include, as mentioned earlier, African American men, Hispanic/ Latino men, Asian American men, gay men, men with differing sexual orientations, transgender men, women, males in different life ages and stages, boys and retired men, and men with differing social class and SES.

African American Men

Researchers have studied the GRS of both college-age and older adult African American men. African American male college students' GRC has been significantly correlated with lower self-esteem; higher anxiety and depression (Lily, 1999; Vinson, 2011); psychological distress (Carter et al., 2005; Manning, 2011; Wester, Vogel, et al., 2006); loneliness, mourning, and grief (Blazina, Novotny, Stevens, & Hunter, 2008); and negative attitudes toward help seeking (White, 2002). Adult African American men's GRC has been significantly correlated with greater depression, lower self-esteem, marital dissatisfaction, and hopelessness (Laurent, 1997), as well as greater feelings of disrespect from others (Brewer, 1998). K. Jones (2010) found that African

American men with low GRC had increased psychological well-being and positive mental health. Malebranche, Gvetadze, Millett, and Sutton (2012) studied unhealthy risk taking and found that African American men who have sex with other men and who have high RE and RABBM were predicted as having a higher rate of unprotected sex with female partners. Three canonical correlation studies have shown that African American adult men's GRC is complex and relates to multiple variables, including class and social position (Brewer, 1998; Stillson, O'Neil, & Owen, 1991); depression, low self-esteem, and hopelessness (Brewer, 1998; Laurent, 1997); and African American identity (Laurent, 1997). These studies suggest that GRC is a reality in African American men's lives, and further research is needed to understand how it develops and is experienced intrapersonally and interpersonally.

How the racial/ethnic identity of African Americans relates to GRC has been an important area for researchers (Carter et al., 2005; Laurent, 1997; Lily, 1999; Manning, 2011; Wade, 1996; Wester, Vogel, et al., 2006; White, 2002), and numerous racial identity categories and attitudes have been found to significantly relate to GRC (Carter et al., 2005; Lily, 1999; Manning, 2011; Wade, 1996; Wester, Vogel, et al., 2006). For example, Black men with high African American cultural identity reported significantly lower GRC and higher self-esteem (Laurent, 1997), and S. C. Walker (2008) found that African American men who were more assimilated into the majority culture reported higher GRC. In the same way, Vinson (2011) found that high ethnic identity predicted lower GRC, but ethnic identity did not moderate the relationship between GRC and both self-esteem and life satisfaction. Furthermore, the relationship between GRC and indexes of psychological functioning has been found to be moderated by traditional African American religious acculturation and Black male identity salience (Lily, 1999). African American men who have a multicultural inclusive racial identity report significantly lower RE and CBWFR and more positive attitudes toward help seeking (White, 2002). Two studies found that higher GRC significantly correlates with pre-encounter states of racial identity, defined as the idealization of Whites and White culture and the denigration of Blacks and Black culture (Carter et al., 2005; Wade, 1996). Two studies found that racial identity either partially or fully mediates the effects of GRC on psychological stress for African American men (Carter et al., 2005; Wester, Vogel, et al., 2006). Wester, Vogel, et al. (2006) found that Black men's internalized racism (self-hatred) mediated the relationship between GRC and psychological stress. This finding is important because it came from one of the first studies to document that internalized oppression interacts with both GRC and psychological stress. Carter et al. (2005) found that the degree to which Black men endorse the norms of the dominant White culture influences the extent to which GRC affects psychological symptoms. This study moves us closer to connecting the macrosocietal level of analysis with the microinterpersonal experience of GRC, psychological problems, and oppression. Finally, in one of the only studies to yield insignificant findings, Manning (2011) found that racial identity did not mediate GRC and stress. Taken together, the overall results of these studies suggest that African American men's GRC is significantly related to negative psychological outcomes and racial/ethnic identity categories.

In summary, the relationships between GRC and low self-esteem and depression are reported by both college-age and older adult African American men. Moreover, the results of these studies suggest that there is complexity in explaining GRC. African American men's GRC is related to class and social position, racial identity, and degrees of assimilation and acculturation to the American culture. Evidence that GRC relates to racial identity categories could suggest that attitudes toward White power and authority are part of the gender role dynamics. This speculation is supported by two studies that found that internalized racism and attitudes toward the White culture are related to GRC and psychological symptoms. These results provide some initial evidence that GRC is a multicultural, sociopolitical issue that relates to racial identity, discrimination, and social justice issues.

Hispanic/Latino Men

Ten studies have assessed Hispanic or Latino men's GRC (Carter et al., 2005; Cox, 2009; J. M. Davis & Liang, 2014; Fragoso & Kashubeck, 2000; Leka, 1998; Liang et al., 2010; Mejias, 2010; Schwartz, Waldo, Bloom-Langell, & Merta, 1998; Silva, 2002; Torres Rivera, 1995). Two found that Mexican American men's stress significantly relates to three of the four patterns of GRC, with SPC and RE being the most consistent predictors (Fragoso & Kashubeck, 2000; Leka, 1998). In another study, higher GRC scores correlated with a desire for muscularity and the perception that muscles were important (Mejias, 2010). Two studies assessed how Hispanic men's GRC relates to help seeking; one found that RABBM predicted negative attitudes toward help seeking (Cox, 2009), and the other found that RE and RABBM related to place of birth (J. M. Davis & Liang, 2014). RE has been significantly associated with higher levels of depression and stress, but the interaction of machismo (see below) and GRC did not predict stress or depression (Fragoso & Kashubeck, 2000).

How acculturation affects Hispanic/Latino men's GRC has been examined in four studies. All of the patterns of GRC have been significantly correlated with lower acculturation, with SPC being the strongest predictor (Leka, 1998; Schwartz et al., 1998). In two other studies, acculturation and ethnic identity issues were not related to GRC in Hispanic/Latino men (Silva, 2002; Torres Rivera, 1995).

Liang et al. (2010) completed a complex and important study on how GRC relates to *machismo* (a narrow and stereotypic description of Latino masculinity described as hypersexualized, aggressive, dominant, and in control of women), *caballerismo* (a positive set of masculinity norms that emphasizes emotional responsiveness, collaboration, caretaking, providing for the family, honor, dignity, and respect for others), and perceived racism. They found that machismo was correlated with all GRC patterns, caballerismo was associated with less RABBM, and higher levels of machismo and RABBM were associated with perceptions of both general and job racism. The authors concluded that the different context in which racism occurs influences the relationship among machismo ideology, caballerismo ideology, and aspects of GRC.

In summary, the studies suggest that Hispanic/Latino men's GRC is related to negative psychological outcomes, but the role of acculturation is less clear. As with African American men, GRC is related to psychological symptoms for Hispanic men, including stress, depression, and negative attitudes toward help seeking. How GRC is related to Hispanic men's acculturation is mixed and unclear from the four studies that have been completed. In one of the only direct tests of whether GRC relates to discrimination, Liang et al.'s (2010) results with perceived racism and RABBM suggest that social injustice issues and GRC are related. More direct studies are needed on how GRC and discrimination are related and affect marginalized groups of diverse men.

Asian American Men

Six studies have assessed Asian American men's GRC (E. J. Kim, O'Neil, & Owen, 1996; Liu, 2002a; Liu & Iwamoto, 2006; Shek & McEwen, 2012; Vu, 2000). Asian American men's GRC has significantly correlated with Asian cultural values, with SPC being the most significant predictor (Liu & Iwamoto, 2006). Using a mixed sample of Asian Americans, E. J. Kim et al. (1996) found that men who reported greater acculturation reported significantly less RE and more SPC than less acculturated men. Liu (2002a) also assessed a mixed sample of Asian American men and found that racial identity attitudes of confusion, ethnocentrism, and integration related to significantly greater GRC. Vu (2000) found that Vietnamese American men's shame and self-esteem were correlated with GRC and that being monocultural versus bicultural increased their GRC. The relationship of GRC to Asian American men's self-esteem has produced contradictory results. One study found no relationship between self-esteem and GRC (Liu & Iwamoto, 2006), but in another study RE, RABBM, and CBWFR were significantly related to lower self-esteem for Asian American men, and racial identity attitudes of conformity, dissonance, and immersion also significantly correlated with the four patterns of GRC (Shek & McEwen, 2012).

As with the previous diverse groups, Asian American men's GRC appears to relate to cultural, acculturation, and racial identity factors. There are too few studies to make any generalizations, but these factors are relevant for future study. The way self-esteem relates to GRC has received mixed results with Asian American men, and within-group differences related to education, SES, and other demographics have not been studied.

Gay Men, Men With Different Sexual Orientations, and Transgendered Persons

During the first wave of research on GRC in gay men (1998–2005), eight studies were completed (Ervin, 2003; D. A. Jones, 1998; Naranjo, 2001; Sánchez, 2005; W. D. Shepard, 2001; Simonsen, Blazina, & Watkins, 2000; Van Hyfte & Rabinowitz, 2001; Wester, Pionke, & Vogel, 2005). Since then, the research on gay men has increased significantly, with 27 studies to date having been completed. The first-wave studies on gay men over age 30 found their GRC to be significantly related to lower intimacy (Van Hyfte & Rabinowitz, 2001), greater depression and anxiety (D. A. Jones, 1998; W. D. Shepard, 2001; Simonsen et al., 2000), less relationship satisfaction (Wester et al., 2005), negative coping styles and attitudes toward help-seeking attitudes (D. A. Jones, 1998; Simonsen et al., 2000), homonegativity, and less psychological well-being (Ervin, 2003). Simonsen et al. (2000) used canonical correlation and found that gay men with greater SPC and CBWFR tended to be angrier, more anxious, and more depressed. Combinations of RE, CBWFR, and homonegativity have also been significantly associated with gay men's decreased psychological well-being (Ervin, 2003). Studies have found that single gay men, compared with gay men in couple relationships, report significantly greater RE and RABBM (D. S. Shepard, 2002; Wester et al., 2005), higher levels of anger and anxiety, and lower self-esteem (W. D. Shepard, 2001). Three studies found that heterosexual men report significantly more RE, RABBM, and SPC than gay men (Naranjo, 2001; W. D. Shepard, 2001; Van Hyfte & Rabinowitz, 2001). On the whole, the results of these studies indicate that older gay men's GRC relates to similar psychological problems in straight men but, overall, gay men report significantly less GRC than heterosexual men.

In the second wave of research, GRC in gay men (2005–2013) was studied in a more focused way. GRC has been correlated with negative feelings about being gay (Sánchez, Westefeld, Liu, & Vilain, 2010), casual sex and relationship satisfaction (Sánchez, Bocklandt, & Vilain, 2009), attachment insecurity and sexual compulsivity (Griffin, 2011), negative identity and attitudes about being "out" (Sánchez, 2005), and eating disorder symptomatology (Blashill & Vander Wal, 2009; Jackson, 2009). Furthermore, a significant area of research has focused on how internalized homonegativity, heterosexism, and homophobia and heterosexist discrimination relate to gay men's GRC and psychological problems. Four studies significantly correlated internalized homonegativity with GRC (Bryce, 2012; M. A. Robinson & Brewster, 2014; Szymanski & Carr, 2008; Zhang, 2014), and SPC, RE, and RABBM were the most consistent predictors of not liking one's sexual orientation. In addition, two studies found that GRC correlated with internalized homophobia, with SPC, RE, and RABBM being the significant predictors in each study (Szymanski & Carr, 2008; Szymanski & Ikizler, 2013).

Moderation and mediation studies have demonstrated the complexity of these issues for gay men. Zhang (2014) studied Chinese gay men and found that GRC significantly mediated the relationship between homonegativity and both shame and guilt. Szymanski and Ikizler (2013) found that gay men with high RABBM and who think that heterosexist discrimination exists are more likely to have internalized heterosexism that may lead to depression. In another study, gay men's internalized heterosexism moderated the relationship between beliefs about parental efficacy and motivation to be a parent (M. A. Robinson & Brewster, 2014). GRC has also been found to directly and indirectly relate to self-esteem through internalized heterosexism and that coping relates to psychological stress (Szymanski & Carr, 2008). In a moderation study, Blashill and Hughes (2009) found that all GRC patterns correlated with psychological stress and that as RE increased so did the distress. Blashill and Vander Wal (2009) found that all the GRC factors correlated with eating disorder symptoms in gay men. Moreover, negative affect and social sensitivity mediated the relationship between GRC and eating disorder symptomatology and body dissatisfaction. These studies of internalized homonegativity and homophobia provide initial evidence that internalized oppression is related to GRC and gay men's psychological problems.

Another study assessed men who sought a sexual orientation change because their homosexual attraction was a source of dissatisfaction (Karten & Wade, 2010). The results indicated that these men reported relatively high RABBM 6 months prior to their sexual orientation change effort and somewhat lower levels of RABBM afterward. Reductions in both RABBM and feelings of disconnectiveness with other men prior to seeking help related to decreases in homosexual feelings and behaviors and increases in heterosexual feeling and behaviors. Furthermore, significantly less RABBM related to self-reports of positive changes in psychological well-being.

Limited research exists on transgendered individuals' GRC, but the topic has been addressed in both clinical and empirical studies. Wester, McDonough, White, Vogel, and Taylor (2010) discussed helping individuals who were seeking change from male to female by coping with their GRC during the stages of awareness, seeking information, exploration, disclosure, and integration. Only one empirical study focused on GRC and young adults who were biologically female but had a masculine gender role identity (Grethel, 2007). The results indicated that female-to-male individuals reported GRC to the same degree as biological males, and the degree of their transition was associated with both less GRC and better body image. Increased attention to transgendered persons' GRC is likely given the greater openness and affirmation of gender role identity changes in U.S. society.

On the basis of the extant research, GRC is related to gay men's lives in major emotional and interpersonal realms, including depression, anxiety, eating disorder symptomatology, and distress. Gay men report less GRC than straight men, and gay men in couples report less GRC than single gay men. There is complexity with GRC in gay men's lives, and perceived discrimination and oppression appear to be linked to negative psychological states, including homonegativity and internalized heterosexism, and these conditions are related to mental health difficulties such as shame, guilt, depression, and lower self-esteem. The relationship between GRC and internalized oppression has some research support for gay men, and this evidence provides a good justification for future research.

Women

Assessing women's GRC may at first seem inappropriate given that the GRCS measures men's GRC. The rationale for assessing women is that females are also affected by patriarchal male norms that produce SPC, RE, RABBM, and CBWFR. Women have been given a modified version of the GRCS in which the pronouns have been changed. The psychometric evaluation of the GRCS for women showed that the factor structure of the revised scale was similar to that of the male version (Borthick et al., 1997). In the 11 studies that have used the GRCS for women, significant sex differences have been found on three of the GRC factors (SPC, RE, and RABBM). Men reported significantly more GRC on these three patterns than women (Borthick et al., 1997; Eicken, 2003; Harnishfeger, 1998; A. M. Hernandez, 2006; S. G. Newman, 1997; Schwartz, Higgins, & He, 2003; Silva, 2002; Zamarripa, Wampold, & Gregory, 2003). Across six studies, CBWFR had consistently shown no differences between men and women. In two other studies, women reported significantly higher CBWFR than men (Eicken, 2003; Schwartz et al., 2003).

Three other studies found that GRC is related to women's psychological symptoms and problems. Daltry (2009) found that women athletes' identity distress tolerance and quality of athletic life correlated with total GRC score. S. G. Newman (1997) found that GRC did not correlate with self-silencing for women; neither did it moderate the relationship between GRC and depression. Schwartz et al. (2003) found that women's low CBWFR and

RE were associated with positive feelings toward their weight and physical conditions.

GRC studies of women raise questions about how the patterns of men's GRC relate to women's psychological functioning and therefore deserve further investigation. There are no formal measures of women's GRC, but such scales are needed to explain the complexity of men's and women's relationships. Enns (2004) indicated "that the literature on male GRC is not integrated with work on women's [GRC] and may subtly support the exaggeration of differences between women's and men's gender related conflicts" (p. 94).

Age and Stage of Life: Boys and Retired Men

How GRC develops as boys and men age is not understood because of a lack of longitudinal research. Cross-sectional studies assessing age differences and GRC have been completed (Birthistle, 1999; Brewer, 1998; Burke, 2000; Cournoyer & Mahalik, 1995; Gough, 1999; Heath & Thomas, 2006; Laurent, 1997; Leka, 1998; Mahalik, Locke, Theodore, Cournoyer, & Lloyd, 2001; Mendelson, 1988; Pytluk & Casas, 1998; Ross, 2004; Stillson et al., 1991; Theodore, 1998; Theodore & Lloyd, 2000; Wade, 1996; Wester et al., 2005). Two studies found no significant differences or mixed results in assessing age differences and the patterns of GRC (Mendelson, 1988; Stillson et al., 1991). However, seven other studies found age differences in regard to GRC (Cournoyer & Mahalik, 1995; Gough, 1999; Heath & Thomas, 2006; Mahalik, Locke, Theodore, Cournoyer, & Lloyd, 2001; Ross, 2004; Theodore & Lloyd, 2000; Wester et al., 2005). Six studies showed that older men, compared with college-age men, report significantly less SPC and RABBM (Brewer, 1998; Burke, 2000, Gough, 1999; Heath & Thomas, 2006; Leka, 1998; Pytluk & Casas, 1998). Two studies of American and Australian college and older adult men found similar results for SPC and CBWFR (Cournoyer & Mahalik, 1995; Theodore & Lloyd, 2000). In both studies, college men reported significantly more SPC and less CBWFR than middle-aged men. In another study, gay men in their early 20s reported significantly more RABBM and SPC than did gay men over age 30 (Wester et al., 2005). One of the most striking conclusions across all of the studies is that RE showed no significant age differences across the different age group. This may suggest that RE is a pattern of GRC that, once learned, is very difficult to modify when living in a sexist and patriarchal society.

GRC studies focused on boys have become more frequent with the publication of the Gender Role Conflict Scale for Adolescents (GRCS–A; Blazina, Pisecco, & O'Neil, 2005). Eight studies with adolescent boys have been completed using the GRCS–A. Boys' reports of family stress and problems with conduct, anger, and emotions were significantly correlated with RE, RABBM, and CBWFR (Blazina et al., 2005; Cadenhead & Huzirec, 2002;

Soublis, 2003; Watts & Borders, 2005). Blazina and Jackson (2009) found that boys' RE correlated with greater depression and that increased RABBM correlated with less depression. In a study of Korean high school boys, GRC demonstrated direct and indirect effects on depression through the mediating variable of self-esteem (Choi, Kim, Hwang, & Heppner, 2010). Steinfeldt and Steinfeldt (2010) found that upperclassman football players reported less GRC than students in lower grade levels. Freshman players reported significantly more RABBM than their teammates, and RE predicted negative attitudes about help seeking. In one of the only qualitative studies, adolescent boys reported all four GRC patterns, and the authors concluded that GRC is a developmental process that starts in adolescence (Watts & Borders, 2005). In one of the only studies of boys outside of the United States, Beaglaoich (2013) found that Irish boys reported GRC, but there were significant differences in how GRC is understood and experienced.

More research on boys is needed, but the initial findings indicate that GRC is related to male adolescent emotional, familial, and athletic experiences. The quantitative studies of boys suggest that GRC exists in adolescence and relates to depression, self-esteem, and family stresses, but qualitative studies may better determine the context of boys' GRC during different ages. Beaglaoich, Sarma, and Morrison (2013) provided a good example of this kind of research using in-depth interviews and developing an Irish GRC scale for boys.

On the other end of the life span, retired men's GRC has been investigated in three studies (Graham & Romans, 2003; W. G. Hill & Donatelle, 2004; Lontz, 2000). Graham and Romans (2003) found that as RE, RABBM, and CBWFR decreased, retirement satisfaction increased, but, unexpectedly, higher SPC predicted significantly greater retirement satisfaction. This may suggest that aspects of GRC negatively affect retirees but that SPC may have some positive impact after retirement. Using canonical correlations and multiple regressions, Lontz (2000) found that retired men's SPC, RABBM, and CBWFR significantly predicted antifemininity and that RE and CBWFR significantly predicted lower satisfaction with life. Research has also shown that older men with GRC limit their perception of social support and their appreciation of supporting relationships (W. G. Hill & Donatelle, 2004).

In summary, the research on age and GRC indicates that men are conflicted with their gender roles across the life span, but in different ways. No research has yet documented how GRC develops or how it changes over different developmental periods and during gender role transitions. No developmental study of GRC has been completed, but the cross-sectional research suggests that GRC can be lifelong. The age differences with SPC, RABBM, and CBWFR are predictable in the context of different developmental tasks across the life span for boys and men (see Chapter 5 and Table 5.2, this volume). Few studies have assessed age as it relates to race/ethnicity, class, and different nationalities.

Class and Socioeconomic Status

Class and SES in the context of GRC is one of the most important but understudied topics in the GRC research program. Class and SES have been the least explored of all diversity variables. Only one study examined SES and men's GRC (Stillson, 1988). The results indicated that the low-SES men reported significantly more GRC than high-SES men and that, as educational and occupational status increased, men's GRC decreased. Theoretical analyses and empirical study of how class relates to men's GRC is a potential growth area for the psychology of men. Important social class models have been proposed (Liu, 2002b; Liu, Ali, et al., 2004; Liu, Soleck, Hopps, Dunston, & Pickett, 2004), but many of these ideas have not been tested empirically. How class and GRC interact needs to be examined in the context of race/ethnicity, sexual orientation, and other diversity variables. Some of the problems with the study of class and SES is how to adequately measure these demographics. As with research on boys, qualitative research may be a good starting point to establish the critical issues and topics related to class and SES that can be used in developing future quantitative research.

THE INTERNATIONAL STUDY OF MEN'S GENDER ROLE CONFLICT

The international study of the psychology of men was established with the publication of *The International Psychology of Men: Theoretical Advances, Case Studies, and Clinical Innovations* (Blazina & Shen-Miller, 2010). This edited book showcased the psychology of men in 12 countries. The editors discussed the importance of contextualizing the psychology of men globally and identified two challenges in internationalizing the psychology of men: (a) recognizing that theories generated within one country may have limited utility in explaining a wide range of cross-cultural phenomena and (b) the need to critically evaluate the generalization of psychological constructs, measures, and empirical findings related to gender from one country and culture to another. This point was implemented well by Beaglaoich et al. (2013) in their study of Irish boys' GRC.

Both of these challenges suggest caution when using American masculinity constructs in other cultures without careful thought and reflection. For example, in regard to the GRC construct, Blazina and Shen-Miller (2010) identified numerous issues that need to be considered. How are contextual definitions of

GRC and masculinity ideology determined within a culture? What, exactly, are cultural masculinities, and do different cultural definitions of *masculinity* require redefining GRC and masculinity ideology for the concepts to be valid? How are constructions of masculinity different or similar across cultures?

In the following sections, I report on international GRC research in the following three areas: (a) Canada, Ireland, Australia, and Great Britain; (b) Europe and the Mediterranean region; and (c) Asia, including Southeast Asia and the Middle East.

Canada, Ireland, Australia, and Great Britain

Studies that have been conducted in English-speaking countries outside the United States are clustered together given a common language and Anglo-Saxon heritage. Five of the seven Canadian studies found that GRC is related to problems in men's lives, including GRC being correlated with problematic coping (Wester, Kuo, & Vogel, 2006), hostility toward women (Chartier, Graff, & Arnold, 1986), less intimacy and low identity development (Chartier & Arnold, 1985), suicidality (Houle, Mishara, & Chagnon, 2008), and rape myths (Senn, Desmarais, Verberg, & Wood, 2000). Two Canadian studies found no correlations between GRC and domestic batterers' attitudes (Mendoza & Cummings, 2001) or change during a group intervention (Nahon, 1992).

Two of the five Irish studies focused on therapists' GRC (Holohan, 2008; Murtagh, 2012). Holohan (2008) found that therapists experienced less GRC than the average population and that therapeutic orientation, age, or academic level was not significantly related to GRC. Murtagh (2012) found that more experienced therapists had less GRC than less experienced clinicians, implying that GRC may occur more in the early days of one's career. In a separate study assessing sexual orientation differences, straight men reported greater RABBM than gay men (McMahon, 2009). Beaglaoich (2013) studied Irish boys using an alteration of the GRCS–A and found that boys' GRC significantly correlated with low self-esteem, depression, and suicide ideation. Finally, Birthistle (1999) found that Irish men's RABBM predicted restraint coping and denial and that RE predicted hopelessness.

In regard to Australian men, two studies found that GRC correlated with negative attitudes toward help seeking (Bevan, 2010; Dolling, 2008), and two other studies found GRC to be related to substance abuse (Gough, 1999; Monk & Ricciardelli, 2003). Heath and Thomas (2006) found age differences in GRC for middle-age and younger men, with older Australian men reporting less SPC but more CBWFR. With Australian men, GRC has been found to correlate with psychological stress (Heath & Thomas, 2006), and stress and diffuse religious orientation (Jurkovic & Walker, 2006). Dolling (2008) found that SPC and RABBM negatively correlated with optimism.

Four studies examined British men's GRC. RE varied by age (Tate, 1998), and it predicted lower self-esteem in two studies (Ross, 2004; Tate, 1998). Baker, Robertson, and Connelly (2010) found that higher RABBM predicted less strain in caregiving, and Fitton (2010) found that British men's expressiveness and instrumentality were predictive of GRC; specifically, when expressiveness increased, RE decreased, and younger men with greater instrumentality experienced higher levels of GRC.

Europe and the Mediterranean Region

Three German studies (Eimer & Kidd, 2010; Gulder, 1999; Wolfram, Mohr, & Borchert, 2009) focused on traditional masculinity, teachers, and students. GRC was related to higher emotional irritation, anxiety, depression, and lower work satisfaction for German schoolteachers, and SPC predicted more traditional gender role values (Wolfram et al., 2009). German students' RE was found to correlate with fears of working with a female career counselor, and both SPC and RE were related to feeling inferior to a female counselor. Two studies were completed in the Mediterranean region of Malta and Turkey: Lease, Ciftci, Demir, and Boyraz (2009) found Turkish men's GRC to be negatively correlated with intimacy and poor work relationships, and Cachia (2001) assessed Maltese men and found that RE predicted fearful attachments.

Asia, Southeast Asia, and the Middle East

Studies conducted in Asia and Southeast Asia have found men reporting GRE in the following countries: South Korea, Taiwan, China, Japan, Indonesia, and Singapore. In South Korea, researchers have found that GRC is correlated with low self-esteem, depression, and anxiety (Jo, 2000); less martial satisfaction (J. Kim, Hwang, & Choi, 2005); social stigma, self-stigma, and less positive attitudes toward counseling (Park & Seok Seo, 2009); and psychological stress (Kang, 2001). Choi et al. (2010) found that Korean men's GRC demonstrated both a direct and indirect effect on depression through the third variable of self-esteem. In a qualitative study, Jun (2009) found that gender role strain affected the spiritual maturity of 80% of the Korean men interviewed. In Taiwan, all of the patterns of GRC predicted negative attitudes toward help seeking (Tsai, 2000), and Zhang (2014) found that gay and straight men's GRC significantly mediated the relationship between internalized homonegativity and shame and guilt. Two studies conducted in Japan found GRC related to anxiety, depression, self-esteem, and affect regulation, and SPC and RE correlated negatively with the likelihood of seeking professional help (Chan & Hayashi, 2010; Hayashi, 1999).

A single study in Singapore and two studies in Indonesia found significant correlations between GRC and other variables. Jin (2012) found that men in Singapore with high GRC were less willing to seek counseling when working with a male versus a female counselor. Two studies in Indonesia found that Indonesian men with RABBM predicted inexpressive behavior (Horhoruw, 1991) and Nauly (2002) found significant differences in SPC, CBWFR, and RABBM within Indonesian cultural groups (Bataks, Minang, and Javanese). Three studies have been completed in the Middle East. Jassim (2012) found that Iraqi ministry employees reported high SPC but no age differences with GRC, whereas Jana-Massri (2011) found that Egyptian men's religiosity did not moderate GRC in any way but that GRC was correlated with negatively attitudes towards help seeking. Chamykarpour, Pourshahbaz, Dolatshahi, and Moshtagh (2012a, 2012b) found that GRC scores with Iranian men correlated with personality factors and temperament.

These international studies have shown that GRC is not just an American phenomenon. In nearly every international study, researchers have found some significant relationship between GRC and a psychological variable. Too few studies exist in any one country to make any generalities, but research does indicate that GRC is a relevant international construct. Validation of the GRCS in countries other than the United States is needed in future research, and numerous studies have found good construct validation for the scale; however, future study is needed. Most important is that studies are contextualized to any country or culture (Beaglaoich et al., 2013; Blazina & Shen-Miller, 2010; O'Neil, 1993, 2011). Also important is that new culturally specific measures of GRC are needed to fully capture the nuances of GRC in different countries and with different ethnic and racial groups.

SITUATIONAL INDEXES OF VULNERABLE MEN

Many GRC studies have examined White, middle-class, heterosexual men who represent mainstream America. In this section, I review research on vulnerable men who are fragile because of life events, psychological problems, low self-esteem, and/or discrimination and societal injustices. As I discussed conceptually in Chapter 3, male vulnerability is hypothesized to be a result of GRC. Male vulnerability is an emotional and cognitive state wherein a man feels emasculated, oppressed, weak, inferior, unmanly, worthless, shameful, or feminine. Vulnerability develops when striving to meet or failing to meet gender role norms of masculinity ideology, but it is also a normal outcome of life's situations. Outcomes of vulnerability include depression, anxiety, personal rigidity, low self-esteem, inadequate empathy for others, and violence toward others.

In the sections that follow, I review several broad categories of research on male vulnerability, including oppressed men who experience or perceive discrimination and social injustice; self-destructive, suicidal, and victimized men; men with low self-esteem; homeless and unemployed men; abusive and violent men; and men in vulnerable work roles.

Oppressed Men Who Experience or Perceive Discrimination and Social Injustice

One of the fundamental assumptions of this book is that GRC and masculinity ideology contribute to personal and societal discrimination and social injustices against men and women. This relationship is shown in Figure 6.1 at Point 7. This topic has been addressed by researchers, but only three studies have assessed the relationship between discrimination and GRC with Hispanic/Latino men (Liang, Salcedo, & Miller, 2011), gay men (Szymanski & Ikizler, 2013), and African American men (Wester, Vogel, et al., 2006). Liang et al. (2011) completed a complex and important study of how GRC relates to machismo, caballerismo, and perceived racism. They found three things: (a) machismo was correlated with all GRC patterns, (b) caballerismo was associated with less RABBM, and (c) higher levels of machismo and RABBM were associated with perception of both general and job-related racism. Furthermore, they found that CBWFR was significantly correlated with perceived racism on the job and in academic, public, and general settings, whereas total GRC scores correlated with perceived racism in the job setting. Wester, Vogel, et al. (2006) found that Black men's internalized racism (self-hatred) mediated the relationship between GRC and psychological stress. Szymanski and Ikizler (2013) found that gay men with high RABBM and who think that heterosexist discrimination exists are more likely to have internalized heterosexism that may lead to depression, and RABBM was associated with perceptions of both general and job racism. These studies represent just the beginning of this important area of research; future empirical study is needed to explain how discrimination and social injustices contribute to men's emotional and psychological problems.

Self-Destructive, Suicidal, and Victimized Men

GRC has also been associated with vulnerability that leads to self-destructiveness, and evidence exists that extreme vulnerability from GRC is related to male suicide. Houle et al. (2008) found that suicidal men reported significantly more GRC than nonsuicidal men. Also, GRC has been found to be correlated with the probability of suicidality (Borthick, 1997; Borthick et al., 1997) and, for suicidal men, GRC is related to less perceived social support and less confiding in family and is mediated by mental health state, help-seeking behaviors, and social support (Houle et al., 2008).

Other areas of vulnerability include being a victim of sexual and emotional abuse, injury, and/or cancer. By definition, being a victim is a vulnerable state. Being a victim and a male are incompatible states because stereotypical masculinity implies not being taken advantage of and having strength, control, and power. Research indicates that GRC is relevant to male victims. In one study, clients who experienced sexual abuse reported significantly greater RE and CBWFR than nonabused clients (P. Thomson, 1995). Tsui (2010) studied male victims of partner abuse and found that GRC related to barriers to help seeking for all scales except RABBM. Hoyt (2009) found that cancer victims' GRC was associated with lower emotional expression, which was associated with greater distress and less coping through emotional expression. In a study of men with serious head injuries, GRC was unrelated to all dependent variables except SPC, which correlated with the number of drinks ingested per drinking episode (Good et al., 2006).

Men With Low Self-Esteem

Not liking yourself or having low self-esteem is a vulnerable state for many men. As one man once told me, "I hate myself, and I don't know what to do about it." Nineteen studies have shown a negative relationship between GRC and positive self-esteem across seven diverse groups, including White college-age American, Japanese, Korean, African American, Mexican American, Asian American, and gay men. These findings have been found with mixed-race samples (A. M. Hernandez, 2006; Vinson, 2011), African American men (Bingham, Harawa, & Williams, 2012), gay men (Szymanski & Carr, 2008), abusive men (Schwartz & Waldo, 2003), Asian American men (Shek & McEwen, 2012), and Korean men (Choi et al., 2010). RE, RABBM, and CBWFR were consistent predictors of low self-esteem across these studies. These results provide strong evidence that GRC is related to the vulnerable state of feeling bad about oneself.

Homeless and Unemployed Men

Nguyen, Liu, Hernandez, and Stinson (2012) found that homeless men's RE was significantly related to negative appraisals of skills and confidence to solve problems, distress, and negative attitudes toward seeking professional counseling. Homeless men's GRC has also been correlated with using drugs and acts of violence (Amato & MacDonald, 2011). In the only study to assess GRC and unemployment, Friedman (2011) found that unemployed men's CBWFR correlated with depression.

Abusive and Violent Men

Men's abuse of and violence against women is epidemic in the United States, and masculinity and GRC are related to the violence. Violence and abuse comprise a context in which to understand men and their masculinity. Many men who victimize others usually have been victimized themselves and are showing their wounds through their abuse. Men who are violent or abusive are considered vulnerable because they resort to force and aggression, instead of their positive power, to achieve their goals.

Twenty-two studies have assessed how GRC relates to men's negative or violent attitudes toward women. Almost all of these studies have focused on White men. Specifically, GRC has been significantly correlated with sexually aggressive behaviors and the likelihood of forcing sex (Kaplan, 1992; Kaplan, O'Neil, & Owen, 1993; Serna, 2004), abusive behaviors and coercion (Schwartz et al., 1998; Senn et al., 2000), dating violence (Harnishfeger, 1998), hostile sexism (Covell, 1998; Schwartz, Tylka, & Hood, 2005), hostility toward women (Rando, Rogers, & Brittan-Powell, 1998; Senn et al., 2000; Serna, 2004), rape myth acceptance (T. L. Davis, 1997; Kassing, Beesley, & Frey, 2005; Rando et al., 1998; Serna, 2004), positive attitudes toward and tolerance of sexual harassment (Covell, 1998; Glomb & Espelage, 2005; Jacobs, 1996; Kearney, King, & Rochlen, 2004), and self-reported violence and aggression (Amato, 2012; Chase, 2000; Cohn & Zeichner, 2006; C. L. Johnston, 2005). M. S. Hill and Fischer (2001) conducted a mediation study and found that masculine gender role components (including SPC, RABBM, and CBWFR) significantly predicted general male entitlement, which in turn predicted sexual entitlement, which then predicted rape-related criterion variables. The results indicated that general and sexual entitlement completely or partially mediated the links between masculinity and rape-related variables. Research also has shown that high and low levels of RE and RABBM significantly differentiate coercive from noncoercive men (Senn et al., 2000), sexually aggressive college men from sexually nonaggressive men (Rando et al., 1998), and domestic abusers from nonviolent men (Walls & Walker, 2002). In one of the only laboratory studies on this topic, Cohn et al. (2010) found that emotional dysregulation mediates the association between RE and aggression. Schwartz and Waldo (2003) found, with abusive men, that SPC correlated with acts of physical abuse and that RE correlated with intimidation and threats. The empirical results linking GRC to men's violation of women and others are sobering. Collectively, they imply that GRC is significantly related to thoughts, attitudes, and behaviors that are abusive of and violent toward others.

There is further evidence that GRC relates to men who have committed crimes. Amato (2012) found that prisoners' tendency to use violence correlated with SPC, RE, RABBM, and total GRC score. He also found that younger prisoners who were not affiliated with a religion reported that SPC and RE were correlated with violence. Prisoners with a history of crime and not affiliated with a religion scored significantly higher on GRC. The lack of religion in a prisoner's life as it relates to higher GRC is interesting and may suggest that having a group of religiously minded peers may decrease one's degree of GRC. Finally, in a study that may address precursors to crime, GRC was found to be uncorrelated with young boys' attitudes toward guns and violence (Dukes, 2007).

The research on vulnerable men is in its earliest stages and directly relates to the forgotten men who could not cope with or who have been victimized by the macrosocietal system (see Chapter 3, this volume). The plight of vulnerable men is directly relevant to significant societal problems, including men's violence against women, male-on-male violence, sex abuse, school shootings, societal discrimination, suicide, poverty, and homelessness, to name just a few. Further conceptualization is needed to understand male vulnerability in the context of masculinity ideology and GRC. Psychometric measures and specific study of different kinds of vulnerability, such as perceived, gendered, and internalized racism (Liang, 2010; Liang et al., 2011); heterosexist discrimination; stigma; internalized homonegativity; and heterosexism are needed.

Men in Vulnerable Work Roles

Men whose work puts them in harm's way or who have stressful roles in helping others also have been studied. The groups studied include police officers, firefighters, and combat veterans; all these men qualify as heroes by risking their health and life daily. Four studies assessed GRC in police officers (Faircloth, 2011; M. A. Peterson, 1991; Rooney, 2011; Wester, Arndt, Sedivy, & Arndt, 2010). Wester, Arndt, et al. (2010) found that police officers' GRC predicted seeing fewer benefits and greater risks associated with their line of work, and a stigma associated with counseling. Furthermore, anticipated benefits did not mediate the relationship between GRC and stigma, but police officers' self and public stigma correlated with all GRC patterns. Rooney (2011) studied female Irish police officers and found that SPC predicted negative attitudes toward mentally ill people. Faircloth (2011) studied both male and female police officers and found that SPC predicted job dissatisfaction for men, RE predicted a lack of job satisfaction for women, and CBWFR predicted job satisfaction for both male and female police officers. Male officers reported significantly more RABBM than women officers, and women officers reported significantly more CBWFR than men. M. A. Peterson (1991) found that overall GRC correlated with police officers' negative attitudes toward professional help seeking.

Only one GRC study has been completed on firefighters, and two have focused on combat veterans. Varvel (2008) studied firefighters and found that GRC was a partial mediator between problem-solving appraisal and psychological functions and that all the patterns of GRC were significantly correlated with firefighters' stress and negative attitudes toward problem solving. The two studies of combat veterans (Baima, 2012; Fleming, 2012) found that negative attitudes toward help seeking was correlated with GRC (Fleming, 2012), and Baima (2012) found significant correlations between GRC and help seeking with veterans but no moderation or mediation effects.

Summary of Diversity Studies on Men's Gender Role Conflict

The studies of GRC and race/ethnicity, age, class, sexual orientation, nationality, and vulnerabilities provide important information on diverse men's experience with GRC. There is evidence that GRC is significantly related to racial/ethnic minority men's psychological issues, such as depression, stress, anxiety, and self-esteem, across various diversity groups. Also, 10 studies have found that GRC relates to such issues as racial identity, racial reference group, African American consciousness, and acculturation. These initial studies suggest that GRC interacts in complex ways with racial/ethnic and cultural beliefs. Men who are less acculturated and who identify mainly with the dominant culture experience greater GRC. African American, Asian American, and Hispanic/Latino American men report racial identity and acculturation issues related to GRC. Furthermore, nine studies have shown that GRC is moderated or mediated by racial/ethnic and acculturation factors. Unfortunately, how GRC relates to White men's racial identity and privileged status has gone unexplored.

Both heterosexual and gay men experience GRC, but gay men report significantly less RE and RABBM. Differences in GRC between gay and straight men may relate to gay men's different socialization experiences with homophobia and the formation of a homosexual identity in a heterosexist society. Gay men may experience GRC in different ways and at earlier developmental points than straight men. No research exists on these developmental questions, but accepting a gay sexual identity while living in a heterosexist culture may force gay men to examine their GRC more proactively and resolve it earlier.

The more recent research on gay men indicates that, in five studies, GRC was correlated with homonegativy, and internalized homophobia and heterosexism are related to GRC in ways that negatively affect mental health. Other studies have found that shame, guilt, and eating disorder symptomatology correlated with gay men's GRC. All of these studies suggest that GRC contributes to aspects of internalized oppression.

Women report GRC to a lesser degree than men, with the exception of CBWFR, which is experienced to the same or greater degree. Other research (see Chapter 7, this volume) indicates that women's report of their partner's GRC is related to their own depression and overall relationship dissatisfaction. Needed are measures of women's GRC based on theories and research in the psychology of women. The measurement of women's GRC could provide an additional contextual perspective to understand men's GRC.

The preliminary age differences in GRC probably relate to different demands and developmental tasks faced by boys and older men. Furthermore, as men age there may be opportunities to resolve GRC by recognizing the futility of restrictive gender roles attitudes and behaviors. Younger men report significantly more SPC and RABBM than older men, but the age differences regarding RE and CBWFR are less clear. The lack of difference in RE across ages may suggest that emotional restriction may not be easily moderated by time or experience. In short, RE may be a more difficult GRC pattern for men to confront and change.

Gaps in the Literature and Future Research

No GRC research has been completed on Native American or Pacific Islander men, gay boys in high school, or bisexual men, and only a single study each exists on physically injured men (Good et al., 2006) and immigrants (Wester, Vogel, et al., 2006). Transgendered people have been assessed in only one study (Grethel, 2007), and only one theoretical analysis has focused on counseling transgendered individuals with GRC (Wester, McDonough, et al., 2010). No studies have been implemented in South America, and only one in China and three in Arab or Middle Eastern countries have been conducted. Differences among single, married, divorced, remarried, and widowed men's GRC have rarely been tested, and class differences in GRC, Class × Race interactions, Class × Ethnicity interactions, and Class × Sexual Orientation interactions are also conspicuously absent in the literature. Research on these topics is necessary to understand the complexity of GRC in the context of different cultures, poverty, classism, racism, heterosexism, and ethnocentrism.

The results of the GRC studies on diverse groups suggest important topics to be pursued in the future. For example, are there GRC differences across the races and nationalities, and, if so, are they related to different racial/ethnic and cultural values related to gender roles? Do the effects of different political systems (e.g., capitalism, communism, socialism), as well as ethnic and family values, contribute to different degrees of GRC for men in different countries? Research on these topics can help explain how macro-societal and microinterpersonal aspects of patriarchal sexism interact in men's and women's lives. How, exactly, does GRC relate to racial identity, family and cultural values, racism, ethnocentrism, and acculturation for men of color and immigrants? Knowledge about how men's gender roles vary by race/ethnicity, nationality, and sexual orientation has accumulated slowly in the psychology of men. The assumption that a single masculinity exists (i.e., White, middle class, heterosexual, American) is erroneous, short-sighted, and biased. Race/ethnicity, class, age, sexual orientation, religious orientation, nationality, and other variables affect men's experience of GRC. Exactly how these diversity variables affect men is one of the most crucial issues to be assessed in the field of the psychology of men.

The research reported in this chapter suggests that a body of knowledge is emerging on diverse men's GRC. The next step in the multicultural study of men and masculinity is to develop more comprehensive research programs that address more than one-shot studies on various topics. The conceptual model illustrated in Figure 6.1 provides one vantage point from which to generate future studies. One of the final questions is this: How well does the empirical research provide support for the current theoretical assumption discussed earlier and the theoretical concepts in Figure 6.1 at both the macrosocietal and microinterpersonal levels?

EMPIRICAL EVIDENCE FOR THE CONCEPTUAL MODEL IN FIGURE 6.1

On the basis of the studies reviewed thus far, what is known about GRC's relationship with multicultural, situational, and contextual indexes? Does empirical evidence support the assumptions specified earlier and the conceptual relationships depicted in Figure 6.1? To review the evidence, I discuss in the following sections eight research questions based on the model in Figure 6.1. The numbered arrows and points (1–7) in Figure 6.1 represent the research questions discussed. In Exhibit 6.1, I summarize the variables that are significantly correlated with GRC and other contextual, situational, and multicultural indexes for racial/ethnic minority men across 10 categories, including (a) contextual, demographic, and multicultural variables correlated with GRC; (b) restrictive masculinity ideologies correlated with GRC; (c) patterns of GRC (SPC, RE, RABBM, and CBWFR) correlated with racial/ethnic minority men's emotional psychological problems; (d) gender role self-devaluations; (e) gender role self-restriction; (f) gender role self-violations; (g) kinds of internalized oppression correlated with racial/ethnic minority men's GRC; (h) emotional psychological problems correlated with racial/ethnic minority men's internalized oppression; (i) moderators of GRC for racial/ethnic minority men; and (j) mediators of GRC for racial/ethnic minority men. I use

EXHIBIT 6.1

Multicultural, Contextual, and Situational Variables Correlated With GRC

Race/ethnicity, class, age, stage of life, sex (women and transgendered people), socioeconomic status, educational level, marital status, work roles, nationality, acculturation and assimilation, racial/ethnic identity, *machismo* and *caballerismo* ideology, cultural values, personal and societal discrimination, states of vulnerability, being violent

Restrictive Masculinity Ideologies Correlated With GRC

GRC and masculinity ideology have been significantly correlated with the following masculinity ideologies measures: the Masculine Role Norms Scale (E. H. Thompson & Pleck, 1986), the Male Role Norms Inventory (Levant et al., 1992), and the Conformity to Masculine Norms Inventory (Mahalik, Locke, et al., 2003). All of these measures have been significantly correlated with the Gender Role Conflict Scale (O'Neil, Helms, Gable, David, & Wrightsman, 1986), with median rs ranging between .32 and .49. for the following scales and subscales: Male Role Norms Scale—Status Norms, Toughness Norms, Anti-Femininity Norms; Conformity to Masculine Norms Inventory—Winning, Emotional Control, Risk Taking, Violence, Power Over Women, Dominance, Playboy, Self-Reliance, Primacy of Work, Disdain for Homosexuals, Pursuit of Status, Total Conformity; Male Role Norms Inventory—Avoidance of Femininity, Fear and Hatred of Homosexuals, Self-Reliance, Aggression, Achievement/Status, Non-Relational Attitudes Toward Sex, Restrictive Emotionality.

Patterns of GRC (Success, Power, and Control; Restrictive Emotionality; Restrictive Affectionate Behavior Between Men; Conflict Between Work and Family Relations) Correlated With Racial/Ethnic Minority Men's Emotional Psychological Problems

Lower self-esteem, anxiety, shame, guilt, psychological distress, loneliness, mourning, grief, negative attitudes toward help seeking, martial and relationship dissatisfaction, hopelessness, unprotected sex, internalized racism, drive for muscularity, perceived racism, negative coping styles, homonegativity, anger, psychological well-being, negative feelings about being gay, attachment insecurity, sexual compulsivity, eating disorders, internalized homonegativity, homophobia, heterosexist discrimination, body dissatisfaction, distress tolerance

Gender Role Self-Devaluations

Internalized heterosexism, homonegativity, negative attitudes toward being out, negative feelings about being gay, self-hate from racism, depression, low self-esteem

Gender Role Self-Restriction

Coping problems, anxiety, stress, alexithymia, hopelessness, intimacy, negative attitudes toward help seeking

Gender Role Self-Violations

Eating disorder symptomatology; substance use and abuse; chronic self-destructiveness; suicidal risk or attempts; internalized homonegativity, homophobia, and heterosexism.

(continues)

Kinds of Internalized Oppression Correlated With Racial/Ethnic Minority Men's GRC

Internalized racism (self-hatred), internalized homonegativity, internalized heterosexism, internalized homophobia, low self-esteem

Emotional Psychological Problems Correlated With Racial/Ethnic Minority Men's Internalized Oppression

Low self-esteem, shame, guilt, depression, parental efficacy, psychological stress

Moderators of GRC for Racial/Ethnic Minority Men

Less ambivalence and confusion about racial identity, Asian identity, self-esteem, assimilation into the majority culture, traditional African American religious acculturation, Black identity salience, multicultural inclusive racial identity, attitudes toward help seeking, pre-encounter state of racial identity, depression, stress, *machismo*, acculturation, monocultural versus bicultural status, distress, *caballerismo*, perceived racism, sex typing of self, homonegativity, environmental mastery, purpose in life, internalized heteroesexism

Mediators of GRC for Racial/Ethnic Minority Men

Racial identity, psychological stress, internalized racism, norms of the dominant White culture, *machismo* ideology, homonegativity, shame, guilt, heterosexist discrimination, internalized heterosexism, self-esteem, negative affect, social sensitivity, internalized heterosexism, avoidant coping, multicultural inclusiveness

Note. References for these categorizations are found throughout this chapter and in the References section.

these categories of research to address Research Questions 2–8. There are no data to report for Questions 1–3.

Research Question 1: Is There Any Evidence That the Macrosocietal Level Shown in Figure 6.1 (Arrows 1, 2, and 3) Directly Influences the Personal Experiences of Men at the Microinterpersonal Level (Points 4–7)?

No GRC research linking the macrosocietal factors with the micro-interpersonal dynamics exists because the GRCS does not directly assess how the larger society influences individual's lives. Scholars in psychology and sociology have made a cogent case for these sociopolitical relationships; specifically, theorists in the psychology of women are leading the way in explaining how societal oppression causes interpersonal and psychological issues for both men and women (see Enns, 2004; Enns & Williams, 2013; Szymanski & Hilton, 2013; Williams & Enns, 2013). The emerging theories in the psychology of men can contribute much to explaining how oppression, stereotypes, and biases against men cause discrimination and social injustice. Concepts such as gendered racism (Liang et al., 2010, 2011, in press) and reactionary masculinity (Hammond & Mattis, 2005; Jamison, 2006) can be incorporated into future research and planned psychoeducational interventions.

Research Question 2: Is There Any Evidence That Gender Role Conflict Correlates With Multicultural, Contextual, and Situational Indices for Racial/Ethnic Minority Men (Point 4 in Figure 6.1)?

Exhibit 6.1 lists 21 multicultural, contextual, and situational variables that have been significantly correlated with GRC. All the diverse groups of men studied have reported that GRC relates to numerous contextual, situational, and multicultural indices. The most commonly used demographics in basic research are related to GRC, including race/ethnicity, class, age, stage of life, sexual orientation, sex (women and transgendered people), SES, educational level, marital status, work roles, and nationality. Other situational and contextual indexes related to GRC are degrees of acculturation and assimilation, racial/ethnic identity, machismo and caballerismo ideology, cultural values, personal and societal discrimination, states of vulnerability, and being violent. Futures studies need to move beyond assessing simple relationships between diversity indexes and dependent variables and focus on situational, interpersonal, and real-life contexts (Addis et al., 2010; K. Jones & Heesacker, 2012).

Research Question 3: Is There Any Evidence That the Patterns of Gender Role Conflict Correlate With Restrictive Masculinity Ideology (Point 5 in Figure 6.1)?

Pleck (1995) indicated that GRC was a cofactor of masculinity ideology, and research has verified this relationship (Levant & Richmond, 2007; O'Neil, 2012b). The convergent validity between GRC and masculinity ideology has been studied by correlating the GRCS with masculinity ideologies measures, including the Masculine Role Norms Scale (E. H. Thompson & Pleck, 1986), the Male Role Norms Inventory (Levant et al., 1992), and the Conformity to Masculine Norms Inventory (Mahalik, Locke, et al., 2003). Exhibit 6.1 provides a brief summary of GRCS correlations with measures of masculinity ideologies. All of these measures have been significantly correlated with the GRCS, with median rs ranging between .32 and .49 with mostly White men. These significant correlations suggest that the GRC is related to masculinity ideology, but the low to moderate correlations suggest that GRC is a distinct construct.

In a recent analysis, seven studies were examined to assess the correlations between GRC and masculinity ideology scales (O'Neil & Denke, in press). The results of this investigation provided additional support that SPC, RE, RABBM are moderately correlated with GRC. CBWFR showed lower correlations and more inconsistent results as a significant correlate of GRC.

The critical question that has not been answered is whether racial/ ethnic minority men's masculinity ideology, as it differentially defined, correlates with GRC. Only one study has found GRC to be significantly correlated with Asian American men's masculinity ideology (Liu, 2005). More research is needed to determine how different kinds of masculinity ideologies across diverse groups of men relate to GRC and other psychological problems.

Research Question 4: Is There Any Evidence That Gender Role Conflict (Success, Power, and Control; Restrictive Emotionality; Restrictive Affectionate Behavior Between Men; and Conflict Between Work and Family Relations) Correlates With Racial/Ethnic Minority Men's Emotional and Psychological Problems and Vulnerabilities (Point 6 in Figure 6.1)?

Exhibit 6.1 also lists 28 emotional–psychological problems or vulnerabilities that have been significantly correlated with racial/ethnic minority men's GRC. The list provides a sobering view of how GRC affects the lives of men who are members of racial/minority ethnic groups. As summarized earlier in this chapter, men of different races, sexual orientations, and nationalities report significant relationships between GRC and emotional–psychological problems.

Research Question 5: Is There Any Evidence That Gender Role Self-Devaluations, Self-Restrictions, and Self-Violations Correlate With Racial/Ethnic Minority Men's Emotional and Psychological Problems (Point 6 in Figure 6.1)?

I completed a separate review of the empirical research to determine whether the patterns of GRC for racial/ethnic minority and international men significantly relate to gender role self-devaluations, self-restrictions, or self-violations. In each of the studies GRC was significantly correlated with a dependent variable that represents self-restrictions, self-devaluations, or self-violations defined by SPC, RE, RABBM, and CBWFR. A review of the studies found that self-devaluations, self-restrictions, and self-violations were related to psychological–emotional problems and vulnerability in 38 studies with racially and ethnically mixed groups, men from other countries, and non-heterosexual men. In the following sections, I review the studies individually using the categories of self-devaluations, self-restrictions, and self-violations.

Self-Devaluations

As shown in Exhibit 6.1, seven symptoms defined self-devaluations: (a) internalized heterosexism, (b) homonegativity, (c) negative feelings toward being out, (d) negative feelings about being gay, (e) self-hate from racism, (f) depression, and (g) low self-esteem. The assumption is that when men experience these seven symptoms, self-devaluation occurs. Research indicates that gay men's GRC relates to internalized heterosexism and homonegativity (Ervin, 2003; Szymanski & Carr, 2008; Zhang, 2014) and to negative feelings about being gay or outness (Sánchez, 2005; Sánchez et al., 2010). For African American men, GRC has been correlated with self-hate related to racism (Wester, Vogel, et al., 2006). When self-devaluations are defined by being depressed, the following diverse groups reported that GRC was related to their negative affect: African Americans (Brewer, 1998), victims of sex abuse (Coonerty-Femiano, Katzman, Femiano, Gemar, & Toner, 2001), Mexican American men (Fragoso & Kashubeck, 2000), Japanese men (Hayashi, 1999), Korean men and college students (Choi et al., 2010; Jo, 2000; Kang, 2001), gay men (D. A. Jones, 1998; Simonsen et al., 2000), and Australian men (Tate, 1998; Theodore, 1998). When self-devaluations are defined by low self-esteem, the following diverse groups reported GRC to be significantly correlated with disliking themselves: Japanese men (Hayashi, 1999), Korean men (Jo, 2000; J. Kim et al., 2005), African American men (Laurent, 1997), and Australian men (Mahalik, Locke, Theodore, Cournoyer, & Lloyd, 2001. Two studies found self-devaluations as shame to be related to GRC for African American men (McMahon, Winkel, & Luthar, 2000) and Chinese gay men (Zhang, 2014).

Self-Restrictions

Self-restrictions are defined as problems with coping, anxiety, stress, alexithymia (difficulty identifying and expressing one's emotions), hopelessness, limited intimacy, and negative attitudes toward help seeking. With these dependent variables, it was assumed that personal gender role restrictions contributed to the inability to cope with anxiety, stress, hopelessness and that a limited behavioral repertoire contributed to intimacy problems and not seeking help. GRC as an aspect of self-restriction was correlated with stress with Mexican American men (Fragoso & Kashubeck, 2000; Leka, 1998); alexithymia with Japanese men (Hayashi, 1999); hopelessness for Irish (Birthistle, 1999) and African American men (Brewer, 1998); and problems with intimacy for gay men (Van Hyfte & Rabinowitz, 2001), Canadian men (Chartier & Arnold, 1985), and Australian men (Theodore & Lloyd, 2000). A single study found restrictions in help-seeking attitudes for Canadian men (James, 2005).

Self-Violations

Studies of GRC as self-violations for diverse men are fewer in number. The five areas of self-violations are (a) eating disorder symptomatology; (b) substance use and abuse; (c) chronic self-destructiveness; (d) suicidal risk or attempts; and (e) internalized homonegativity, homophobia, and heterosexism. GRC as an aspect of self-violation was correlated with eating disorder symptomatology for gay men (Blashill & Vander Wal, 2009), substance abuse and use for Korean and Australian men (Kang, 2001; Monk & Ricciardelli, 2003), chronic self-destructiveness for gay men (Naranjo, 2001), and suicide attempts or suicide risk with Canadian men (Houle et al., 2008). Furthermore, research on gay men's GRC relates to internalized heterosexism and homo-negativity (Ervin, 2003; Szymanski & Carr, 2008; Zhang, 2014) and negative feelings about being gay or about outness (Sánchez, 2005; Sánchez et al., 2010). All of these aspects of GRC can be experienced as self-violations.

Unfortunately, there is no direct evidence that GRC from others causes personal oppression, discrimination, or serious mental health problem. One study indirectly assessed the relationship between discrimination and GRC. Liang et al. (2010) found that Latino men's CBWFR significantly correlated with perceived racism on the job and in academic, public, and general settings, whereas total GRC score correlated with perceived racism in the job setting. These results suggest that there is a relationship between GRC and perceived discrimination in diverse men's lives, but direct devaluations, restrictions, and violations by others need further study.

Research Question 6: Is There Any Evidence That the Patterns of Gender Role Conflict (Success, Power, and Control; Restrictive Emotionality; Restrictive Affectionate Behavior Between Men; and Conflict Between Work and Family Relations) and Gender Role Devaluations, Restrictions, and Violations Relate to Internalized Oppression for Racial/Ethnic Minority Men (Point 6 in Figure 6.1)?

There is both direct and indirect evidence that gender role devaluations, restrictions, or violations of gay men relate to aspects of personal oppression or other indexes of poor mental health. Exhibit 6.1 lists six symptoms of internalized oppression that have been correlated with GRC, including negative feelings about being gay (Sánchez et al., 2010), attachment insecurity and sexual compulsivity (Griffin, 2011), negative identity and attitudes about being out (Sánchez, 2005), and eating disorder symptomatology (Blashill & Vander Wal, 2009). A significant area of research has focused on how internalized homonegativity, heterosexism, homophobia, and heterosexist discrimination relate to gay men's GRC and psychological problems. Four studies have significantly correlated internalized homonegativity with GRC

(Bryce, 2012; M. A. Robinson & Brewster, 2014; Szymanski & Carr, 2008; Zhang, 2014), with SPC, RE, and RABBM being the most consistent predictors of not liking one's sexual orientation. Two studies have found that GRC correlated with internalized homophobia, with SPC, RE, and RABBM being the significant predictors in each study (Szymanski & Carr, 2008; Szymanski & Ikizler, 2013)

Evidence also exists that GRC correlates with internalized oppression. Moreover, many studies have correlated contextual–multicultural factors to GRC and internalized oppression with diverse groups of men. For gay men, research has documented that GRC is related to internalized oppression in terms of homonegativity, internalized heterosexism and homophobia, and negative feelings about being gay. If *internalized oppression* is defined as low self-esteem, then the research indicates that GRC and disliking oneself are significantly correlated for African American, Asian American, and gay men. The research does not indicate that internalized oppression is externalized through violence and abuse of others; however, because more than 20 studies have found correlations between GRC and violence toward women, it is likely that men's internalized oppression is projected onto women and others. In terms of discrimination, gay men report that GRC is related to heterosexist discrimination (Szymanski & Ikizler, 2013), and for African American and Hispanic men, racism was significantly correlated with GRC in two studies (Wester et al., 2005; Liang et al., 2010).

Research Question 7: Is There Any Evidence That the Patterns of Gender Role Conflict, Gender Role Devaluations, Restrictions, and Violations, Emotional–Psychological Problems, and Internalized Oppression Lead to Personal and Societal Discriminations and Social Injustice Against Men and Women (Points 6 and 7 in Figure 6.1)?

Point 7 in Figure 6.1 depicts the relationship between all of the gender related and psychological problems at the microinterpersonal level with the personal, societal, and institutional aspects of discrimination and social injustices against both men and women. This relationship links the personal and interpersonal issues related to GRC to the larger macrosocietal level as discussed earlier in the chapter. From a GRC perspective, personal and societal oppression occurs because of men's abuses of power, destructive competition, homophobia, and interpersonal violence that maintain privilege and power over others. The personal pain of oppression is visible in our society, but patriarchal masculinity has rarely been factored into explaining the injustice. An obvious theoretical relationship exists between GRC, discrimination, and social injustices, but no direct research exists documenting this relationship.

As reported earlier, studies that provide indirect evidence for the relationship represented by point 7 indicate that GRC is significantly related to stereotyping of women, homophobic and antigay attitudes, racial bias, and violence against women and others. For example, two studies found men's perception of racism and heterosexist discrimination related to GRC (Liang et al., 2011; Szymanski & Ikizler, 2013). Both Latino and gay men reported experiencing discrimination that was related to their GRC and emotional problems but whether GRC was a part of discrimination was not assessed. These studies link discrimination and potential injustice to GRC, but the research does not document the direct causes and processes that result in personal and institutional oppression. What is unknown is how both victimizers and victims act out their vulnerability and gender related wounds against themselves or others. Situational and contextual research is needed to explore how oppression and GRC interact to cause social injustice. The research models presented in Chapters 3 and 8 are designed to promote this kind of study of men's real life experiences. The relationship between GRC and restrictive masculinity ideologies and societal discrimination, oppression, and injustice toward both men and women should be a high priority for any call to action in the psychology of men over the coming decades.

Research Question 8: Is There Any Evidence That Multicultural, Contextual, and Diversity Variables Moderate and Mediate Gender Role Conflict or Any Evidence That GRC Mediates These Same Variables?

How GRC is moderated and mediated by third variables is another critical multicultural issue. Moderators and mediators of GRC are not shown in Figure 6.1, but in Chapter 8, I present four research paradigms that depict the importance of looking at more complex relationships instead of simple correlations. The research reviewed does indicate that numerous variables moderate and mediate GRC. This final research question promotes more complex thinking about how contextual variables moderate and mediate GRC.

Exhibit 6.1 lists 21 moderators and 16 mediators of GRC for racial/ethnic minority men. A perusal of these items suggests a complexity in explaining the multicultural psychology of men. The moderation and mediation studies support the model in Figure 6.1 and help shape future research directions. For example, moderating and mediating results of GRC have been consistent in research on cultural, racial/ethnic, and religious identity and indexes such as acculturation, assimilation, racism, and social position. With African American men, GRC was moderated or mediated by the following contextual–multicultural factors: African American identity, racial identity, a pre-encounter state of racial identity, African American cultural identity, ethnic identity, multicultural inclusive racial identity, assimilation into the majority culture, African American religious acculturation, internalized racism, endorsement of the White culture, and class and social position. For Asian American men, the multicultural factors were Asian cultural values, acculturation, racial identity, and ethnocentrism. For Hispanic men, the factors were acculturation, ethnic identity, and perceived racism. These findings suggest that researchers are moving away from studying categorical variables (e.g., race, sexual orientation) as simply being present in a dependent variable to a more nuanced approach where race, for example, is related to perceived racism, racial identity, internalized homonegativity, and diverse cultural values. It is my hope that future researchers can use the past moderation and mediation research and the new contextual research paradigms in Chapter 8 to design research that explains the complexity of multicultural psychology of men.

Summary of Empirical Evidence for the Multicultural Psychology of Men Model

On the basis of correlational data, evidence supports four of the theoretical relationships found in Figure 6.1 that promote future research and increased discussion about the lives of racial/ethnic minority men. Theoretical analyses convey that the macrosocietal level of men's experience includes patriarchy, stereotypes and biases, and discrimination and social injustices (see Arrows 1–3 in Figure 6.1). Furthermore, how the macrosocietal levels interact with the microinterpersonal level also has theoretical justification, but no GRC research can link these two levels of men's lives. Additional theory and new methodological approaches need to be developed to help document the interaction of the macrosocietal and the microinterpersonal levels of men's experience.

Empirical support exists for Research Questions 4, 5, and 6, related to the microinterpersonal level of diverse men's experiences. Strong support exists that the multicultural, contextual, and situational indexes significantly correlate with GRC. In addition, research on masculinity ideology demonstrates that masculinity norms and conformity to male role norms also correlate with GRC. There is strong support indicating that both GRC and masculinity ideology significantly correlate with diverse men's emotional–psychological problems and vulnerability. Furthermore, there is emerging evidence that gender role devaluations, restrictions, and violations are correlated with men's GRC and emotional–psychological problems. How men's GRC and emotional problems relate to internalized oppression has some support with samples of gay men, African American men, and men who have low self-esteem or are violent towards others or themselves. The analyses are limited by the use of correlational data, but the moderation and mediation studies used more elaborate statistical procedures. Further theory is needed to continue to operationalize the concepts in Figure 6.1, and future research needs to assess the situational experience of racial/ethnic minority men with their GRC in the context of racial identity, discrimination, and oppression.

FINAL COMMENT: RESISTANCE TO UNDERSTANDING MEN'S DIVERSITY AND OPPRESSION

I have often wondered how Martin Luther King Jr. would react to the multicultural psychology of men model illustrated in Figure 6.1; specifically, would he see GRC and masculinity ideology as relevant to his societal agenda of eradicating injustices toward men of color and restoring equal opportunity and human rights for all? There is no way to know how King would have reacted to the model and the data; however, it is likely that he would be disappointed in our limited capacity to discuss race relations, diversity, and multiculturalism in America. He would agree with Derald Sue (2005) that a conspiracy of silence exists in the United States regarding race and race relations. This conspiracy of silence also includes understanding how patriarchy, masculinity ideology, GRC, and oppression exist in men's and women's lives.

Men's oppression is difficult to discuss because it produces uncomfortable interpersonal dynamics between racial/ethnic majority and minority groups. For example, White guilt and fears about appearing racist, sexist, and heterosexist have hampered dialogues that could promote personal and social change and greater equality for all. Many people lack contexts in which to engage in dialogue about men's and women's oppression and have difficulty thinking outside of the patriarchal status quo. One of the problems is that many of us have learned that the United States was founded on principles of equality and human rights, with checks and balances that protect racial/ethnic minorities from discrimination and injustice. The truth is that these checks and balances often fail or do not exist. Patriarchal, sexist, heterosexist, and racist practices remain discriminatory and cause much human pain and turmoil. Racial profiling and killings, violence against women, discrimination and violence against sexual minorities, job discrimination, and micro-aggressions are still commonplace.

The oppressed are usually those men and women who deviate from the gender role standards and norms of a White, middle-class, wealthy, and heterosexual culture. If a White, male, heterosexual, middle-class, Eurocentric American is the expected norm, then the majority of people in the United States deviate from these standards. As the research reviewed here suggests, these deviations have significant and negative mental health implications for diverse groups of men and women.

An obvious but difficult truth exists: American society is structured in such a way that there are oppressive outcomes for specific groups of men, women, and children. Americans grow up in an oppressive, racist, and sexist society in which they consciously or unconsciously learn oppressive attitudes and behaviors toward others who are different from them. This does not imply that everyone acts in racist, sexist, or oppressive ways but that under the right circumstances everyone has the capacity for discriminatory attitudes and behaviors. Only the full acceptance of this oppressive reality can free people from the defensive silence and promote more dialogue about men, masculinity, GRC, and oppression.

As soon as the oppressive realities are exposed to the majority culture, strong defense mechanisms are activated to cover the resultant threat, embarrassment, guilt, shame, and fear. People who are in denial or are defensive may dispute that discrimination and oppression actually exist, or they may blame the victim. Furthermore, strong political, cultural, and religious forces that promote denial about societal discrimination exist. In some situations, outright lies and propaganda are created about minority groups to deceive or confuse the public about the sources of the oppression. In my opinion, the best example of this was the ongoing challenge to President Barack Obama's citizenship and birthplace as a way to nullify his right to be the first African American president of the United States. If extremists can devalue and discredit the legitimacy of the president, everyone is a potential target and at risk for abuse.

Other people accept societal inequities based on essentialist gender role beliefs, natural laws, religious principles, or evolutionary biological reductionism. Furthermore, truths about discrimination are sometimes difficult to accept if you are rewarded by the system or see yourself as less oppressed than others. Many citizens are so invested in (or unconscious of) the injustices that are built into the U.S. political system that it is difficult for them to see what is really happening. Acceptance of the status quo exists in particular if you are not being oppressed in any way.

How to change societal oppression is an overwhelming issue for those who are aware of it. Many feel powerless to do anything about such an enormous societal problem, and those who actively address these social and political issues can be at risk. Activists who expose oppression are many times targeted for telling the truth (Albee, 1981) because exposing the truth jeopardizes established power relationships and economic gains made from the oppression. Destructive capitalism surely generates profits from discrimination and oppression, and those who have vested interests usually protect their advantage and position.

Finally, being oppressed is a very private, embarrassing, and shameful reality to admit; therefore, talking about it is difficult. Many people do not have outlets to discuss their oppression, and some do not even know why and how they are oppressed. Some blame themselves and repress the anger as a way of coping. Eventually, the anger turns to rage, apathy, or depression, and sometimes it turns to violence, permanently damaging the human spirit.

For these reasons, GRC has both political and personal implications for the psychology of men. More correctly, GRC has human rights implications because everyone in U.S. society is promised justice and equal opportunity under the law, and everyone—including men—should be free from GRC, personal oppression, and unjust discrimination. Social injustice that emanates from patriarchal masculinity and sexism can appear to be political in nature but is in fact a violation of democratic and human rights principles. The multicultural psychology of men has to become a priority if the discipline is to be a credible agent of change. How to expose and eradicate men's and women's oppression in our democratic society is what the psychology of men can be about, and that goal represents the most important call to action in this book.

7

SUMMARY OF THE GENDER ROLE CONFLICT RESEARCH PROGRAM

As I pointed out in Chapter 1, men's gender roles have not received much scientific attention in the history of psychology, and research about men was conspicuously absent in the psychological literature until the late 1970s. Very little was known about how men's gender role socialization contributes to their psychological and emotional problems. Over the past 20 years, slowly but systematically, the psychology of men has emerged as an important area for scientific inquiry and clinical intervention.

In this chapter, I provide an update of gender role conflict (GRC) research conducted since the publication of a special issue of *The Counseling Psychologist* in 2008 (O'Neil, 2008b). That special issue summarized 232 studies, but now more than 350 have been completed. I combine the new studies with the earlier findings to provide a new synthesis of what is known about men's GRC.

Some sections of this chapter were adapted from "Summarizing Twenty-Five Years of Research on Men's Gender Role Conflict Using the Gender Role Conflict Scale: New Research Paradigms and Clinical Implications," by J. M. O'Neil, 2008c, *The Counseling Psychologist, 36*, pp. 358–445. Copyright 2008 by Sage Publications. Adapted with permission.

http://dx.doi.org/10.1037/14501-008

Overall, the complexity of GRC is apparent from the research, and the challenge now is how to interpret the results for future researchers and clinicians who are helping men.

This review of men's GRC is important for several reasons. First, research reviews of men's psychological problems have been lacking in the literature, and those that have been published have been based on small numbers of studies (Levant & Richmond, 2007; O'Neil, Good, & Holmes, 1995). In the current review, I summarize men's GRC by evaluating many empirical studies, published over a 30-year period. Second, lacking has been a comprehensive review of empirical studies that assess whether GRC relates to men's mental health problems. Empirical research has not fully confirmed that men's psychological problems relate to conflicts with their socialized gender roles. Little has been known about how men's gender roles relate to depression; anxiety; violence; suicide; poor health care; homophobia; academic failure; bullying; racial/ethnic oppression; and dysfunctional relations with women, men, and children. These problems negatively affect the quality of people's lives and the overall soul of our society. Very little is known about the contexts of GRC in terms of the historical, situational, developmental, and immediate experiences of men's lives. Enns (2000) discussed GRC as an important area for future research in psychology but did not specify the particular areas to study. In Chapter 8 of this volume, I provide recommendations for future research on these contexts. Furthermore, diagnostic models are needed to assess GRC in therapy, and therapy approaches based on GRC are needed (see Chapters 9–12). Finally, summaries of the GRC studies are needed to guide future research paradigms on men. New ideas and more expansive measures of GRC are also needed. In the review I provide in this chapter, I challenge readers to improve the GRC construct through future research, therapeutic interventions, and preventive programming.

Given the large number of studies, the review has a prescribed structure and is sequentially organized. The four goals of this research summary are to (a) describe the methods of locating, analyzing, and synthesizing the GRC studies; (b) summarize major findings on men's GRC in three contexts—intrapersonal, interpersonal, and therapeutic; (c) summarize how well the empirical research supports the GRC theory proposed in the early 1980s; and (d) suggest research topics that should be pursued in the future.

This chapter does not include all the research that has used the Gender Role Conflict Scale (GRCS; O'Neil, Helms, Gable, David, & Wrightsman, 1986) or information about the GRC research program. For example, the question of whether GRC significantly relates to contextual variables such as race/ethnicity, nationality, age, sexual orientation, and other diversity variables was discussed separately, in Chapter 6. There may be some overlap between some chapters in certain parts of each. The demographics related to past studies and psychometrics of the GRCS are found in Chapters 4 and 6. Criticism of the entire database is found in Chapter 3, and the new contextual GRC research paradigms based on this review are found in Chapter 8. Readers are directed to these chapters for information and research on these topics and to the GRC research web page (http://jimoneil.uconn.edu) for those studies not reported in this chapter because of space limitations.

THE METHODOLOGY OF ANALYZING
THE GENDER ROLE CONFLICT STUDIES

Two specific questions about men's GRC organize this review. First, is there evidence that GRC significantly relates to men in the context of their intrapersonal, interpersonal, and therapeutic lives? Second, how well does the research program provide support for the developing theory on men's GRC? I used a defined method and specific strategies to locate and synthesize the research on men's GRC. First, I studied release forms from researchers who used the GRCS and sought out papers presented at the Annual Conventions of the American Psychological Association from 1995 to the present. In addition, to locate the studies, computer searches from 1980 to the present were implemented in PsycINFO, *Dissertation Abstracts International*, and ERIC. Quantitative and qualitative studies and published and unpublished papers are included in the review to provide the most comprehensive summary of the research program.

I followed a prescribed process in analyzing the studies:

- The research studies were read and numerical counts were made to determine the demographics of the studies by race, age, sexual orientation, and nationality.
- The numbers of published and unpublished studies, dissertations, and convention presentations were calculated.
- The studies were then read again to determine the vital information on sample characteristics, the measures used, the hypotheses tested, the statistical method used, the results, and any limitations to the study.
- The vital information was transferred to a single-sheet summary abstract.
- Abstracts were then sorted into various groupings to facilitate the analysis and summarization of the findings.
- Separate sorts were implemented in three categories, including major dependent variables related to (a) the intrapersonal, interpersonal, and therapeutic contexts; (b) diversity categories

of race, age, nationality, sexual orientation, and socioeconomic status; and (c) statistical methods using simple correlations, canonical correlations, multiple regressions, factor analyses, and structural equation modeling.

Within the three areas listed in the last step, I conducted additional sorting. Each sorting was the basis for writing the summaries and establishing the current status of the research.

The primary areas of the literature review were determined by the groupings of the studies. The groupings were demographic categories of nationality, race, sexual orientation, class, and age and dependent variables in the context of men's GRC in intrapersonal, interpersonal, and therapeutic realms. The analysis was reduced to a single grid sheet with the number of statistically significant relationships among the four GRC patterns (Success, Power, and Control [SPC]; Restrictive Emotionality [RE]; Restrictive Affectionate Behavior Between Men [RABBM]; and Conflict Between Work and Family Relations [CBWFR]) and any dependent variable (i.e., depression, anxiety) recorded. To determine whether there was evidence of significance relationships between GRC and dependent variables, the number of studies that reported a significant relationship between GRCS and dependent variables was recorded using a cutoff probability level of $p < .05$ or lower. Other studies that used canonical correlations, multiple regressions, and structural equation modeling techniques to assess moderators or mediators of GRC were also summarized.

Both conceptual and methodological issues required that some studies be excluded, and therefore criteria for exclusion were specified. Independent ratings from objective others were not used to exclude any studies. Only 17 studies were excluded from the review. Only seven studies were excluded because of a major limitation (e.g., sample size of 26, no valid or reliable dependent measures, confusing methodology and interpretation of the data). The other 10 studies were excluded because they used samples that were extremely narrow or peripheral or the topics were conceptually outside the scope of the literature review.

SUMMARIZING MAJOR FINDINGS ON MEN'S GENDER ROLE CONFLICT IN THE INTRAPERSONAL CONTEXT

In this section, I discuss how men experience GRC internally or as an intrapersonal reality. The internal, unconscious, and intrapsychic correlates of men's GRC are important because they have been inadequately explained in the psychological literature, except for some early discussion by Freud and his followers. During the early years of psychoanalysis, psychodynamic theorists described men's problems as the *femininity complex* (Boehm, 1930), *dread of women* (Horney, 1932), *repudiation of femininity* (Freud, 1937), and *masculine protest and inferiority* (Adler, 1936). Connell (2005) provided an intriguing summary of how masculinity and femininity were salient topics in these early days of psychology and how men's and women's psychological issues were approached and then avoided from 1910 through the 1970s. Controversial topics such as "male femininity" and the unconscious dynamics of masculinity and femininity are significantly different from the dominant perspective today in the psychology of men: social constructivist views of gender roles.

GRC theory from the very beginning has emphasized both social constructionist and unconscious–intrapsychic frameworks to explain how men learn masculinity ideologies and harbor fears about femininity (O'Neil, 1981b, 1982, 1990, 2006). Therefore, GRC is assumed to be not only learned from the larger patriarchal system in schools and families but also experienced as an unconscious phenomenon in terms of the fear of femininity. The research summarized below is limited to research on men's conscious self-report of GRC. The relationships of SPC, RE, RABBM, and CBWFR to 27 psychological and interpersonal categories are summarized in Table 7.1. The studies in these 27 categories are cited by the author(s) and publication date and the full citations are found in the references.

Depression

U.S. society now "lets" men be depressed, but it has been only about 10 years since men's depression finally came "out of the closet" in society and psychology. The likely reason that men's depression has been neglected over the decades lies in biases about men's emotions (Heesacker et al., 1999) and an inability to understand male vulnerability because of gender role stereotypes. That no major books were written in psychology on men and depression until the late 1990s is evidence that we have been unable to accept men as human beings with negative emotionality. Over the past decade both self-help and scholarly books in psychology have discussed men's depression (Cochran & Rabinowitz, 2000; Lynch & Kilmartin, 1999). Cochran and Rabinowitz (2000) indicated that "it is remarkable and disconcerting that so little attention has been devoted to men's suffering from depression" (p. xvi). How men's depression relates to GRC has been one of the most studied areas in the psychology of men.

The relationship between GRC and depression has been assessed in 33 studies (see Table 7.1 for the citations). All but three studies (Bursley, 1996; Good, Heppner, DeBord, & Fischer, 2004; Sharpe & Heppner, 1991) found a significant relationship between depression and GRC. All of the patterns of GRC have significantly correlated with depression; RE has been

TABLE 7.1
Gender Role Conflict (GRC) and Dependent Variable References

Depression	Anxiety and stress	Help-seeking attitudes
Blazina & Jackson (2009)	Blazina & Watkins (1996)	Bevan (2010)
Blazina & Watkins (1996)	Burke (2000)	Blazina & Marks (2001)
Brewer (1998)	Bursley (1996)	Blazina & Watkins (1996)
Burke (2000)	Cournoyer & Mahalik (1995)	Bursley (1996)
Bursley (1996)	F. Davis (1988)	Cortese (2003)
Choi et al. (2010)	Hayashi (1999)	J. M. Davis & Liang (2014)
Coonerty-Femiano et al. (2001)	Kang (2001)	Englar-Carlson (2001)
Cournoyer & Mahalik (1995)	Jo (2000)	Good & Wood (1995)
Fragoso & Kashubeck (2000)	D. A. Jones (1998)	Good et al. (1989, 2006)
Friedman (2011)	Mertens (2000)	Goodwin (2008)
Good & Mintz (1990)	Sharpe & Heppner (1991)	Groeschel et al. (2010)
Good et al. (1996)	Theodore & Lloyd (2000)	James (2005)
Good & Wood (1995)	Fragoso & Kashubeck (2000)	Mansfield et al. (2005)
Hayashi (1999)	Good et al. (1996)	Jana-Massri (2011)
Hoyt (2009)	J. A. Hayes & Mahalik (2000)	Lane & Addis (2005)
Jo (2000)	Hetzel (1998)	Larma (2006)
D. A. Jones (1998)	Liu et al. (2005)	Mendoza & Cummings (2001)
Kang (2001)	Kratzner (2003)	Osborne (2004)
Kelly (2000)	Leka (1998)	Pederson & Vogel (2007)
J. Kim et al. (2006)	Van Delft (1998)	Robertson & Fitzgerald (1992)
Larma (2006)	S. C. Walker (2008)	Rogers (2009)
Mahalik & Cournoyer (2000)	Blashill & Hughes (2009)	Segalla (1996)
Magovcevic & Addis (2005)	Liang et al. (2011)	Shepherd (2009)
S. G. Newman (1997)	Szymanski & Carr (2008)	Simonsen et al. (2000)
F. Peterson (1999)	Wester, Vogel, et al. (2006)	Steinfeldt & Steinfeldt (2010)
Sharpe & Heppner (1991)	Wolfram et al. (2009)	Tsai (2000)
Sharpe et al. (1995)	Hoyt (2009)	Vogel et al. (2014)
D. S. Shepard (2002)	Sbaratta (2011)	White (2006)
Simonsen et al. (2000)	Wester et al. (2007)	Wisch et al. (1995)

Stigma	Discrimination	Religion and spirituality	Coping and problem solving
	Tate (1998)	Wester, Kuo, & Vogel (2006)	Mendoza & Cummings (2001)
	Theodore & Lloyd (2000)	Blashill & Hughes (2009)	D. A. Thompson (2009)
	Thomas (2008)	Stillson (1988)	
	Wolfram et al. (2009)	Hetzel (1998)	
T. E. Rogers (2009)	Liang et al. (2011)	Baima (2012)	Bergen (1997)
Steinfeldt et al. (2009)	M. A. Robinson & Brewster (2014)	Heard (2009)	Birthistle (1999)
Park & Seok Seo (2009)	Bryce (2012)	Jurkovic & Walker (2006)	D. A. Jones (1998)
Wester et al. (2010)	Szymanski & Carr (2008)	Lammy (2011)	Stanzione (2005)
Shepherd (2009)	Zhang (2014)	Laurent (1997)	Strom (2004)
Vogel et al. (2014)	Szymanski & Ikizler (2013)	Lily (1999)	Szymanski & Carr (2008)
Magovcevic & Addis (2005)	Sánchez et al. (2010)	Mahalik & Lagan (2001)	Wester, Kuo, & Vogel (2006)
		Reiman (1999)	Chamberlin (1993)
		Wilkinson (2004)	Good et al. (2004)
			Varvel (2008)

Self-esteem	Personality	Psychoeducational interventions	Men's interpersonal and sexual violence toward women and others
Bingham et al. (2012)	Cortese (2003)	McAnulty (1996)	Kaplan (1992)
Bursley (1996)	Schwartz, Buboltz, et al. (2004)	T. L. Davis & Liddell (2002)	Kaplan et al. (1993)
Choi et al. (2010)	Chamykarpour et al. (2012b)	Kearney et al. (2004)	McDermott et al. (2014)
Cournoyer (1994)	Fischer (2007)	Schwartz, Magee, et al. (2004)	Serna (2004)
F. Davis (1988)	Kratzner (2003)	Blazina & Marks (2001)	Schwartz & Waldo (2003)
Hayashi (1999)	Serna (2004)	Robertson & Fitzgerald (1992)	Schwartz et al. (1998)
Hernandez (2006)	Sipes (2005)	Rochlen et al. (2006)	Senn et al. (2000)
Hobza & Rochlen (2009)	Tokar et al. (2000)	Schwartz & Waldo (2003)	Harnishfeger (1998)
Jo (2000)	Arnold & Chartier (1984)	Gertner (1994)	Covell (1998)
Laurent (1997)	Chartier & Arnold (1985)	Maton et al. (1998)	Schwartz et al. (2005)

(continues)

TABLE 7.1
Gender Role Conflict (GRC) and Dependent Variable References *(Continued)*

Self-esteem	Personality	Psychoeducational interventions	Men's interpersonal and sexual violence toward women and others
Lily (1999)	Chamberlin (1993)	Braverman et al. (1992)	Rando et al. (1998)
Mahalik et al. (2001)	Kratzner (2003)	Brooks-Harris et al. (1996)	Senn et al. (2000)
Schwartz et al. (1998)		Nahon (1992)	Serna (2004)
Sharpe & Heppner (1991)		Moore (1993)	T. L. Davis (1997)
Sharpe et al. (1995)			Kassing et al. (2005)
Schwartz & Waldo (2003)			Glomb & Espelage (2005)
Shek & McEwen (2012)			Jacobs (1996)
Swenson (1998)			Kearney et al. (2004)
Vinson (2011)			Chase (2000)
Szymanski & Carr (2008)			Cohn & Zeichner (2006)
			Johnston (2005)
			M. S. Hill & Fischer (2001)
			Amato & MacDonald (2011)
			Amato (2012)
			O'Neil et al. (1994)

Overall interpersonal functioning	Clients and therapists	Intimacy, self-disclosure, and relationships with fathers	Marital satisfaction, family dynamics, and couple's GRC
Bruch et al. (1998)	Burke (2000)	Chartier & Arnold (1985)	Alexander (1997)
Bruch (2002)	Coonerty-Femiano et al. (2001)	Cournoyer & Mahalik (1995)	Brewer (1998)
Davenport et al. (1998)	Cusack et al. (2006)	Fischer & Good (1997)	Campbell & Snow (1992)
Breiding (2004)	Good et al. (1996)	Good et al. (1995)	Leka (1998)
Breiding et al. (2008)	J. A. Hayes & Mahalik (2000)	Lindley & Schwartz (2006)	Scott (2001)
Celentana (2000)	Mertens (2000)	Odes (2008)	Sharpe et al. (1995)
Land et al. (2011)	Noyes (2004)	Sileo (1996)	Breiding (2004)
Rochlen & Mahalik (2004)	Van Delft (1998)	Sharpe & Heppner (1991)	Breiding et al. (2008)
	Schaub & Williams (2007)	Rainwater (2011)	Celentana (2000)

	Wisch et al. (1995) M. M. Hayes (1985) P. Thomson (1995) Wisch & Mahalik (1999)	Sharpe et al. (1995) Theodore & Lloyd (2000) Van Hyfte & Rabinowitz (2001)	Rochlen & Mahalik (2004) Windle & Smith (2009)
Career development	**Attachment, bonding, and family individuation**	**Body image and muscularity**	**Alcohol and substance abuse**
Dodson & Borders (2006) Jome & Tokar (1998) Rochlen et al. (2002) Rochlen & O'Brien (2002) Wolfram et al. (2009) Eimer & Kidd (2010) Graef et al. (2010) Faircloth (2011) Rochlen et al. (2009)	Blazina, Novotny, et al. (2008) Blazina & Watkins (2000) Cachia (2001) Covell (1998) DeFranc & Mahalik (2002) Fischer (2007) Fischer & Good (1997) Griffin (2011) James (2005) Land et al. (2011) Napolitano et al. (1999) Schwartz, Waldo, & Higgins (2004) Selby (1999) Siffert (2012)	Hobza & Rochlen (2009) Howells (2010) McConville (2004) McCreary et al. (2005) Mejias (2010) Murray & Lewis (2014) Schwartz et al. (2010) Shepherd & Rickard (2012) Schwartz & Tylka (2008)	Blazina & Watkins (1996) Fahey (2003) Good et al. (2006) Groeschel et al. (2010) Howells (2010) Kang (2001) Korcuska & Thombs (2003) McMahon et al. (2000) Monk & Ricciardelli (2003) F. Peterson (1999) Uy et al. (2013)

Alexithymia	**Shame and guilt**	**Training**	**College student development**
Berger et al. (2005) Eicken (2003) Fischer & Good (1997) Hayashi (1999) D. S. Shepard (2002) Levant et al. (2006)	D. Thomson (2005) McMahon et al. (2000) Segalla (1996) Thompkins & Rando (2003) Thomas (2008) D. Thomson (2005) Vu (2000)	Wester et al. (2004) Spillman (2007) Sbaratta (2011) Holohan (2008) Murphy (2001) Murtagh (2012) Wester & Vogel (2002)	T. L. Davis & Liddell (2002) Goodwin (2008) Sosoka (2001) Syzdek et al. (2005) Stanzione (2005)

the most consistent predictor, suggesting that restricted emotions may be a marker for a man who is depressed.

Studies of various special groups of males have reported that GRC is related to depression, including high school boys in both the United States and South Korea (Blazina & Jackson, 2009; Choi, Kim, Hwang, & Heppner, 2010), German schoolteachers (Wolfram, Mohr, & Borchert, 2009), adult cancer patients (Hoyt, 2009), veterans with erectile dysfunction (Larma, 2006), unemployed men (Friedman, 2011), and combat veterans (D. A. Thompson, 2009).

Diversity trends were evident in the depression studies. An empirical link was found between GRC and depression across diverse racial (Brewer, 1998; Fragoso & Kashubeck, 2000; Good, Robertson, Fitzgerald, Stevens, & Bartels, 1996), sexual orientation (D. A. Jones, 1998; Simonsen, Blazina, & Watkins, 2000; Szymanski & Ikizler, 2013), and cross-cultural samples of men (Choi et al., 2010; Hayashi, 1999; Jo, 2000; Kang, 2001; Tate, 1998; Theodore & Lloyd, 2000; Wolfram et al., 2009). Depression was significantly associated with the four GRC patterns in groups of White, African American, Hispanic, and gay men as well as in men from Great Britain, Korea, Japan, Germany, and Australia.

Moderation and mediation effects have been found with depression and other social psychological factors. Mexican American men's higher levels of machismo and RE both predicted higher depression and White men's self-silencing moderated the relationship between GRC and depression (Fragoso & Kashubeck, 2000; S. G. Newman, 1997). A complex mediation effect was found with depression for gay men and Korean high school students. Gay men reporting RABBM and heterosexist discrimination were more likely to experience heterosexism that leads to depression (Szymanski & Ikizler, 2013). For Korean high school students, SPC, RE, and RABBM predicts low self-esteem, and this mediated higher levels of depression (Choi et al., 2010). These moderating and mediating studies provide evidence that men's restrictive gender roles relate to their depression in complex ways. Greater depression occurs with men who restrict their feelings, restrict their affections toward other men, have restrictive attitudes toward SPC, and struggle with work and family conflicts. The results of GRC and depression studies of samples of diverse men, in various countries, and numerous situational contexts help destroy the illusion that depression is a women's issue and that it has little to do with masculinity ideology.

How and why depression relates to GRC and masculinity issues remain unknown. Does male depression occur when men are unable to demonstrate their masculinity, or does it occur when negative affect is internalized because of RE? The situations and interactions that cause men's depression are important topics to pursue in the future. The diversity trends noted in the depression studies suggest that male depression transcends cultural differences, but more research is needed.

Anxiety and Stress

Discrepancy strain has been hypothesized to exist when men do not meet the demands of masculine ideologies (Pleck, 1981, 1995), causing anxiety and stress in their lives. How men's gender roles relate to stress has been conceptualized with the masculine gender role stress paradigm and the GRC paradigm (Eisler, 1995; Eisler, Skidmore, & Ward, 1987; O'Neil, 2008c; O'Neil et al., 1995).

The research I reviewed indicates that more than 90% of the 32 studies on stress and anxiety were significantly correlated with GRC (see Table 7.1). Furthermore, stress has been significantly correlated with all the patterns of GRC in nine studies. Anxiety and GRC have been correlated in four countries outside of the United States, that is, Korea, Japan, Germany, and Australia (Hayashi, 1999; Jo, 2000, Kang, 2001; Theodore & Lloyd, 2000; Wolfram et al., 2009); across race and sexual orientations (Blashill & Hughes, 2009; D. A. Jones, 1998; Leka, 1998; Liang, Salcedo, & Miller, 2011; Szymanski & Carr, 2008; S. C. Walker, 2008; Wester, Kuo, & Vogel, 2006); and with special populations of college and doctoral students, cancer patients, Chinese Canadians students, and German schoolteachers (Hoyt, 2009; Sbaratta, 2011; Wester, Christianson, Vogel, & Wei, 2007; Wester, Kuo, & Vogel, 2006; Wolfram et al., 2009).

Complexity exists in determining how anxiety and stress are related to GRC. In a study of gay men, Blashill and Hughes (2009) found that higher levels of femininity and RE predicted higher levels of distress; as RE increased, so did the levels of distress. A study of Mexican American men revealed that higher levels of machismo predicted higher levels of stress (Fragoso & Kashubeck, 2000). Wester et al. (2007) found that RABBM and social support moderated college students' level of distress. GRC has been found to correlate with specific kinds of stress, including physical and psychological strain (Stillson, 1988), global levels of psychological stress (Hetzel, 1998), competition/comparison strain, physical inadequacy, and performance failure (Davenport, Hetzel, & Brooks, 1998).

Numerous studies have found that anxiety and stress related to GRC are mediated by third variables. Two studies indicated that gay men's stress is mediated by GRC and other variables. GRC predicted lower self-esteem that in turn related to avoidant coping that produced higher levels of stress (Szymanski & Carr, 2008). Blashill and Hughes (2009) found that femininity and GRC were correlated, and a significant Femininity × GRC interaction was found, suggesting that feminine gay men with high GRC are at increased risk for general stress. A similar interactive pattern was found for Chinese Canadian students in that SPC, RE, and RABBM were mediated by avoidant and exaggerated coping that contributed to psychological stress (Wester, Kuo, & Vogel, 2006). With African Americans, internalized racism (self-hatred) partially mediated the relationship between GRC and psychological distress (Wester, Vogel, Wei, & McLain, 2006), and in another study social support mediated RE in terms of psychological distress (Wester et al., 2007). Finally, Hoyt (2009) found that cancer victims' GRC was related to low emotional expression that caused greater distress.

Two studies yielded insignificant findings between GRC and stress. Good et al. (2004) found that GRC was not associated with psychological stress and that GRC and problem-solving attitudes did not mediate psychological stress. Olsen (2000) failed to find that anxiety and GRC interacted with anger.

The studies just reviewed support Eisler's (1995) hypothesis that men's gender roles are stressful but more moderating and mediating studies are needed to determine how, when, and why men experience anxiety related to GRC. The factors that moderate and mediate relationships between GRC and anxiety deserve greater attention by researchers. For example, five of the studies discussed above indicated that either RE or RABBM was moderated or mediated by third variables, suggesting that emotional and affectionate restrictions interact with stress and anxiety. The specific situations and interactions that link GRC to stress in harmful way for boys and men remain unknown.

Psychological Well-Being/Satisfaction With Life

GRC has been defined as the opposite of psychological well-being, with restrictive gender roles resulting in devaluations, restrictions, and violations of the man and others (O'Neil, 1990, 2008c; O'Neil et al., 1995). The relationship between GRC and psychological well-being has been assessed in four studies. Sharpe and Heppner (1991) found that college students' RE, RABBM, and CBWFR were correlated with poor psychological well-being, but with adult men this relationship existed only for RE (Sharpe, Heppner, & Dixon, 1995). K. Jones (2010) studied gay Black men's well-being and found that low GRC predicted positive mental health, positive homosexual identity, multiculturalism, and resilience. Tokar, Fischer, and Schaub (1998) found that men who reported greater psychological well-being were less likely to report concerns with RE and CBWFR.

These four studies provide initial evidence that GRC and poor psychological well-being are related. What is missing in the research are the personal qualities and experiences that promote healthy, positive masculinity

(Kiselica, 2011; Kiselica & Englar-Carlson, 2010). In addition, research that documents how psychosocial development and family experiences help men overcome sexism and restrictive gender roles can help move the focus away from what is wrong with men to how men can generate positive growth that improve their lives and society.

Low Self-Esteem

Poor psychological well-being usually implies low self-esteem. *Self-esteem* is a positive impression of oneself that includes self-respect and positive self-regard. Many men are reluctant to talk about their lack of self-esteem because this disclosure could threaten their power base in close relationships and at work. The private feeling of not liking oneself is often isolating and experienced as loneliness and self-objectification, which have also been found to significantly correlate with GRC (Blazina, Settle, & Eddins, 2008; Schwartz, Grammas, Sutherland, Siffert, & Bush-King, 2010). One of the negative outcomes of GRC is low self-esteem and gender role strain (O'Neil, 1981a; Pleck, 1995), and 20 studies found that GRC is correlated with self-esteem (see Table 7.1). Eighteen of the 20 studies (90%) showed a negative relationship between GRC and positive self-esteem. All of the GRC patterns have been found to be significantly related to low self-regard. Furthermore, positive self-esteem has been negatively correlated with GRC across seven diverse groups, including White American students, Japanese, Koreans, African Americans, Mexican American men, Asian Americans, and gay men. This finding suggests that the relationship between GRC and poor self-esteem has cross-cultural and ethnic/racial importance.

Complexity exists in regard to self-esteem in terms of how other variables moderate or mediate GRC and self-esteem. Abusive men with low self-esteem who do express emotions (low RE) report greater use of intimidation and threats (Schwartz & Waldo, 2003), and SPC, RE, and RABBM have been shown to correlate with low self-esteem that affects higher levels of depression (Choi et al., 2010). In a study of gay men, Szymanski and Carr (2008) found that GRC was directly and indirectly correlated with poor self-esteem and that low self-esteem and internalized heterosexism expressed through avoidant coping increased psychological distress. Shek and McEwen (2012) found that Asian American men with low RE and high clarity about their involvement in their racial identity had higher self-esteem. Hobza and Rochlen (2009) studied body esteem, self-esteem, and drive for muscularity and found no moderating or mediating effects among these potentially related concepts.

The overall results provide strong evidence for a significant relationship between men's GRC and low self-esteem. Future research should investigate more complex questions about how third variables affect men's self-esteem.

Furthermore, whether GRC causes men's lower self-esteem or whether lower self-esteem causes GRC deserves future study, as do the situational conditions that activate both dynamics. The finding that GRC correlates with self-esteem across diverse groups is important, but what needs to be assessed more fully is how gender role devaluations, restrictions, and violations are part of these cultural differences (see Chapters 3 and 9).

Shame and Guilt

Personal devaluation, fragmentation of the self, and sometimes personality disorganization define *shame*, a powerful emotion that was not theoretically linked to GRC in the early conception of the theory (O'Neil, 1981a, 1981b, 1982). Shame has emerged as an important part of understanding men's problems and personal development (Krugman, 1995; Schenk & Everingham, 1995). Shame is related to men's GRC because negative feelings can occur when a man fails to meet the masculine norms or when meeting them hurts other people. Seven studies have assessed GRC's relationship to shame or guilt (see Table 7.1). In these studies, all the patterns of GRC significantly correlated with shame, with RE and CBWFR being the most strongly correlated. Thomas (2008) examined the relationship between interpersonal guilt and GRC and found four kinds of guilt that correlated with GRC: (a) SPC, RE, and CBWFR predicted *survivor guilt*; (b) SPC, RE, and RABBM predicted *self-hate guilt*; (c) SPC, RE, and RABBM predicted *separation guilt*; and (d) SPC, RE, RABBM, and CBWFR predicted *omnipotent guilt*. Regression analyses revealed that guilt was more predictive of GRC than depression and that shame-proneness mediated the relation between GRC and depression (Thomas, 2008). These collective results support Krugman's (1995) theoretical proposition that guilt is a significant variable in men's lives and therefore an important clinical area on which to focus when working with men. The antecedent contexts of feeling shame and guilt related to GRC need to be explored in relation to suicide, self-destruction, addiction, and violence toward others.

Discrimination: Internalized Homophobia, Homonegativity, Heterosexist Discrimination, and Perceived Racism

The relationship among GRC, discrimination, and internalized oppression is one of the main premises of this book. The research reported in this section directly relates to the models presented in Chapters 3 and 6 on how GRC interacts with discrimination and oppression. Only one study has assessed how perceived racism is related to GRC. Liang et al. (2011) found in a study of Latino men that perceived racism in different settings (job, academic, public, and general settings) correlated with CBWFR and that total GRCS scores were correlated with perceived racism in the job setting. Six studies found that GRC is correlated with discrimination defined as internalized homonegativity, internalized homophobia, heterosexist discrimination, and negative feelings about being gay (see Table 7.1). In five studies, complex relationships were found between GRC and other variables. For example, M. A. Robinson and Brewster (2014) found that both GRC and internalized heterosexism moderated the relationships between perceived parenting efficacy and motivation for parenthood for gay and bisexual men. Szymanski and Ikizler (2013) found that sexual minority men who had RABBM and thought that heterosexist discrimination exists were more likely to have internalized heterosexism that may lead to depression. Szymanski and Carr (2008) found that GRC relates to self-esteem both directly and indirectly, through internalized heterosexism, and that self-esteem relates to psychological stress directly and indirectly, through coping. Sánchez, Westefeld, Liu, and Vilain (2010) found that RABBM and CBWFR were correlated with negative feelings about being gay, and Bryce (2012) found that RE and RABBM were correlated with homonegativity, relationship dissatisfaction, and outness (of being gay).

These studies provide ample evidence that GRC is related to discrimination and internalized states of oppression (see Chapter 6 for more on this topic). The results are important because they provide initial evidence that GRC is related to harmful attitudes toward members of racial and sexual minority groups. Furthermore, as I discuss in Chapters 3 and 8, how internalized oppression is caused and experienced in gender-related situations requires more contextual research.

Self-Destructiveness, Hopelessness, and Suicide

More extreme aspects of GRC have been studied in terms of self-destructiveness, hopelessness, and suicide. RE has significantly predicted men's chronic self-destructiveness (Naranjo, 2001) and hopelessness (Birthistle, 1999; Brewer, 1998), suggesting that unexpressed emotion may have severe negative outcomes for vulnerable men. Suicide probability has been found to be correlated with GRC (Borthick, 1997; Borthick, Knox, Taylor, & Dietrich, 1997); suicidal men have reported significantly more GRC than nonsuicidal men (Houle, Mishara, & Chagnon, 2008); and the effects of GRC on suicidal behavior have been found to be mediated by mental state, help-seeking behaviors, and social support (Houle et al., 2008). These few studies suggest that GRC is related to feelings of desperation in men, and therefore more research is definitely needed in this area, given that male suicide is epidemic and preventable. Vulnerable and at-risk men with GRC are a critical group to study, and qualitative research may be the first step toward understanding GRC's relationship to men's suicide and other self-destructive behaviors.

Alcohol and Substance Abuse

In the past several years, there has been a significant increase in studies assessing how GRC relates to alcohol and substance use and abuse. Substances may temper gender role expectations, help manage conflict from restricted gender roles (Capraro, 2000), and be used to prove one is "one of the boys." Eleven studies have assessed the relationship between men's GRC and substance use and abuse (see Table 7.1). Four studies found no relationship between GRC and alcohol use/abuse, but 7 other studies identified significant relationships between GRC and use/abuse of substances. Using an Australian sample, Monk and Ricciardelli (2003) found that higher RE was associated with greater alcohol and cannabis use. Furthermore, in a study of college students, alcohol-related consequences were partially mediated by GRC but not by drinking motives (Groeschel, Wester, & Sedivy, 2010). Using path analysis, Uy, Massoth, and Gottdiener (2013) found that GRCS total score significantly predicted drinking to cope, number of drinks consumed in one sitting, and drinking problems. They also found that GRC had a mediating effect on drinking-to-cope motives in the context of traditional masculinity ideology and alcohol consumption.

The overall results of these studies indicate that problems with increased alcohol use or substance abuse are significantly related to SPC, RE, and RABBM. In the past, there has been speculation about how drinking and masculinity related to each other (Capraro, 2000), but research is providing emerging evidence that GRC and substance use and abuse are correlated. These results could be useful to substance abuse counselors and professionals who conduct alcohol and substance abuse programming.

Coping and Problem Solving

Problematic coping has been considered in ten studies, and RE, RABBM, and SPC were found to be significantly related with negative coping methods (see Table 7.1), but exactly how this occurs is unclear from the research. Two studies found that dysfunctional coping mediated GRC and other factors (Szymanski & Carr, 2008; Wester, Kuo, & Vogel, 2006). In the first study, GRC and internalized heterosexism predicted low self-esteem and were mediated by avoidant coping that resulted in psychological stress (Szymanski & Carr, 2008). In the second study, avoidant and exaggerated coping mediated SPC, RE, and RABBM and psychological distress (Wester, Kuo, & Vogel, 2006).

How GRC relates to problem-solving attitudes (Heppner, Witty, & Dixon, 2004) has been assessed in three studies (Chamberlin, 1993; Good et al., 2004; Varvel, 2008). In all three studies, RE was significantly related to problem-solving attitudes characterized by approach–avoidance and low problem-solving confidence. Two studies assessed GRC and the mediating effects of other variables on problem-solving attitudes (Good et al., 2004; Varvel, 2008). Good et al. (2004) failed to find any mediation effect among GRC, problem-solving appraisal, and psychological distress. Firefighters' GRC was found to be a partial mediator between problem solving and psychological stress and lower psychological functioning (Varvel, 2008).

Collectively, these studies indicate that GRC relates to men's poor coping and problem solving, but more studies are needed on each topic. Knowing which men cope and do problem solving, and how psychosocial experiences foster these important life skills, could guide more effective psychoeducational programming for boys and men across the life cycle (see Chapter 12, this volume).

Body Image and Muscularity

Nine studies found that GRC significantly relates to body image and the drive for muscularity for both college-age and older men (see Table 7.1). Body dissatisfaction and GRC have been found to be significantly correlated for men between the ages of 50 and 70 years (Murray & Lewis, 2014). Younger men had higher levels of muscle and height dissatisfaction, but body fat dissatisfaction was experienced similarly for both young and old, and age moderated the relationship between GRC and muscle body dissatisfaction but not with height dissatisfaction (Murray & Lewis, 2014).

Numerous studies have assessed the moderating and mediating effects of other variables with GRC and body image/muscularity issues. McCreary, Saucier, and Courtenay (2005) found that as SPC and CBWFR increased, so did the drive for muscularity, and in a second study self-assertive entitlement mediated the relationship between RE and CBWFR and body esteem (Schwartz & Tylka, 2008). In another study, GRC did not predict muscularity, but high RE did predict pressure to have low body fat, and low RABBM predicted a lack of concern about this issue (Schwartz et al., 2010). Blashill and Vander Wal (2009) found in a study of gay men that all GRC patterns predicted body satisfaction and that social sensitivity solely mediated the relationships between GRC and body dissatisfaction. Mejias (2010) studied Latino men and found that increased GRC significantly correlated with desire for muscularity. Shepherd and Rickard (2012) found that GRC mediates the relationship between the drive for muscularity and intentions to seek help and, finally, Hobza and Rochlen (2009) found no moderation or mediation effects for body esteem, self-esteem, and drive for muscularity.

Body image and muscularity have emerged as a significant area of research in the psychology of men, but still little conceptualization exists on why and how muscularity and masculinity are related to overall emotional and physical health. More definitive concepts on this topic are warranted.

Personality

The 12 studies on personality found that GRC significantly relates to personality styles and types, models of personality, ego identity, and authoritarianism (see Table 7.1). GRC has been found to be significantly correlated with the five-factor model of personality in five studies (Fischer, 2007; Kratzner, 2003; Serna, 2004; Sipes, 2005; Tokar, Fischer, Schaub, & Moradi, 2000), and two other studies found that low ego identity significantly relates to higher GRC and lower intimacy (Arnold & Chartier, 1984; Chartier & Arnold, 1985). The personality styles of Neuroticism, Introversion, Extraversion, Openness, Agreeableness, aggressiveness, narcissism, and dependency have been found to be correlated with GRC (Cortese, 2003; Kratzner, 2003; Schwartz, Waldo, & Higgins, 2004). Little is known about how GRC relates to positive and negative aspects of men's personality; integrative principles are needed so that personality can be studied in the context of GRC. Studies of men of different races, sexual orientations, ethnicities, and nationalities could deepen our understanding of how GRC and personality relate to each other.

Religion and Spirituality

Nine studies have examined GRC's relationship to religion and spirituality (see Table 7.1). Less GRC has been found with men who have a more internal/spiritually focused religious orientation (Jurkovic & Walker, 2006; Mahalik & Lagan, 2001; Reiman, 1999). Lammy (2011) found that Christian college students' religious grandiosity and instability correlated with RABBM and GRC total score. Heard (2009) found that low existential well-being (an aspect of religiosity) was significantly correlated with RABBM, and Baima (2012) studied male veterans and found that their spiritual well-being was correlated with GRC. In one of the only studies from the Middle East, conducted with Egyptian students, Islamic religiosity was found to be correlated with GRC but did not moderate help seeking (Jana-Massri, 2011). Lily (1999) found that traditional African American religious acculturation moderated GRC and indexes of psychological functioning. Furthermore, Laurent (1997) found that African American men who did not attend church or have religion in their life had higher GRC. In a qualitative study, Jun (2009) studied how 15 Korean men's GRC affected their spirituality and identity. A majority of the men indicated that GRC affected their views of religion, spirituality, and power. Wilkinson (2004) found that Christian orthodoxy did not correlate with any of the GRC factors. These studies provide an initial foundation for the continued study of how GRC affects spiritual development and religious processes. Few theoretical analyses have linked GRC with religious experiences even though RE, power, and control are all obvious impediments to full spiritual identity and development. Later in this chapter, I discuss how religion and spirituality are an area of priority for future research.

Alexithymia

Alexithymia—the inability to describe one's feelings in words (Levant, 1995)—has been related to men's GRC, but the theoretical relationship has been vague and unclear (Levant et al., 2006). As expected, research has found that GRC and alexithymia are significantly related to RE; six studies found such results (see Table 7.1). Fischer and Good (1997) found that RE predicted unique variance in alexithymia and that RABBM predicted unique variance with difficulty in identifying and describing feelings. McGill (2011) studied African American men and observed that as all GRC factors increased so did problems with both identifying and expressing emotions. Also, he noted that RE was associated with identifying emotions rather than expressing them. All four of the patterns of GRC significantly correlated with alexithymia in one of the first published Japanese studies, which used a modified version of GRCS (Hayashi, 1999). Overall, the collective studies indicate that GRC relates to alexithymia, but exactly how it interacts with masculinity ideology and negative male behavior has not been tested and deserves further study.

Summary of Research on Gender Role Conflict in the Intrapersonal Context

The internal experience of GRC is significantly correlated with numerous psychological problems for men as identified in the research reviewed, which has moved us beyond the mere psychodynamic explanations of men's problems described decades ago (Adler, 1936; Boehm, 1930; Freud, 1937; Horney, 1932). Depression, anxiety, low self-esteem, stress, and other psychological experiences are related to GRC and can negatively affect men's lives. Depression and low self-esteem are correlated with GRC across diverse racial, sexual orientation, and cross-cultural samples, suggesting some universality with this finding. Whether there are differences across these groups on depression and self-esteem and what factors cause these differences need further exploration. No research has yet assessed whether there might be other contextual factors that may differentially affect GRC in these different groups of men. How contextual factors such as racial/ethnic identity, age, sexual orientation, and the situational demands of being a man affect GRC is unknown. A critical question is whether GRC causes depression and self-esteem or whether these problems cause GRC. Furthermore, except for the 29 studies of mediation I reviewed in Chapter 6, how GRC affects third variables is mainly unknown. Mediation studies that move beyond correlational designs can begin to answer more complex questions about what variables cause GRC in the context of loss, marital conflict, failure, health problems, sexual dysfunction, violence, and homophobia. More complex research focused on interacting variables of GRC could help in the preparation of effective preventive interventions for boys and men (see Chapters 12 and 13).

Summary of Major Findings on Men's Gender Role Conflict in the Interpersonal Context

In the new conceptual models described in Chapters 3, 6, and 9, men's GRC has been hypothesized to negatively affect others at an interpersonal level. Other authors have discussed how GRC contributes to interpersonal problems such as poor parenting, marital conflicts, homophobia, antigay attitudes, racism, sexual harassment, and violence toward women (Betz & Fitzgerald, 1993; J. A. Hayes & Mahalik, 2000; Pleck, 1995; Wade & Rochlen, 2013). The research I describe in this section summarizes the negative outcomes of men's GRC in an interpersonal context in six separate areas: (a) overall interpersonal functioning; (b) attachment, bonding, and family individuation; (c) men's intimacy, self-disclosure, and relationships with fathers; (d) marital satisfaction, family dynamics, and couples' GRC; (e) stereotyping, attitudes toward women, egalitarianism, homophobia, and racial bias; and (f) men's interpersonal and sexual violence toward women.

Overall Interpersonal Functioning

Mahalik (2000) assessed restriction of men's interpersonal behavior because of GRC; he found that SPC significantly predicted rigid and dominant interpersonal behavior and that RE and RABBM were correlated with hostile and rigid interpersonal exchanges. Other interpersonal functions have been assessed and RE has been found to be significantly associated with problems with sociability and intimacy (Sharpe et al., 1995), a lack of interpersonal competence/closeness, and less intimate self-disclosure (Bruch, Berko, & Haase, 1998). Shyness and emotional inexpressiveness been found to be significantly correlated with RE and RABBM (Bruch, 2002; Bruch et al., 1998; Davenport et al., 1998). In an examination of complex relationships, Bruch et al. (1998) found that RE both mediated the effects of shyness in terms of interpersonal competence and served as a mediator of intimate self-disclosure. GRCS total score predicted avoidance of close relationships, suppression of emotional regulation, negative parental and maternal bonding, and negative mood regulation, and four other studies found that men's GRC relates to women's depression, anxiety, and marital satisfaction (Breiding, 2004; Breiding, Windle, & Smith, 2008; Celentana, 2000; Land, Rochlen, & Vaugh, 2011; Rochlen & Mahalik, 2004).

These studies imply that GRC relates to deficits and problems that affect men's interpersonal functioning. The specific contexts of the restrictions in interpersonal behavior and what causes the inhibited emotional and relational dynamics based on masculinity ideology and GRC are missing from the research. The studies that have shown that men's GRC relates to women's negative emotional states supply initial evidence that GRC has negative consequences for others.

Attachment, Bonding, and Family Individuation

Attachment, bonding, and family individuation are not fully conceptualized in the psychology of men, but the relationships between boys' attachment problems and GRC have been hypothesized using concepts such as disidentification with the mother, the fragile masculine self, and a traumatic abrogation of the early holding pattern (Blazina, 2001; Blazina & Watkins, 2000; Pollack, 1995). Researchers have argued that early parent–son dynamics affect male bonding in ways that can contribute to problems with attachment, separation, individualization, disidentification, and conflictual independence (Blazina & Watkins, 2000; DeFranc & Mahalik, 2002; Fischer & Good, 1998; Schwartz, Waldo, & Higgins, 2004).

Attachment to parents and GRC has been investigated in 14 studies (see Table 7.1). All the patterns of men's GRC have significantly correlated with attachment problems to both mothers and fathers. Six studies have used either canonical correlations or structural equation modeling to assess GRC's relationship to attachment (Blazina & Watkins, 2000; DeFranc & Mahalik, 2002; Fischer, 2007; Fischer & Good, 1998; Napolitano, Mahalik, & Kenny, 1999; Selby, 1999). Complex and significant findings have been found between GRC and measures of attachment, separation, and individuation problems (Blazina & Watkins, 2000); affective attachment (Siffert, 2012); attachment quality (Fischer, 2007); attachment styles (Blazina, Novotny, Stevens, & Hunter, 2008; Cachia, 2001; Schwartz, Waldo, & Higgins, 2004; Selby, 1999); perceptions of father's GRC (DeFranc &

Mahalik, 2002); conflicts with mothers (Fischer & Good, 1998); and identity development (Napolitano et al., 1999). For example, in a study of college men, Blazina and Watkins (2000) found that as GRC increases, so did problems of attachment, separation, and individuation in regard to parents. In another study, higher levels of SPC, RE, and RABBM were significantly related to fearful and avoidant attachment styles, and increases in GRC predicted higher attachment avoidance scores (Cachia, 2001). Siffert (2012) found that autonomy from parents and affective attachment were correlated negatively with RE, RABBM, and CBWFR. He also studied self–object dimensions and found that that maladaptive self–object orientation was associated with the GRC patterns. Land et al. (2011) found that the GRCS total score negatively predicted maternal bonding care and parental bonding and that GRC did not mediate the relationship between maternal bonding care and adult attachment avoidance. In a study of African American men, all GRC patterns were related to unhealthy attachment styles (Blazina, Novotny, et al., 2008). Finally, Griffin (2011) found a nonsignificant mediational effect of GRC on the relationship between attachment insecurity and sexual compulsivity.

The initial studies on attachment suggest that GRC is related in complex ways to bonding and separation from parents. More research is needed to unravel how early parent–child bonding affects gender role development and GRC. In Chapter 5, I provided more theories on how psychosocial issues affect development tasks and psychosocial crises that could be useful to both future researchers and therapists. The overall results of the studies just described support the call for greater attention to the developmental and familial aspects of attachment and gender roles in the context of GRC.

Men's Intimacy, Self-Disclosure, and Relationships With Fathers

Intimacy and self-disclosure are two areas where men struggle because of their gender role socialization. GRC has been hypothesized to restrict men's intimacy, self-disclosure, and male friendships. In 12 studies, both college-age and adult men's GRC was negatively related to intimacy (see Table 7.1). GRC and self-disclosure have been assessed in three studies, with higher levels of GRC significantly predicting lower self-disclosure (Bruch, Berko, & Haase, 1998) and lower RE and CBWFR significantly predicting greater self-disclosure (Swenson, 1998). Odes (2008) observed that self-disclosure in close same-sex male friendships was a partial mediator of including close relationships in one's self-concept. In a study of Indonesian men, RABBM was found to be significantly correlated with unexpressive behavior (Horhoruw, 1991), and Sileo (1996) found that RE, RABBM, and

SPC were significantly related to American men's lack of intimacy and male friendship.

Men's perceptions of their fathers and GRC also have been studied. Men who perceive their fathers and themselves to have less GRC report closer attachments to and less psychological separation from both parents (DeFranc & Mahalik, 2002). Another study found that drug-dependent men who had a restricted definition of fathering had higher RE (McMahon, Winkel, & Luthar, 2000). Other studies have found no significant or mixed results when studying GRC's relationship to father mutuality (Marrocco, 2001), sex offenders' father–son relationships (Gullickson, 1993; Todryk, 1999), and attachment to parents (Covell, 1998; Swenson, 1998). The results of these initial studies indicate that GRC significantly relates to men's lack of intimacy, self-disclosure, and connection with other men. The research on GRC and fathers is less clear, and the topic deserves further investigation. For example, whether a father's GRC causes a son's GRC could help explain the intergenerational transmission of masculinity conflicts.

Marital Satisfaction, Family Dynamics, and Couples' Gender Role Conflict

GRC's relationship to marital satisfaction and family life has been assessed in six studies (Alexander, 1997; Brewer, 1998; Campbell & Snow 1992; Leka, 1998; Scott, 2001; Sharpe et al., 1995). Four studies found that each of the GRC patterns negatively correlates with marital satisfaction (Alexander, 1997; Brewer, 1998; Campbell & Snow, 1992; Sharpe et al., 1995). Furthermore, three studies found that RE negatively relates to dyadic adjustment and that SPC significantly relates to low relationship satisfaction (Breiding, 2004; Brewer, 1998; Campbell & Snow, 1992). Two studies assessed racial/ethnic minority men's martial satisfaction and family issues. African American men who experience RE, RABBM, and CBWFR report significantly less marital satisfaction and cohesion in their relationships (Brewer, 1998), and Mexican American men who emphasize the family report significantly more CBWFR and SPC (Leka, 1998). Pierce (2012) found that total GRC score predicted less support in romantic relationships and that men with higher GRC were more likely to provide low support to others.

Family dynamics also have been assessed in the context of men's GRC. Alexander (1997) found that RE was significantly related to parenting dissatisfaction and a lack of parenting self-efficacy. He also found that when men's RE increased, fathering self-efficacy and fathering satisfaction decreased. Furthermore, college men's RE, RABBM, and CBWFR have been significantly correlated with family conflict, avoidance, and enmeshment/disengagement as well as decreased cohesion with both parents (Scott, 2001). M. A. Robinson and Brewster (2014) studied gay men's views about parenting and found that both GRC and internalized heterosexism moderated the relationship between positive parenting efficacy and motivation for parenthood. The results of these studies indicate that men's GRC significantly relates to family dynamics, but exactly how this occurs requires future research.

In the past decade, researchers have examined how men's GRC relates to couple dynamics and psychological functioning (Breiding, 2004; Breiding et al., 2008; Celentana, 2000; Rochlen & Mahalik, 2004; Windle & Smith, 2009). SPC, RE, RABBM, and total GRCS score have significantly related to decreased marital adjustment, lower daily marital happiness, greater depressive symptomatology, and greater negative affect for both men and women (Breiding, 2004; Breiding et al., 2008; Celentana, 2000). Two studies have assessed how women's perception of men's GRC relates to the women's relationship satisfaction and psychological health (Breiding et al., 2008; Rochlen & Mahalik, 2004). Wives' assessments of husbands' GRC are significantly correlated with wives' decreased marital adjustment and happiness, increased depressive symptomatology, and negative affect (Breiding, 2004). Furthermore, women's reports of their partners' high RE and SPC significantly predict less relationship satisfaction, greater depression, and anxiety (Rochlen & Mahalik, 2004). In addition, women's reports of partners' lower RABBM predict women's greater depression and anxiety. One interpretation of this finding is that when men indicate no conflict with showing affection toward other men, this may raise women's concerns about the man's sexual orientation and manifest as greater anxiety and depression.

Two studies assessed how GRC actually affects couple's interactions and dynamics. Husbands' GRC has been significantly related to increased levels of reported spousal criticism (Breiding et al., 2008). Furthermore, in this same study, husbands' criticism mediated the relationship between husbands' GRC and wives' marital adjustment and depressive symptoms. Also, self-criticism and wives' criticism mediated relationships between their GRC and wives' depressive symptoms. Windle and Smith (2009) found that RE and RABBM were significantly related to husbands' marital communications and withdrawal and that, furthermore, the husband's withdrawal moderated the association between GRC and marital adjustment during a communication process. In another study, husbands with high GRC engaged in hostile behaviors during marital interactions and, more important, husbands' hostility mediated the relationship between husbands' GRC and wives' marital adjustment (Breiding, 2004).

These studies indicate that men's GRC affects couple dynamics negatively, adversely affects women's psychological functioning, and relates to men's hostility during marital interactions. Future research with couples could explore how GRC relates to other marital problems, such as emotional abuse and the high rates of violence against women (Harway & O'Neil, 1999; O'Neil & Nadeau, 1999). Moreover, the situational antecedents and causes of couple's conflict, as well as other indexes of martial satisfaction and family interaction patterns, should be studied further.

Stereotyping, Attitudes Toward Women, Egalitarianism, Homophobia, and Racial Bias

Researchers have assessed relationships between GRC and men's attitudes toward women, egalitarianism, homophobia, and racial bias. One or more patterns of GRC have significantly correlated with men's traditional attitudes toward women (Blazina &Watkins, 2000; Jacobs, 1996; R. Mintz & Mahalik, 1996; D. T. Robinson & Schwartz, 2004; Wood, 2004), sex role stereotyping (Rando, Rogers, & Brittan-Powell, 1998), and stereotypic beliefs about men's emotions (Heesacker et al., 1999). Three studies found that low sex role egalitarianism relates to significantly higher GRC for both college and high school students (Addelston, 1995; Englar-Carlson & Vandiver, 2002; Tokar et al., 2000). Overall, these studies indicate that stereotypic thinking about women correlates with men's GRC. Although the evidence is indirect, the research does imply that GRC relates to potential inequality toward women and attitudes that are restrictive of women's rights and roles.

Research is developing on how GRC relates to biases toward racial/ ethnic groups, including gay/lesbian/bisexual/transgendered persons and other oppressed groups. In one study, White males' RABBM and SPC were found to be significantly correlated with negative attitudes toward African Americans (D. T. Robinson & Schwartz, 2004). Six studies found that SPC, RE, and RABBM were significantly related to homophobic and antigay attitudes (Kassing, Beesley, & Frey, 2005; Lindley & Schwartz, 2006; McDermott, Schwartz, Lindley, & Proietti, 2014; Schwartz, Tylka, & Hood, 2005; D. F. Walker, Tokar, & Fischer, 2000; Wilkinson, 2004).

Overall, these studies suggest that men's GRC significantly relates to stereotypic and negative thinking about women, sexual minorities, non-heterosexuals, and African Americans. They indicate that gender-conflicted men's homophobic and antigay attitudes are related to the devaluation of sexual minorities. These results, combined with research on sexual minorities who report both discrimination and GRC (see Chapter 6), provide initial evidence that GRC expressed toward others exists in the context of homophobic and antigay attitudes.

Men's Interpersonal and Sexual Violence Toward Women and Others

Betz and Fitzgerald (1993) reviewed men's issues in their overview of diversity in the field of counseling psychology. They identified male violence against women as a missing variable in men's studies research:

> In reviewing this work, however, we are struck by the absence of any serious discussion of what could arguably be considered the most problematic aspect of the male role: the socialization of male violence. Conspicuous by its absence is any sustained attempt to analyze and intervene in what can only be considered one of the most serious social problems of our age—male violence against women. (p. 361)

Twenty years later, there is some evidence that scholars in the field of the psychology of men have been responding to Betz and Fitzgerald's (1993) critique (Brooks & Silverstein, 1995; Harway & O'Neil, 1999; Mendoza & Cummings, 2001; O'Neil & Egan, 1993; O'Neil & Nadeau, 1999). Twenty-five studies have assessed how GRC relates to men's negative or violent attitudes toward women and others (see Table 7.1); specifically, GRC has been significantly correlated with sexually aggressive behaviors and the likelihood of forcing sex, abusive behaviors, coercion, threats and intimidation, dating violence hostile sexism, hostility toward women, rape myth acceptance, positive attitudes toward and tolerance of sexual harassment, and self-reported violence and aggression. M. S. Hill and Fischer (2001) conducted a mediation study and found that masculine gender role components (including SPC, RABBM, and CBWFR) significantly predicted a sense of general male entitlement, which in turn predicted sexual entitlement, which finally predicted rape-related criterion variables. Their results indicated that general and sexual entitlement completely or partially mediated the links between masculinity and rape-related variables. Covell (1998) found that age, GRC, and sexist attitudes mediated likelihood of sexual harassment. Finally, some studies have shown that high versus low levels of RE and RABBM significantly differentiate coercive from noncoercive men (Senn, Desmarais, Verberg, & Wood, 2000), sexually aggressive college men from sexually non-aggressive college men (Rando et al., 1998), and domestic abusers from nonviolent men (Walls & Walker, 2002). Schwartz and Waldo (2003) found that abusive men who have low self-esteem and low RE reported higher use of intimidation and threat.

Research on prisoners and homeless men also provide evidence that violence and GRC are related (Amato, 2012; Amato & MacDonald, 2011). Older homeless men who report violence and using drugs have greater GRC than other homeless men (Amato & MacDonald, 2011). Younger prisoners who report high GRC and who are not affiliated with religion and conform to traditional gender roles report higher levels of violence (Amato, 2012). Younger prisoners with a family history of crime not affiliated with religions score higher on GRC and report greater levels of violence in their lives (Amato, 2012).

The empirical results of studies linking GRC to men's violation of women are sobering. Collectively, they imply that GRC is significantly related to thoughts, attitudes, and behaviors that are abusive and violent toward women and others. These studies provide some initial data supporting the conceptual models illustrated in Figures 3.1 and 6.1 that link GRC to violence toward others. Greater efforts are needed to better understand the situational cues (i.e., triggers) of men's violence toward women, children, and other men. These results may be useful to professionals who are creating violence prevention programs and treating abusive and violent men.

Summary of Research on Men's Gender Role Conflict in an Interpersonal Context

The overall results of the extant research indicate that GRC is significantly related to dysfunctional patterns in men's relationships, including interpersonal restrictions, attachment problems, and marital dissatisfaction. Furthermore, couples' dynamics, family interaction patterns, and problems with intimacy and self-disclosure have all been significantly related to GRC. A consistent pattern of significant findings suggests that GRC is related to negative interpersonal problems for men and others. Moreover, research indicates that GRC is related to restrictive and negative attitudes toward women, gays, and, in one study, members of racial/ethnic minority groups. Even more striking and disturbing is that GRC has been significantly correlated with positive attitudes toward sexual harassment, rape myths, hostile sexism, and self-reported sexual and dating violence toward women. The results suggest that GRC significantly relates to dysfunctional and dangerous interpersonal outcomes for men and others. The research supports what feminists have communicated for years about how restrictive gender roles are potential mental health issues for both men and women.

At present, few studies exist that explain why GRC occurs and how it operates in both male and female relationships. No studies have yet assessed how men's GRC affects other men. Exactly how and what kinds of male and female interactions activate GRC are unknown. Documentation of the interpersonal triggers of men's GRC needs to be pursued in future contextual research. For example, the existing research does not explain how conforming to or deviating from masculine norms produces GRC in relationships. Future studies should examine how the cognitive and emotional restrictions of GRC result in men's behavioral conflicts with others. Many studies indicate that GRC is significantly related to attitudes that are dysfunctional, but only a few studies have found that GRC is correlated with actual negative, destructive, or violent behavior toward others (Amato, 2012; Breiding, 2004; Breiding et al., 2008; C. L. Johnston, 2005; Kaplan, O'Neil, & Owen, 1993). Behavioral outcome studies need to establish that GRC results in negative outcomes for men, women, and children. More quantitative research is needed in this area, but well-designed qualitative research may also uncover the complexity of the interpersonal dynamics of GRC.

MAJOR FINDINGS: GENDER ROLE CONFLICT IN A THERAPEUTIC CONTEXT

Recommendations for conducting therapy with men have discussed the fragile masculine self (Blazina, 2001), deepening (Rabinowitz & Cochran, 2002; Robertson, 2006), men's cognitive distortions (Mahalik, 1999a), masculinity scripts (Mahalik, Good, & Englar-Carlson, 2003), the stages and process of change (Brooks, 2010), men's depression (Cochran & Rabinowitz, 2000), authoritarian men (Robertson, 2012), clinical practice with men (Rochlen & Hoyer, 2005), men's emotional behavior (Wong & Rochlen, 2005), men's psychotherapy (Englar-Carlson, 2006; Mahalik, 1999b; Rabinowitz & Cochran, 2002), women as therapists of men (Sweet, 2012), case studies of men's therapies (Englar-Carlson & Stevens, 2006), and training counselors who work with men (Wester & Vogel, 2002). These publications identify GRC as a relevant therapeutic construct when doing therapy with men. However, even though the authors cite research to support their recommendations, a limited amount of research on men's therapy actually exists. Moreover, how to effectively help men in therapy has not been studied for very long, nor has it been a research priority. In the sections that follow, I review the research on GRC in a therapeutic context in the following categories: (a) clients' and therapists' GRC; (b) help-seeking attitudes and preferences for help; (c) stigma and GRC; (d) career development; (e) psychoeducational interventions; (f) training of therapists, supervisors, and supervisees; and (g) GRC and college student development.

Clients' and Therapists' Gender Role Conflict

Only eight clinical studies have assessed whether clients' GRC relates to psychological problems (see Table 7.1). Two studies found that male counseling center clients' GRC significantly related to psychological distress, including problems with hostility, compulsiveness, social discomfort, paranoia, psychoticism, obsessive–compulsivity, and interpersonal sensitivity (Good et al., 1996; J. A. Hayes & Mahalik, 2000). Four other studies found that clients experience more RE and RABBM than nonclients (Burke, 2000;

Coonerty-Femiano, Katzman, Femiano, Gemar, & Toner, 2001; Mertens, 2000; Van Delft, 1998). Clients' RE has been found to be inversely related to perceptions of treatment helpfulness but not to help-seeking intentions or the therapeutic bond (Cusack, Deane, Wilson, & Ciarrochi, 2006). In one study, clients who had experienced sex abuse reported significantly greater RE and CBWFR than nonabused clients (P. Thomson, 1995). In another study, sex abuse victims reported that their abuse traumas were significantly related to SPC, RE, RABBM, and total GRCS score (Coonerty-Femiano et al., 2001). In one of the only process-and-outcome studies, Noyes (2004) found that GRC did not significantly relate to dropping out of therapy or predict rates of improvement in therapy. The existing research on client's GRC comes primarily from college counseling center clients and suggests that GRC is significantly related to mental health problems.

Therapists' GRC and their clinical judgments of male clients were assessed in two studies (M. M. Hayes, 1985; Wisch & Mahalik, 1999). Therapists with high RABBM reported significantly less liking of male clients, less empathy toward nontraditional male clients, and identified more maladjustment in non-traditional male clients (M. M. Hayes, 1985). Therapists reporting SPC and RABBM had significantly less liking for, empathy with, and comfort with male clients and were less willing to see clients who were homosexual and those who were angry but not sad (Wisch & Mahalik, 1999). Furthermore, therapists with significantly less RABBM were more comfortable seeing a homosexual client and reported better prognosis for such clients in therapy. In both of these studies, RABBM related to therapists' feelings and thoughts about clients who were nontraditional or homosexual. This suggests that training may be necessary to help some therapists resolve their RABBM and biases about men who deviate from masculinity ideology.

GRC's relationship to men's defenses, treatment fearfulness, perceptions of counselors, expectations about counseling, and therapy supervision (Englar-Carlson, 2001; Schaub & Williams, 2007; Wester, Vogel, & Archer, 2004; Wisch et al., 1995) has also been assessed. A study that examined GRC's relationship to men's psychological defenses found that SPC, RE, and RABBM were significantly related to immature and neurotic defenses (projection, denial, and isolation) and that men who reported SPC and RE reported defenses that are turned against others (Mahalik, Cournoyer, DeFranc, Cherry, & Napolitano, 1998). GRC has also significantly predicted treatment fearfulness (Englar-Carlson, 2001), and men with higher GRC have rated counselors as significantly less expert and trustworthy (Wisch et al., 1995). GRC has also been found to significantly relate to men's expectations about counseling. Men who reported RE, RABBM, and SPC had significantly higher expectations that counselors would be an expert therapist and lower expectations of taking responsibility during the counseling process (Schaub & Williams, 2007).

Jin (2012) found that the degree of GRC did not affect men's willingness to see either a male or female therapist but men with high GRC were less willing to enter into therapy with a male therapist when the message was related to distress than men with low GRC, regardless of the kind of therapist or type of outreach message. In one of the only studies of supervisory relationships and GRC, male supervisees who reported high RE reported significantly lower self-efficacy as counselors than supervisees with low RE (Wester et al., 2004). Wester, McDonough, White, Vogel, and Taylor (2010) used GRC theory to present a therapeutic approach to working with transgendered clients and their unique problems and potentials. The studies reviewed provide preliminary information on clients' and therapists' GRC and should be expanded to include more process-and-outcome research on men's therapy.

Help-Seeking Attitudes and Preferences for Help

The relationship between help seeking and men's GRC was first conceptualized by Glenn Good in the late 1980s. Since his landmark dissertation (Good, Dell, & Mintz, 1989), research on help seeking and GRC has become an important knowledge area for therapists. Addis and Mahalik's (2003) *American Psychologist* article brought men's help seeking to the attention of mainstream psychology. Thirty-one studies (see Table 7.1) have assessed how men's help-seeking attitudes relate to GRC, and all but one study (Mendoza & Cummings, 2001) found the patterns of GRC to be significantly related to negative attitudes toward seeking psychological help. A significant relationship between GRC and help-seeking attitudes has been found across diverse groups of men, including adult men (Cortese, 2003), Taiwanese men (Tsai, 2000), Japanese men (Chan & Hayashi, 2010), Costa Rican men (Lane & Addis, 2005), Canadian men (James, 2005), Australian men (Bevan, 2010; Dolling, 2008), Egyptian men (Jana-Massri, 2011); gay men (Simonsen et al., 2000), African American men (White, 2002), Mexican American and Latino men (Cox, 2009; J. M. Davis & Liang, 2014), veterans (Larma, 2006), men with serious injuries (Good et al., 2006), high school football players (Steinfeldt & Steinfeldt, 2010), male victims of partner abuse (Tsui, 2010), and White male college students (Blazina & Marks, 2001; Blazina & Watkins, 1996; Bursley, 1996; J. M. Davis & Liang, 2014; Good & Wood, 1995; Good et al., 1989; Goodwin, 2008; Groeschel et al., 2010; Lane & Addis, 2005; Osborne, 2004; T. E. Rogers, 2009; Segalla, 1996; Shepherd, 2009; Tsan, Day, Schwartz, & Kimbrel, 2011; Vogel, Wester, Hammer, & Downing-Matibag, 2014). These results suggest that GRC and negative attitudes about help seeking are related to men across different ages, nationalities, races, sexual orientations, and special health circumstances. The stigma of seeking help because of masculinity conflicts appears to be a universal problem for the samples that have been assessed.

Three studies indicated that GRC is correlated with specific barriers to seeking help, with SPC, RE, CBWFR and the total GRCS score all showing significance (Shepherd, 2009; Tsui, 2010). Moreover, research on special populations indicates that help seeking is contextual and situation specific. For example, African American men who support multicultural inclusiveness and low RE have more positive views of help seeking (White, 2002). In regard to high school football players, boys who had higher levels of RE and were younger had more negative views of help seeking (Steinfeldt & Steinfeldt, 2010).

Some of the help-seeking studies have assessed complex relationships between GRC and other variables. Vogel et al. (2014) found that men with RE were less likely to refer friends and family to seek mental health treatment and that RABBM was also linked to less willingness to refer someone to seek treatment, through the mediated effect of stigma. J. M. Davis and Liang (2014) found that Latino men's RE partially mediated the association between machismo ideology and attitudes toward help seeking: As more positive attitudes toward seeking help increased, their concerns with RABBM decreased. In the only study of an Egyptian sample, Jana-Massri (2011) found that Islamic religion was not a moderator of GRC and help seeking but that religiosity was significantly correlated with GRC. T. E. Rogers (2009) found that stigma correlated with GRC, and the more GRC men experienced the less likely they were to perceive other important people in their lives as supportive of their intentions to seek psychological help. Goodwin (2008) found that college students' RE correlated with negative attitudes toward help seeking and an avoidance orientation pattern of help seeking. They concluded that RE negatively affects academic and psychological help-seeking attitudes.

These studies have established that GRC is related to attitudes that prohibit men from seeking help with their problems. What remains unknown is how to change these attitudes. Examining exactly how men think and feel about help seeking in the context of their masculinity could elucidate what messages need to be communicated to clients and others who need help but are too embarrassed to seek it.

Stigma and Gender Role Conflict

Stigma is the experience of disgrace whereby a person is set apart and categorized as a member of a stereotyped group and thus vulnerable; stigma involves ridicule, prejudice, and discrimination. How stigma and GRC relate to men's help-seeking or other behaviors has recently been studied by numerous researchers. Studies have focused on college students (T. E. Rogers, 2009; Vogel et al., 2014), football players (Steinfeldt & Steinfeldt, 2010), Korean students (Park & Seok Seo, 2009), and police officers (Wester, Arndt, Sedivy,

& Arndt, 2010). In all these studies, stigma was significantly correlated with GRC. Researchers have found multiple factors that moderate or mediate GRC. Shepherd (2009) found that GRC partially mediated the relationship between the drive for muscularity and the self-stigma of seeking help. Park and Seok Seo (2009) found that Korean students' GRC had a negative effect on attitudes toward counseling when mediated by social stigma and self-stigma. Wester, Arndt, et al. (2010) studied police officers and found that both self-stigma and public stigma were correlated with all factors of the GRCS but that anticipated risks and benefits did not mediate the relationships between GRC and stigma. Men's stigma is likely part of self-gender role devaluation and restrictions (see Chapters 3 and 9, this volume), and the early research suggests that these problems are related to men's issues with negative attitudes toward help seeking. Future research should investigate exactly how stigma develops and how it can be remediated so that men freely seek the help that they need.

Career Development

One of the least researched areas is how GRC relates to men's career attitudes and behaviors. The lack of research is ironic because men's work has been defined as primary to male identity and self-worth. Four studies assessed how GRC relates to men's career attitudes and needs (Dodson & Borders, 2006; Jome & Tokar, 1998; Rochlen, Blazina, & Raghunathan, 2002; Rochlen & O'Brien, 2002). Two of these indicated that men with GRC report greater career counseling stigma; decreased willingness to engage in career counseling; and greater needs for self-clarity, career information, and assistance with career indecisiveness (Rochlen et al., 2002; Rochlen & O'Brien, 2002). In addition, GRC appears to be more evident with men in traditional male careers and to predict career choice traditionality (Jome & Tokar, 1998; Tokar & Jome, 1998).

Wolfram et al. (2009) found that German teachers' GRC was correlated with work dissatisfaction and that those higher levels of GRC were related to emotional irritation, anxiety, and depression. German students were assessed about their views of career counseling. Students with high RE feared having a women counselor, their RE and SPC correlated with feeling inferior to a female counselor, and their RABBM and SPC were significantly related to preference for cognitively focused career counseling (Eimer & Kidd, 2010). Graef, Tokar, and Kaut (2010) found that college men's RABBM and RE were correlated with stigma about career counseling and that RE uniquely predicted stigma toward career counseling. Using a mixed sample of male and female police officers, Faircloth (2011) found that SPC predicted job dissatisfaction for males, RE predicted dissatisfaction for females, and CBWFR predicted job dissatisfaction for both sexes but that the women had more CBWFR than the men. Finally, unemployed men's GRC significantly correlated with depression (Friedman, 2011). The lack of research on GRC and men's careers makes it a primary area for theorists and researchers to pursue in the future.

Psychoeducational Interventions

Whether psychoeducational interventions can change socialized GRC related to emotions, control, and success is an important therapeutic question. Eleven studies have used the GRCS to evaluate interventions related to parenting, rape prevention, spouse abuse, sexual harassment, and dating violence with diverse groups of men who were divorced, alcoholic, or undergraduate students. Five studies have used the GRCS to assess change from a structured program. Australian fathers enrolled in a parenting program reported no difference in GRC immediately after the program, but SPC was significantly lower 8 weeks later (McAnulty, 1996). T. L. Davis and Liddell (2002) evaluated a socialization-focused rape prevention program and found that men with lower GRC reported a significantly greater comprehension of consent and more liberal attitudes toward women. The effects of a sexual harassment tolerance training program indicated that college men who had lower SPC reported a greater reduction of harassment tolerance (Kearney, King, & Rochlen, 2004). A 4-week group intervention to prevent dating violence demonstrated that RE can be significantly decreased and healthy entitlement can be increased (Schwartz, Magee, Griffin, & Dupuis, 2004).

Three studies assessed GRC and men's preferences for seeking help using counseling brochures (Blazina & Marks, 2001; Robertson & Fitzgerald, 1992; Rochlen, McKelley, & Pituch, 2006). Robertson and Fitzgerald (1992) found that men who reported high GRC were significantly more likely to prefer a nontraditional counseling brochure (i.e., describing workshops or classes) over a direct-service counseling brochure. This implies that men with high GRC are more comfortable with services outside of therapy. Rochlen et al. (2006) found that men with low GRC rated "Real Men. Real Depression" brochures as more appealing and effective than men in two other conditions. Men have also been tested using three different treatment brochures describing individual therapy, a psychoeducational workshop, and a support group (Blazina & Marks, 2001). Men who reported high GRC had negative reactions to all three treatment formats and power dynamics were significantly related to men's treatment preferences and negative help-seeking attitudes.

Can a specific treatment change GRC? Studies have yielded some positive and mixed results. A 10-week GRC resolution intervention for Mexican American spouse abusers was tested, and RABBM and RE were significantly decreased for the treatment compared with the control group (Schwartz & Waldo, 2003). Gertner (1994) assessed the impact of a one-semester men's studies course and found a significant decrease in RE for the treatment versus control groups. Maton, Anderson, Burke, Hoover, and Mankowski (1998) assessed the Mankind Project and found significant decreases in the participants' SPC, RABBM, and RE 1 month later. Evaluation research has also found that college men can learn about GRC and recognize the merits of seeking assistance to resolve it (Braverman, O'Neil, & Owen, 1992). Three studies found no significant effects in changing the GRC of college men (Brooks-Harris, Heesacker, & Mejia-Millan, 1996), divorced men (Nahon, 1992), and alcoholics (Moore, 1993).

One area in which the psychology of men lacks needed empirical research is evidence-based studies on programs that help men. The studies reviewed above are a start, but more theoretically based, empirically driven research is needed if programming for boys and men is to become a major area of service (see Chapters 12 and 13).

Training of Therapists, Supervisors, and Supervisees

A number of studies have assessed GRC in therapists, supervisors, and supervisees. Wester et al. (2004) found that interns with high RE reported a turn-against-self style and that greater RE was correlated with lower level of self-efficacy. Second, male supervisees working with male supervisors reported a poorer level of a working alliance than those who worked with a female supervisor. Spillman (2007) studied empathy with male counselors in training and found no relationship between GRC and the capacity to empathize Sbaratta (2011) studied male doctoral students and found that distress and multicultural awareness significantly correlated with RE and CBWFR and that they reported less overall GRC than men in general but more CBWFR. Holohan (2008) studied Irish therapists and found that they experienced less GRC than the overall population and that no relationship existed between GRC and therapeutic orientation, age, or academic level. Murphy (2001) studied male and female therapists and found that their GRC was lower than a normative group of nontherapists. Finally, Murtagh (2012) compared 20 experienced counselors with 20 inexperienced counselors and found that the experienced counselors reported less GRC than inexperienced counselors. The results of these initial studies of therapists and their supervisees suggest that GRC is a relevant concept that deserves further study and conceptualization.

Gender Role Conflict and College Student Development

Two recently published books have made masculinity issues more mainstream in college student development (Harper & Harris, 2010; Laker & Davis, 2011). Only five studies have addressed GRC and college student development (T. L. Davis, 2002; Goodwin, 2008; Paciej, 2010; Sosoka, 2001; Syzdek, Beatty, Kellom, & Farr, 2005). Goodwin (2008) found that RE negatively affected college students' academic and psychological help seeking, and Paciej (2010) found that RE significantly correlated with emotional barriers to affect the college experience. Sosoka (2001) found that RE and RABBM were higher for underclassmen compared to graduating seniors and that SPC was significantly higher for graduating seniors compared to first-year students. Syzdek et al. (2005) found that RE, SPC, CBWFR, and GRCS total score were different for individual students compared to how they perceived their peers' GRC. In general, men view male peers as more stereotypically masculine and as having more GRC than themselves. Only these few GRC studies have been conceptualized using college student development theory; therefore, in Chapter 12, I make a theoretical justification for this kind of research and issue a call to action for more campus programming for college men (O'Neil & Crapser, 2011).

SUMMARY OF GENDER ROLE CONFLICT IN A THERAPEUTIC CONTEXT

How GRC relates to therapeutic processes is just now emerging as a critical area of research. An important finding is that GRC significantly relates to male clients' psychological distress, but scholars have not assessed whether the problems are related to GRC and, if they are, how. Furthermore, no research exists on how to treat GRC in therapy; therefore, evidence-based interventions are needed. There is some early evidence that GRC relates to men's treatment fearfulness, help-seeking attitudes, psychological defenses, and perceptions of counselors. Two studies suggested possible clinical biases of therapists who have GRC (M. M. Hayes, 1985; Wisch & Mahalik, 1999), and another study suggested that supervisees' GRC affects their self-efficacy (Wester et al., 2004). Assessment of clients', therapists', and supervisees' GRC should be a fertile area for future clinical research. The significant relationships between attitudes toward help seeking, stigma, and GRC are critical for therapists to recognize given the consistent findings across the diversity areas of race, age, sexual orientation, and nationality. GRC's significant relationship with negative help-seeking attitudes makes conceptual sense because expressing feelings and vulnerabilities and giving up some power and control can be experienced as violations of a man's masculinity ideology and threaten his male identity. Therapists can use the help-seeking findings to facilitate men's adjustment in therapy and to be more vigilant to premature terminations of therapy. Furthermore, therapists can increase their skills of treating GRC by reading Mahalik's scholarly papers on GRC and men's depression (Mahalik & Cournoyer, 2000), cognitive distortions (Mahalik, 1999a), and interpersonal psychotherapy with men (Mahalik, 1999b). Case studies of men in therapy (Blazina, 2004; Englar-Carlson & Stevens, 2006; Mahalik, 1999a; O'Neil, 2006), and four important books (Brooks, 2010; Rabinowitz & Cochran, 2002; Robertson, 2012; Sweet, 2012) provide clinically important information for therapists. In Chapter 9, I propose a diagnostic schema for assessing men's GRC in therapy for practitioners to consider. Additionally, I offer my own approaches to men's therapy in Chapter 10 and in Chapter 11 I describe a case study of GRC with one of my current clients based on gender role journey therapy.

OTHER STUDIES ON GENDER ROLE
CONFLICT AND VARIED TOPICS

Other studies on a variety of topics do not fit neatly into the intrapersonal, interpersonal, and therapeutic categories I have just discussed. For example, there have been studies on gay fathers (Kosmopoulos, 2008) and stay-at-home fathers (Columbo, 2008). Other studies have included an intergenerational analysis of GRC (Heath & Thomas, 2006) and a 25-year, cross-temporal meta-analysis of GRC over the past three decades (McGinness, 2011). Women's athletic identity distress tolerance has been studied (Daltry, 2009), and energy drinks and jock identity have been assessed in the context of GRC (Wimer & Levant, 2013), and the moral atmosphere in sports as it relates to GRC has been examined (Steinfeldt, Steinfeldt, England, & Speight, 2009). All of these studies provide valuable new information on GRC and expand our knowledge base in diverse directions.

HOW WELL DOES THE EMPIRICAL RESEARCH SUPPORT
GENDER ROLE CONFLICT THEORY?

Thirty years ago, my main assertion was: "Men are also oppressed and restricted by rigid gender role socialization that limits their potential to be fully functioning and whole human beings" (O'Neil 1981b, p. 205). Over the past three decades, the GRC research program has provided evidence that men's psychological problems do relate to restrictive gender roles. A man's restricted thoughts, feelings, and behaviors about masculine gender roles predict serious psychological and interpersonal problems. This has never before been empirically documented.

Overall, the extant research provides support for parts of the GRC model developed in the early 1980s. The hypothesis that men experience GRC in major domains of life was supported in three of five areas of men's lives. The research indicates that GRC significantly relates to men's psychological problems, is experienced in an interpersonal context, and has relevance for men's home and family lives. Little research has assessed how GRC relates to men's career development and work behaviors, and thus far no research has tested how men's GRC relates to physical health.

The psychological domains of GRC (cognitive, affective, behavioral, and unconscious) have received mixed empirical support. Good support exists relating GRC to men's cognitive and affective processes. The affective aspects of GRC are evident from significant correlations with men's reports of anxiety, depression, homonegativity, negative identity, anger, and low self-esteem. The cognitive aspects of GRC are evident through significant correlations with traditional attitudes toward women, stereotyping, antigay attitudes, homophobia, and low sex role egalitarianism. In the behavioral domain, significant correlations exist between GRC and hostile behavior, spousal criticism, sexually aggressive behaviors, and health risk behaviors. The unconscious domain of GRC has gone unexplored. In addition, the situational contexts of GRC have been supported by research indicating that GRC is related to intrapersonal processes (within the man) and in an interpersonal context in families and couple relationships (Alexander, 1997; Breiding, 2004; Breiding et al., 2008; Rochlen & Mahalik, 2004; Scott, 2001). There is also positive evidence for men's personal experiences of GRC (gender role devaluations, restrictions, and violations). Men's GRC relates to gender role restrictions through depression, alexithymia, problems with intimacy and self-disclosure, and negative attitudes toward help seeking. Self-devaluations are evident in that GRC relates to low self-esteem, homonegativity, depression, and shame. The research also indicates that GRC relates to men's potential to restrict, devalue, or violate others. These restrictions, devaluations, and violations of others are apparent from GRC's relationship to positive attitudes toward sexual harassment, homophobia, antigay attitudes, sexual coercion, hostility toward women, rape myths, and violence against women.

In Chapter 5, I discussed GRC in the context of the gender role strain paradigm, specifically, Pleck's (1981, 1995) concept of gender role dysfunction strain. The data on the four patterns of GRC provide rather substantial support for Pleck's concept. GRC significantly relates to areas of dysfunction that have negative consequences for men and others. SPC, RE, RABBM, and CBWFR have been significantly related to psychologically dysfunctional symptoms of depression, anxiety, anger, alexithymia, low self-esteem, stress, shame, marital dissatisfaction, homonegativity, homophobia, and negative attitudes and behaviors toward women.

Three discernible diversity trends are evident in the research reviewed here: (a) depression and GRC significantly correlate for men across racial, sexual orientation, and cross-cultural samples; (b) negative help-seeking attitudes significantly correlate with GRC for diverse groups of men, including White college students, adult men, older gay men, African American men, and Taiwanese men; and (c) self-esteem negatively correlates with GRC for men across different races and nationalities. GRC appears to be relevant to men outside the United States in many different countries (see Chapter 6, this volume, for summaries of international studies). In nearly every international study, a GRC pattern was related to a significant issue in men's lives. These international findings are tentative, but the results do suggest that GRC transcends the American culture.

Overall, the empirical research provides support for the GRC constructs developed more than 30 years ago. There is now considerable empirical research indicating that men's psychological problems relate to conflict with their socialized gender roles. The positive research findings support new directions for future research and result in more elaborate GRC theory and research paradigms; they also support new contextual domains, hypotheses, and research paradigms.

RESEARCH OF PRIORITY FOR THE FUTURE

Future researchers should give priority to several areas within the psychology of men. Specifically, more studies are needed on men's spirituality, religious experience, and GRC; men and forgiveness; masculinity and preventing men's violence; and the psychology of boys.

Men's Spirituality, Religious Experience, and Gender Role Conflict

One of the most understudied topics in the psychology of men is spirituality and men's religious experience. The spiritual aspects of men's lives are important because they function as portals (Rabinowitz & Cochran, 2002; Robertson, 2006) to men's inner lives and help them discern their life's purpose. Furthermore, spirituality and religion can be sources of strength during difficult times when gender role identity is developing or changing. Over 80% of people in the United States have a belief in a transcendent power (i.e., God; Newport, 2011), and gender role attitudes are very relevant to the quality of people's religious experience. Exactly how gender roles interact with spiritual development and religious practice is what needs to be explored in the future.

The critical question is how GRC affects spiritual development, specifically, how SPC and RE limit men from deepening their relationship with God. Religious experiences are usually emotional, and therefore how RE inhibits men from using their deeper feelings about their spiritual selves is a critical question. If, by definition, religious experience implies giving up some power and control, how does SPC interfere with the process of turning oneself over to the higher power? If spirituality is about embracing one's human vulnerability, how does this ownership conflict with men's view of themselves as self-reliant, all powerful, and invincible, all parts of restrictive masculinity ideology? How do masculine and negative attitudes toward help seeking, self-reliance, and masculine individualism keep men from developing spiritual resources with others?

Much of religious experience relies on being able to believe in what cannot be seen and to have flexible thought patterns that may not always correspond to what is deemed to be rational deductive thinking. How can a cognitively rigid man who can process his life only rationally engage the divergent thought and feelings needed to deepen his spiritual life? If religious experience means prayer, an active relationship between a person and God, how does a man who has restricted relational skills develop this process? How does RE limit men's ability to pray or process feelings toward the higher power? Finally, how does GRC limit fathers' ability to teach their sons and daughters about religious and spiritual issues? These questions could be pursued in future research and expand our knowledge of how men's GRC affects men's spirituality and religious experiences.

Men and Forgiveness

Forgiveness is a process that helps people release their anger, resentment, and negative emotions toward those who have hurt them. Forgiveness is a universal human concept that has existed throughout the centuries in nearly all world religions (Rye et al., 2000). Forgiveness, although known as a religious construct, is also a complex psychological process on both the emotional and cognitive levels. Most theorists believe that forgiveness is a process of giving up anger, resentment, negative judgment, and attachment to the hurt. Furthermore, forgiveness can allow for greater empathy and compassion for the offender, perceptual shifts, and greater contextual understanding of the offense. All of this requires the person to take responsibility for his or her feelings; reframe the injury; and change the grievance story, releasing the pain, anger, hurt, and need for revenge. Those who forgive move away from blaming, accept that the injustice has happened, and move on to strategies to relieve the hurt. They come to the same conclusion as Mahatma Gandhi that "the weak can never forgive. Forgiveness is the attribute of the strong" (http://thinkexist. com/quotation/the_weak_can_never_forgive-forgiveness_is_the/215848.html).

How GRC negatively affects men's capacity to forgive is an important question for future researchers. GRC issues such as RE, control, power, and rigid thinking about strength and self-reliance all could affect the degree to which men consider and complete the forgiveness process.

Masculinity and Preventing Men's Violence

Perhaps the most critical question in the psychology of men is what causes men's violence against women, children, and other men (Harway & O'Neil, 1999; O'Neil & Nadeau, 1999). Physical violence is everyone's fear in today's society, and men are the primary victimizers. Many discussions of men's violence become derailed by anger, blame, defensiveness, and outright helplessness given the enormity and severity of the problem. Psychologists need to lead the way past these understandable but unfortunate arguments with research and preventive programs. One way to do this is to generate masculinity hypotheses about men's violence (O'Neil & Nadeau, 1999). For example, how, when, and why do masculinity ideology and GRC stimulate threat, intimidation, and violent retaliation by men? The research cited in this chapter indicates that masculinity ideology and GRC and stress are significantly correlated with negative and angry attitudes toward others, coercive and abusive behavior and violence, and aggression. Future research needs to document why and how violence is related to GRC. Furthermore, more study of how oppressive and discrimination against men stimulates violence toward others is needed. How men's emotional and psychological processes contribute to violence deserves a separate call to action in our violence-prone society.

Promoting the Psychology of Boys

The psychology of boys has been slow to develop as a specialty in the psychology of men. The publication of specific books on boys (Horne & Kiselica, 1999; Pollack, 1998b) and media debates about the "boys' crises" (Hoff Sommer, 2000; Tyre, 2006; Von Drehle, 2007) have now given the psychology of boys a central place in the psychology of men. There is a great need to accelerate efforts to assess GRC in boys and create prevention programs for boys and men in public schools and the community (O'Neil & Lujan, 2009b; see Chapter 13 for examples of evaluated programs). Curricula for boys need to be developed to promote their psychological development, and strategies to implement such programming into public schools need to be generated.

Many parents and educators are unaware of how sexism and restrictive gender roles negatively affect boys' lives, and there is denial about boys' problems that emanate from sexist stereotypes. The axiom "Boys will be boys" is frequently used to dismiss and thus ignore the significant problems of male youth. The assumption that boys will outgrow their problems is seriously flawed because it represents a superficial assessment of boys' lives and does not capture the deeper and unidentified sources of boys' GRC. Future research can help make the case that programs for boys are needed and that they are useful in solving problems that I described in Chapter 1.

Interventions and Research on Men's Health Issues

Courtenay's (2000b, 2000c, 2011) call to action for men's health issues is one of the most important areas for researchers and practitioners to pursue. Courtenay identified many health risk factors for men, including use of health and dental services and frequency of physical checkups; obesity, eating habits, diet, and sleep problems; stress, exercise, hypertension, and heart disease; sexual dysfunction and sexually transmitted diseases; self-examination for cancer, prostate cancer tests, and monitoring of cholesterol levels; alcohol/ drug/tobacco use, reckless risk taking, and sport injuries; and suicide, violence toward others, or being a victim of violence.

To pursue men's health issues, scholars in the field of the psychology of men must venture into an exploration of how the biological bases of behavior interact with psychological and gender-related factors for men. How masculinity ideology and GRC moderate and mediate men's physical problems deserves more expansive conceptualization (O'Neil, 2008c; Schopp et al., 2006). Courtenay's (2000a) health agenda for men includes more than 30 male behaviors that increase men's risk of disease, injury, and death. Teams of psychologists could work with teams of medical experts in developing research and prevention interventions that literally have life-and-death implications for men.

Promoting Positive Healthy Masculinity

The fields of the psychology of men and the GRC research program have focused primarily on men's problems instead of on men's potentials and possibilities. Another important direction for the field is to create research programs related to positive, healthy masculinity (Kiselica, 2011; Kiselica & Englar-Carlson, 2010). More elaborate conceptualizations of healthy and positive aspects of masculinity are needed (O'Neil, 2008c, 2012b; O'Neil & Lujan, 2009b). Patterns of positive masculinity can help men and boys learn alternatives to sexist attitudes and behaviors that cause GRC. Positive conceptualizations of healthy masculinity are needed now to help men aspire to what is noble and sacred in life. Positive masculinity is about changing the dialogue to emphasize the qualities that men can strive for that transcends their sexist socialization. Diagnostic schemas that assess men's positive and healthy masculine attitudes and behaviors are needed and should be tested empirically to determine whether they are helpful to men. This healthy masculinity schema would help men mobilize their potential with confidence and hope and change sexism against both sexes.

Men's strengths and potentialities could focus on themes such as responsibility, courage, altruism, resiliency, service, protection of others, social justice, positive fathering, perseverance, generativity, and nonviolent problem solving. Positive masculinity moves away from what is wrong with boys and men by identifying the qualities that empower males to improve themselves and society. Programs and research on healthy masculinity could change the common misperception that the psychology of men is about documenting what is "wrong" with boys and men.

8

FOUR CONTEXTUAL PARADIGMS FOR GENDER ROLE CONFLICT RESEARCH

Disinformation is most effective in a very narrow context.
—Frank Snepp

For me context is the key—From that comes the understanding of everything.
—Kenneth Noland

Most scholars of masculinity recognize that future research in the psychology of men needs be contextual and assess how situations and environmental contingencies affect behavior. How to organize this kind of research is challenging for a number of reasons. First, the psychology of men has few well-defined and empirically based concepts that help us understand contextual behavior and gendered social learning (Addis, Mansfield, & Syzdek, 2010). Second, there exist few measures that are specifically designed to capture the contextual aspect of gendered behavior, and therefore assessment relies on adaptation of current measures. Third, there have been few published summaries of what the critical contextual questions are in the psychology of men. I have argued that perhaps qualitative studies are needed to

Certain sections of this chapter are from "Summarizing Twenty-Five Years of Research on Men's Gender Role Conflict Using the Gender Role Conflict Scale: New Research Paradigms and Clinical Implications," by J. M. O'Neil, 2008, *The Counseling Psychologist*, 36, pp. 358–445. Copyright 2008 by Sage Publications. Adapted with permission.

http://dx.doi.org/10.1037/14501-009

answer how, when, and why men become gender conflicted and that this kind of research could expand the field (O'Neil, 2008c). Furthermore, contextual research many times needs to be in controlled environments or laboratories, and only a few scholars in the field of masculinity have done this kind of research. Finally, many of the past studies have not used behavioral measures that assess men's behavior in situational contexts.

In this chapter, I discuss future contextual research on gender role conflict (GRC) with these limitations in mind. In Chapter 3, I presented a full description of contextualism along with both a descriptive and functional model explaining contextual perspectives. Those models are directly relevant to the research paradigms discussed here. I discuss four research paradigms that can move the research closer to a more comprehensive contextual research paradigm: (a) GRC as a predictor and GRC moderators, (b) GRC as a predictor and GRC mediators, (c) situational contexts of GRC with GRC as mediators, and (d) situational contexts of GRC with GRC as outcomes (see Figures 8.1–8.4). According to the correlational research, GRC is significantly related to both intra- and interpersonal variables. One of the primary limitations of the past research has been the simplicity of the correlational studies. Complex relationships among independent, dependent, and intervening variables (moderators and mediators) have not been frequently tested. Only 23 studies have assessed how moderators affect GRC, and only 37 have examined the mediators of men's GRC. Currently, too little research exists on the moderators and mediators of men's GRC to develop a robust theory explaining how gender roles negatively affect men and others. Heppner (1995) stated the need for moderator and mediator studies when he indicated that "it would be most informative to examine more complex relationships between GRC and psychological maladjustment by investigating moderating and mediating relationships" (p. 20).

To assess moderators, mediators, and causal factors, the contextual dimensions of men's GRC need to be more fully developed. As I discussed in Chapters 3 and 7, men's GRC has been previously assessed in three contexts: (a) intrapersonal, (b) interpersonal, and (c) therapeutic. These contextual dimensions represent only a partial framework to help understand men's GRC; they need to be expanded to include more comprehensive domains. The critical contextual questions are how, when, and why does GRC occur? To answer these questions, moderator and mediator studies are needed. The contextual variables that moderate, mediate, and cause men's GRC need to be specified, and research questions need to be tested. In the next sections, I discuss seven contextual domains and 18 related research questions about men's GRC. These domains and questions provide a theoretical foundation for developing more complex moderation and mediation studies and studying men's behavior in situational contexts.

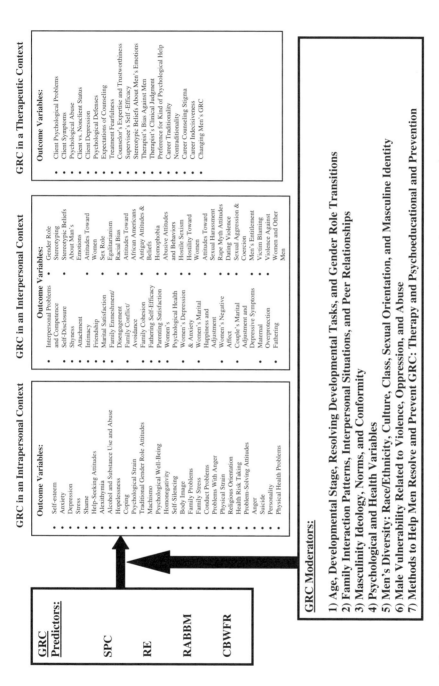

GRC Predictors:

SPC
RE
RABBM
CBWFR

GRC in an Intrapersonal Context

Outcome Variables:

- Self-esteem
- Anxiety
- Depression
- Stress
- Shame
- Help-Seeking Attitudes
- Alexithymia
- Alcohol and Substance Use and Abuse
- Hopelessness
- Coping
- Psychological Strain
- Traditional Gender Role Attitudes
- Machismo
- Psychological Well-Being
- Homonegativity
- Self-Silencing
- Body Image
- Family Problems
- Family Stress
- Conduct Problems
- Problems With Anger
- Physical Strain
- Religious Orientation
- Health Risk Taking
- Problem-Solving Attitudes
- Anger
- Suicide
- Personality
- Physical Health Problems

GRC in an Interpersonal Context

Outcome Variables:

- Interpersonal Problems and Competence
- Self-Disclosure
- Shyness
- Attachment
- Intimacy
- Friendship
- Marital Satisfaction
- Family Enmeshment/ Disengagement
- Family Conflict/ Avoidance
- Family Cohesion
- Fathering Self-Efficacy
- Parenting Satisfaction
- Women's Psychological Health
- Women's Depression & Anxiety
- Women's Marital Happiness and Adjustment
- Women's Negative Affect
- Couple's Marital Adjustment and Depressive Symptoms
- Maternal Overprotection
- Fathering

- Gender Role Stereotyping
- Stereotypic Beliefs About Man's Emotions
- Attitudes Toward Women
- Sex Role Egalitarianism
- Racial Bias
- Attitudes Toward African Americans
- Antigay Attitudes & Beliefs
- Homophobia
- Abusive Attitudes and Behaviors
- Hostile Sexism
- Hostility Toward Women
- Attitudes Toward Sexual Harassment
- Rape Myth Attitudes
- Dating Violence
- Sexual Aggression & Coercion
- Men's Entitlement
- Victim Blaming
- Violence Against Women and Other Men

GRC in a Therapeutic Context

Outcome Variables:

- Client Psychological Problems
- Client Symptoms
- Psychological Abuse
- Client vs. Nonclient Status
- Client Depression
- Expectations of Counseling
- Psychological Defenses
- Treatment Fearfulness
- Counselor's Expertise and Trustworthiness
- Supervisee's Self-Efficacy
- Stereotypic Beliefs About Men's Emotions
- Therapist's Bias Against Men
- Therapist's Clinical Judgment
- Preference for Kind of Psychological Help
- Career Traditionality
- Nontraditionality
- Career Counseling Stigma
- Career Indecisiveness
- Changing Men's GRC

GRC Moderators:

1) **Age, Developmental Stage, Resolving Developmental Tasks, and Gender Role Transitions**
2) **Family Interaction Patterns, Interpersonal Situations, and Peer Relationships**
3) **Masculinity Ideology, Norms, and Conformity**
4) **Psychological and Health Variables**
5) **Men's Diversity: Race/Ethnicity, Culture, Class, Sexual Orientation, and Masculine Identity**
6) **Male Vulnerability Related to Violence, Oppression, and Abuse**
7) **Methods to Help Men Resolve and Prevent GRC: Therapy and Psychoeducational and Prevention**

Figure 8.1. Gender role conflict (GRC) predictor variables, outcome variables in three contexts, and seven moderators. SPC = Success, Power, and Control; RE = Restrictive Emotionality; RABBM = Restrictive Affectionate Behavior Between Men; CBWFR = Conflict Between Work and Family Relations. From "Summarizing Twenty-Five Years of Research on Men's Gender Role Conflict Using the Gender Role Conflict Scale: New Research Paradigms and Clinical Implications," by J. M. O'Neil, 2008, *The Counseling Psychologist, 36*, p. 412. Copyright 2008 by Sage Publications. Adapted with permission.

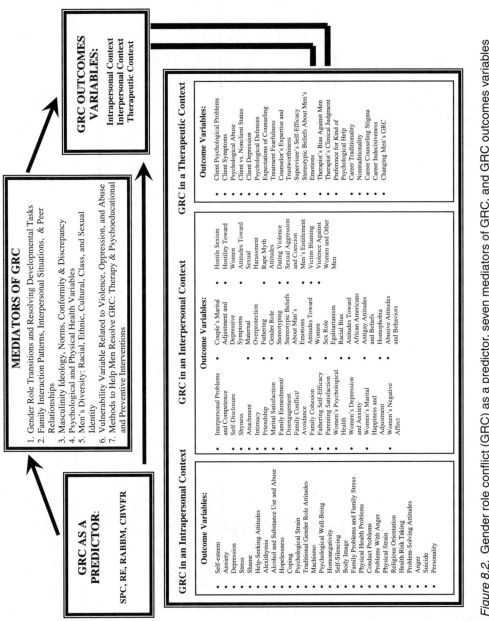

GRC AS A PREDICTOR:

SPC, RE, RABBM, CBWFR

MEDIATORS OF GRC

1. Gender Role Transitions and Resolving Developmental Tasks
2. Family Interaction Patterns, Interpersonal Situations, & Peer Relationships
3. Masculinity Ideology, Norms, Conformity & Discrepancy
4. Psychological and Physical Health Variables
5. Men's Diversity: Racial, Ethnic, Cultural, Class, and Sexual Identity
6. Vulnerability Variable Related to Violence, Oppression, and Abuse
7. Methods to Help Men Resolve GRC: Therapy & Psychoeducational and Preventive Interventions

GRC OUTCOMES VARIABLES:

Intrapersonal Context
Interpersonal Context
Therapeutic Context

GRC in an Intrapersonal Context

Outcome Variables:

- Self-esteem
- Anxiety
- Depression
- Stress
- Shame
- Help-Seeking Attitudes
- Alexithymia
- Alcohol and Substance Use and Abuse
- Hopelessness
- Coping
- Psychological Strain
- Traditional Gender Role Attitudes
- Machismo
- Homonegativity
- Psychological Well-Being
- Self-Silencing
- Body Image
- Family Problems and Family Stress
- Physical Health Problems
- Conduct Problems
- Problems With Anger
- Physical Strain
- Religious Orientation
- Health Risk Taking
- Problem-Solving Attitudes
- Anger
- Suicide
- Personality

GRC in an Interpersonal Context

Outcome Variables:

- Interpersonal Problems and Competence
- Self-Disclosure
- Shyness
- Attachment
- Intimacy
- Friendship
- Marital Satisfaction
- Family Enmeshment/ Disengagement
- Family Conflict/ Avoidance
- Family Cohesion
- Fathering Self-Efficacy
- Parenting Satisfaction
- Women's Psychological Health
- Women's Depression and Anxiety
- Women's Marital Happiness and Adjustment
- Women's Negative Affect

- Couple's Marital Adjustment and Depressive Symptoms
- Maternal Overprotection
- Fathering
- Gender Role Stereotyping
- Stereotypic Beliefs About Man's Emotions
- Attitudes Toward Women
- Sex Role Egalitarianism
- Racial Bias
- Attitudes Toward African Americans
- Antigay Attitudes and Beliefs
- Homophobia
- Abusive Attitudes and Behaviors

- Hostile Sexism
- Hostility Toward Women
- Attitudes Toward Sexual Harassment
- Rape Myth Attitudes
- Dating Violence
- Sexual Aggression and Coercion
- Men's Entitlement
- Victim Blaming
- Violence Against Women and Other Men

GRC in a Therapeutic Context

Outcome Variables:

- Client Psychological Problems
- Client Symptoms
- Psychological Abuse
- Client vs. Nonclient Status
- Client Depression
- Psychological Defenses
- Expectations of Counseling
- Treatment Fearfulness
- Counselor's Expertise and Trustworthiness
- Supervisee's Self-Efficacy
- Stereotypic Beliefs About Men's Emotions
- Therapist's Bias Against Men
- Therapist's Clinical Judgment
- Preference for Kind of Psychological Help
- Career Traditionality
- Nontraditionality
- Career Counseling Stigma
- Career Indecisiveness
- Changing Men's GRC

Figure 8.2. Gender role conflict (GRC) as a predictor, seven mediators of GRC, and GRC outcomes variables in three contexts. SPC = Success, Power, and Control; RE = Restrictive Emotionality; RABBM = Restrictive Affectionate Behavior Between Men; CBWFR = Conflict Between Work and Family Relations.

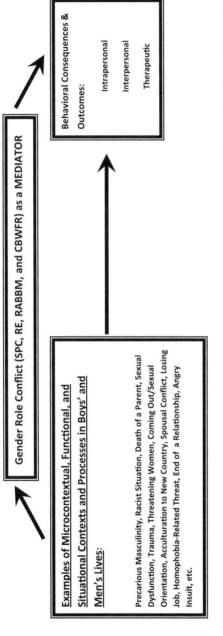

Figure 8.3. Microcontextual, functional, and situational contexts as predictors, mediated by gender role conflict and behavioral consequences in three contexts. SPC = Success, Power, and Control; RE = Restrictive Emotionality; RABBM = Restrictive Affectionate Behavior Between Men; CBWFR = Conflict Between Work and Family Relations.

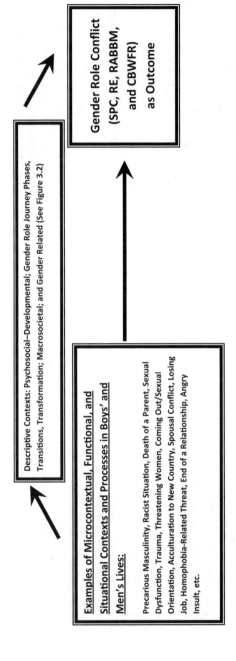

Descriptive Contexts: Psychosocial–Developmental; Gender Role Journey Phases, Transitions, Transformation; Macrosocietal; and Gender Related (See Figure 3.2)

Gender Role Conflict (SPC, RE, RABBM, and CBWFR) as Outcome

Examples of Microcontextual, Functional, and Situational Contexts and Processes in Boys' and Men's Lives:

Precarious Masculinity, Racist Situation, Death of a Parent, Sexual Dysfunction, Trauma, Threatening Women, Coming Out/Sexual Orientation, Acculturation to New Country, Spousal Conflict, Losing Job, Homophobia-Related Threat, End of a Relationship, Angry Insult, etc.

Figure 8.4. Microcontextual, functional, and situational contexts as predictors, mediated by descriptive contexts, and gender role conflict as an outcome. SPC = Success, Power, and Control; RE = Restrictive Emotionality; RABBM = Restrictive Affectionate Behavior Between Men; CBWFR = Conflict Between Work and Family Relations.

SEVEN CONTEXTUAL DOMAINS OF AND 17 RESEARCH QUESTIONS ON MEN'S GENDER ROLE CONFLICT

The seven contextual domains of men's GRC are based on the research I review in this book as well as earlier previous research and theory in the psychology of men. The domains are (a) age, developmental stage, resolving developmental tasks, and gender role transitions; (b) family interaction patterns, interpersonal situations, and peer relationships; (c) masculinity ideology, norms, and conformity; (d) psychological and physical health variables; (e) men's diversity, including race/ethnicity, culture, class, religious, sexual orientation, and masculine identity issues related to these categories; (f) male vulnerability related to violence, oppression, and abuse; and (g) methods to help men resolve and prevent GRC through therapy and psychoeducational interventions. These seven domains provide an expanded theoretical basis for understanding the potential moderators and mediators of men's GRC and the functional and microcontextual aspects of men's experiences in specific situations. To operationalize the seven contextual domains, in Exhibit 8.1, I enumerate 17 moderator, mediator, and causal research questions. These research questions, which can be pursued in the future, are described below.

Age, Developmental Stage, Resolving Developmental Tasks, and Gender Role Transitions

Developmental perspectives on how gender roles affect human functioning over the life span have not been fully conceptualized (Smiler, 2004). Heppner (1995) noted, "At this point, counseling psychologists know very little about gender role conflict across the lifespan or about gender role conflict within specific developmental issues like the midlife crisis" (pp. 21–22). Moreland (1980) discussed age and change in adult gender roles and came to three conclusions: that (a) men at different periods of their lives have different conceptions of masculinity, (b) men question and evaluate their gender standards during different periods and transitions, and (c) men experience stress associated with the evaluation of gender role standards and age norms. These premises provide a vantage point from which to assess how age and developmental stage affect boys and men's GRC. Some research has indicated specific age differences in GRC for men across the life cycle. As shown in Exhibit 8.1, Research Questions 1 through 3 indicate that age, developmental stage, resolving developmental tasks, and gender role transitions either moderate, mediate, or cause GRC. What moderates, mediates, and causes GRC can be studied during different developmental periods or ages, in the context of developmental tasks, and during critical gender role transitions. These research questions imply that at certain ages, and during certain

EXHIBIT 8.1
Moderator, Mediator, and Causal Research
Questions for Seven Contextual Domains of the
Gender Role Conflict (GRC) Research Paradigm

Domain 1: Age, Developmental Stage, Resolving Developmental Tasks, and Gender Role Transitions
1. Do age, developmental stage, or gender role transitions moderate or mediate men's and boys' GRC in terms of problem outcomes for boys and men?
2. Does resolving developmental tasks and psychosocial crises or failure to complete them moderate, mediate, or cause GRC for boys or men?

Domain 2: Family Interaction Patterns, Interpersonal Situations, and Peer Relationships
3. Do family interaction patterns, interpersonal situations, and peer relationships moderate, mediate, or cause men's GRC in terms of negative problem outcomes for men and others?
4. Do families' racial/ethnic, class, religious, and cultural values moderate, mediate, or cause men's GRC in terms of negative problems outcomes for men and others?
5. Do intimacy, friendships, marital conflicts, parenting, and sexual functioning moderate, mediate, or cause men's GRC in terms of negative outcomes for men and others?

Domain 3: Masculine Ideology, Norms, and Conformity
6. Do masculinity ideology and norms moderate, mediate, or cause GRC in terms of negative problem outcomes for men and others?
7. Does conformity to masculine ideology/norms or violation of them moderate, mediate, or cause GRC?

Domain 4: Psychological and Health Variables
8. Do psychological and physical health problems moderate, mediate, or cause GRC for men and others?

Domain 5: Men's Diversity: Race/Ethnicity, Culture, Class, Sexual Orientation, and Masculine Identity
9. Do race/ethnicity, class, religious, cultural, and sexual orientation moderate or mediate GRC in terms of problem outcomes for men and others?
10. Do internally and externally defined racial/ethnic, class, religious, cultural, and sexual identities moderate, mediate, or cause GRC in terms of problem outcomes for men and others?
11. Does acculturation to status quo norms (White, middle class, heterosexual, capitalist) moderate, mediate, or cause problem outcomes for men and others?

Domain 6: Male Vulnerability Related to Violence, Oppression, and Abuse
12. Does men's vulnerability to violence, oppression, abuse, and discrimination against others moderate, mediate, or cause GRC in terms of problem outcomes for men or others?
13. Does being a victim of oppression (racism, classism, ageism, sexism, ethnocentrism, heterosexism) moderate, mediate, or cause GRC in terms of problem outcomes for men or others?
14. Does being a victim of violence moderate, mediate, or cause GRC in terms of problem outcomes for men and others?

Domain 7: Methods to Help Men Resolve and Prevent GRC: Therapy and
Psychoeducational Interventions

15. Do different methods of helping (techniques, theoretical approaches) moderate,
mediate, or lessen GRC in terms of positive outcomes for men in therapy and
psychoeducational programs?

16. Do clients' and therapists' qualities, gender role attitudes, and behaviors moderate, mediate, or promote successes and failures during therapy with men and
during psychoeducational programming?

17. Do different ways of marketing men's psychological or health services contribute
to men's use of the services?

Note. From "Summarizing Twenty-Five Years of Research on Men's Gender Role Conflict Using the
Gender Role Conflict Scale: New Research Paradigms and Clinical Implications," by J. M. O'Neil, 2008,
The Counseling Psychologist, 36, p. 406. Copyright 2008 by Sage Publications. Adapted with permission.

developmental stages, tasks, and transitions, men may experience high or low
GRC that can affect dysfunctional behavior as well as provide opportunities
for positive growth and change. The questions also imply that developmental mediators affect GRC as predictors. In other words, facing and resolving
developmental tasks and going through gender role transitions may mediate
how GRC is experienced in the context of psychological, interpersonal, and
therapeutic outcomes in men's lives.

Family Interaction Patterns, Interpersonal Situations, and Peer Relationships

The second contextual domain broadens our understanding of GRC
in families, with peers, and in various interpersonal contexts. The existing
research indicates that GRC significantly relates to interpersonal processes,
family issues and attachment, and peer relationships (Beatty, Syzdek, &
Bakkum, 2006). Research Questions 4 through 6 in Exhibit 8.1 imply that
family interaction patterns, interpersonal relationships, and peer relationships
may moderate, mediate, or cause GRC in terms of intrapersonal, interpersonal, and therapeutic outcomes. The research questions also imply that the
family, relationships, and peers may mediate or cause GRC in the context of
intrapersonal, interpersonal, and therapeutic outcomes. These research questions significantly expand the assessment of the relational aspects of GRC
interpersonally and in families. Furthermore, Research Question 5 emphasizes
how family diversity (racial/ethnic, class, religious, and cultural values) affects
GRC in terms of outcome variables. Also, this contextual domain implies that

interpersonal interaction in families, intimate and sexual relationships, friendships, work relationships, and parenting roles may moderate, mediate, or cause boys' and men's GRC in terms of outcomes. How GRC and interpersonal dynamics affect children, partners, friends, and work relationships has gone largely unexplored. Research is needed in this interpersonal/familial domain because little is known about how GRC develops in families and whether it is transmitted intergenerationally.

Masculinity Ideology, Norms, and Conformity

The third domain indicates that masculinity ideology, norms, and conformity moderate, mediate, and cause GRC. Research Questions 6 and 7 are supported by theory from the gender role strain paradigm (Pleck, 1995) and conformity to and endorsement of masculine norms (Levant et al., 1992; Mahalik, Locke, et al., 2003). No study has yet assessed whether conformity to masculinity ideology moderates, mediates, or causes GRC in terms of outcome variables. Research could examine whether conforming to or violating masculine norms affects the degree of GRC or mediates GRC in terms of outcomes such as self-esteem, anxiety, depression, and other interpersonal variables. Qualitative research may first need to identify situational areas in which boys and men violate or conform to masculine norms. Measuring violations of masculinity ideology may require new psychometric measures, and controlled laboratory studies may be needed so that conformity and violation can be simulated.

Psychological and Physical Health Variables

Contextual Domain 4 includes one research question on how psychological and physical health problems relate to GRC and the intrapersonal and interpersonal outcomes in men's lives. Whether and how men's psychological and physical health variables moderate, mediates, or causes GRC has been a neglected area of research. Many of the empirical studies reviewed in this book support further examination of how psychological problems moderate and mediate GRC. The most comprehensive summary to date of how gender roles relate to men's health problems was completed by Will Courtenay (2000a, 2000b, 2000c, 2011). His important health agenda for men includes more than 30 behaviors that increase men's risk of disease, injury, and death (Courtenay, 2000a; see also Chapter 7, this volume). Physical health variables could be studied contextually in regard to men's GRC. Research on men's physical and emotional health is a critical area for scholars in the field of the psychology of men to pursue over the coming decades.

Men's Diversity: Race/Ethnicity, Culture, Class, Religion, Sexual Orientation, and Male Identity

Contextual Domain 5 addresses how diversity and multicultural variables moderate, mediate, and cause GRC. I discussed the topic of diversity in Chapter 6, where I presented a multicultural psychology of men model to help guide future research. Research Question 9 asks how race/ethnicity, culture, class, religion, and sexual orientation moderate GRC in terms of outcomes variables. Research Question 10 questions how internally and externally defined racial/ethnic, cultural, class, religious, and sexual identities mediate GRC in terms of outcome variables. These diversity variables have gone mostly unexplored in the psychology of men, and how they moderate or mediate GRC is mostly unknown. Research Question 11 addresses how acculturation to the status quo affects men's GRC. This topic has implications for immigrants or anyone who feels marginalized by the larger U.S. economic system or systematically discriminated against because of race/ethnicity, class, or sexual orientation. As reported earlier, seven studies have found that race and acculturation moderate GRC (Fragoso & Kashubeck, 2000; E. J. Kim, O'Neil, & Owen, 1996; Laurent, 1997; Lily, 1999; Shek, 2006; Wade, 1996; White, 2002), and two have found mediating effects of racial identity on GRC (Carter, Williams, Juby, & Buckley 2005; Wester, Kuo, & Vogel, 2006). These studies represent a promising but limited database on which to base explanations of the complex ways diversity variables relate to GRC.

Male Vulnerability Related to Violence, Oppression, and Abuse

Male vulnerability was discussed in Chapter 6 and defined as an emotional and cognitive state in which a man feels emasculated, weak, inferior, unmanly, worthless, shameful, or feminine. Vulnerability can develop when one is striving to meet or failing to meet gender role norms of masculinity ideology. It also can arise from experiencing oppression or discrimination; being poor, unemployed, or feeling that one is of a lower class; becoming addicted, hopeless, or chronically ill; and having no purpose, confidence, or positive identity. Furthermore, vulnerability can result from being harassed or bullied; experiencing physical, psychological, or sexual victimization; or experiencing personal or institutionalized oppression (racism, classism, ethnocentrism, homophobia, and ageism). Vulnerability is sometimes masked as defensiveness to avoid being seen as weak or to decrease the chance of being humiliated, shamed, or personally attacked. Other outcomes of vulnerability include depression, anxiety, personal rigidity, low self-esteem, inadequate empathy for others, and interpersonal violence.

Research Questions 12 through 14 relate men's vulnerability and GRC to discriminating against, abusing, or being violent toward others; being personally victimized by others; and being victimized by institutional oppression. Previous research has correlated men's GRC with negative, abusive, or violent attitudes toward women and others. Research has not assessed how vulnerability to committing acts of violence is moderated, mediated, or caused by GRC (Research Question 12). Some research suggests that men with GRC are more violent and abusive than other men (Rando, Rogers, & Brittan-Powell, 1998; Senn, Desmarais, Verberg, & Wood, 2000; Walls & Walker, 2002). How this violence moderates or mediates GRC in terms of psychological outcome variables remains unknown. Another important question is whether vulnerable males with GRC are discriminatory, biased, and oppressive toward others. Do sexist, racist, ethnocentric, homophobic, and classist men have greater GRC than other men?

Research Question 13 relates to situations in which men are personal victims of oppression from racism, sexism, classism, ethnocentrism, and heterosexism. Victims are hypothesized to be more vulnerable to GRC and traumatic outcomes are presumed to be related to being oppressed. How oppression moderates, mediates, or causes GRC and emotional and physical health is an important question. Personal oppression is emasculating because it threatens a man's masculine identity and denies him human rights and confidence to succeed in life. No research has found a correlation between men's GRC and being a victim of societal discrimination or oppression. Research could explore whether GRC relates to being a victim and, if it does, exactly how.

The third area of male vulnerability relates to being a victim of emotional abuse or physical violence. Research Question 14 asks whether being a victim of violence relate to GRC and, if so, how any trauma moderates, mediates, or causes men's GRC and negative psychological outcomes. GRC, trauma strain (Pleck, 1995), and conforming to masculinity ideology (Mahalik, Locke, et al., 2003) are theoretically linked with this vulnerability question. Victimizing experiences that may relate to GRC include sex abuse, threats of a homophobic nature, bullying, physical or emotional harassment, physical assault, child abuse and neglect, war experiences, serious accidents, and other traumatizing events. How abuse and trauma moderate or mediate GRC in terms of psychological well-being is a critical area for future research.

Methods to Help Men Resolve and Prevent Gender Role Conflict Through Therapy and Psychoeducation

The last contextual domain raises questions about the efficacy of therapeutic interventions to moderate, mediate, or promote success and failure when trying to help men (Research Questions 15–17). Assessing how to help men resolve GRC in therapy or in preventive interventions should be a high-priority area for future research. Research Question 15 asks what specific therapeutic interventions best help men. Therapy-related research needs to focus on both clients' and therapists' GRC (L. Mintz & O'Neil, 1990). Little is known about which client and therapist qualities and attitudes help change GRC (Research Question 16). How do clients' perceptions of therapists and their expectancies of therapy moderate or mediate GRC in the therapy process? Do biased therapists or those with GRC moderate or mediate the possibility that GRC can be remediated?

Increased experimentation is also needed in regard to preventive and psychoeducational programs for men (Research Question 17). What gender role curricula are most effective, under what conditions, with which different groups of men who have various patterns of GRC, with what positive outcomes? Research could assess whether men's attitudinal change about GRC translates to behavioral changes over different time periods. Finally, researchers need to look at how to market therapeutic services to men with GRC (Rochlen & Hoyer, 2005; Rochlen, McKelley, & Pituch, 2006). What public relations approaches and media campaigns increase the likelihood that men will use therapeutic services and are helped by them? Explorations of methods that effectively moderate or mediate men's GRC and decrease the barriers to their help seeking (Mansfield, Addis, & Courtenay, 2005) will be critical for the marketers of men's services.

CONTEXTUAL RESEARCH PARADIGMS THAT ENCOURAGE MODERATION AND MEDIATION STUDIES

In this section, I synthesize into new research paradigms the previous correlational research and seven contextual domains of GRC. I propose contextual research paradigms to guide future research on men's GRC and encourage more complex research designs. The contextual research paradigm is depicted by four conceptual diagrams shown in Figures 8.1–8.4. The predictor, moderator, mediator, and causal variables of men's GRC are shown in these paradigms and represent the programmatic areas for future research with men's GRC.

Predictive and Moderating Models of Gender Role Conflict

Figure 8.1 shows the predictive, moderating, and outcome variables related to men's GRC. The purpose of this figure is to help researchers generate prediction and moderator studies using the past research and theory. The box on the left side of Figure 8.1 shows the GRC predictors (Success, Power, and Control [SPC]; Restrictive Emotionality [RE]; Restrictive Affectionate Behavior Between Men [RABBM]; and Conflict Between Work and Family

Relations [CBWFR]) relating to outcomes in the three GRC contexts shown in the top rectangles. These GRC contexts are the same research areas reviewed throughout this book and include GRC in an intrapersonal context, GRC in an interpersonal context, and GRC in a therapeutic context.

Prediction studies assess the variables to which GRC is significantly related. As shown in Figure 8.1, GRC patterns (SPC, RE, RABBM, and CBWFR) have predicted 88 outcome variables shown in the three contextual rectangles. The overall prediction question is this: What demographic, psychological, physiological, racial, cultural, social, familial, interpersonal, or situational variables significantly predict men's GRC?

Moderator variables assess when or for whom a variable most strongly predicts or causes an outcome variable (Frazier, Tix, & Barron, 2004). Moderator variables affect the direction and/or the strength of a relation between independent variables (predictors) and a dependent or criterion variable (outcome; Baron & Kenny, 1986). Moderation effects explain interaction effects or how one variable depends on the level of others. Figure 8.1 depicts how moderator studies can be conceptualized. The longer arrow on the left in Figure 8.1 shows the seven GRC moderators affecting the relationship among the four GRC predictors (SPC, RE, RABBM, and CBWFR) and the outcome variables in the three GRC contexts (intrapersonal, interpersonal, and therapeutic). The seven moderators of men's GRC are the contextual domains discussed in the previous sections.

Moderator studies assess how variables contribute to fluctuations of high and low GRC. The overall moderator question is the following: How do demographic, psychological, physiological, racial, religious, cultural, social, familial, interpersonal, or situational variables significantly affect the direction and strength of GRC in predicting psychological outcomes for boys, men, and others? In other words, what contextual factors and situational contingencies differentiate those men who experience negative effects of GRC from those who do not? For moderation studies, theoretical rationales for hypothesized interactions are needed before hypotheses can be posed (Frazier et al., 2004). The previous elaborations on the seven contextual domains provide an initial theoretical rationale for assessing GRC moderator effects. Furthermore, 23 studies have found GRC to be moderated by different variables (see Chapters 6 and 7, this volume). These previous studies and the correlational data reported in this review provide initial empirical justification for testing the moderators of men's GRC shown in Figure 8.1.

Mediating Model of Gender Role Conflict

Mediator variables assess how and why one variable predicts or causes an outcome variable. Mediators assess the mechanism whereby a predictor influences an outcome and the underlying change process. Simply put, mediators are the mechanisms through which an effect occurs. Figure 8.2 shows how mediator studies can be conceptualized. The overall research question is how mediation variables explain relationships between GRC and outcome variables. Figure 8.2 shows the GRC predictors (SPC, RE, RABBM, and CBWFR) in the upper left rectangle as being directly related to the seven mediators (top center rectangle) as well as related to the outcome variables in the far right and the large bottom rectangles. The mediators of GRC are the seven contextual domains defined earlier. The question captured by Figure 8.2 is this: How and why does GRC cause men's psychological problems, and what variables mediate the relationship between GRC and those problems? In other words, do demographic, psychological, physiological, racial, religious, cultural, social, familial, social, interpersonal, and situational variables relate to GRC in producing negative outcomes for men and, second, what variables mediate GRC in terms of these outcomes? As I reported in Chapters 6 and 7, the variables that mediate GRC have been examined in 37 studies.

There is both empirical and theoretical justification for the mediational research paradigm shown in Figure 8.2. For mediation analyses, predictors need to be significantly related to outcome variables (Frazier et al., 2004). As this research review has shown, SPC, RE, RABBM, and CBWFR have been significantly correlated with the 88 outcome variables in the large rectangle in Figure 8.2 (see the long arrow in the middle of Figure 8.2 for an illustration of this relationship). Presumed predictors must also be theoretically related to the mediators (Frazier et al., 2004). Men's GRC has been empirically or theoretically related to the proposed mediators as shown in Figure 8.2 (see the short arrow in the upper left corner).

In summary, researchers can use Exhibit 8.1 and Figures 8.1 and 8.2 to generate predictor, moderating, and mediating hypotheses for their own studies. Researchers can hypothesize what constitutes a predictor, moderator, mediator, or outcome variable of GRC using both the empirical and theoretical literature. The seven contextual domains in Figure 8.1 and 8.2 represent future programmatic areas of research for men's GRC.

Functional and Microcontextual Research Paradigms: Gender Role Conflict as a Mediator and Dependent Variable

Since the last GRC research models were presented (O'Neil, 2008c), two major critiques of the GRC research have been published (Addis et al., 2010; K. Jones & Heesacker, 2012). Both critiques are very important in terms of expanding the options for researchers to study more focused contextual and situational issues. Addis et al. (2010) discussed the previous GRC research as limited and recommended a gendered social learning approach, and K. Jones and Heesacker (2012) made a case for microcontextual research with GRC (see Chapter 3, this volume). Both Addis et al. and K. Jones and Heesacker suggested similar directions for future masculinity research. Using different terminology, they argued for contextual, microcontextual, situational, and environmental cues and factors as independent variables that may be mediated by GRC. I agree with this analysis and add another perspective that promotes research where GRC is the dependent variable. I addressed these contextual issues more fully in Chapter 3 and address them further in the next section.

Based on these new critiques and recommendations, Figures 8.3 and 8.4 depict additional ways to conduct GRC research in which GRC is more than a predictor variable. In each figure, microcontextual, functional, or situational contexts are predictors, and GRC is either a mediator or the dependent variable. More than 10 examples of microcontextual and situational predictors are shown in Figures 8.3 and 8.4, and many more could be specified.

In regard to Figure 8.3, the research question is how and why antecedent contexts (historical, situational, developmental, and men's immediate experiences) cause men's psychological problems, and how GRC mediates the relationship between contextual variables and men's problems. In other words, does GRC (SPC, RE, RABBM, and CBWFR) relate to the contextual and microcontextual variables in producing negative outcomes for men and, second, how does GRC mediate the contextual variables in terms of these outcomes? In regard to Figure 8.4, the question is how and why situational contexts cause GRC (SPC, RE, RABBM, and CBWFR) and what other contextual variables mediate situations.

The purpose of both figures is to encourage future research on gendered social learning (Addis et al., 2010) and microcontexts (K. Jones & Heesacker, 2012). They expand GRC's role from simply being a predictor of men's problems to both a mediator and outcome of situational contingences. This expansion can generate many new research questions about how GRC is affected by environmental and situational cues in men's lives.

In the previous models, the assumption made was that men's socialization experiences, including masculinity ideology, were the causes of men's GRC. In the two new research models, microcontexts or situations can be the cause of GRC, or GRC can be a mediator of a cause that has negative intrapersonal, interpersonal, or therapeutic outcomes. The new contextual research paradigms support the study of both the macrosocietal and micro-interpersonal levels of men's experience (see Chapters 3 and 6). How racism, traumas, acculturation, or other situations stimulate GRC, or how GRC mediates those events, can both be studied. Furthermore, these new contextual paradigms also have implications for understanding the developmental issues I discussed in Chapter 5. How are the processes of demonstrating, resolving, reevaluating, or integrating aspects of masculinity affected by contexts that result in GRC (SPC, RE, RABBM, CBWFR)? Also, how does failing to master developmental tasks or resolve psychosocial crises cause GRC? Furthermore how do the social/political issues related to multiculturalism, diversity, social injustices, and oppression issues discussed in Chapter 7 cause GRC, or how does GRC mediate those causes? In addition, the paradigms allow GRC from others and toward others to be more completely conceptualized and assessed (see Chapters 3 and 9). Finally, how can therapeutic contexts affect the causes or mediation of GRC when men experience psychotherapy or during psycho-educational interventions (see Chapters 10–14)? These questions represent the future direction of the GRC research program and can generate more useful research on how men experience conflicts with masculinity and femininity. This kind of contextual research is one of the most important calls to action in this book.

IV

PRACTICAL APPLICATIONS FOR GENDER ROLE CONFLICT IN THERAPY AND PREVENTIVE PROGRAMS

9

THERAPEUTIC ASSESSMENT
OF GENDER ROLE CONFLICT IN
COUNSELING AND PSYCHOTHERAPY

Gender role conflict may be man's wound, may conceal a man's wound, and may be a vehicle to discovering a man's wound.

—Jim O'Neil

In the preceding chapters, I reported what is known about gender role conflict (GRC) and possible directions for future research. In the rest of the book, I focus on what can be done to help men in therapy or to create and implement effective prevention programs. The best theories are the ones that are applicable and improve the human condition, and therefore in the next chapters I discuss how GRC can be used by psychologists, educators, and other human services providers.

Over the past decade, more information has been published on assessing men in therapy, but Glicken (2005) indicated that "diagnosing male problems seem particularly fraught with ambiguity, worker bias, and politically correct notions of men as dysfunctional without question" (p. 67). In response to these kinds of problems, Cochran (2005) recommended that

Sections of this chapter appeared in "Gender Role Conflict Research 30 Years Later: An Evidence-Based Diagnostic Schema for Boys and Men in Counseling," by J. M. O'Neil, 2013, *Journal of Counseling & Development*, 91, pp. 490–498. Copyright 2013 by the American Counseling Association. Adapted with permission.

http://dx.doi.org/10.1037/14501-010

masculine-sensitive and evidence-based assessment should consist of three kinds of information: (a) research-based evidence pertaining to diagnosis and treatment, (b) recommendations based on clinical expertise, and (c) client values or preferences.

In this chapter, I respond to Glicken's (2005) criticism that the assessment of men is ambiguous by providing two specific appraisal schemas that apply to therapy with men. One schema is global (see Figure 9.1), and the other is specific to assessing gender role revaluations, restrictions, and violations (see Table 9.1). Furthermore, the two models respond to Cochran's (2005) recommendations that assessment paradigms be based on clinical experience and empirical research. Using theory and empirical evidence from the GRC research program (see Chapters 6 and 7, this volume), and my own clinical experience, I discuss a 13-part diagnostic schema and present an evidence-based assessment model that can be used with individual clients. No assessment approach is complete without a consideration of how multicultural and diversity variables and societal oppression affect clients and their therapies (O'Neil, 2008c; Wade & Rochlen, 2013; Wester, 2008a); therefore, I also summarize the GRC research that specifically supports the evidence-based model for diverse men.

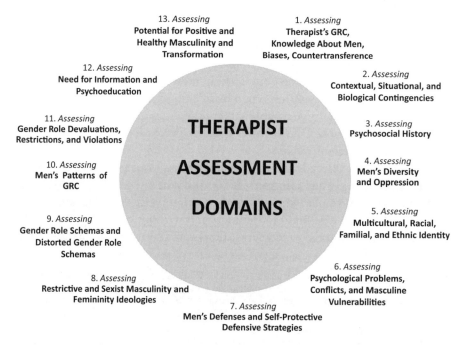

Figure 9.1. Therapist Assessment Domains. GRC = gender role conflict.

TABLE 9.1

A Diagnostic Schema to Assess Men's Gender Role Conflict (GRC)

Personal experience and outcomes of GRC: SPC, RE, RABBM, CBWFR	Within self	Caused by others	Expressed toward others
D. Gender role devaluations	**D₁ Self-devaluation** How does the man devalue himself because of masculinity ideology and GRC?	**D₂ Devaluation by others** How is the man devalued by others because of masculinity ideology and GRC?	**D₃ Devaluation of others** How does the man devalue others because of their masculinity ideology and GRC?
R. Gender role restrictions	**R₁ Self-restriction** How does the man restrict himself because of masculinity ideology and GRC?	**R₂ Restriction by others** How is the man restricted by others because of masculinity ideology and GRC?	**R₃ Restriction of others** How does the man restrict others because of their masculinity ideology and GRC?
V. Gender role violations	**V₁ Self-violation** How does the man violate himself because of masculinity ideology and GRC?	**V₂ Violation by others** How is the man violated by others because of masculinity ideology and GRC?	**V₃ Violation of others** How does the man violate others because of their masculinity ideology and GRC?

Note. SPC = Success, Power, Competition; RE = Restrictive Emotionality; RABBM = Restrictive Affectionate Behavior Between Men; CBWFR = Conflict Between Work and Family Relations. From "Gender Role Conflict Research 30 Years Later: An Evidence-Based Diagnostic Schema for Boys and Men in Counseling," by J. M. O'Neil, 2013, *Journal of Counseling & Development, 91*, p. 494. Copyright 2013 by John Wiley and Sons. Adapted with permission.

PAST DIAGNOSTIC SCHEMAS, TYPOLOGIES, AND PROBLEM AREAS RELATED TO GENDER ROLE CONFLICT

The two most developed assessment paradigms for men in therapy are (a) *deepening* (Cochran & Rabinowitz, 2003) and (b) the *transtheoretical therapy model* (Brooks, 2010). I elaborate on both in Chapters 10 and 11. The process of deepening means identifying masculine-specific conflicts; finding portals to men's wounds; working with clients' defenses; and assessing four interacting and overlapping dimensions, including (a) psychological history, (b) formative experiences, (c) cultural upbringing, and (d) current functioning. Brooks (2010) discussed male-specific diagnostic assessment that emphasizes a gender role strain analysis. He adapted the concepts of the transtheoretical therapy model (Prochaska & DiClemente, 2005; Prochaska & Norcross, 2001) and recommended assessing men's stages and processes of change, motivational hurdles, and a long list of very innovative and practical approaches that fosters the therapeutic alliance.

Other typologies for assessing men in therapy include masculine scripts (Mahalik, Good, & Englar-Carlson, 2003), critical problem areas (Gilbert & Scher, 1999; Good & Sherrod, 2001) distorted cognitive schemas (Mahalik, 1999a; O'Neil & Nadeau, 1999), integrative approaches (Good & Mintz, 2001), and categories of depressive disorder—male and disorder of the self—male type categories (Pollack, 1998a, 2001). Three GRC diagnostic schemas to assess men have been previously published (O'Neil, 1990, 2006, 2008c), but whether they have been useful to clinicians is unclear.

Approaches to assessing men are in development, but some of the past assessment models (including my own) have been vague and not operationalized for use. Most assessment models focus on men's socialization (Good & Sherrod, 2001; Mahalik, Good, & Englar-Carlson, 2003; Rabinowitz & Cochran, 2002), but the connection between male-oriented appraisal and intervention lacks clarity. In addition, past assessment models have not been evidence based, and only a few have addressed the multicultural implications of doing therapy with diverse men (see Brooks, 2010, for the exception). Only a few models appear to be based on clinicians' experience (Brooks, 2010; Gilbert & Scher, 1999; Good & Sherrod, 2001; Mahalik, Good, & Englar-Carlson, 2003; Rabinowitz & Cochran, 2002). Assessment of men in therapy could be strengthened by summarizing empirical research on men's GRC and identifying the assessment domains that help therapists find the portals through which to promote stage- and process-based change with men (Brooks, 2010; Rabinowitz & Cochran, 2002). This chapter provides both a global assessment paradigm and a specific, evidence-based diagnostic paradigm that can be used with men in therapy. The evidence-based paradigm has empirical support, with categories including *gender role devaluations*, *restrictions*, and *violations*.

A GLOBAL DIAGNOSTIC SCHEMA TO ASSESS MEN
AND THEIR GENDER ROLE CONFLICT

The global diagnostic schema shown in Figure 9.1 expands on my previous models (O'Neil, 1990, 2006, 2008c; O'Neil & Lujan, 2009a). The model has 13 therapist assessment domains that are clustered into three assessment areas. Domains 1 through 5 represent parameters related to the therapist's situation, contextual contingencies, psychosocial development, and diversity and multicultural indexes. Domains 6 through 11 focus on the client's problem and defenses; masculinity and femininity ideologies; GRCs and schemas; and gender role devaluations, restrictions, and violations. Domains 12 and 13 include the assessment of clients' need for information and psychoeducation and the man's potential for creating positive healthy masculinity. In the following sections, I briefly define each of these domains; a more elaborate discussion of them is found elsewhere (O'Neil, 2008c).

The first five assessment domains are critical to understanding the client's background and life history. The first domain, in which biases are assessed (Robertson & Fitzgerald, 1990), includes three interrelated processes: (a) the therapist's assessment of his or her own biases toward men, (b) assessment of client biases, and (c) assessment of transference and countertransference issues between the therapist and client. Assessing contextual, situational, and biological contingencies is the broadest area in the assessment paradigm and represents everything that the client discloses about his or her life that affects the therapeutic process. The context could be some historical event, a current illness, a serious loss, even an unknown, unconscious variable. As I discussed in Chapter 5, psychosocial–developmental history of the client is a critical assessment area because it relates to gender role transitions and developmental changes in a man's life. Assessing how GRC may have affected psychosocial development is relevant to understanding the client's presenting problems. Assessing men's diversity and oppression involves determining whether the man has experienced discrimination and oppression. If he has, how this has affected his masculinity ideology and male identity is a critical therapeutic variable to be assessed. The assessment of multicultural, racial/ethnic, and familial identity is designed to determine how GRC interacts with the client's race/ethnicity, class, age, religion, sexual orientation, and other cultural values. Racial/ethnic identity and acculturation have been found to moderate and mediate GRC, but how these diversity variables affect the therapeutic process is still unknown.

Domains 6 through 11 represent the important masculinity-related parameters that make therapy with men unique and challenging. Assessment of men's psychological problems, conflicts, and masculine vulnerabilities relates to clients' presenting problems, but there are usually layers of problems to be probed and discovered. Masculinity ideology and GRC can help define the problem with greater precision and clarity. Unresolved GRC produces vulnerability or hidden feelings of weakness, fragility, and psychological symptoms that add to men's negative gender role identity and sense of self. Masculine vulnerability is an emotional and cognitive state in which a man feels emasculated, weak, inferior, unmanly, worthless, shameful, or feminine. It occurs when men fail to meet expected masculine gender role norms. Sources of vulnerability include institutional and personal oppression and discrimination; poverty; unemployment; being addicted, hopeless, or ill; having no purpose, confidence, or positive identity; being bullied; and physical, psychological, or sexual victimization. Furthermore, the assessment of defenses is important because defensiveness can mediate powerful emotions, help men cope with fears of femininity or of being emasculated, and defend against perceived losses of power and control. These defensive functions are important vantage points to consider when conducting therapy with men.

The assessment of restrictive masculinity and femininity ideologies involves determining how a man thinks about gender roles and the ways rigid thinking limits human functioning. Internalizing restrictive masculinity ideologies can produce distorted gender role schemas (Mahalik, 1999a; O'Neil & Nadeau, 1999)—exaggerated thoughts and feelings about masculinity ideology in a man's life (O'Neil & Nadeau, 1999) that occur when men experience pressure, fear, or anxiety about meeting or not meeting stereotypic notions of masculinity—and patterns of GRC that are potentially damaging to men and others. Men's distorted cognitive schemas are assessed because they are related to men's psychological problems. The assessment of the patterns of GRC can be accomplished through direct questioning or by administrating the Gender Role Conflict Scale (GRCS; O'Neil, Helms, Gable, David, & Wrightsman, 1986) or the Gender Role Conflict Checklist (O'Neil, 1988c). Assessing patterns of GRC can stimulate disclosure about the personal experience of being a man. Assessing a man's gender role restrictions, devaluations, and violations is accomplished by means of sensitive listening and through questions that help him understand his gender role journey. The therapist listens to the client's story about being a man, interprets the story from a gender role perspective, and provides support for making healthy change.

In Domain 12, the therapist also needs to assess the degree the man needs information about being a man or other psychoeducational experience that support the therapy. Finally, in Domain 13, the therapist assesses the man's potential to embrace positive and healthy masculinity and transform himself.

Most of the 13 assessment domains provide information that can help therapists find men's portals (Rabinowitz & Cochran, 2002) and provide insights that facilitate the stage-based change Brooks (2010) recommended.

These domains are useful, but they do not address in a substantive way how masculinity ideology and GRC are personally experienced by the client. The second assessment model, described next, addresses in a more direct way men's gender role devaluations, restrictions, and violations.

ASSESSMENT OF MEN'S GENDER ROLE CONFLICT USING AN EVIDENCE-BASED DIAGNOSTIC SCHEMA

The most critical clinical question at hand is whether the GRC research reviewed in Chapters 6 and 7 supports the idea that evidence-based approaches should be used when counseling men. The research I have reviewed documents that GRC is related to psychologically negative outcomes for men and others. The evidence is strong, but do the studies provide any guidance regarding how to counsel men? The GRC research provides useful information about how to assess men in the early stages of counseling and psychotherapy. To demonstrate how this research guides assessment, in the following sections I present a diagnostic assessment schema based on both GRC theory and empirical research. My intent is to help counselors assess GRC in the context of men's symptoms and presenting problems.

Lacking in the previous GRC assessment models are approaches that help clinicians assess GRC in the context of a client's specific symptoms and presenting problems. Conspicuously absent in the therapy literature are specific diagnostic schemas that assess men's presenting problems in the contexts of the masculinity ideology and GRC. For example, how can a client's chronic anxiety, depression, loss, substance abuse, interpersonal conflicts, or other psychological symptoms be conceptualized in the context of his socialized masculine norms and ideology? How does the therapist understand a client's presenting problem in the context of his socialized masculinity and GRC? The complex relationship between a client's sense of masculinity and his problems needs to be assessed for any deepening to occur (Rabinowitz & Cochran, 2002).

AN EXPANDED DEFINITION OF MEN'S GENDER ROLE DEVALUATIONS, RESTRICTIONS, AND VIOLATIONS

Men's personal experiences of GRC are missing links in the comprehensive assessment of men in therapy. Many of men's problems emanate from rigid masculinity ideologies and GRC experienced as gender role devaluations, restrictions, and violations. GRC theorists have hypothesized that these three experiences of GRC negatively affect men's interpersonal, career, family, and health lives (O'Neil, 1981a, 1981b, 1990, 2008c; see also Chapters 3 and 6, this volume). Devaluations, restrictions, and violations provide an operationally defined way to describe men's personal experience of GRC and their presenting problem.

The summarizing of men's personal experience of GRC into just three categories may appear to be simplistic and overly reductionist. Nonetheless, devaluations, restrictions, and violations do provide a heuristic-based way to understand what happens to men because of GRC. The definition of GRC from the beginning has included these three experiences of intrapersonal and interpersonal realities. Moreover, almost 70% of the items on the GRCS measure or imply restrictions, devaluations, violations of self because of socialized gender roles. These GRCS items address thoughts and feeling and, to a lesser extent, behaviors. After years of reflection, I have concluded that most of men's gender role problems directly relate to gender role devaluations, restrictions, and violations.

Gender role devaluations, restrictions, and violations were operationally defined in Chapter 3. In this section, I provide expanded descriptions of how devaluations, restrictions, and violation are personally experienced by men. This has implications during therapy as well as explanatory power in connecting a client's presenting problems to masculinity issues, including GRC. *Gender role devaluations* are negative critiques of the self or others when conforming to, deviating from, or violating stereotypic gender role norms of masculinity ideology. Devaluations result in a lessening of status, stature, and self-esteem. When this occurs, fear and anger can be turned inward, causing depression and feelings of isolation. Men can devalue themselves, be devalued by others, or devalue someone else. For example, when a man cannot conform with the expected masculine norms that are based in masculinity ideologies, he may devalue and blame himself.

Self-devaluations are damaging to a man's sense of self and psychological stability. They diminish a man's sense of positive well-being and personal worth. Men devalue themselves when they don't succeed, when they lose in a competition, when they can't solve their own problems, or when they must admit they need help. Self-devaluations may occur when men fail to perform sexually, can't process complex interpersonal exchanges or find the words to express emotions, and when work–family conflicts or demands occur. Other times, self-deprecation occurs because a man's career advancement stalls, fathering is failing, or when not enough money is being made. Devaluation can happen when a man loses status, power, or a dream and thus feels like a failure.

Devaluations of others represent the direct and negative criticism of others when they deviate from or conform to gender role norms. Devaluations can be projections of the man's own worries and fears that are made at someone else's expense. This can occur when weakness, emotions, affect, and vulnerability are shown. Sexual minorities and other cultural groups can be devalued when they deviate from expected gender role norms. Devaluation of others is a way of feeling superior to and subordinating others and, many times, reflects the fact that one does not feel good about oneself.

Gender role restrictions imply that GRC confines the self or others to stereotypic and restrictive norms of masculinity ideology. Confining oneself or others in terms of gender roles implies that conformity to expected gender role norms is expected. These restrictions result in attempts to control people's behavior, limit other people's potential, and decrease human freedom. Gender role restrictions occur when restrictive masculine and feminine norms limit flexibility in work situations and negatively affect family and interpersonal relationships. Restrictions limit options, deny people's needs, and can result in manipulative control and abuses of power. The costs of restricting oneself or others include feelings of loss, guilt, anger, and powerlessness.

Self-restrictions imply having a limited behavioral repertoire and the narrowing of one's responses to life events. Self-imposed restrictions inhibit growth and problem solving, causing stress and psychological problems. Self-restrictions are evident in the form of limited communication, avoidance of expressing emotions, failure to cope and manage stress, being highly self-reliant, and thinking narrowly about an issue. A man restricts himself by not seeking help that he needs, having limited adaptability interpersonally, defining success and intimacy narrowly, and having a limited group of friends. A self-restricted man would be vulnerable to what he perceives as stigmatizing therapy and rigid in how he sees the world and himself.

Restrictions of others involve having control over others to maintain power and dominance. Many times this restriction includes protecting one's masculinity ideology or resources and controlling the environment and people in it. This may be manifested by limiting emotional expression, demanding conformity to rigid norms, and stereotyping or stigmatizing others, and these restrictions may be manipulative, authoritarian, or threatening.

Gender role violations represent the most severe kind of GRC because direct harm can be inflicted on the self or others. Gender role violations occur when one harms the self, harms others, or is harmed by others because of gender role norms of masculinity ideology. Gender role violations can cause gender role trauma strain that results in severe negative outcomes in terms of psychological functioning.

Self-violations involve doing oneself harm through maladaptive thoughts, feelings, and behaviors. Self-violations put a person at risk for future problems, pain, and suffering. They block the possibility for renewal and change. Violating oneself can take the form of not taking care of one's health, limited body awareness, engaging in unsafe sex, not eating well, and consuming excessive food or alcohol. The potential for self-violations occurs through the use of dangerous drugs, engaging in risky activities, and not getting regular medical checkups. A pattern of self-destructive behavior that can lead to early death and suicide is observed. Overall, a man who violates himself feels invulnerable to harm or simply does not care about himself and his life.

Violations of others involves the direct harming of others through emotional or physical abuse. The violations can be intentional or unintentional, but hurt is directed toward others. They are characterized by threat, emotional abuse, stereotyping, and homophobic-based reactions to others. Rape, sexual abuse, harassment, bullying, stalking, and assault also represent violations of others. Devaluations, restrictions, and violations toward others follow the same pattern, only in this instance the man is doing the devaluing, restricting, and violating to others.

As described in Chapter 3, men are devalued, restricted, and violated by others when violating, deviating from, or adhering to restrictive masculinity ideology norms. Gender role devaluations from others can be painful. How gender role devaluations, restrictions, and violations from others occur and the psychological effects are the least known aspects of GRC.

Therapists can assess clients' gender role devaluations, restrictions, and violations in the context of their presenting problems. They can be portals (Rabinowitz & Cochran, 2002) or pathways to understanding men's problems. In the next section, I propose a diagnostic schema that uses devaluations, restrictions, and violations in therapy and report the GRC research that supports it.

DIAGNOSTIC SCHEMA TO ASSESS MEN'S GENDER ROLE CONFLICT

A diagnostic schema that assesses men's GRC during counseling and psychotherapy is depicted in Table 9.1. On the left of the table are the personal experiences and outcomes of GRC, including gender role devaluations, gender role restrictions, and gender role violations. Across the top of the table are shown the three situational contexts of these experiences: (a) within self, (b) caused by others, and (c) expressed toward others. These three are defined on the basis of how and from whom GRC is experienced by an individual man. These contexts demonstrate that devaluations, restrictions, and violations can exist within a man (the intrapersonal context), emanate from others, or be expressed toward others (the interpersonal contexts).

Table 9.1 contains nine assessment cells that therapists can use when assessing client's personal experience of GRC. For example, self-devaluation from GRC is found in Cell D_1, whereas GRC devaluation by others or devaluation of others are represented by Cells D_2 and D_3, respectively. Likewise, gender role restrictions and violations within self, caused by others, or expressed toward others are represented by Cells R_1, R_2, and R_3 and Cells V_1, V_2, and V_3, respectively.

A careful study of the nine cells provides an operationally defined method of understanding clients' personal experience of GRC and connecting it to their presenting problem or symptom. Each cell contains a diagnostic question that therapists can ask when assessing clients' GRC and masculinity ideology. For GRC within self (Cells D_1, R_1, and V_1), the question is, "How does the client devalue/restrict/violate himself because of masculinity ideology and GRC?" Answering this question in the context of the client's presenting symptoms can help explain how masculinity ideology and GRC contribute to the man's problems. For GRC caused by others (Cells D_2, R_2, and V_2), the question is, "How is the client devalued/restricted/violated by others because of his masculinity ideology and GRC?" Answers to this question can help the client see how he is treated by others who demand conformity or nonconformity to expected gender roles. For GRC expressed towards others (Cells D_3, R_3, and V_3), the question is, "How does the client devalue/restrict/violate others because of his masculinity ideology and GRC?" This question focuses on how the client treats others when endorsing or rejecting traditional gender roles. The nine cells in Table 9.1 provide the most personal, contextually sensitive, and situationally focused ways to assess clients' personal experiences of GRC in the context of their presenting problem. In Chapter 12, in which I present a case study of one of my clients, I use both the global schema and the nine diagnostic cells described in Table 9.1.

EMPIRICAL EVIDENCE SUPPORTING THE DIAGNOSTIC SCHEMA

The empirical question at hand is whether the GRC research reviewed in Chapters 6 and 7 and elsewhere (O'Neil, 2008c, 2010) supports the diagnostic schema shown in Table 9.1. Is there any direct or indirect empirical evidence that the gender role devaluations, restrictions, and violations in the nine cells of Table 9.1 relate to men's psychological and interpersonal problems (O'Neil, 2008c, 2010; O'Neil, Good, & Holmes, 1995)? Specifically, do gender role devaluations, restrictions, and violations as assessed by the GRCS correlate with men's psychological and interpersonal problems, including depression, anxiety, self-esteem, homophobia, marital conflict, violence toward women, and substance abuse? For example, is there any evidence that self-devaluations (D_1) and devaluation of others (D_3) relate to any patterns of GRC (Success, Power, and Control [SPC]; Restrictive Emotionality [RE]; Restrictive Affectionate Behavior Between Men [RABBM]; and Conflict

Between Work and Family Relations [CBWFR]). If there is, what are the negative psychological outcomes related to self-devaluations and devaluations of others? For example, is there any evidence that self-devaluations (Cell D_1) and devaluation of others (Cell D_3) relate to any patterns of GRC (SPC, RE, RABBM, and CBWFR), and, if so, what are the negative psychological outcomes related to self-devaluations and devaluations of others? Is there empirical evidence that gender role self-devaluations (Cell D_1) and devaluations of others (Cell D_3) are empirically correlated with men's actual emotional and mental health problems? In a similar way, have the other cells in Table 9.1 related to gender role restrictions and violations been significantly correlated with negative psychological outcomes for men?

I conducted an evaluation of the GRC research to determine whether empirical support exists for the diagnostic schema depicted in Table 9.1. I reviewed empirical studies that showed significant correlations ($p < .05$) between the patterns of GRC (SPC, RE, RABBM, and CBWFR) and men's psychological and interpersonal problems (O'Neil, 2008c, 2010) for the nine cells in the table. As I discussed in Chapter 4, over 60% of the items on the GRCS assess men's personal experience of GRC in terms of gender role violations, restrictions, and violations. In my review of the literature, I identified GRC studies that had dependent variables that were theoretically associated with gender role devaluations, restrictions, and violations. Those dependent variables that are significantly correlated with GRCS were identified and categorized in the nine cells of the diagnostic schema.

In Table 9.2 are shown the dependent variables and psychological problems that have been found to be significantly correlated with the GRCS subscales (SPC, RE, RABBM, and CBWFR) for five of the nine cells in Table 9.1. These problem areas have been significantly correlated with men's personal experience of gender role devaluations, restrictions, and violations. For five of the nine cells in Table 9.1, empirical evidence links GRC to negative psychological and interpersonal symptoms. Empirical evidence links GRC patterns and devaluations, restrictions, and violations to men's psychological problems in the following cells: D_1, D_3, R_1, V_1, and V_3.

Sixty-five specific symptoms that have been empirically correlated with SPC, RE, RABBM, and CBWFR are listed in Table 9.2. Forty-six of the psychological problems relate to men's possible self-devaluations, restrictions, and violations. Another 19 problem areas relate to men's devaluations, restrictions and violations by and of others. A careful review of each cell provides evidence-based information about how gender role devaluations, restrictions, and violations relate to men's psychological problems. For example, Cell D_1 includes 9 important psychological symptoms related to self-devaluations, including depression, shame, low self-esteem, internalized forms of oppression related to racism, homophobia, heterosexism, and

TABLE 9.2

Dependent Variables and Psychological Problems Correlating With Gender Role Devaluations, Restrictions, and Violations Using the Gender Role Conflict Scale (GRCS)

Personal experience and expression of GRC	GRC within self	GRC caused by others	GRC expressed toward others
Gender role devaluations (SPC, RE, RABBM, CBWFR)	**D₁ Self-devaluations** Depression, low self-esteem, shame, internalized racism, perceived racism, homonegativity, negative attitudes toward "outness," internalized heterosexism, negative feelings about being gay	**D₂ Devaluation by others** No research in this cell	**D₃ Devaluation of others** Stereotyping of women, homophobic attitudes, racial bias, antigay attitudes, low sex role egalitarianism; spousal criticism, negative attitudes toward African Americans
Gender role restrictions (SPC, RE, RABBM, CBWFR)	**R₁ Self-restrictions** Stress; anxiety; alexithymia; coping problems; personality problems; negative attitudes toward help seeking; negative attitudes toward problem solving; acculturation stress; inexpressiveness; hopelessness; shyness; intimacy problems; attachment, separation, and individuation problems; lack of parenting self-efficacy; poor marital adjustment; lack of male friendships; limited self-disclosure; traditional attitudes toward women; social and self-stigma; stigma associated with counseling; stigma associated with career counseling; stigma associated seeking psychological help; difficulty identifying feelings; loneliness; emotional irritation; emotional dysregulation	**R₂ Restriction by others** No research in this cell	**R₃ Restriction of others** No research in this cell

(continues)

TABLE 9.2

Dependent Variables and Psychological Problems Correlating With Gender Role Devaluations, Restrictions, and Violations Using the Gender Role Conflict Scale (GRCS) *(Continued)*

Personal experience and expression of GRC	GRC within self	GRC caused by others	GRC expressed toward others
Gender role violations (SPC, RE, RABBM, CBWFR)	**V₁ Self-violations** Alcohol/substance abuse, negative alcohol-related consequences, high-risk behaviors, self-objectification, eating disorder symptomatology, self-destructiveness, suicide, high suicidal probability, suicide attempts, suicide acceptability	**V₂ Violation by others** No research in this cell	**V₃ Violation of others** Violence against women, rape myth acceptance, sexual harassment, hostility toward others, sexually aggressive behaviors, greater likelihood of forcing sex, abusive behavior, coercion, dating violence, hostile sexism, positive attitudes and tolerance for sexual harassment, self-reported violence and aggression

Note. GRC = Gender Role Conflict; SPC = Success, Power, and Control; RE = Restrictive Emotionality; RABBM = Restrictive Affectionate Behavior Between Men; CBWFR = Conflict Between Work and Family Relations. From "Gender Role Conflict Research 30 Years Later: An Evidence-Based Diagnostic Schema for Boys and Men in Counseling," by J. M. O'Neil, 2013, *Journal of Counseling & Development, 91*, p. 496. Copyright 2013 by John Wiley and Sons. Adapted with permission.

negative attitudes about being gay. Cell R_1 lists 27 psychological symptoms related to self-restrictions that are associated with GRC including stress, anxiety, coping problems, hopelessness, loneliness, and various stigma associated with seeking help, to name a few. Cell V_1 indicates that GRC is correlated with 10 self-violating symptoms, including substance use and abuse, high-risk behavior, eating disorder symptoms, self-objectification, self-destructiveness, and indexes related to suicide.

Two other areas in which empirical research links gender role devaluations, restrictions, and violations to specific problems and symptoms in men's lives are represented by Cells D_3 (devaluation of others) and V_3 (violations of others). The devaluation of others (Cell D_3) has been empirically linked to seven insulting attitudes, including stereotyping of women, homophobic and antigay attitudes, racial bias, sex role equalitarianism, and spousal criticism. Likewise, with violations of others (Cell V_3), GRC has been found to be correlated with 11 different ways to hurt other human beings including violence against women, sexual harassment, sexually aggressive behavior, likelihood of forced sex, hostility toward women, dating violence, hostile sexism, rape myths, abusive behavior and coercion.

The specific studies that have documented the fact that gender role devaluations, restrictions, and violations are associated with negative psychological symptoms are listed in Exhibit 9.1. Empirical evidence now exist that gender role devaluations, restrictions, and violations are correlated to men's problems in both an intrapersonal and interpersonal context. There is little empirical evidence for how gender devaluations, restrictions, and violations caused by others (Cells D_2, R_2, and V_2) results in negative psychological outcomes for men. Also, research has yet to document how the restriction of others (Cell R_3) has a negative psychological impact in interpersonal relations. The diagnostic schema does provide a more evidence-based approach to assessing men than previous assessment models have (O'Neil, 1990, 2006, 2008c; O'Neil & Lujan, 2009b). The evidence presented in Exhibit 9.1 provides greater empirical support that the schema can be useful when counseling men. Most of the research has been conducted with nonclinical populations, and therefore more research is needed to directly assess actual clients who seek help.

MULTICULTURAL AND DIVERSITY EVIDENCE FOR THE DIAGNOSTIC SCHEMA

One of the limitations of past assessment models has been the lack of attention to diversity and multiculturalism. Not only have models been narrowly defined, but they also have lacked empirical support. The critical question is how well the research supports assessments regarding men with

EXHIBIT 9.1
Research on Gender Role Devaluations, Restrictions, and Violations Using the Gender Role Conflict Scale

Self-devaluations		
Internalized heterosexism M. A. Robinson & Brewster (2014) Szymanski & Carr (2008) Szymanski & Ikizler (2013)	**Self-objectification** Schwartz et al. (2010)	**Perceived racism** Liang et al. (2010)
Negative feeling about being gay Sánchez et al. (2010)	**Internalized racism** Wester, Vogel, et al. (2006)	**Homonegativity** Bryce (2012) Ervin (2003) Sánchez et al. (2010)
Self-esteem Berko (1994) Bursley (1996) Choi et al. (2010) Cournoyer (1994) F. Davis (1988) Hayashi (1999) Jo (2000) J. Kim et al. (2006) Laurent (1997) Mahalik et al. (2001) Schwartz et al. (1998) Sharpe & Heppner (1991)	**Depression** Blazina & Watkins (1996) Brewer (1998) Burke (2000) Bursley (1996) Choi et al. (2010) Coonerty-Femiano et al. (2001) Cournoyer & Mahalik (1995) Fragoso & Kashubeck (2000) Good et al. (1996) Good & Mintz (1990) Good & Wood (1995) Hayashi (1999) Jo (2000) D. A. Jones (1998) Kang (2001) Magovcevic & Addis (2005) S. G. Newman (1997) F. Peterson (1999) Sharpe et al. (1995) Sharpe & Heppner (1991) D. S. Shepard (2002) Simonsen et al. (2000) Tate (1998) Theodore (1998) Kelly (2000) J. Kim et al. (2006) Mahalik & Cournoyer (2000)	
Negative attitudes toward "outness" Sánchez (2005) Sánchez et al. (2010)	**Shame and shame proneness** McMahon et al. (2000) Segalla (1996) Thompkins & Rando (2003) D. Thomson (2005)	

EXHIBIT 9.1
Research on Gender Role Devaluations, Restrictions, and Violations
Using the Gender Role Conflict Scale   *(Continued)*

Self-restrictions		
Emotional irritation Wolfram et al. (2009)	**Emotional dysregulation** Cohn et al. (2010)	**Stigma toward career counseling** Graef et al. (2010)
Hopelessness Birthistle (1999) Brewer (1998)	**Physical and psychological strain** Stillson (1988)	**Social and self-stigma** Park & Seok Seo (2009) Shepherd & Rickard (2012) Vogel et al. (2014)
Stigma associated with counseling Wester, Arndt, et al. (2010)	**Difficulty identifying feelings** Wong et al. (2006)	**Global levels of psychological stress** Hetzel (1998)
Greater emotional inexpressiveness Davenport et al. (1998)	**Loneliness** Blazina, Settle, & Eddins (2008)	**Self-disclosure** Horhoruw (1991) Swenson (1998)
Shyness Berko (1994) Bruch (2002) Bruch et al. (1998)	**Lack of intimacy and male friendship** Sileo (1996)	**Dyadic adjustment** Breiding (2004) Brewer (1998) Campbell & Snow (1992)
Stigma for seeking psychological help Steinfeldt et al. (2009)	**Negative attitudes toward problem solving** Chamberlin (1993)	**Parenting dissatisfaction and a lack of parenting self-efficacy** Alexander (1997)
Coping Bergen (1997) Birthistle (1999) D. A. Jones (1998) Stanzione (2005) Strom (2004) Wester, Kuo, & Vogel (2006)	**Marital satisfaction** Alexander (1997) Brewer (1998) Campbell & Snow (1992) Sharpe et al. (1995)	**Greater career counseling stigma, decreased willingness to engage in career counseling** Rochlen et al. (2002) Rochlen & O'Brien (2002)
Personality styles: Neuroticism, introversion, extraversion, openness, agreeableness, aggressiveness, narcissism Cortese (2003) Kratzner (2003) Schwartz, Buboltz, et al. (2004)	**Immature and neurotic defenses (projection, denial, and isolation) and defenses that are turned against others** Mahalik et al. (1998)	**Alexithymia** Berger et al. (2005) Fischer & Good (1997) Hayashi (1999) D. S. Shepard (2002)

(continues)

Intimacy
Chartier & Arnold (1985)
Cournoyer & Mahalik (1995)
Fischer & Good (1997)
Good, Heppner, et al. (1995)
Lindley & Schwartz (2006)
Sharpe & Heppner (1991)
Sharpe et al. (1995)
Theodore & Lloyd (2001)
Van Hyfte & Rabinowitz
  (2001)

Anxiety
Blazina & Watkins (1996)
Burke (2000)
Bursley (1996)
Cournoyer & Mahalik (1995)
F. Davis (1988)
Hayashi (1999)
Kang (2001)
Jo (2000)
D. A. Jones (1998)
Mertens (2000)
Sharpe & Heppner (1991)
Theodore & Lloyd (2000)

**Personality: Styles, types,
  models, ego identity,
  and authoritarianism**
Arnold & Chartier (1984)
Chamberlin (1993)
Chartier & Arnold (1985)
Cortese (2003)
Schwartz, Buboltz, et al.
  (2004)
Kratzner (2003)
Serna (2004)
Sipes (2005)
Tokar et al. (2000)

Stress
Fragoso & Kashubeck
  (2000)
Good et al. (1996, 2004)
J. A. Hayes & Mahalik (2000)
Hetzel (1998)
Kratzner (2003)
Leka (1998)
Van Delft (1998)

**Psychological distress,
  including problems with
  hostility, compulsive-
  ness, social discomfort,
  paranoia, psychoticism,
  obsessive–compulsiv-
  ity, and interpersonal
  sensitivity**
Good et al. (1996)
J. A. Hayes & Mahalik
  (2000)

**Negative attitudes toward
  help seeking and pref-
  erence for help**
Bevan (2010)
Blazina & Marks (2001)
Blazina & Watkins (1996)
Bursley (1996)
Chan & Hayashi (2010)
Cortese (2003)
Englar-Carlson (2001)
Englar-Carlson & Vandiver
  (2002)
Good et al. (1989, 2006)
Good & Wood (1995)
James (2005)
Lane & Addis (2005)
Osborne (2004)
Robertson & Fitzgerald
  (1992)
Segalla (1996)
Simonsen et al. (2000)
Tsai (2000)
White (2002)
Wisch et al. (1995)

**Marital adjustment,
  lower daily marital
  happiness, greater
  depressive symp-
  tomatology, and
  greater nega-
  tive affect toward
  women**
Breiding et al. (2008)
Celentana (2000)

**Attachment problems
  to parents**
Blazina & Watkins
  (2000)
Cachia (2001)
Covell (1998)
DeFranc & Mahalik
  (2002)
Fischer & Good (1998)
James (2005)
Napolitano et al. (1999)
Schwartz, Waldo, &
  Higgins (2004)
Selby (1999)

EXHIBIT 9.1
Research on Gender Role Devaluations, Restrictions, and Violations Using the Gender Role Conflict Scale *(Continued)*

	Self-violations	
Low and high health risk Courtenay & McCreary (2011)	**Chronic self-destructiveness** Naranjo (2001)	**High-risk behaviors** Courtenay & McCreary (2011)
Negative alcohol-related consequences Groeschel et al. (2010)	**Eating disorder symptomatology** Blashill & Vander Wal (2009)	**Suicide attempts, acceptability, and risk** Houle et al. (2008)
Self-objectification Schwartz et al. (2010)	**Substance/alcohol abuse** Blazina & Watkins (1996) Fahey (2003) Kang (2001) Korcuska & Thombs (2003) McMahon et al. (2000) Monk & Riccuardelli (2003) F. Peterson (1999) Uy et al. (2013)	**Suicidal probability, amount of GRC for suicidal versus nonsuicidal men** Borthick (1997) Borthick et al. (1997) Houle et al. (2008)
Devaluations by others No data to report	**Restrictions by others** No data to report	**Violations by others** No data to report
	Devaluation of others	
Husbands' GRC/reported spousal criticism Breiding et al. (2008)	**Sex role stereotyping** Rando et al. (1998)	**Negative attitudes toward African Americans** D. T. Robinson & Schwartz (2004)
Homophobic and antigay attitudes Kassing et al. (2005) Lindley & Schwartz (2006) McDermott et al. (2014) Schwartz et al. (2005) D. F. Walker et al. (2000) Wilkinson (2004)	**Low sex role egalitarianism** Addelston (1995) Englar-Carlson & Vandiver (2002) Tokar et al. (1998)	**Restrictions of others** No data to report
	Violation of others	
Hostile sexism Covell (1998) Schwartz et al. (2005)	**Abusive behaviors and coercion** Schwartz et al. (1998) Senn et al. (2000)	**Dating violence** Harnishfeger (1998)

(continues)

EXHIBIT 9.1
Research on Gender Role Devaluations, Restrictions, and Violations
Using the Gender Role Conflict Scale   *(Continued)*

Sexually aggressive behaviors and likelihood of forcing sex	Hostility toward women	Rape myth acceptance
Kaplan (1992)	Rando et al. (1998)	T. L. Davis (1997)
Kaplan (1993)	Senn et al. (2000)	Kassing et al. (2005)
Serna (2004)	Serna (2004)	Rando et al. (1998)
		Serna (2004)
Positive attitudes toward and tolerance for sexual harassment	**Self-reported violence and aggression**	**Actual destructive or violent behavior toward others**
Covell (1998)	Amato (2012)	Amato (2012)
Glomb & Espelage (2005)	Chase (2000)	Breiding (2004)
Jacobs (1996)	Cohn & Zeichner (2006)	Breiding et al. (2008)
Kearney et al. (2004)	C. L. Johnston (2005)	C. L. Johnston (2005)
		Kaplan et al. (1993)

different racial/ethnic backgrounds, nationalities, and sexual orientations using the diagnostic schema described earlier. As I reported in Chapter 6, analyses were completed to determine which studies, and how many, support the devaluations/restrictions/violations paradigm for men of different racial/ethnic backgrounds, nationalities, and sexual orientations.

A second review of the pertinent studies revealed that self-devaluations, self-restrictions, and self-violations are significantly related to negative psychological outcomes for racially and ethnically mixed (non-White) groups of males, men from five countries, and gay men. In 26 studies, 19 psychological symptoms were correlated with gender role devaluations, restrictions, and violations. Five symptoms defined self-devaluations: (a) internalized homonegativity and heterosexism/negative feelings about being gay, (b) racism/self-hate, (c) depression, (d) low self-esteem, and (e) shame. Self-restrictions were defined by problems with coping, anxiety, stress, alexithymia, hopelessness, limited intimacy, and negative attitudes toward help seeking. Fewer studies related GRC to self-violations for diverse men. The four areas of self-violations are (a) eating disorder symptomology, (b) substance abuse, (c) chronic self-destructiveness, and (d) suicidal attempts or risk.

USING THE DIAGNOSTIC SCHEMA IN THERAPY WITH MEN

The evidence suggests that the diagnostic schema in Table 9.1 has some validity and can be useful to therapists in finding portals to men's GRC. The presenting problem of the client is the starting point for using the schema.

Respecting and affirming a client's own views of his problems is critical in developing the therapeutic alliance and setting the stage for deepening (Rabinowitz & Cochran, 2002) and the internal emotional work that is many times necessary. The first two major questions are (a) "What masculinity ideology has the client internalized?" and (b) "Which patterns of GRC is he experiencing?" A third critical question is, "Is masculinity ideology and GRC interacting with the client's symptoms and presenting problem?" If the answer to this question is yes, then the assessment questions should address which masculinity ideology norms and patterns of GRC relate to the man's presenting problem and any gender role devaluations, restrictions, and violations (see Table 9.2).

Therapists have a number of options to assess masculinity ideology; GRC; and the devaluations, restrictions, and violations described in Tables 9.1 and 9.2. The client may need to read about male socialization or discuss it fully in the sessions to have a frame of reference for any gender role transitions to occur. Working the gender role questions from the diagnostic schema (see Table 9.1) into the counseling is the direct approach. Another option is to administer a masculinity ideology measure or the GRCS. Administering such measures, along with assigning some carefully selected readings, can provide both personal assessment and theoretical grounding for the client's further exploration. Another approach is to conduct a full assessment of the client's psychosocial development to determine how past GRC has affected his adult functioning. A review of a client's early gender role socialization and how it affects his current views of masculinity and femininity also are important to establish. Investigating the source of a client's self-devaluations, restrictions, and violations in childhood and the family can be critical in uncovering current GRC. Finally, inquiries about whether the client experiences gender role devaluations, restrictions, and violations from others (Cells D_2, R_2, and V_2 in Table 9.1) and towards others (Cells D_3, R_3, and V_3 in Table 9.1) can help explain complex interpersonal dynamics that might otherwise go unexplored.

Helping men see how their socialized masculinity contributes to their problems is very important for any permanent change to be effected in men's lives. Table 9.1 can be useful in connecting men's symptoms to empirically correlated aspects of GRC in terms of gender role devaluations, restrictions, and violations. Explaining to clients how gender role devaluations, restrictions, and violations relate to their psychological and interpersonal symptoms can help them understand their GRC. Conceptualizing from this diagnostic schema can help counselors get down to the heart of the matter with complex problems that emanate from men's restrictive gender roles.

From the empirical analysis, calls to action in research are appropriate in a couple of the diagnostic cells in Table 9.1. Two areas that prompt further research are (a) how devaluations, restrictions, and violations caused by others result in psychological and emotional problems (Cells D_2, R_2, and V_2) and (b) how the restrictions of others (Cell R_3) cause problems.

SOME FINAL THOUGHTS ON ASSESSING MEN IN THERAPY

New assessment directions need to be pursued to improve therapy services for men. The diagnostic schemas in Tables 9.1 and 9.2 focus mostly on men's GRC problems and what might be wrong with a man. A new direction would be to create positive paradigms of healthy masculinity. Future research and conceptualization on affirmative and positive aspects of masculinity are needed (Kiselica, 2011; Kiselica & Englar-Carlson, 2010; O'Neil & Lujan, 2009b). Patterns of positive masculinity can help men and boys learn alternatives to sexist attitudes and behaviors that cause GRC.

In the future, diagnostic schemas that assess men's positive and healthy masculine attitudes and behaviors are needed. A real breakthrough can occur if therapists begin to more proactively assess the positive qualities men have or need to develop. This healthy masculinity schema would help men mobilize their potential with confidence and hope. The promotion of positive, healthy masculinity is needed to change sexism against both sexes and thereby decrease the suffering that men, women, and children experience as a result of restrictive gender roles.

10

GENDER ROLE JOURNEY THERAPY WITH MEN

Listen to me. If I talk to you and it turns me into a fag, I'll kill you. You understand?

—Paul Vitti, a potential client of Dr. Ben Sobel,
in the movie *Analyze This*

One of the best portrayals of working with a difficult male client is the classic exchange between Dr. Ben Sobel (played by Billy Crystal) and mobster Paul Vitti (played by Robert De Niro) in the movie *Analyze This* (Rosenthal, Weinstein, & Ramis, 1999). Sobel doesn't know what to do with Vitti, whose aggressive style is apparent within the first few minutes of the session. "You guys are supposed to be so great when it comes to listening," Vitti complains. "You can't remember what I said two seconds ago. I have to tell you, Doc, I'm not thrilled with the level of service up to this point."

Vitti goes on to say he came to therapy not for himself, but for "a friend," who is

a very powerful guy. Never had a problem dealing with things, you know? Now, all of a sudden, he's falling apart. He cries for no reason. He's having trouble sleeping. And then he started having these attacks. You know, can't breathe, dizzy, chest pains—like you think you're gonna die.

http://dx.doi.org/10.1037/14501-011
Men's Gender Role Conflict: Psychological Costs, Consequences, and an Agenda for Change, by J. M. O'Neil

Sobel identifies these symptoms as a panic attack, and Vitti immediately becomes defensive: "What's with all you doctors and the fuckin' panic? Did I say panic?"

Sobel then goes out on a limb: He guesses Vitti's "friend" is Vitti. His client is taken aback: "You—you—you—you God bless you, have a fuckin' gift," he stammers. "Just getting that off my chest, I feel better already."

When Sobel protests he didn't do anything, Vitti disagrees. "You did something," he says. "The load? Off. Where is it? Don't know. You're good, Doctor."

Vitti commits to the therapy but with a final, menacing caveat to Sobel: "Listen to me. If I talk to you and it turns me into a fag, I'll kill you. You understand?"

Sobel replies, "Could we define 'fag'? Because some feelings may come up." Vitti silences him with a wave of his hand: "I go fag, you die. Got it?"

In that one scene, Sobel and Vitti showcase the stigma of therapy for men, gender role conflict (GRC), male vulnerability, defensiveness, projection, denial, therapeutic relief, threat, confrontation, and therapy as homophobia and heterosexual threat. Restrictive Affectionate Behavior Between Men (RABBM) as a pattern of GRC makes Vitti feel that having another man listen to him about his problems will make him vulnerable to being gay. His association of therapeutic listening with the possibility of becoming a homosexual is so scary to him that, in true mafia style, he declares he will kill Sobel if it happens.

Sobel actually connects these homophobic reactions to having feelings and, no doubt, Vitti's panic attacks are actually caused by extreme Restrictive Emotionality (RE). On some unconscious or irrational level, Vitti must have deduced something like this: Expressing your feelings and being listened to by a man is feminine. Feminine is not masculine or male. If you are not male, you are female, and if you are a man who is female, then you are a homosexual. This kind of illogical reasoning reflects Vitti's need to protect his masculine identity from any possibility of becoming a homosexual because of the proposed therapy.

GRC could have been a therapeutic context for Sobel's counseling of Vitti. The empirical research I reviewed in Chapter 7 indicates that GRC is correlated with men's anxiety and homophobic fears. None of the research would assist Sobel in deciding how to help Vitti, and although the GRC diagnostic schema I discussed in Chapter 9 could help establish more about Vitti's masculinity ideology and GRC in the context of his anxiety, even organizing this diagnostic assessment information would not necessarily point to strategies for therapeutic change. If therapists are to help men like Vitti, another therapeutic paradigm is needed that addresses GRC in the context of the stages and processes of change—in other words, what is called the *transtheoretical approach* to therapy (Brooks, 2010; Prochaska & Norcross, 2001).

One of the more challenging issues for therapists is how to help men resolve their GRC during psychotherapy. Men often bring anxiety, depression, and grief to therapy, and many times the way to help them is unclear. How often do therapists conceptualize men's symptoms in the context of socialized gender roles? For the clinicians who recognize men's symptoms as GRC, how often is the insight used to foster therapeutic growth? Brooks (2010) suggested that mental health professionals have failed boys and men in their therapeutic approaches to help them, and almost all the experts agree therapy with men is difficult, complex, and problematic.

The gender role journey metaphor has been used in psychoeducational workshops for many years (O'Neil, 1996; O'Neil & Roberts Carroll, 1988; see also Chapter 13, this volume), but it has not been fully discussed as a paradigm for counseling men. In this chapter, I discuss a new way of conceptualizing men's therapy using the gender role journey and GRC. First, I define the gender role journey in terms of the three phases and aspects of the transtheoretical therapy approach (Brooks, 2010; Prochaska & Norcross, 2001) and the deepening framework (Rabinowitz & Cochran, 2002). Next, I identify three critical contexts of gender role journey therapy (GRJT) by conceptualizing GRC as a diagnostic and process variable. On the basis of the theories and contexts, I discuss six principles of GRJT as the theoretical foundation for facilitating men's change during therapy. Next, I discuss the therapeutic process of GRJT, using the stages and processes of change (Brooks, 2010; Prochaska & Norcross, 2001) and the gender role journey phases, along with how therapists can respond to clients' symptoms. I close the chapter with suggestions on helping clients move from one stage of therapy to another and therapeutic strategies to resolve GRC.

THE GENDER ROLE JOURNEY: ONE WAY TO CONCEPTUALIZE MEN'S THERAPY

As defined in Chapters 3 and 5, the gender role journey is a metaphor to help people examine how their emotional, psychological, and interpersonal lives have been affected by their gender role socialization, sexism, and other forms of oppression (O'Neil, Egan, Owen, & Murry, 1993). The journey involves evaluating thoughts, feelings, and behaviors about gender roles, sexism, and GRC (O'Neil & Egan, 1992a) and includes a retrospective analysis of early family experiences with gender roles and an assessment of one's present situation with regard to sexism. Part of the journey process is to gain an understanding of how GRC develops in the family, with peers, and in schools and how it comes from the larger society. The gender role journey also calls for the identification of gender role transitions and a reexamination of gender role schemas (see Chapter 5, this volume) over the life span (O'Neil & Egan 1992b; O'Neil & Fishman, 1992; O'Neil, Fishman, & Kinsella-Shaw, 1987). In other words, the journey is a reevaluation of how masculinity and femininity has affected one and what can be done about it personally, professionally, and politically.

Called "deconstruction of traditional gender roles," the evaluation process involves the critical analysis of destructive gender role stereotypes and the assessment of unverified sex differences that are the basis for sexism for both men and women. Alongside the deconstruction of sex and gender roles can occur a parallel deconstruction process with reference to racial/ethnic, class, and sexual orientation indexes. The deconstruction process can also involve analyzing the status quo's investment in sexism and the dominant culture's potential to oppress groups (including women, people of color, sexual minorities, immigrants, and even White men) through personal and institutional forms of sexism, racism, classism, heterosexism, ethnocentrism, or any other kind of discrimination. The deconstruction process and oppression become directly associated with stereotyping, sex discrimination, poverty, sexual assault and harassment, emotional abuse, and violence.

On a personal level, reevaluating gender roles means looking inward and assessing how masculinity and femininity have both enhanced and restricted one's interpersonal growth. Moving through the phases of the journey stimulates important personal questions, such as "How do sexism and GRC limit human potential and negatively affect my interpersonal relationships?" and "How can gender role schemas be discerned and redefined, and how can gender role transitions be managed positively?"

As I reported in Chapters 4 and 5, the gender role journey concept has empirical support (McDermott & Schwartz, 2013; McDermott, Schwartz, & Trevathan-Minnis, 2012; O'Neil et al., 1993). The Gender Role Journey Measure (O'Neil et al., 1993) was created to help both men and women determine which phase of the gender role journey their current condition most closely approximates (O'Neil et al., 1993). The three empirically derived phases of the journey are (a) acceptance of traditional gender roles; (b) gender role ambivalence, confusion, anger, and fear; and (c) personal and professional activism (O'Neil et al., 1993). Exhibit 3.1 contains descriptions of the attitudes and behaviors associated with these three phases that are relevant to men's therapy. The exhibit shows the phases separately and implies a natural, linear progression from one to the next in positive gender role growth. In actuality, regression in the phases and fluctuation in attitudes about gender roles may occur, depending on the person's situation and environmental contingencies.

In Phase 1, characterized by acceptance of traditional gender roles, the person embraces traditional stereotypes of masculine and feminine attitudes and behavior. Societal and family structures usually endorse and reward conformity to these stereotypes and expect individuals to build their identities on them. The extreme male stereotype is the "macho man"; for a woman, it is the "beauty queen." Acceptance of roles based on these stereotypes implies endorsing highly sex-typed behavior and restrictive views of gender roles for men and women. This phase is typical of most people's gender role socialization in childhood and adolescence.

Some men in Phase 1 believe that male and female roles are based on biological and essentialist imperatives. Men should be in charge at work and in the home, and women should provide the primary child care; men should be stereotypically strong and not show weakness or emotions, and women should be more passive, submissive, and unassertive. Individuals in Phase 1 have limited awareness of how sexism hurts people, believe that feminism has caused problems between men and women, and do not problems of sexism and discrimination exist. Often, they devalue and dislike people who violate gender role stereotypes at work and in family relationships.

In Phase 2, marked by gender role ambivalence, confusion, anger, and fear, the person's consciousness has been raised regarding the problems with restrictive gender roles and sexism, but confusion about gender role stereotypes remains, along with fear about deconstructing them and ambivalence about taking the gender role journey. The person vacillates between accepting the stereotypes and recognizing that they negatively restrict people's lives and relationships and between their new gender role consciousness and the safety of the old stereotypes of masculinity and femininity. Although this ambivalence implies dissatisfaction with or doubts about the value of stereotypical gender roles, questioning or changing gender role stereotypes is frightening, and the person needs help and support with the process.

As well as being fearful, the person in Phase 2 feel angry about sexism but is not sure why, or what to do about it. Sometimes the anger emanates from the realization of potential lost in Phase 1 of the gender role journey—from the recognition that the stereotypes are insufficient to build a human identity and that the person has been a victim of sexism and restrictive gender role socialization. The more anger is expressed, the more conflict is experienced, but the person may fear taking action that could produce negative consequences and reactions from others. The result of all the ambivalence, confusion, anger, and fear is psychological warfare in the form of combat among the different parts of the person's psyche, as the desire to retain the old self clashes with the quest to create a new one. The person may think about giving up the struggle and reverting to Phase 1. In Phase 2 there is no closure with the issues, and the person is left in a state of ambivalence and confusion.

Anger is pivotal in moving the person to the third phase of the journey. The real issue is how to use one's anger constructively. Staying angry or getting stuck in one's anger is counterproductive. Only when this negative state worsens or persists to the point that the person tires of it, however, does he or she become willing to risk changing him- or herself and challenge the status quo by moving on to action.

This brings us to Phase 3, characterized by personal and professional activism, which means changing oneself by integrating the anger and making commitments to reduce sexism in one's own life and the lives of others. Activism really begins when just talking has not worked and personal change is perceived as a better course to pursue. The person attempts to live free from restrictive gender role stereotypes and sexism and feels an inner strength and power based on rejecting them. He or she feels responsible for reducing sexism and believes something can be done to prevent it. Anger, pain, and emotions are channeled into positive efforts to raise other people's consciousness through teaching and other activist interventions. Increased self-communication is required to remain in the activism stage, and joining a network of support is helpful to avoid getting burnt out. People in Phase 3 have greater compassion for themselves and for other people in their gender role journeys.

The gender role journey is a male-friendly way of analyzing the self and may appeal to men who find deep introspection threatening. Full theoretical descriptions of its phases can be found in earlier publications (O'Neil, 1996; O'Neil et al., 1993; O'Neil & Egan, 1992a; O'Neil & Roberts Carroll, 1988). In the next section, I integrate the gender role journey phases with therapeutic processes and the transtheoretical model's stages of change, creating a base for GRJT.

THEORIES AND CONCEPTS RELATED TO THE GENDER ROLE JOURNEY THERAPY

The deepening concept (Rabinowitz & Cochran, 2002), the transtheoretical approach (Prochaska & Norcross, 2001), and an adaptation of the transtheoretical model (Brooks, 2010) provide the foundation for using the gender role journey phases in therapy. Each provides paradigms of change and intervention and therefore offers greater clinical application of the empirical and theory discussed throughout this book. Both Brooks (2010) and Rabinowitz and Cochran (2002) have mentioned the gender role journey as ways to organize therapy, but neither of them fully integrated the gender role journey phases into the therapy process. These heuristic models help explain how journeying with gender roles can result in resolving GRC and promoting positive healthy masculinity.

Rabinowitz and Cochran's (2002) "Deepening of Psychotherapy" and the Gender Role Journey

GRC can be unconscious, and addressing it in therapy may require the therapist to penetrate men's defenses to reach their wounds, pain, and suffering. Therapeutic deepening (Rabinowitz and Cochran, 2002) is valuable in accomplishing this penetration. *Deepening* is a therapeutic process that helps the person move through layers of socially imposed and personally constructed defenses to deeper levels of human experience. On a man's journey with his gender roles, he can uncover and elucidate masculine-specific conflicts experienced on an emotional level (Rabinowitz & Cochran, 2002), the identification and resolution of which may be blocked by GRC. These conflicts may include ambivalence about independence and dependence in significant relationships; prohibition about emotionality and problems with grief, loss, and disappointment; issues with self-structure related to gender role identity in the masculine culture of the United States; and conflicts between being and doing (Rabinowitz & Cochran, 2002).

The gender role journey implies therapeutic deepening as the man confronts his GRC and the masculine-specific conflicts in his life. Success, Power, and Competition (SPC), with its emphasis on power and control, and RE's and RABBM's restrictions on feelings, can be obstacles to uncovering masculine-specific conflicts. Furthermore, with deepening, a critical task for therapists is identifying the *portal*: the central or focal conflict around which to organize thematic schemas in the male client's narrative, which provides an entry to its deeper, emotional elements (Rabinowitz & Cochran, 2002). By listening empathically and making sense of the client's life story, the therapist finds the portal through the wounds—defined as "shortcomings, frustrations with life's expectations, failure to live up to cultural masculine ideals, and rejection in relationships" (Rabinowitz & Cochran, 2002, p. 37)—all of which challenge his basic sense of self and destabilize his sense of well-being. GRC may be part of the central conflict, or it may cover the portal up so the real issue cannot be addressed.

With deepening, Rabinowitz and Cochran (2002) recommended assessing four interacting and overlapping dimensions of male experience: (a) psychological history, (b) formative experiences, (c) cultural upbringing, and (d) current functioning. These dimensions are relevant to the gender role journey because they are areas to be explored in making any gender role transition. In short, deepening is directly related to journeying with one's gender roles because it describes a dynamic and therapeutic process of change that deepens a man's experience of himself and the world he experiences.

Prochaska and Norcross's (2001) Transtheoretical Model's Relationship to the Gender Role Journey

A second theoretical perspective related to the gender role journey is the transtheoretical model of change proposed by Prochaska and Norcross (2001), which may be the most coherent, useful, and research-based approach for conducting therapy with men. The transtheoretical stages and processes of change have been documented empirically, and their value in doing therapy with clients is widely acclaimed. In transtheoretical therapy, the therapist focuses on contextual levels of the client's problems by taking into account multiple orientations and interventions and making note of factors in a client's life that maintain problems and constrain change (Prochaska & Norcross 2001). Sexism, restrictive gender roles, and GRC are contextual problems that can inhibit therapeutic changes and reinforce dysfunctional attitudes and behaviors.

The transtheoretical approach defines five stages of therapeutic change: (a) precontemplation, (b) contemplation, (c) preparation, (d) action, and (e) maintenance. These stages parallel the phases of the gender role journey described earlier and therefore have explanatory power in connecting GRC to psychotherapeutic practice. Each stage represents a period of time and a set of tasks to be accomplished before one can move to the next stage. The time one spends in each stage may vary, but the tasks are assumed to be invariant, although different change processes and relational stances produce optimal progress in accomplishing them. Definitions of the stages are provided below, along with the implications of the change process during the gender role journey that I discuss later in the chapter.

The *precontemplation* stage of therapy is when the client has no intention of changing his or her behavior in the near future but has an increasing awareness of the need to change. Although most clients in this stage are unaware of their problems, families or friends are often well aware of them and may put pressure on the precontemplators to face them. The precontemplators may wish to change, but they also resist: "I may have faults, but there is nothing I can do about them." If they are to alter their behavior, they need to own their problems. Phase 1 of the gender role journey is similar because clients in this phase are unaware of their GRC and the negative aspects of sexism and restrictive gender roles.

Contemplation is the stage in which clients are aware a problem exists and are seriously thinking about overcoming it but have not yet made a commitment to take action. They need to be motivated to change and have greater confidence in their ability to do so. Contemplators struggle with their positive evaluations of their dysfunctional behavior and the amount of effort, energy, and loss required to overcome it. Because it is easy to get stuck in this phase, some clients become chronic contemplators who are unable to take action. The contemplation stage of therapy is similar to Phase 2 of the gender role journey.

The *preparation* stage can be seen as analogous to a transition between Phases 2 and 3 of the gender role journey. Individuals in the preparation stage intend to take action soon, and they report small behavioral changes. Their problem behavior has been reduced, but their efforts cannot yet be considered effective action. The client has to negotiate a plan, set goals, use the insights developed in the contemplation stage and, finally, make a full commitment to the change process.

Action is the stage of therapy in which individuals change their behavior, experiences, and environments to overcome their problems through a full commitment to change that corresponds directly to Phase 3 of the gender role journey. Clients are in the action stage if they have successfully altered their dysfunctional behavior for a period ranging from 1 day to 6 months. Action involves the most overt behavioral changes and requires considerable commitment of time and energy, and clients in this stage have developed skills and can use them.

In the *maintenance* stage, which extends from 6 months to an indeterminate period past initial action, individuals work to prevent relapses and consolidate the gains attained during the action stage. The therapist should encourage active problem solving to achieve this. Remaining free of the problem and/or consistently engaging in a new behavior for more than 6 months are the criteria for being in the maintenance stage. Maintenance equates to ongoing personal and professional activism phase of the gender role journey.

Transtheoretical theory also describes seven processes of change that relate to each stage and to the transition from one stage to another: (a) consciousness raising, (b) catharsis, (c) environmental reevaluation, (d) self-reevaluation, (e) self-liberation, (f) contingency management, (g) counterconditioning, and (h) stimulus control. In *consciousness raising*, observations, confrontations, and interpretations help clients become more aware of the causes and consequences of, and the solutions to, their problems. In the context of the gender role journey, the therapist can provide an opportunity for clients to review their GRC. The deconstruction of gender roles and the consideration of new models of positive masculinity are part of consciousness raising in the gender role journey. With *catharsis*, or dramatic relief, the therapist provides clients with helpful affective experiences that can raise emotions related to problem behaviors. *Environmental reevaluation* means evaluating how one's behavior affects others, and *self-reevaluation* involves assessing which values clients will actualize and which they will exclude from their lives. During the gender role journey a similar process of reevaluating relationships and personal values occurs, related to gender roles and sexism. *Self-liberation* means not only believing one has the autonomy to change one's life but also recognizing that coercive forces may block efforts, so self-efficacy is needed. *Contingency management* is rewarding oneself or receiving positive affirmation from others by establishing contingencies related to overt and covert reinforcement, whereas *counterconditioning* and *stimulus control* are ways to cope with external circumstances that may cause a relapse. Both contingency management and counterconditioning can be applied to the gender role journey, in particular, when one is making the transition from one phase to another. These behavioral techniques can be developed in therapy with the help of the therapist; all are relevant to facilitating the gender role journey.

Brooks's (2010) Contribution to the Transtheoretical Model

Gary Brooks (2010) used the transtheoretical approach to explain how the stages and processes of change relate to men's therapy. His elaborate model provides a very useful theoretical and clinical foundation for therapy with men, offering a comprehensive approach based on eight central concepts. Like Rabinowitz and Cochran (2002), Brooks recommended performing male-specific diagnostic assessment by evaluating a man's gender role socialization as part of his problem, as well as assessing his motivation and the different kinds of pressure that might affect his engagement in therapy. He diagrammed four types of male therapy seekers that are very useful in assessing clients' motivation and pressure to change. He discussed motivational hurdles for clients and described the therapeutic alliance in terms of goals, tasks, and bonds. Brooks provided a complete review of user-friendly therapies for boys and men and discussed the challenges of dealing with diverse masculinities and the importance of multicultural competence. Finally, he applied Prochaska and DiClemente's (2005) transtheoretical approach to therapy in terms of the processes and stages of change.

GRJT builds on Brooks's excellent adaptation of the transtheoretical analysis and extends it in new ways. Brooks indicates that the gender role journey metaphor used in workshops (see Chapter 13, this volume) is relevant to therapy: "Although O'Neil described his workshops as more or less freestanding from psychotherapy, it is easy to see how the consciousness-raising aspects would dovetail with it by facilitating many men's transition from precontemplation to greater consideration of entering therapy" (p. 59). Brooks's adaptation of the transtheoretical approach and his contributions to therapy with men are integrated later in the chapter with the discussion of GRJT processes.

THREE CLINICAL CONTEXTS OF GENDER ROLE CONFLICT IN MEN'S THERAPY AND THE GENDER ROLE JOURNEY

Besides developing broad theoretical foundations, the way GRC operates during the therapeutic process is critical to facilitating the client's gender role journey. Three clinical contexts are critical to explaining how GRC can affect men's therapy and the development of the therapeutic bond, each with implications for the therapeutic process and positive therapy outcomes. The three clinical contexts are GRC (SPC, RE, RABBM, CBWFR): (a) as the client's presenting problem and symptoms, (b) as how clients enter and experience the therapy, and (c) as the client–therapist therapeutic dynamics.

First, the patterns of GRC can be associated with clients presenting such problems as depression, anxiety, or stress. Most empirical research (see Chapters 6 and 7, this volume) has documented a relationship between GRC and a variety of intrapersonal and interpersonal problems. Often, clients' GRC is unconscious; therefore, clients may not be able to understand the relationship between GRC and their psychological symptoms and problems. Both unconscious GRC and denial are critical contexts for therapists to assess in the early parts of therapy.

A second clinical context is based on the possibility that the therapy process itself is an experience in GRC for the client. Rochlen and Hoyer (2005) suggested that because the therapy process runs counter to almost everything men have learned about being a man, coming to therapy is an exercise in conflict. Remember that GRC is a psychological state in which negative consequences occur because of restrictive gender roles and self-devaluations, self-restrictions, and self-violations. This context implies that GRC occurs in just *coming* to therapy because it amounts to an admission that the client has failed as a man by not solving his problems on his own. Furthermore, starting a therapeutic relationship that requires being introspective and vulnerable and asking for help can feel like a negative consequence. More than 25 studies have suggested that men's GRC is significantly correlated with negative attitudes toward seeking help (O'Neil, 2008c), implying that receiving help could also be a negative or fearful situation.

The third GRC context is based on client–therapist dynamics, which implies that both the client's and therapist's GRC can be activated during the therapy process. For the client, the GRC may relate to fears about being vulnerable, trust issues, losses of control, and homophobia. GRC as a transference is highly relevant with men in therapy and can be addressed or used in therapy. The therapist's GRC and biases about men can also impede the therapeutic process and be a form of countertransference; this is most likely to happen with therapists who have limited information about male socialization, unconscious or conscious heterosexism and homophobia, or unfinished business with men (in many cases, their fathers). The interaction of GRC in the therapy dyad challenges the therapist to get the process going and keep it moving by approaching it with insight and skill.

All three of these contexts are important to consider when helping men journey with their gender roles because they imply complexity when counseling men using GRJT.

PRINCIPLES OF GENDER ROLE JOURNEY THERAPY

To *journey* is to move through time and space for a reason and reach a new place, and therapy can be conceptualized the same way. The notion of a journey can lessen the stigma attached to therapy that can keep men from seeking help. Regardless of whether the path is predictable or the direction unknown, journeying implies movement and change. The goal of the gender role journey is to resolve GRC and promote healthy and positive masculinity.

I conceptualized the process of journeying with one's gender roles from observing students during the gender role journey workshop that was offered for 22 consecutive summers at the University of Connecticut (O'Neil, 1996; O'Neil & Roberts Carroll, 1988; see also Chapter 13, this volume). More than 700 men and women participated in this 6-day, psychoeducation experience, and my evaluations of the students' change processes as they considered whether and how to journey with their gender roles were critical in helping define the gender role journey therapeutic process. On the basis of those evaluations and past conceptions of men's therapy reviewed above, I present in Exhibit 10.1 six specific principles of GRJT and elaborate on them later in the chapter when I describe the stages and processes of change in GRJT.

GRJT establishes a structure for the male client to evaluate his experiences with gender roles and determine how his restrictive socialization in a sexist society contributes to any of his mental health problems. The therapist begins by assessing the client's posture toward change using the transtheoretical stages (precontemplative, contemplative, preparation, etc.; see Brooks, 2010; Prochaska & Norcross, 2001, and above) and his motivation and readiness to journey with his gender roles using Brooks's (2010) four types of therapy seekers framework. The client is offered an opportunity to evaluate how restrictive gender roles, sexism, and other forms of oppression have affected his life personally, professionally, and politically. He is invited or encouraged to complete a retrospective analysis of early family experiences with gender roles, make an assessment of his present situation with sexism, and create prospects for the future.

The phases of the gender role journey are a way for a man to discover his specific masculine conflicts and wounds in terms of GRC devaluations, restrictions, and violations (see Chapter 9, this volume). The journey facilitates therapeutic deepening and helps the therapist identify the portals to men's inner

EXHIBIT 10.1
Principles of Gender Role Journey Therapy

1. The three phases of the gender role journey phases can be used as a therapeutic framework to conduct therapy with men. Clients need to be assessed in regard to the phase of the gender role journey they most closely approximate and their readiness and motivation for change. Therapists can invite or encourage clients to take the gender role journey by asking them if they are open to evaluating how restrictive gender roles, sexism, and oppressions have affected them.

2. The three phases of the gender role journey parallel the stages of change in therapy (precontemplation, contemplation, preparation, action, maintenance) and relate to the context of a client's problems and the factors that maintain problems and constrain change (Brooks, 2010; Prochaska & Norcross, 2001). Phases 1 and 2 of the gender role journey are considered to be unhealthy, or at least unsettled, phases and reinforce masculine-specific conflicts and other problems in men's lives.

3. The gender role journey can be a way of helping men discover their masculine-specific conflicts and emotional wounds experienced as gender role devaluations, restrictions, and violations. Facilitating a client's gender role journey allows for deepening of the therapy (Rabinowitz & Cochran, 2002) and prompts gender role transitions. The gender role journey serves as a possible portal to men's problems in therapy. In this regard, the gender role journey and gender role conflict (GRC) become a "a way to organize the thematic elements in the male client's narrative as well as an entry or key to the deeper, emotional elements of images, words, thematic elements of the client's inner psychological life" (Rabinowitz & Cochran, 2002, p. 26).

4. Providing clients macrosocietal and diversity contexts to their gender role journey can help them discern how sexism and other oppressions have contributed to their psychological problems, including internalized oppression. Deconstructing masculine and feminine gender roles and stereotypes is the primary way to experience the gender role journey and help men resolve their GRC. Therapists have options when facilitating the gender role journey by using interviews, consciousness-raising exercises, psychoeducation, bibliotherapy, and masculinity measures. Psychosocial assessment of clients' development, their gender role transitions, and distorted gender role schemas can facilitate the gender role journey.

5. GRC is a multifaceted dynamic for both clients and therapists and needs to be monitored during therapy for positive therapy outcomes. Clients' GRC (Success, Power, and Competition [SPC]; Restrictive Emotionality [RE]; Restrictive Affectionate Behavior Between Men [RABBM]; and Conflict Between Work and Family Relations [CBWFR]) can be a defense that hides the portal and the masculine-specific conflicts and inhibits movement through the gender role journey phases and the levels and processes of therapeutic change (Brooks, 2010; Prochaska & Norcross, 2001). Psychological defenses may need to be assessed and worked with during the gender role journey. Assessing a man's masculinity ideology, patterns of GRC, and distorted gender role schemas is critical during therapy. Helping clients transition from one phase of the gender role journey to another by assessing and resolving the patterns of GRC (SPC, RE, RABBM, and CBWFR) can increase the deepening that occurs during the therapeutic process. Assessing how the man devalues, restricts, and violates himself and others is key to finding the portal and resolving the GRC. Healing from gender role devaluations, restrictions, and violations requires insight, assertiveness, self-efficacy, risk taking, and personal and professional activism.

6. Normalizing human vulnerability, wounds, and pain is critical to facilitating the gender role journey. Contextually, GRC may be a man's wound, may conceal a man's wounds, and may be a vehicle to discovering a man's wounds. The critical issue of transitioning men from one stage of change to another through the phases of the gender role journey occurs best with the resolution of the RE, SPC, homophobia, and control issues.

experience (Rabinowitz & Cochran, 2002). The journey involves the deconstruction of gender roles to identify any masculine specific conflict (i.e., GRC). The therapist uses a variety of therapeutic and psychoeducational techniques to facilitate the journey. In addition, there are a number of critical diagnostic questions for the therapist to pursue (see Chapter 9 for details). For example, what is the client's masculinity ideology, and how does it relate (if at all) to his presenting problem? Second, how does the man devalue, restrict, or violate himself for conforming to or deviating from expected gender role norms? Two other processes include a (a) psychosocial and (b) developmental appraisal of the man's life that assess gender role transitions and distorted gender role schemas (see Chapter 5). Furthermore, a macrosocietal and diversity context is introduced in the therapy, allowing the man to assess how sexism has contributed to his psychological problems, including internalized oppression (see Chapter 6).

During the therapy, the GRC of the client, the therapist, and the therapeutic interaction is monitored. Furthermore, human vulnerability, wounds, pain, and psychological defenses are discussed as important topics, and the therapist monitors how these critical issues hide the portal and men's GRC. GRC is construed as being a man's wounds, concealing a wound, or being a vehicle to discover the wound. Transitioning from one phase of the gender role journey to another may depend on working with the critical issues of RE, SPC, homophobia, and control issues during therapy sessions. Moving toward personal and professional activism of the gender role journey requires deepening insights, assertiveness, self-efficacy, risk taking, and activism.

THE GENDER ROLE JOURNEY THERAPY PROCESS: STAGES AND PROCESSES OF THERAPEUTIC CHANGE

The GRJT process integrates the stages of change put forth in the transtheoretical model (Brooks, 2010; Prochaska & DeClemente, 2005; Rabinowitz & Cochran, 2002; see above) with the three phases of the gender role journey (O'Neil et al., 1993), providing a developmental perspective on the therapy process in the context of a man's gender role socialization and GRC. In the sections that follow, I describe the man's cognitive, affective, and behavioral state for each stage of change, followed by therapeutic options and interventions for the therapist. The developmental perspectives and interventions are not meant to be fully prescriptive but instead to provide clinicians with many ways to think about gender-aware approaches to men's therapy. For the purpose of illustration, generalized statements about the stages and processes of change are enumerated. Not all of these would apply to every man, but they provide examples of how GRJT can be conceptualized and implemented.

Precontemplative Men in Phase 1 of the Gender Role Journey (Acceptance of Traditional Gender Roles)

In the first stage, many salient dynamics occur as the man decides whether to change and, if so, how. A man in the precontemplative stage is usually unaware he has any problems with GRC and denies that anything is significantly wrong. His unconscious GRC affects his views of masculinity and femininity cognitively, emotionally, and behaviorally. His endorsement of traditional gender roles is part of his dualistic thinking about masculinity and femininity—a black-and-white, essentialist way of looking at gender roles and the world. A man in this phase usually lacks awareness of how sexism restricts and violates people, may receive rewards for acting in stereotypical ways, and becomes angry when others violate or question traditional gender role stereotypes. He may devalue, restrict, or violate others who fail to meet his standards of masculine norms or share his categorical way of thinking about masculinity and femininity. He is likely to be homophobic and have negative attitudes toward gay, lesbian, bisexual, and transgendered men, or at least be confused or anxious by sexual diversity. He may limit his male friends to those men who share his restrictive world view of gender roles ("good old boys"), and these relationships may be superficial, not emotional or personally intimate, and affected by RABBM. Privately or unconsciously, he may even devalue, restrict, and violate himself for not meeting the masculine stereotypes or not consistently proving his masculinity.

Also in this stage, rigid defenses may block any consciousness about how sexism affects the man's life or the lives of others, and he creates an attitude of denial: "There are no wounds, nothing to really feel bad about." These defenses are maintained by RE that negatively affects the man's intrapersonal dynamics and interpersonal interactions. He devalues emotional expression (i.e., catharsis) as unnecessary and believes men should be strong and "suck it up." Emotions are considered inferior to rational thought, and others who do have feelings may be labeled as too sensitive, out of control, or overreacting. Anger may be the only emotion that is easy to access, but this too is tightly controlled and tucked away; only under the right conditions (threat or loss of control) might he express it, and sometimes explosively. Work or other time-consuming activities (e.g., sports) may be used to avoid emotions and stimulate Conflict Between Work and Family Relations (CBWFR).

Success, power, control, and competition (i.e., SPC) are important to a precontemplative man because he needs them to maintain an advantage and protect his masculine persona. Distorted gender role schemas related to control, power, emotions, sexual orientation, and competition emanating from his restrictive views of gender roles may reinforce how he thinks and behaves. A precontemplator may have a masked vulnerability: a fragility that may remain invisible until he confronts a challenge to his worldview, a crisis, or a loss of control in his intimate or his "close" relationships. Therapy may involve these kinds of challenges and vulnerabilities.

Politically, men who typify this group have very limited awareness of how macrosocietal factors—specifically patriarchy, hegemonic masculinity, and sexism—affect their lives and shape their gender role identities. Furthermore, they have little awareness of how psychosocial development is negatively affected by stereotyped masculinity and femininity ideologies and essentialist perspectives. Precontemplators are also unaware of how sex, race/ethnicity, class, and sexual orientation shape masculinity ideology and how oppression is a psychological problem for men and women. Gender role transitions are difficult to complete in this stage because rigid thinking and rules about gender roles prohibit change and renewal.

Finally, a man in this stage is unaware of how gender role devaluations, restrictions, and violations contribute to his psychological problems. SPC problems are likely to operate during therapy—that is, assuming the man begins or sticks with therapy at all. A high percentage of male clients in this stage will not come to therapy, will be no-shows, or will terminate therapy as soon as their defenses are tested or their real problems are confronted.

This stage and phase of change has the greatest number of issues to consider and therefore is the most challenging and complex stage of therapy with men. How does the therapist work with a client who cannot see his problem and lives in denial, with restricted gender roles? How does the therapist promote deepening, find the portal, and organize the therapy (Rabinowitz & Cochran, 2002)? Changing a man's dualistic thinking or gender role identity after years of sexist gender role socialization is complex and requires patience, experimentation, and strategic interventions.

Brooks (2010) provided a number of important insights regarding what needs to happen with precontemplative men. He suggested that the relational bond is critical, and therapists should invest highly in gaining the client's trust. Encouraging clients to look at therapy as involving "masculine" tasks, such as coaching, goal orientation, and using teamwork to get a job done, normalizes the process of helping and decreases the possibility that the man will feel "small" or "less than" the therapist. As Englar-Carlson suggested in the DVD *Engaging Men in Psychotherapy*, small talk may help break the ice and begin the early bonding (American Psychological Association, 2011). The use of humor or brief self-disclosures by the therapist can make these early moments of therapy evolve into a fluid exchange between two strangers. The therapist should show the client a high level respect and honor him during the critical entry period. For example, the client's strength and courage need to be acknowledged by making statements that directly affirm the client's efforts. The therapist can assess whether the therapy process itself is an experience in GRC for the client that stimulates personal devaluations, feelings of failure, and shame. If so, helping the client see that seeking help can be a sign of intelligence, strength, and courage instead of a personal failure can decrease the stigma of therapy quickly.

A critical task in the early minutes of the first session is to assess how easily the client does talk therapy. How comfortable is he having an intimate conversation about himself with another human being? This assessment allows the therapist to decide how much control to take in the first session. Seeking permission from a highly resistant man to ask questions or make comments can give the client a sense that he is in control of what is happening and mediate any power conflicts.

In the early sessions, the therapist also needs to assess the client's stage of change. Does he deny he has a problem (precontemplative), admit he has problem but does not know what to do about it (contemplative), or want solutions (preparation) or is ready to take action (Prochaska and DiClemente (2005)? Brooks (2010) also conceptualized very well the issue of the precontemplative client's readiness to change with his 2 × 2 paradigm describing how the client's motivation to change is affected by external pressure placed on him to change. Another part of assessing a man's stage of change is hypothesizing what emotions (e.g., anger, fear of failure, loss) might block the change process.

Listening to the client's story and understanding what he experiences is much of what the first sessions are about. A precontemplative client may covertly feel a loss of control as he discloses personal information, which contradicts a key imperative he has been taught as a man: "Don't expose any weakness, because you will be hurt or lose your advantage." The therapist can mediate losses of control and shame by giving affirmation and full support for the client's strength and courage and also use selective self-disclosure to mediate the potential emotional fallout of sharing power with another man.

According to Brooks (2010), the therapist should offer opportunities and options to the client and is the change agent that sells the therapy. The options need to be tailored to the client; they should not be too much or too little for the individual. For more tentative or distrusting clients, adhering to the generality that "things can probably get better" may be best, whereas with more secure clients the therapist can propose the idea that, as men, they need to tell the truth about their lives.

Another issue to address in the first or early sessions is establishing a structure for the therapy and setting mutually agreed-on goals. Many men like structure in ambiguous situations, and establishing an articulated process can give the client a sense of what to expect. Also common among men is a pragmatic attitude toward therapy: "I want you to fix me or help me fix myself"; "I want to get over this." Therapists need to be clear that it is the client's responsibility to change himself, with the therapist's help. Setting achievable goals together can demonstrate that power sharing is part of the therapeutic process.

Because a precontemplative client is in denial and unaware that anything is wrong with his masculinity, the next step to be taken is consciousness raising and psychoeducation in the context of his presenting problem (Brooks, 2010; Prochaska & Norcross, 2001). Because the therapeutic portal (Rabinowitz & Cochran, 2002; see also the earlier discussion in this chapter) is usually unclear, this step is needed to help the man understand the problem so he can move to the next stage of therapy, where change is acknowledged and worked on.

Consciousness raising is designed to specify the problem in more detail and identify its source. At some point, the process needs to be centered specifically on masculine socialization to determine its relevance to the presenting problem. At first, bibliotherapy, to help explain the restrictive aspects male socialization, may be useful, but ultimately the client needs to be asked whether his problems relate to masculinity ideology, distorted gender role schemas, and GRC. A planned and sequential approach to introducing these issues may be needed if his defenses are strong and his resistance is high.

Once the problem has been identified, its negative consequences need to be discussed, Brooks (2010) indicated, so that "the client sees what hasn't been seen before" (p. 29). Directive questions such as "Tell me what the consequences will be over the next 10 years if you do nothing about this problem now" can drive home the severe seriousness of inaction. This is "truth time" for the client and is always a complex moment to get through because the closer one gets to the truth, the higher the probability that psychological defensiveness, resistance, and fear will follow.

Under these circumstances, the assessment of the client's defensive structure is essential to determining strategies for change. Highly defensive men may need psychoeducation on what defenses are and how, though they are necessary for coping, they also can obstruct finding the truth and making change. Bibliotherapy that addresses defenses, emotionality, or other men's issues may be necessary before genuine truth telling occurs. From the information they read about men's lives through bibliotherapy, clients can learn they are not the only ones with problems and perhaps discern how the larger society sets both men and women up for sexism and dysfunction.

Brooks (2010) suggested that the therapist address directly how masculinity contributes to the man's problem by exploring questions such as "What does it mean to be a man?" This question is a direct assessment of the client's masculinity ideology and designed to deepen the therapy and bring the masculinity issues to a head. Of course, the answer is what is important. Can the man conceptualize how his socialized masculinity has implications for his mental health? Specific masculinity constructs may need to be directly introduced into the therapeutic process, including masculinity ideology, GRC, gender role transitions and schemas, and the gender role journey process. Furthermore, how sexism and other forms of oppression emanate from families, peers, and school experiences can be offered as a way to understand a man's problems. This leads to an analysis of the man's psychosocial development in terms of the mastery of developmental tasks and the resolution of psychosocial crises. The critical question is how restrictive gender roles delay psychosocial growth. The false assumptions and promises about gender role stereotypes and the illusions about the rewards of highly sex-typed behaviors can be part of the discussion.

The therapist can administer the Gender Role Conflict Scale (O'Neil, Helms, Gable, David, & Wrightsman, 1986), the Gender Role Journey Measure, or some other masculinity measure and then follow up with questions about what the man is currently doing in terms of his masculine gender role identity. After a personal assessment of the client's GRC (SPC, RE, RABBM, CBWFR), the next question is how the GRC and the client's problems developed—a question that in turn prompts the critical macrosocietal question "How do patriarchal societies oppress men, and what is the role of oppression in men's lives?" The man's experiences with oppressions can be discussed by explaining how internalized oppression (i.e., turning oppression back at oneself) is a serious mental health issue.

At the same time, the client can be encouraged to increase self-dialogue around these issues and the entire therapy process. The client can be prepared or taught how to manage emotions, including how to label, experience, and express strong feelings from a position of strength and positive health. Physical health problems related to psychological functioning also should be discussed, and the interaction of race/ethnicity, class, and other diversity variables with the learning of gender role values add to the mixture of ideas. Finally, the client should be presented with the reality that all men are vulnerable, have wounds, and experience pain from the past that contribute to their current problems and that the gender role journey is a way to understand these issues and feel better. Because the introduction of the notion of working with wounds and emotional pain may stimulate memories of past abuses, trauma, and emotions for the client (Brooks, 2010), the preparation for emotional management mentioned earlier is critical so he will not get blown away by floods of emotions he cannot handle.

I agree with Brooks (2010) that attribution of blame needs to move away from exclusive self-blame and take into account the way macrosocietal factors contribute to a client's problems. This usually produces relief for the man and a new way of looking at his problems. At the same time, the therapist reinforces the man in regard to taking personal responsibility for making change to address his problems. The acknowledgment of positive, healthy masculinity as an alternative to GRC and sexism is critical and center stage.

Contemplative Men in Phase 2 of the Gender Role Journey (Gender Role Ambivalence, Confusion, Anger, and Fear)

In this stage of change, a man recognizes he has a problem and knows that something needs to be done about it, but he has no firm commitment to change. Following the work in the precontemplative stage, he is more open to evaluating himself cognitively and emotionally, more open to evaluating his behavior toward others (Brooks, 2010), and may see himself differently in masculine and feminine terms than he did before, but he may be unsure of how to actualize the changes with concrete and corrective action. Although he now accepts that GRC has affected his life (Brooks, 2010), confusion about gender roles and his problem lingers, and he still periodically has bouts with denial. He never fully experiences the deeper emotional aspects of the problem (i.e., fear and anger), and he may get stuck in his negative emotions and begin procrastinating about addressing the problem.

To move through this stage, a man must accept the reality of his problem and have some trust in the process, the therapist, and himself. Having hope for positive outcomes can act like a buoy as he vacillates on whether to follow through on specific actions and how to do so effectively, and between the safety of stereotypical gender roles and the excitement and anxiety of possible gender role change. On a cognitive level, the man experiences dissatisfaction with stereotypical notions of gender roles, understands their restrictiveness, and is more aware that societal sexism violates people—and is perhaps even angry about it—but the personal meaning of these insights may still be vague or only partially understood. Although the man begins to recognize how restrictive gender roles and sexism have limited his own human potential and identifies the distorted gender role schemas that affect him, redefinition of these salient cognitive structures is still difficult, and the costs and benefits of giving them up are difficult to calculate and reconcile. Taking action to address GRC still seems risky, and he is beset by fears and worries about losing his masculine identity and having no basis on which to clearly establish his life. Despite any consideration he might be giving to changing his gender role attitudes and behaviors, no major gender role transition can occur until alternative assumptions about self and the world are more fully processed.

At the contemplative stage of change, the therapist may still be looking for the portal to organize thematic elements in the client's narrative, and deepening may need to occur (Rabinowitz & Cochran, 2002). The therapist should recommend increased internal dialogue (self-talk) as a way of bringing out the salient gender role issues. Distorted gender role schemas may need to be directly assessed and corrected. The false assumptions and lies about gender role stereotypes can be discussed on a more emotional level than in the preceding stage. Brooks (2010) indicated that during this stage the client can identify those people who have evaluated and judged him for adhering to or deviating from traditional gender roles. From a GRC perspective, this means identifying how the man has devalued, restricted, and violated himself because of GRC and masculinity ideology. Furthermore, the man can be directly assessed in regard to how he has devalued, restricted, and violated others and himself as well. This kind of soul searching may produce guilt, anger, and shame that become part of the deepening and, ultimately, of letting go of the pain.

The therapist may need to define *gender role loss* (i.e., giving up or deconstructing the stereotypes) so that the man can accept it as a necessary part of the gender role journey. Losses, if they are presented as opportunities to develop new life structures that serve the man better and more fully, can be turned into gains. The therapist should introduce the notion of risk and ask the client to monitor the triggers of intense emotions.

Central to this discussion is the acknowledgment of positive, healthy masculinity as an alternative to GRC and sexism. To resolve the vacillation and ambivalence toward making changes to accept that alternative, additional reflective homework activities and bibliotherapy may be necessary. Discussing the research evidence for the negative effects of GRC may help move the client to the next stage of preparation and action, as may having him calculate again the costs versus the benefits of changing. The therapist needs to exercise patience in letting these processes play themselves out, providing maximum support and care to avert any possibility of the client's opting out of the gender role journey.

At this point, the client himself may grow impatient with the therapy and may blame the therapist for the slowness of the process. This kind of projection may be a sign that the therapy needs to move to a much deeper emotional level, and it should be discussed and worked through, along with any power struggles that might inhibit moving the therapy to the next stage. The therapist may need to return to the man's wounds and pains discussed in the first stage, presenting vulnerability as a sign of strength and a useful emotional state from which to change one's life.

To get to the deeper emotions—in particular, anger, loss, and fear—the therapist may need to orchestrate emotional catharsis, perhaps stimulating the full impact of the gender role devaluations, restrictions, and violations. The client may need to face his internalized oppression and trust the process of letting go of his pain that is associated with it. The result may be defensiveness and "pushback" from the client, and more power struggles may occur. The defense mechanisms identified in Phase 1 may need to be rearranged so the man can process more complex thoughts and feelings. The client needs to feel the past, present, and future losses from the GRC and experience the anger as a vehicle for change. In short, the client's emotions need to accumulate to the point of discomfort so that he will put the insights and emotional turmoil into action. At the same time, he should be encouraged to create metaphors for healing as a vehicle for change and transformation.

Preparation, Action, and Maintenance Stages for Men in Transition From Phase 2 to Phase 3 of the Gender Role Journey (Personal and Professional Activism)

Preparation is the stage in which a man is intending to take action "soon" (e.g., in the next month) and reports some small behavioral changes (baby steps). The client fully commits to making changes in the very near future, but any minor change he has already made is not yet enough to call transformative or significant. The therapy goal now is self-liberation, whereby the man chooses a new life path that is not constrained by biology or past socialization (Brooks, 2010) and plans out a process to change his life. Because the client lacks a plan or map to make the personal changes with his gender role identity, he needs assertiveness and increased self-confidence to move the process along.

At this stage, the client expresses more negative emotions about sexism to others, which results in increased stress and anxiety because of people's reactions. The man's circle of friends may narrow to those who understand, empathize with, and can support his process. Sometimes the man gets stuck in his anger, becomes immobilized, and does not know what to do. A reduction in problem behavior has occurred, but a criterion for effective action has not yet been reached. The client has to develop a plan using the insights developed in the contemplation stage and make a commitment to it. The gender role changes he should make may still be unclear.

The client is now less ambivalent about resolving GRC, although he still does not have enough positive energy to act. He may wonder how the gender role transition will play out and whether he can actually pull it off. Defenses still operate, but with less negative impact because he has decided how to use his anger to make personal changes, possibly going as far as becoming an activist against sexism and other oppressions.

In the action stage individuals modify their behavior, experiences, and/ or environment to overcome their problems. Action involves the most overt behavioral changes and requires a considerable commitment of time and energy. As noted earlier, individuals are classified as being in the action stage if they have successfully altered the dysfunctional behavior for a period lasting from 1 day to 6 months.

Maintenance is the stage in which people work to prevent relapse and consolidate the gains attained during action. During this stage the therapist should encourages active problem solving. This stage begins at 6 months past the initial action and lasts for an indeterminate period. As I mentioned earlier, the criteria for it are remaining free of the problem and/or consistently engaging in a new, incompatible behavior for more than 6 months.

The preparation stage is all about getting ready to take action, and the therapist is a resource, "cheerleader," and supporter of this process. Calculated risk taking is discussed as a means of deciding what to act on and how. The therapist may be quite helpful in a coaching capacity by stimulating brainstorming and developing different behavioral options for the client. Part of the process is the creation of a supportive network of friends or colleagues to help the man take action. As he has learned how to channel anger and negative emotions into constructive action, it is time to generate possible action steps and review triggers of vulnerability. Giving the client insight into how others have managed this gender role transition to action may be quite useful and effective. People and situations that are likely to disconfirm change and not be supportive should be identified and discussed and strategies for dealing with inevitable disconfirmation devised.

Personal and professional activism means modifying oneself and becoming involved in changing situations and structures that are oppressive. In this phase, the client commits to personal and professional activism and develops a maintenance plan, using a timeline and taking charge of environmental contingencies. He is open to modifying plans of change if they are ineffective or do not meet the criteria of success or the desired outcome. A behavioral plan is also used to prevent any relapse and to continue the development of a healthy male lifestyle. The client engages in ongoing alteration of his environment to continue the changes. When successful action occurs, the probability is high it will bring about both positive confirmation and disconfirmation. Disconfirmation of the activism can come from family and friends who are not sure how to react to the man's changes and activities; in fact, negative reactions from others can be the stimulant for not being able to maintain the changes over time. Role models and mentors may be useful to help process the reactions to the man's activism.

With maintenance, the client has broken free from his problems over an extended period of time and has fully internalized any gender role transitions. Many times he will have become involved with individuals or organizations committed to the same course of action. This activity helps maintain the change and becomes a useful outlet for emotions and thoughts about the psychological problems that have been solved.

Summary of the Stage and Phase Analysis
for Gender Role Journey Therapy

Exhibit 10.2 is a summary of the stages and phases of change for male clients and their therapists during the gender role journey, including a list of possible client symptoms and dynamics in each phase of the gender role journey or stage of change as well as possible therapist interventions. The exhibit lists 91 client symptoms or therapeutic states and enumerates almost 80 action-oriented interventions for the therapist. The summary of this information defines GRJT in very operational terms and adds to the early work Brooks (2010) did integrating transtheoretical therapy with masculinity conflicts. The list should be useful in preparing diagnostic process-oriented assessments and interventions during men's gender role journeys. The exhibit can be used to find men's portals (Rabinowitz & Cochran, 2002) and determine their readiness for change (Brooks, 2010). Because every client and therapy process is different, Exhibit 10.2 can serve as a template for generating hypotheses about how to intervene, when to intervene, and what outcomes to expect, based on the stage of change and phase of the gender role journey.

MOVING FROM ONE STAGE OR PHASE TO ANOTHER

Because GRC is a portal or gateway to men's other problems (e.g., depression, anxiety, poor performance), having strategies to resolve it is critical to promoting change and the healing process. My workshops and clinical experience suggest that helping men resolve GRC with RE, SPC, and homophobia are the most important issues for therapists to focus on in facilitating the transition process. In the next paragraphs, I discuss why these problem areas are important.

RE is critical because resolving feelings is essential to solve inevitable problems in life. Many of life's problems cannot be addressed through rational thought; solving them requires emotional intelligence and the ability to label, experience, and express emotions. Emotional processing brings about the necessary insights for problem solving in interpersonal situations, both at work and in intimate relationships. Moreover, most men face intrapersonal emotional turmoil that rational thought cannot really help with, either. This is particularly true when it comes to trauma, loss, grief, and tragedy, which require emotional discharge, or what I call "emptying." Men who cannot process emotions are severely limited, suffer in silence, and struggle with their life problems.

SPC and control issues are also very useful avenues to promote change because they dominate male socialization and the course of men's lives. Men

EXHIBIT 10.2

Client Symptoms and Dynamics and Therapist Interventions for Each Phase of the Gender Role Journey

Precontemplative Stage and Phase 1: Acceptance of Traditional Gender Roles

Client Symptoms and Dynamics

- Is unaware of any gender role problems
- Has dualistic-categorical thinking
- Has unconscious gender role conflict (GRC)
- Receives rewards for stereotypic attitudes and behaviors
- Is unsure whether there is a problem
- Has limited awareness about sexism
- Has limited awareness about how sexism devalues, restricts, and violates people
- Is irritated when traditional gender roles are violated
- Devalues, restricts, and violates self and others
- Restricts friends to those who endorse his gender role values
- Has mostly superficial and distant relationships with others
- Has Restrictive Emotionality and Restrictive Affectionate Behavior Between Men
- Has rigid and strong defenses
- Devalues emotional expressions
- Has anger, perhaps the only emotion
- May work to preoccupy self to avoid emotions
- Thinks power and control are important to protect self
- Has distorted gender role schemas
- Has masked vulnerability
- Is unaware of macrosocietal effects of sexism and oppression
- Has limited awareness about his psychosocial development
- Has limited appreciation for diversity and multiculturalism
- Experiences difficulties making gender role transitions
- Becomes a no-show or terminates therapy prematurely
- Feels therapy stigmatizes him

Possible Interventions for Therapists in Phase 1 (Precontemplative)

- Define the gender role journey
- Experiment with strategic interventions
- Show patience and invest in bonding with client
- Use masculine terms for helping (i.e., coaching)
- Use small talk if appropriate
- Assess stage of change, readiness, and motivation
- Use humor to connect with client
- Make self-disclosures to deepen the therapy
- Show high respect and honor the client
- Affirm client's strength and courage
- Recognize that therapy may involve GRC for the client
- Explore false assumptions about gender roles
- Assess client's capacity for talk therapy
- Administer masculinity measures
- Get permission to ask questions and make comments
- Address self-blame and blaming others
- Listen to the client's story
- Assess client's experience with losses of control
- Encourage increased self-talk
- Offer options and opportunities
- Tailor options to client's comfort
- Introduce a pain paradigm
- Establish a therapy structure
- Make mutually agreed-upon goals
- Explain how diversity affects men
- Do consciousness raising around men's issues
- Consider bibliotherapy with client
- Assess distorted gender role schemas
- Define internalized oppression
- Discuss the negative consequences of GRC
- Ask how masculinity conflicts affect functioning
- Introduce masculinity concepts into therapy
- Introduce psychosocial concepts into therapy
- Prepare client for emotional management
- Assess physical health issues

(continues)

EXHIBIT 10.2

Client Symptoms and Dynamics and Therapist Interventions for Each Phase of the Gender Role Journey   *(Continued)*

Contemplative Stage and Phase 2: Gender Role Ambivalence, Confusion, Anger, and Fear

Client Symptoms and Dynamics

- Accepts the reality of his problem
- Has some trust of the process, the therapist, and self
- Has hope for positive outcome
- Vacillates on whether to follow through
- Gets stuck in thinking and procrastinates
- Identifies those who have judged him
- Is confused about gender role identity
- Vacillates between safety of stereotypes and eliminating them
- Deconstructs gender roles
- Has openness to change and gender role transitions
- Is ambivalent about the usefulness of stereotypes
- Has greater awareness of macrosocietal oppression
- Continued dissatisfaction with stereotypic gender roles
- Has increased awareness that sexism violates people
- Has some vagueness on how sexism operates
- Slips into denial about effects of gender roles
- Is confused by the emotional aspect of his problem
- Recognizes in a greater way that sexism hurts people
- Identifies distorted gender role schema
- Experiences difficulty redefining distorted gender role schemas
- Experiences difficulty calculating costs/benefits of changing
- Experiences difficulty taking action with GRC
- Has worries and fears about giving up old masculine identity
- Experiences losses as gender roles are deconstructed
- Contemplates making change
- Has no firm commitment to change
- Has lingering confusion about his problem
- Understands the seriousness about the problem but is not ready to act
- Becomes more flexible in evaluating himself cognitively and emotionally
- Takes baby steps with his problem
- Has no real plan to change
- Is ambivalent about taking action
- Sees himself differently but is unsure how to actualize the change
- Becomes more open to evaluate his behavior
- Accepts that he has GRC
- Experiences impatience with therapy

Possible Interventions for Therapists in Phase 2 (Contemplative)

- Look for the portal
- Deepen the therapy
- Recommend increased internal dialogue
- Bring out more salient gender role issues
- Assess distorted gender role schema
- Address false assumptions on an emotional level
- Assess and discuss devaluations, restrictions, and violations
- Assess shame and guilt
- Introduce the pain paradigm again
- Encourage journeying and letting go of pain
- Help calculate costs versus benefits of changing
- Assess gender role losses
- Introduce the notion of risk
- Encourage monitoring of emotion triggers
- Prepare the client for being blamed or criticized
- Monitor power issues with client
- Refocus client on pain and wounds
- Discuss the strength of vulnerability
- Help client work through internalized oppression
- Stimulate deep emotions about damaging GRC
- Help client use anger as a vehicle for change
- Help client create metaphors for healing
- Create discomfort that prompts action

Preparation Stage and Phase 2: Gender Role Ambivalence, Confusion, Anger, and Fear

Client Symptoms and Dynamics

- Intends to act soon
- Reports baby steps
- Has increased negative emotions about sexism
- Has increased stress about sexism and personal change
- Narrows circle of friends to those who support him
- Gets stuck in his anger sometimes
- Feels immobilized sometimes
- Is confused and doesn't know what to do
- Knows he needs to develop a plan
- Needs to make a commitment to change
- Is uncertain about what gender role issues need to change
- Feels less ambivalent but still can't act
- Has doubts how gender role transitions will work out
- Is unsure how to pull off the personal change
- Decides how to use his anger
- Decides whether to become an activist
- Continue to work on assertiveness
- Continue to work on increasing self-confidence

Possible Interventions for Therapists in Phase 2 (Preparation)

- Help client negotiate plan
- Brainstorm a plan with client
- Coach client on plan
- Give examples of others who changed their GRC
- Encourage client to read about other men
- Encourage positive use of anger
- Discuss self-liberation
- Discuss calculated risk taking
- Help create a network of support
- Review triggers of vulnerability
- Review plans of action
- Prepare client for disconfirmation
- Help client develop plan for disconfirmations

Action–Maintenance Stage and Phase 3: Personal and Professional Activism

Client Symptoms and Dynamics

- Takes positive action
- Modifies his behavior to overcome problems
- Reaffirms commitment to change
- Devotes considerable amount of time to making change
- Continues to change self
- Becomes involved in changing oppressive structures
- Implements plan of action
- Deals with disconfirmation
- Continues to seek role models and mentors
- Stays healthy
- Monitors possible relapse
- Celebrates success in renewing and transforming self

Possible Interventions for Therapists in Phase 3 (Action–Maintenance)

- Affirm client activism
- Give ongoing affirmation and support
- Encourage independence from therapy
- Help troubleshoot when there are problems
- Encourage client to build in reinforcers
- Celebrate client's renewal and transformation

who buy into highly sex-typed masculine stereotypes about success, power, control, and competition usually wake up in their 40s and acknowledge that these stereotypes are lies and illusions (Levinson, Darrow, Klein, Levinson, & McKee, 1978). The obsession with power, competition, and control is a defensive measure designed to ensure that men are not devalued or emasculated and do not appear feminine, in particular in front of other men. Also, if, as Kimmel (2005) suggested, one has to continuously prove one's masculinity, having an edge over everyone else is essential to being in full control. The reality, of course, is that many things are constantly out of our control. Healthy people understand that real control is being able to tolerate being out of control and effectively solve the problem with the least amount of stress. Helping men redefine the gender role schemas about control, power, and success can liberate them from the sexist illusions and distortions they have learned. This issue of power and control as a therapeutic vehicle for change is brought to life in the case study of Thomas I provide in Chapter 11.

Homophobia is another critical issue to address with men but a more difficult one to use as an avenue to change. Many men struggle with their sexual identities and fears because heterosexism rules U.S. society. Homophobia activates men's fears about femininity and their worries that other men will emasculate and humiliate them by challenging their sexual orientation. Being called gay can be pretty threatening, and men learn how to devalue and restrict each other in this way to give themselves an advantage and an edge and to finally "win." When men face their homophobia, they face their deepest fears, and this can liberate them from their sexism and restrictive socialization. Discussions about the homonegativity that oppresses gay, lesbian, bisexual, and transgendered people can generate compassion and deeper understanding of sexual minorities. In addition, I recommend that therapists encourage men to become close to other men because masculine connection can be healing and renew the male spirit.

THERAPEUTIC STRATEGIES TO RESOLVE GENDER ROLE CONFLICT IN THERAPY

Of course, the real question is how to help men in therapy with their GRC in a very practical sense. Exhibit 10.3 lists the four patterns of GRC—SPC, RE, RABBM, and CBWFR—and specific strategies that can be implemented to resolve it and promote movement toward problem solving and healing. Helping men learn how to label, experience, and discharge emotions may be the most important activity to pursue. Changing RE requires both factual knowledge about emotions and practice in expressing feelings. SPC also needs to be redefined, and exposing the illusions about success, control, and

EXHIBIT 10.3
Therapeutic Strategies to Resolve Patterns of Gender Role Conflict:
Success, Power, and Competition; Restrictive Emotionality;
Restrictive Affectionate Behavior Between Men; and Conflict
Between Work and Family Relations

Success, Power, and Competition
- Recognize the difference between power/control over others, sharing power, empowerment, and other categories of power
- Accept the lack of control in certain situations and being comfortable and confident with letting go of control "if necessary"
- Redefine success outside the capitalist and economic realms; humanize success
- Discuss other ways to validate ourselves than through winning and competing against ourselves
- Redefine *losing* as not representing failure as a man
- Engage in noncompetitive activities

Restrictive Emotionality
- Teach emotional vocabulary
- Read about emotional intelligence
- Discuss advantages of a fluid emotional life
- Project the cost of emotional restriction over 10-year period
- Analyze emotionally charged scripts
- Keep an emotion diary, log, or journal
- Redefine *emotional* in human terms
- Role-play feelings
- Use Perl's (1968) empty chair technique of "talking to your feelings"
- Analyze family members', peers', and colleagues' emotional capacity

Restrictive Affectionate Behavior Between Men
- Define and understand homophobia and heterosexism
- Understand how homophobia and heterosexism separate and restrict men
- Differentiate sexual issues from human intimacy and affection
- Explore body awareness
- Practice giving men compliments and receiving them
- Understand body–mind splits
- Practice self-disclosure with other men

Conflict Between Work and Family Relations
- Redefine success at work and in the home
- Learn time management skills
- Show self-compassion in regard to work/family stressors
- Prioritize and plan more
- Take turns in household responsibilities with a spouse
- Learn stress management
- Lower criteria for success at work and home on the basis of situations and contingencies

power can be eye openers, in particular when the severe costs incurred are identified. When RABBM is worked through, the client has more opportunities to actually practice getting close to other men and deconstruct homophobic and heterosexist attitudes. Exploring body awareness and engaging in more self-disclosure with other men as part of therapy homework assignments can be useful activities that move the man along to action and activism. In the same way, therapy can be a laboratory in which men resolve CBWFR through learning better time management, prioritizing, and managing stress in new ways.

SUMMARY OF GENDER ROLE JOURNEY THERAPY

The integration of GRC and gender role journey phases with previous therapeutic models provides new ways to think about therapy with men. GRJT explains how restrictive gender roles, sexism, and other oppressions are mental health issues for men, women, and children. The three clinical contexts of GRC (client's presenting problem, the therapy itself, and the client–therapist dynamics) expand both the assessment and intervention options with men. Stages-of-change assessment and gender role appraisal guide therapists' interventions. Moreover, GRJT helps clinicians find portals to men's problems, thereby promoting the deepening process. With this kind of therapy the assumption is that GRC is operative in some way during it and that it can thus be assessed, addressed, and used in constructive ways.

One critical insight about the journey has become clear from my work with clients and workshop students over the years: When consciousness is raised and people see that the sexist society sets them up to be oppressed, confused, and conflicted about gender roles, breakthroughs and transformations become a real possibility. With that single insight, both men and women can stop blaming themselves and others for their GRC, sexism, and other oppressions. They can let themselves off the "sexist hook" and consider how to recover through personal growth and societal activism. If either of these change processes occurs, then GRJT has been effective in changing people's lives.

11

USING GENDER ROLE JOURNEY THERAPY: THE CASE STUDY OF THOMAS

In this chapter, I present a case study of Thomas (a pseudonym), whom I currently see as a client. The case study provides an example of using gender role journey therapy (GRJT), the concept of deepening (Rabinowitz & Cochran, 2002), and transtheoretical theory processes and methods (Brooks, 2010; Prochaska & Norcross, 2001). The therapy comprised a process of deepening to find portals to Thomas's overt wounds as well as his buried wounds. Assessing Thomas's stage of change and determining the processes of change were a central dynamic in therapy. Like most men, Thomas had unresolved issues with power, control, and authority, so the multimodal treatments that promoted self-understanding and regulation were central to my therapeutic processes (Robertson, 2012). The two assessment paradigms I described in Chapter 9 were used in the therapy, and the case study illustrates the use of concepts discussed in Chapters 3 (gender role conflict [GRC] theory), 5 (psychosocial development), 6 (diversity and vulnerable men), 9 (assessment) and 10 (GRJT).

http://dx.doi.org/10.1037/14501-012

The case study has an ordered sequence and includes the following parts. First, I summarize Thomas's background and history, followed by my overall impressions of his presenting problem. Second, I detail my diagnostic process using GRJT processes and the assessment paradigms presented in Chapter 9. Third, I discuss the therapy process in a general way, and I close the case with a discussion of eight dynamic interventions or events that were part of the therapy. Thomas has read this case study, verified its accuracy, and has given me his permission to use it in this book.

THOMAS'S BACKGROUND AND HISTORY

Thomas presented himself as a very bright, 32-year-old White man with a history of extreme, intractable obsessive–compulsive disorder (OCD). From ages 14 to 24—his entire adolescence and early adulthood—Thomas experienced extreme fear, anxiety, nail biting, depression, facial tics, twitches, blinking, vocal tics, repetitive hand motions, suicidal ideations, ongoing music in his ears, the inability to track written words, and hopelessness. This is best described as a lost childhood and adolescence. Because of these severe problems, he attended a special math and science school where he received special accommodations and help. Thomas saw dozens of doctors and mental health professionals and tried more than 20 different medications to control the OCD. None of them worked, and for 10 years he was in a drug-induced daze from the medications' side effects, which contributed to his already severe symptoms.

Thomas had tried many different kinds of talk therapy and reported that cognitive behavior therapy was "useless" and made no difference with his OCD and swinging emotional states. He was able to finish high school because of his giftedness and the special help he received. He was accepted to college and was awarded a National Merit Scholarship, even though his symptoms persisted. When he reported to me that he attended college with this severe OCD still untreated, I knew that Thomas possessed extraordinary fortitude and was a person of great persistence and courage. These qualities helped him get into college, but the OCD made it impossible to manage the rigors of college life, and he dropped out, broke up with his girlfriend, and felt hopeless and suicidal after repeated failures with the drug therapy.

This was the low point for Thomas. He wrote,

> At different points, I dealt with growing breasts, inability to sleep, sleeping all the time, gaining 20 lb, hallucinations, akathisia, dystonia, fainting spells from hypotension, liver enzyme panels due to high dosages, and more than one doctor telling me I must have written something down wrong because "no one takes that dosage of this medication."

Furthermore,

> I wasn't that worried however—after all, since I could no longer read, could not date, could increasingly not do the martial arts I'd come to love, would never hold a job, and was watching everyone else from my cohort graduate, go to medical and law school, get married, have children, and so forth—well, I figured I'd move to my dad's house, and give it a few years, and when things didn't get better, I'd kill myself. I hadn't told anybody about this final plan; it wasn't a cry for help or a look for attention, it was simply the logical long-term plan for the life I had been dealt. Around this time, I also considered having an irreversible cingulotomy[1] that had only a 30% chance of helping my illness.

The big breakthrough came for Thomas when his psychiatrist at the time began to investigate alternatives to a cingulotomy. A deep brain stimulation (DBS) operation appeared to be the promising alternative to pursue. This experimental approach involves having electrodes implanted in the brain that deliver short pulses of electricity. This alters the patterns of activity in the brain, thereby reducing or eliminating the OCD.

This neurosurgical procedure changed Thomas's life by decreasing the OCD significantly, which helped him function better. He was able to sleep, drive, read, and function much more effectively in his interpersonal relations. He graduated from college with honors, worked as a high school teacher, and had only mild symptoms of OCD, including music always playing in his ears as well as lingering anxieties, fears, and bouts of depression. There were also numerous psychosocial problems because of what he missed from ages 14 through 24. Anyone who lived through this kind of life would naturally have an aftermath of problems to work out.

A few years later, the severe OCD symptoms began to return, and so did Thomas's previous terror and worries. He said, "It's all coming back." He described this return of the symptoms as traumatic. He consulted a major medical center and found out the electrodes and wiring that controlled the electrical impulses needed repair because of Thomas's recent 30-lb weight loss. The operation to repair the wiring was successful, and things returned to normal, but the hopeless and terrifying emotions of the past that had flooded him for months brought back his boyhood vulnerability of anger, loss, emotional dysregulation, and dealing with authority figures, worries, and fears about failure.

---

[1]A type of psychosurgery, usually an option considered only after all other efforts have failed, to treat unremitting severe OCD and depression.

INITIAL IMPRESSIONS OF THOMAS
AND HIS PRESENTING PROBLEM

Thomas presented himself as a very likable, perceptive young man who was highly motivated to try therapy again. His beard and long hair made him look like a 1960s hippie, and one participant at the National Psychotherapy With Men Conference, where I first presented this case (O'Neil, 2012a) and (with his permission) showed Thomas's picture, said that Thomas looks like Jesus Christ. My response was, "Can you imagine what it would be like to do therapy with Jesus?" Doing therapy with someone who looks like Jesus did touch me at some deep level, particularly when Thomas discussed his Christian beliefs and religious life as a resource for coping with his emotional pain.

During Thomas's first session it was quite apparent that he was extremely bright and gifted. The speed with which he talked was very rapid, and I struggled somewhat to comprehend all that he verbalized. The intensity and depth of his self-disclosures and delivery of personal history were highly animated, intellectualized, and powerful. Thomas was entertaining as he shared his extensive knowledge across numerous disciplines (including science, philosophy, and religion) in the context of his personal history. He discussed the helpful support of his fiancée and extended family during his life with severe OCD. He indicated that he was engaged to be married in a few months, and I immediately thought of this event as a major gender role transition in his life.

He articulated two presenting problems: (a) how to choose a career in the context of his ongoing OCD and emotional challenges and (b) lingering anxieties about how his OCD would limit his life and affect his family. Our work focused on career issues; managing life events; and identifying the triggers to his OCD, anxieties, and depression. This identification of triggers was very important because he wanted his marriage and family life to be positive and healthy. I was very impressed with Thomas's strength, determination, and courage in pursuing options to have a normal life, something that had escaped him during most of his adolescence and early adulthood. We were able to develop a good working alliance by attending to the complex dynamics of our therapeutic process, which certainly included our colliding masculinities and GRC as we worked together.

Establishing trust and a positive working relationship with a male client requires thought and care. I had some credibility with Thomas on the basis of the referring person's recommendation that I worked well with men, so maybe he had a little more hope that therapy with me could work better than his past therapies. He was dubious from the beginning as to whether it would work, but he wanted to check me out. He had seen a local social worker before coming to me and reported that it had been okay but that the therapy simply involved maintenance, limited change, and no progress with his lingering OCD and bouts with depression. I set positive expectations and did the "sales pitch," as I describe later in the chapter. Thomas challenged the therapy structure, but overall he got invested.

Thomas told me that he wanted to confront the lingering career issues that had been unresolved for over a decade. I told him that I do career counseling and that he had come to the right place. He also wanted to improve his management of his current OCD problems because he had trouble sleeping, was depressed, and found his anxieties and obsessions consuming at least some of the time. He had a polite and likable demeanor, and he impressed me with his knowledge and wit, but at times he was impatient and irritated if I directed the process or took too much control. I sensed masked depression and anger, lack of confidence, fears about failure, and real worries about the future. His self-presentation was strong and together, but there were moments of intense fear, vulnerability, worry, and rage as he told me about his past life with OCD, in particular from the years between the ages of 14 and 24. I knew that there was a canyon of vulnerability in Thomas, and his defenses were strong and difficult to penetrate with his rapid speech, perceptiveness, and quick reasoning. I was wondering how to get to the real issues (deepening). I sensed that his long-term OCD suffering was still traumatic for him, even though the severe symptoms were gone. I proposed that we meet for six sessions and then review whether the process was working and had the potential to resolve the career issues and his fears about not being able to manage his OCD in the future.

DIAGNOSTIC ASSESSMENT PROCESS USING GENDER ROLE JOURNEY THERAPY

In this section, I detail how I implemented my assessment and therapeutic process using aspects of GRJT. In describing this information I give more specific details about Thomas and our therapy interaction. I used the 13 therapist assessment domains depicted in Figure 9.1 to assess Thomas's psychological problems and potentials for change. I comment on each briefly next and elaborate in greater detail some of these assessment domains in subsequent sections of the chapter.

The first assessment domain—the therapist's GRC, knowledge about men, biases, and countertransference issues—was important to consider. My knowledge about men was adequate given my academic background and previous therapy with men, so there were few biases operating against Thomas, but countertransference issues were activated by Thomas. I felt some ambivalence about treating a severe case of OCD that had been so intractable, so I told Thomas that I was not a neuropsychologist and that other consultations may be necessary. Whether I could actually help him given his past failed therapies produced some self-imposed pressure on myself, and his intensely powerful outbursts of anger and hurt did activate my safety concerns, given that each session he put his pocket knife down on my coffee table and that he was a kung fu teacher and could take me out in a second. I assessed the risk to be minimal, and we discussed the purpose of carrying a knife when traveling anywhere.

The contextual, situational, and biological contingencies and the stages of change were important given Thomas's long history of OCD that had never been effectively treated and his strong desire to recover and have a normal life. The biological and situational issues from the past in Thomas's life were very important because they were constants and not likely to change. In terms of stages of change (Brooks, 2010; Prochaska & Norcross, 2001), Thomas straddled the precontemplative and contemplative stages and could be categorized as being in Phase 2 (characterized by ambivalence, confusion, anger, and fear of the gender role journey; see Chapter 10, this volume). He knew he had problems but did not trust that anyone could help him, basing this conclusion on his past failed attempts with talk therapy. He was eager to move to the action and activism stages of therapy, but there were barriers to work out before he could realize the human potential he had lost over his short life span.

Thomas's psychosocial history was assessed to be delayed because numerous developmental tasks had not been mastered and numerous psychosocial crises were unresolved. These psychosocial issues became portals (Rabinowitz & Cochran, 2002) for Thomas's healing. In terms of oppressions and being a victim, Thomas definitely met the criteria for each of these, given that he had been systematically discriminated against and stigmatized most of his life because of people's reaction to his OCD, facial tics, and his at-times-unusual interpersonal behavior. The multicultural, racial/ethnic, and familial identity areas of assessment were relevant to the extent that his White, southwestern U.S. socialization in a middle-class family played out in the therapy. One of Thomas's relatives was a mental health professional, and as a consequence Thomas was familiar with how therapy processes can work and other times be ineffective. Thomas had much vulnerability as a man, and he understood his problems with OCD quite well, but his postsurgery situation left him unsure about the status of his psychological functioning. There were also other emotional problems of which Thomas was unaware that we uncovered as the deepening began. Thomas's highly developed defenses had helped him cope through the many years of hopelessness, but now intellectualizing, rationalization, denial, and projection were blocking his growth and development. Thomas was conceptually aware of GRC issues for men, but they were not personalized or emotional realities for him. His masculinity and femininity ideologies at times seemed unrestricted, but, over time, distorted gender role schemas related to control, power, and perfectionism became quite apparent. These distortions and rigidities related to his unresolved psychosocial issues and contributed to his inability to redefine himself postsurgery.

Thomas's patterns of GRC were obvious as we talked, and I made some assessments using the Gender Role Conflict Scale (GRCS; O'Neil, Helms, Gable, David, & Wrightsman, 1986) and the Gender Role Restrictions, Devaluations, and Violations Worksheet (O'Neil, 1988b). Thomas needed information on various topics, so psychoeducation and bibliotherapy were used throughout the therapy on topics such as psychological defenses and working with emotional pain. I had him read *Survivors: Stories and Strategies to Heal the Hurt* (Preston, 2002) on how to overcome emotional pain and trauma. My overall assessment was that Thomas had an excellent chance to develop a positive and healthy sense of masculinity and transform himself from his tragic past.

Using the 13 assessment domains (see Figure 9.1) provided an overall appraisal of Thomas's psychological functioning but it did not provide enough information to create a treatment plan that would resolve his long-term suffering and fears about the future. In the next section, I describe more focused assessment that deepened the therapy and gave direction to the therapeutic process.

MORE FOCUSED ASSESSMENTS AND QUESTIONS

On the basis of the weekly sessions, I concluded that Thomas's OCD was still a problem postsurgery, and I felt his symptoms could be reduced more by journeying with his gender roles and resolving his psychosocial issues. The emotional wounds were evident from his disclosures, but the exact portal for deepening was unclear for many sessions. There were layers of socially imposed and personally constructed defenses that blocked the gender role journey and problem solving.

I pondered a number of clinical questions. First was the issue of how to move Thomas into the contemplative stage of change (see Chapter 10) so that he could prepare to take action and be responsible for solving his problems. Furthermore, helping him accept the ambivalence and confusion he felt about his own masculinity ideology and identity (Phase 2 of the gender role journey) without the burdens of severe OCD was essential if his self-confidence and personal security were to develop. Finally, I needed to understand how to help him redefine control and power, process emotions without obsessing about them, and embrace pain without turning it into a state of bad feelings and depression, which would be essential for his new roles as spouse and soon-to-be father. I was aware that the deconstruction of power and control as distorted gender role schemas was critical for Thomas's liberation from his GRC. Thomas was also unaware of his gender role devaluations, restrictions, and violations and how they affected his emotional functioning, and therefore how to bring this issue out in the open was a significant question.

The psychosocial–developmental assessment indicated delays in the following areas of psychological and emotional functioning:

- low self-esteem;
- both self-devaluation and feelings of superiority;
- lack of confidence, fears of failure, and limited self-efficacy in certain areas;
- difficulties with emotional labeling and regulations;
- situational problems with self-control;
- problems with order, discipline, and taking responsibility;
- situational defensiveness and the use of various self-protective defensive strategies;
- episodic authoritarianism;
- interpersonal impatience; and
- perfectionism and rigid standards for success and achievement.

The most significant issues to be resolved psychosocially were emotion regulation, personal control, self-efficacy, and anger management. Thomas's opportunity to learn emotion regulation and control in the past had been severely limited because of the medication and ongoing anxieties he experienced during his adolescence. Before becoming a more effective manager of his emotions, his defenses would need to be altered so he could more effectively journey with male emotionality and develop a healthier conceptualization of control and power. Thomas's defense mechanisms kept him from taking risks and exploring his intense emotions in productive ways.

The emotion regulation issues directly related to his OCD and his masculine socialization. We worked on these issues by redefining control, mapping his emotional triggers, and observing how these issues play out in our therapy together. We made some progress on these issues, and his success made Thomas feel better and more confident. One of the best tests of his growth and emotional intelligence would be how he handled the upcoming birth of his son. His marriage to his fiancée and future parenting became two of the main topics in the therapy. Would he be able to deal with the worries and fears that surround any uncertainty about his son's health and create a healthy marital life?

The assessment of Thomas's gender role transitions (see Chapter 5) was also important because these changes were directly related to redefining certain distorted gender role schemas that maintained his defensiveness and emotional problems. The most significant gender role transition was his brain stimulation operation, which had brought back the possibility of having a normal life. With more complete control of the OCD, how to be a productive man became a central issue. Furthermore, two other gender role transitions (getting married and having a child) could motivate him to look more closely at his problems, including his GRC and other wounds. Some of these transitions included reevaluations of gender role schemas that had developed during his adolescence.

USING THE GENDER ROLE CONFLICT SCALE AND GENDER ROLE CONFLICT CHECKLISTS AND WORKSHEETS

As mentioned earlier, Thomas filled out the GRCS, and the Devaluations, Restrictions, and Violations Worksheet, as well as the GRC Checklist (O'Neil, 1988a). The results provided additional insight into how he viewed his GRC and masculinity issues. Thomas's GRCS results indicated that he was low on all the factors of GRC (Success, Power, Competition [SPC]; Restrictive Emotionality [RE]; Restrictive Affectionate Behavior Between Men [RABBM]; and Conflict Between Work and Family Relations [CBWFR]). Only five items were at the middle range or better on the scale, and four of those items were from the SPC scale. On the GRC Checklist, he reported "some" power and control issues, "a little" RE, homophobia, competition issues, and "no" RABBM or SPC. Only health care problems were rated "very much."

The Devaluations, Restrictions, and Violations Worksheet asks respondents to answer nine questions on whether they have devalued, restricted, or violated themselves; been devalued, restricted, or violated by others; or devalued, restricted, and violated others because of their gender role roles or psychological problems. Thomas reported that he had devalued himself and been devalued by others because of his OCD and psychological problems. There was no report of any other devaluations, restrictions, and violations from others or toward others. Overall, the degree of Thomas's self-reported GRC was considered very low and was somewhat discrepant with what I observed during our sessions. The main purpose of this gender role-related assessment with Thomas was not only to document his GRC but also to facilitate discussion about his gender role journey in the context of his problems.

USING THE GENDER ROLE DIAGNOSTIC SCHEMA TO ASSESS THOMAS'S GENDER ROLE CONFLICT

In Chapter 9, I presented a gender role diagnostic schema to assess men's GRC that included a 3×3 nine-cell model that operationally defined a client's personal experience of GRC in terms of gender role devaluations, restrictions, and violations. Table 11.1 contains a summary of my assessment of Thomas using this schema. These results were taken from our sessions and the paper-and-pencil assessments described above. Thomas's self-devaluations resulted

TABLE 11.1
Thomas's Gender Role Devaluations, Restrictions, and Violations

Personal experience and outcomes of gender role conflict: SPC, RE, RABBM, CBWFR	Within self	Caused by others	Expressed toward others
D. Gender role devaluations	**D$_1$ Self-devaluations** Depression, low self-esteem, shame, hopelessness	**D$_2$ Devaluation by others** Relatives thinking he was crazy; devaluation by others because of OCD behaviors	**D$_3$ Devaluation of others** Authoritarian and superior attitudes toward others
R. Gender role restrictions	**R$_1$ Self-restrictions** Stress, anxiety, coping, personality problems, emotional control and anger problems	**R$_2$ Restriction by others**	**R$_3$ Restriction of others**
V. Gender role violations	**V$_1$ Self-violations** Past suicidal ideation	**V$_2$ Violation by others**	**V$_3$ Violation of others**

Note. SPC = Success, Power, Competition; RE = Restrictive Emotionality; RABBM = Restrictive Affectionate Behavior Between Men; CBWFR = Conflict Between Work and Family Relations; OCD = obsessive–compulsive disorder. From "Gender Role Conflict Research 30 Years Later: An Evidence-Based Diagnostic Schema for Boys and Men in Counseling," by J. M. O'Neil, 2013, *Journal of Counseling & Development, 91*, p. 496. Copyright 2013 by the American Counseling Association. Adapted with permission.

in depression, low self-esteem, shame, and hopelessness. His self-restrictions related to his stress, anxiety, coping problems, and emotional control and anger problems. There were no actual self-violations, but Thomas's past suicidal ideation was evidence of his potential to hurt himself. He reported being devalued by his relatives because of his OCD, and as the therapy continued he became more aware of other people's devaluations of him during his bouts with OCD. He also devalued others and had an authoritarian attitude toward others and believed that he was superior to others in intellect and general ability. I used these results to plan interventions and help guide the therapy process.

THE THERAPY PROCESS: AN OVERVIEW

At the outset of therapy, Thomas and I focused on career counseling—specifically, which career he would like to pursue and whether graduate education would be a viable, acceptable option for him—as well as on the deepening process and on work within the contemplation stage of change.

Career Counseling

We addressed a mix of issues in the first six sessions, but the overall focus was on the advantages and disadvantages of a professional career, such as becoming a doctor, scientist, or university professor, versus a career with less stature and prestige. Each week Thomas's worries, fears, and anger about managing the OCD were the main topic of our career counseling as well as a review of suitable careers that would engage his well-developed intellect and varied interests. We reviewed many different career options in the context of his OCD and anxieties. During this process, Thomas reevaluated his success and status schemas in terms of becoming a professor, doctor, or public school educator. We also reviewed his uneven academic record, including his successes and failed attempts to finish courses in which he lost interest. He was adamant and cynical about the hypocrisy of status quo graduate education and the rewards of selling your soul to the system for the promise of a high-status career. His arguments about the inadequacies of higher education and the grueling process graduate students endure were very well-thought-out and convincing. Overall, I agreed with his critical analysis but added that there are many exceptions and that there are pockets of integrity and excellence in many institutions that should temper his cynical generalities. His critical attitude reminded me of my own adolescent critique of "the military and industrial complex" back in the 1960s. My support of his position was helpful in gaining creditability and connection. Thomas's cost–benefit analysis of spending 3 to 5 years in a graduate program at 30, without any certainty that he could land a job, combined with his cynical view of graduate education, all yielded a negative decision on pursuing a graduate degree or traditional professional career.

During all of these sessions, our focus was his career issues, but each week Thomas's worries, fears, and anger about his past and present OCD increased. He complained that the anxiety still got in the way of feeling good about himself and hopeful about the future. He sorted through all of his conflicting emotions about success and status and how to use his potential. After redefining the gender role schema of success, achievement, and personal worth, he was able commit to a career in permaculture, that is, small-scale farming and food production with minimal environmental cost and maximum community benefits. As Thomas reevaluated the gender role schemas around success and prestige, he experienced profound sadness and anger about what he had lost from ages 14 to 24 in terms of opportunities and experiences. Anger about the loss was like acid in his heart. We resolved the career questions in about 10 sessions, and during those sessions additional emotional issues related to Thomas's adolescence and psychosocial development became most obvious.

Deepening and Contemplation Stage of Therapy

During all of these sessions, Thomas was constantly hearing music in his head, he was experiencing difficulties sleeping, and he reported mild to moderate depression. The intensity of the sessions increased significantly as his intellectualizing brought limited relief from storms developing underneath his carefully guarded portal. There was some critical commentary that things were not moving along fast enough. On two occasions there was a dramatic outpouring of negative emotions that included screaming out his anger and pain at me about his fears about the future. The intense expression of these raw emotions was a relief to Thomas and affected both of us. What was most important was that he could let loose his feelings with me by emptying some of the rage that he had been holding in for years. The therapeutic alliance was developing, and we decided to move on after the initial six sessions to the next part of Thomas's work.

On the basis of my approach with men (see Chapter 10), we moved on to Thomas's psychosocial development and his relationship with his family. He reported a good relationship with both of his parents but difficulty with both of them when they divorced in his early 20s. A review of his parental relationships months later revealed other important issues with both his mother and father. There were numerous psychosocial delays and developmental tasks that were not mastered between ages 14 and 24 while he was maximally medicated. During this time, he missed out on numerous important developmental tasks that continued to complicate his life. I indicated that those developmental issues could be resolved with work in therapy and that doing so could help him gain more confidence, a more positive sense of identity as man, and increased self-efficacy.

My work with Thomas appeared to be helping him process the many years of anger, loss, pain, and suffering. A family-of-origin assessment allowed him to see his life in the context of how he was treated by his mother and father and how their problems contributed to his own. Furthermore, we analyzed the academic and personal failures resulting from the side effects of the medications and the OCD. As one can imagine, there was an accumulation of unexpressed emotions attached to this history, all of which impeded his full recovery and his transition to a new life.

Thomas's greatest fear was that OCD would come back with full strength and that the DBS would stop working. He reported this fear as traumatic and stated that he had been unable to discuss this with anyone over the last 2 years. Thomas arranged a consultation at Brown University to discuss a voltage issue with his DBS and received more expert advice about how to manage his worries and fears. He wondered whether an increase in the voltage in his DBS could help with the symptoms that persisted. He still heard music playing almost all of the time in his head, continued to have twitches and tics, and experienced some ongoing compulsions and intrusive thinking. In an earlier session, I had given him a book on how to journey with his pain (Preston, 2002), and I introduced my pain paradigm (which I describe later in the chapter) so that he could see that strong emotions could be worked through in a constructive way.

My impressions of Thomas at this point were the following:

- his career decision-making is only one problem to be solved;
- OCD management may be the greater problem to solve;
- his rate of speech is a defense that required a special kind of information processing for me;
- masked anger and depression were apparent;
- psychosocial–developmental delays interacted with the OCD;
- fears about failure and lack of confidence were apparent;
- masked authoritarian tendencies, feelings of superiority, and perfectionism were part of Thomas's psychological processes;
- his demeanor was polite, perceptive, and cordial, but he was also quick to become irritated and impatient under certain circumstances; and
- strong defenses of intellectualization, rationalization, and denial were quite visible during most sessions.

EIGHT INTERVENTIONS WITH THOMAS

In this section, I have selected some of the major interventions with Thomas that demonstrate how the assessment information translated to our therapy process. Each intervention provides more information on how GRJT can be used with men.

1. Challenging the Efficacy of Therapy, the Expectancy Setting, and Establishing Hope for Healing

Thomas was doubtful about whether I could help him; after all, he had seen many previous therapists and none of them had really helped. He told me that talk therapy, although well intentioned, had been a total failure. Underneath his strong exterior were doubt, hopelessness, desperation, and worries about the future. I felt some pressure to break the cycle of ineffectiveness and wondered whether Thomas's neurological issues were just too dominant for any kind of combination of medication and talk therapy to work. We discussed the past therapies and disappointments and the anger resulting from his apparent helplessness, given that no one seemed to be able to help him with his severe OCD. He confronted me one day by saying in an angry tone, "Nobody has ever helped me; what makes you think you can?"

That kind of challenge got my attention and heightened the pressure and my emotions. First, I thought, maybe he is right: I have met my match! His failed therapeutic history weighed on me during and after the first sessions and a lot in between sessions. With this kind of client, the session doesn't end when he or she leaves the room. Fortunately, I recently had had success with some really difficult clients who had decade-long problems that nobody else could help. My confidence was high; moreover, I really liked this young man. He impressed me with the way he had coped through such suffering and loss. He represented to me a truly courageous man who persevered and never gave up. This positive aspect of his masculinity seemed heroic, and it moved me. My daily prayers told me, "I am the one who is supposed to help Thomas heal himself."

I have seen many hopeless and angry clients over my 40 years as a therapist, but Thomas's affect was different. He touched my sense of human fragility and of human resilience and hope. The song that played in my head was "We Shall Overcome." But there was a good deal of ambiguity, doubts, and questions, and Thomas expressed chronic hopelessness. When clients lack hope, we therapists provide it, even if the road to recovery is unclear.

This confrontation with Thomas about whether I could really help him was the first power and control dynamic (SPC) that entered into the therapy. It also was my first test with Thomas. With my own GRC issues of SPC and countertransference hanging out in front of me, we moved forward to find the portal (Rabinowitz & Cochran, 2002) to Thomas's real problems and positive mental health.

In the first few sessions, I felt Thomas had one foot out the door, and I knew it was time for an intervention. It was a sort of now-or-never situation. It was sales pitch time, as Gary Brooks (1998) so well named it. I had to convince Thomas to give this therapy a try. In fact, this was more than a sales pitch: It was a reaching out for the health and strength in this man's soul. I could feel in the room not only his vulnerable and damaged spirit but also his exceptionality and giftedness. I wanted him to be free from his emotional prison.

The sales pitch went like this. I told him that I did not know what was possible, that I have no magic wands for emotional healing, but I did have a track record of helping people heal who felt hopeless after being hurt. After that statement, I decided to put the responsibility on him for choosing to get better rather than choosing more hopelessness, depression, and despair.

I told Thomas that a lot depended on him and his attitude and ability to believe that he could do it. I told him, "No one has ever changed or healed unless they first believed they can. Expectations matter!" I asked him, "Do you believe you can change?" There was a long silence of inner conflict and anxiety, grief, and loss. I let the silence go on for a long while and then said, "Let's return to that question again after we both have had more time to reflect on what is at stake with your life." I then ended the intervention with this thought: "We can try, or we can walk away and give up before we try."

I then provided some self-disclosure: "My life, and my work with my clients, has been based on *not* walking away." I added, "Thomas, you have to answer that existential question 'about trying' for yourself. Furthermore," I continued, "We are usually *more* capable of doing difficult things in life than we think we are. You have to decide whether you believe that for yourself." I finished by saying that I thought we could achieve some positive changes and that we should give it a try and push beyond the past defeats to positive hope. I told him, "Hope sucks up worry and fear and replaces it with possibilities and options to be pursued. Hope and possibilities exist as long as we are alive." I told him that my daily reflections indicated that was why he ended up here with me: to decide what to do, to produce options, and to create a new way of living.

During the next session, it was clear that Thomas had bought the sales pitch of optimism, positive energy, and my challenge. I believed everything that I said, but the unpredictable neurological issues beyond both our controls weighed in my mind. What if Thomas's brain took over again?

This was the second power and control exchange between Thomas and me in which our mutual SPC issues interacted. Whose masculinity ideology was going to dominate during our process? The tone of the encounter was not competitive or power related. It was instead tactful compassion and an invitation for Thomas to consider. I wanted to transcend the masculinity ideologies (SPC) that were operating and put it in hopeful human terms.

2. Building the Human Bond: More Tests

Whenever two men sit in the therapy room there are power, control, competition, and homophobia issues operating on either a conscious or an unconscious level. The control, power, and competition issues between Thomas and me were apparent, but for some reason homophobia did not feel like a barrier. He appeared quite comfortable talking to me as a man. Maybe it was Thomas's experience with kung fu that helped him here, for it was a discipline in which both physical and emotional contact with other men and women are involved.

I invested in connecting with Thomas in a deep way because all the research suggests that the therapeutic bond/alliance is the most critical variable for positive therapy outcomes. Thomas's therapy posed numerous tests of my competence (or maybe my manhood), including the following:

- Could I keep up with his very fast mind and narrative? (Sometimes I could, and sometimes I would miss ideas because of the amount of words and the speed of the dialogue.)
- Would I value his intelligence and agree with his counter-cultural perspectives?
- Could I handle the depth of his emotions, which had been pent up for years?
- Would I understand his lectures on Plato, Aristotle, Hegel, and Eastern religious thought?

In terms of this last question, I remember being thankful for my Jesuit education, which brought so many philosophers into my consciousness and who will remain there until the day I die. I could discuss philosophy with Thomas and relate to him on that level, and in therapy this kind of deep connection really mattered.

In one session I told him that he was courageous for facing his fears and persisting through the 10 years of hell he had experienced and that I admired him greatly. He became uncomfortable, but he liked the feedback, although he rationalized it away immediately by asking, "Did I have any choice?" I said, "Yes, you had a choice and you chose to keep fighting—not everybody does." He devalued or minimized my comment, but I know that it helped us build our working relationship. He felt less alone with the fears and worries. He had an ally.

Besides honoring him and his struggle, I worked in two major gender role issues during those early sessions. I told him that we would need to share power and control if we were to get down to the heart of the matter in his life. Second, I stated the necessity of focusing not just on thoughts but also on emotions. Emotions are scary for some clients with OCD because they can trigger undesired and uncontrollable thoughts, obsessions, and compulsions. Thomas had learned to avoid emotions and to use his rational mind to cope. I sensed that the emotions would be central to his journey with his GRC. Although the therapeutic alliance was established, it might not be enough for the therapy to be successful, and there were more tests to come.

3. Initial Catharsis: Discharge of Loss, Suffering, and Pain

In the early parts of the therapy, we set specific goals related to career exploration. I told Thomas that I did career counseling like I did psychotherapy: looking at all the available psychological and emotional issues. I won't go into detail about the career counseling, but it was resolved by redefining the gender role schemas of SPC and reviewing what Thomas labeled "the hypocrisy of most work settings, particularly in higher education." This label reminded me that I had this attitude as a college student in the 1960s.

After the career-planning process was in full swing, Thomas began to tell his story. Part of therapy with men is really listening to their stories. Master therapists (e.g., John Robertson, Fred Rabinowitz, Sam Cochran, Mark Stevens, Matt Englar-Carlson, Gary Brooks) all agree that listening to men's stories is critical. Men want to talk about their lives, and Thomas had some things to say about the years from ages 14 to 24, when his OCD was unbearable. He gave the tragic details of his life, including being highly drugged while the OCD symptoms increased with greater and greater frequency. There were the shame and embarrassment; there was intense anger about what he lost, what he did not experience. The grief was raw, vulnerable, and highly emotive. The intensity of the disclosures and pain and speed of the speech left me dazed by the end of each session.

There was emotional catharsis in two sessions that was very intense and very loud. Thomas was screaming at the top of his lungs when the catharsis occurred; the repressed affect was no longer dulled by the medications, so all his emotions were being discharged so new emotional spaces could be created. I fastened my emotional seat belt so I could stay in there and let it happen. That is where the therapists of men need to shine, creating or helping men create new emotional spaces for themselves.

Even though Thomas's DBS had significantly diminished the OCD symptoms, he was still living in that old place of fear, compulsions, and hopelessness, and he did not possess the psychosocial skills to fully function as a 31-year-old man who is extremely talented but unable to actualize that talent. Having human potential and not being able to actualize it is one of the most painful experiences in life, and I knew that Thomas was screaming to use his potential on that emotional day.

4. Emptying: Another Test

I interpreted Thomas's intense emotional outbursts as a sign that he had courage (the ability to face his fears) and that he was willing to take risks and trust me with his process. The relationship was becoming established on an emotional level. Something else was going on with the intense emotional outbursts: a test about whether I could handle this kind of affect. Could he trust me with it? I wondered whether he had been able to get to this level of affect with other therapists while on medication. It really did not matter; what was important was that he was expressing his rage. Yes, I was concerned when he became so animated, nearly jumping out of his chair with his anger and rage over what he had lost from ages 14 to 24 and what he would never tolerate again. He yelled loud enough for the gynecologist in the far corner of the building to hear him, and I am sure the dentist working on the floor beneath my office stopped drilling.

Thomas disclosed intense fears about the OCD coming back again without the DBS. He described the emotions in the context of posttraumatic stress, meaning they involved traumatic ruminations and intrusive memories. I immediately thought of my concept of GRC trauma in which there is a tragic event or victimization resulting in extreme stressors with powerful lingering memories but no way to process it because of GRC and a restrictive masculinity ideology. I decided to not mediate the intensity but to honor the traumatic stress and respect that the emotions needed to be released. What Thomas needed to know was that I could handle the pain—and that he could too. All of this was important for his movement forward past the pain and fear to healing and transformation.

5. Psychoeducation: Emotional Management—Introducing the Pain Paradigm as a Structure

This couple of sessions was very emotional. I wondered whether the intense affect would scare Thomas because it was so powerful. I decided to provide a structure for his emotions (and perhaps mine as well) because I thought it would normalize the emotions.

I shared my working-with-pain paradigm (O'Neil & Egan, 1992a) with Thomas. This paradigm includes the following four components:

1. Embracing Pain: labeling the pain, telling the truth about the pain, and letting pain be pain;
2. Journeying with the Pain: beginning to do something positive with the pain;
3. Letting Go of the Pain: releasing the negative emotions permanently, using any method possible; and
4. Deriving the Benefit of Pain: developing new energy, vitality, a new and positive way of experiencing life.

I used a handout that describes the four phases of working with pain and shows the famous sculpture "Freedom" (see http://zenosfrudakis.com/sculptures/public/Freedom.html), which depicts what most people experience when working with their pain. This pain paradigm provided a meaningful structure for whatever strong emotions would develop and a way to see pain as a potentially positive development.

6. Psychosocial–Developmental Analysis of Thomas's Problems

Thomas's anxieties, career fears, lack of discipline, emotional deregulation, and anger became the focal points of our work. The DBS was continuing to work, and the remaining symptoms, although still present, in my opinion could be reduced even more. He asked me why his emotional problems were continuing after the DBS, and asked a series of questions: Why am I unable to following through on course assignments? Why do I lack confidence, fear failure, and have many worries about success? Why don't I have confidence in my interpersonal relationships? Why do I like to argue with others and convince them that I am right? Answers to these questions required discussing the psychosocial analysis in the context of masculinity ideology and GRC.

The critical questions were which developmental tasks had he not mastered and which psychosocial crises had he missed from ages 14 through 24 because of his severe OCD. The psychosocial analysis needed to be done in the context of GRC, masculinity ideology, and gender role transitions that he was currently experiencing (see Chapter 5). This kind of analysis was critical to my treatment plans and Thomas's ongoing therapy.

Early and later adolescent stages of development were the focus of the psychosocial analysis. For example, later adolescence (18–24 years) includes the following developmental tasks: autonomy in relation to parents, gender identity, internalized morality, and career choice. The psychosocial crisis of this stage of development is individual identity versus identity confusion; the primary ego adaptive quality is fidelity to values and ideologies. The central process was role experimentation, and the core pathology was repudiation.

The question was determining the developmental delays Thomas experienced because of his medicated and secluded life during his severe OCD. What developmental tasks and psychosocial crises had he missed (i.e., not completed) from ages 14 through 24? My assessment included the following psychosocial issues, which were relevant to his current functioning: emotional development and processing, need for power and control, emotional regulation and anger management, positive and negative self-evaluation, lack of confidence and self-efficacy, fears about failure, perfectionism, taking responsibility and becoming disciplined, delayed and unexplored career choice, and perspective taking (being able to consider other people's perspectives), and redirecting energies toward new roles. The reason that Thomas was still having emotional turmoil is that these issues were unresolved and consequently were barriers to his full maturity. These psychosocial issues were the areas on which we would focus in therapy. The psychosocial analysis was useful to Thomas because he had an explanation for why he was struggling with psychological issues. He could stop blaming himself, get to work, and have more hope that his life could get even better.

7. A Major Breakthrough: Testing Defenses and Redefining Control and Power

There had been some relief for Thomas thus far, but no big breakthroughs. The new insights had been helpful, but they were insufficient for the big gain. He and I could sense it was possible for a breakthrough, but we needed a portal. The scene had been set, the foundation had been laid, and Thomas was eager to go further. He expressed impatience with the therapy process and perhaps with me. He wanted things to go faster and to not be so repetitive. He complained that there was too much thought and not enough emotion in the sessions. After disclosing this, he would spend the entire session intellectualizing about the past, the present, or the future. What he was saying to me was that he did know how to get to the deeper emotions, and RE was a problem. I knew that was true, but also there was the issue of SPC in the relationship.

He wanted me to push the process harder, and I agreed to take more charge. I decided an intervention might help get to the emotions by taking more direct control of the therapy process. As I took more control, he became annoyed, irritated, and angry. The major intervention was this: I asked him how he was going to cope with upcoming fears and worries about becoming a father since he was about 6 months from becoming a father; specifically, I asked him, "What worries and fears do you have?" "What needs to be done to get ready?" "What resources do you need to develop, and how can you plan?" and "What other issues contribute to your difficulty processing your worries and fears?" His response was very provocative. He was highly irritated and animated and gave heavy and negative criticism about what I was doing. He said:

> What do you mean? I don't get it! That's not why I am here. It will only increase my fears and OCD by reviewing it. [I'm] not going to think about it until it happens. I did not come here for this. You are making it more difficult for me. Working with my fears brings on my OCD. I don't need that. I will deal with the fathering issues and pregnancy problems when they happen.

I just listened and acknowledged his angry reaction and displeasure. The session ended shortly after that. We processed all this in the next session, and I explained to Thomas that I was doing what he asked me to do: taking control and moving the process along. I explained what was happening with his inability to regulate his emotions, his loss of control that he was experiencing, and how his defenses had been challenged. The GRC patterns of RE and SPC (and control) were operating in our relationship. The portals of control, power, and defensiveness had been exposed.

Thomas had a vague understanding of defenses but did not understand what I was doing. I repeated a similar testing of the defenses 2 weeks later, and the outcome was the same: emotional outbursts but with more tolerance and understanding. We had a pattern to work with, and it was time again to discuss sharing power and control in the sessions.

8. Psychoeducation on Psychological Defenses and Masculine Control

Overall, my intervention was designed to get to the issues of Thomas's defenses because they were so tight that he could not grow emotionally or catch up on his psychosocial growth. He needed education on psychological defenses. I gave Thomas a paper to read on defenses and asked him to do an Internet search on defenses to determine which ones he had that might affect our process and his growth and development.

Teaching him a new way to define control and regulate his emotions was also a goal. First, we did a review of the triggers in his emotional life. What, in particular, activated his negative emotions was the priority. Next, we discussed how to handle these triggers without taking control verbally or behaviorally intervening—how to think and reflect before he let his feelings kick in and activate negative emotions and controlling behaviors.

Thomas's gender role schema of control needed to be redefined. First, I established that being out of control in situations is quite common and something to get used to. I convinced him that he needed more comprehensive definitions of *control* and *power* and that his current definitions were very narrow and restrictive (i.e., gender role restriction) and were contributing to his fears and anxieties. I suggested that his narrow definition of *control* had developed psychosocially as a way to cope with the OCD and protect himself from those who devalued or ignored him. I told him he needed a broader definition of *control* to cope in his marriage and when he became a father.

I asked Thomas if he could redefine *control* in a more productive way. This was very difficult for him, and he said he didn't know where to start. I asked him to work on it over a week's time. Still, there was no new definition. I offered a new definition of *control* for him to consider: "being able to tolerate being out of control and believe that you will survive, believing that you can handle the unpredictable, and that you have options if the situation worsens." This gave Thomas a new way to think about control and options for new ways to internally process emotions and thoughts in uncertain or difficult situations. This was a significant breakthrough. I asked him to experiment with thinking before feeling in situations in which he was out of control. He did and was able to gradually tolerate many more situations in which he was observing and reflecting on the dynamic rather than obsessing or getting fearful. This gave him confidence that he could control his thoughts and feelings in an interpersonal context. This was a major breakthrough that had implications for his career, marriage, parenting, and social interactions.

SUMMARY AND IMPLICATIONS

Thomas's therapy continues, and there have been repeats of the power and control dynamics described above. I assert my therapy agenda, and he gets irritated and pushes back that it is not helpful. Every time this happens, we go deeper into his emotional triggers and GRC issues. His psychological defenses are still quite operative, and more work is needed for him to get comfortable with being out of control. Our work has moved to some of the marital issues between him and his wife and how to better handle obsessive thinking and emotional regulation.

Thomas still reports significant improvements in overall functioning, but there are still emotional regulation issues to resolve. He received an increase in voltage for his DBS, and this has helped with the constant music in his ears. After being a stay-at-home father for more than a year, he is now ready to pursue his career in alternative ways to produce food on a farm that he has decided to purchase. The journey with Thomas's GRC is not yet finished, but the progress he has made so far encourages me that he will regain the potential that he lost in childhood and before his DBS. I hope this case study provides an example of GRJT (see Chapter 10) and how to use the GRC construct in therapy.

12

THEORETICAL AND EMPIRICAL JUSTIFICATION FOR PSYCHOEDUCATIONAL PROGRAMMING FOR BOYS AND MEN

Education is the most powerful weapon you can use to change the world.
—Nelson Mandela

Consider the following hypothetical situation: A group of energetic university resident assistants and progressive student development professionals called a meeting with the vice president for student affairs and other campus administrators to present a proposal for the development of special services for men over a 5-year period. They wanted to develop a comprehensive service delivery system that included a men's center that provides services equal to the well-developed ones for women on campus. They prepared for the meeting by reviewing the literature but found only scattered references to men's issues in college student development literature and a limited empirical base in the psychology of men. There were also no theoretically written publications that justified what they were proposing.

Certain sections of this chapter are from "Using the Psychology of Men and Gender Role Conflict to Promote Comprehensive Service Delivery for College Men: A Call to Action" (pp.16–49), by J. M. O'Neil and B. Crasper, in *Masculinities in Higher Education: Theoretical and Practical Considerations*, by J. A. Laker and T. Davis (Eds.), 2011, New York, NY: Routledge. Copyright 2011 by Routledge. Adapted with permission.

The presentation was carefully prepared and effectively delivered with details about program possibilities and a detailed budget. Although the presentation was effective, it was a hard sell. Administrators strapped by economic cutbacks said they did not have any extra funds, and they also were skeptical about the need for these services. As one prominent administrator said defensively, "Our boys seem to be doing just fine here." The women professionals attending immediately worried about their special funding being cut for their programs and whether men's programming would reinforce the same old sexist norms that they thought had contributed to a recent increase in sexual assaults on campus.

After the presentation was made, the vice president asked three questions in rapid succession: (a) Is there any evidence that men have problems and need more services? (b) If there is evidence, does research document that college men's problems are related to gender roles? and (c) What is the theoretical rationale for having special services for men?

A hush came over the room because nobody could answer these questions. Finally, someone spoke but gave ambiguous responses to all the questions. In essence, the vice president was asking for data-based, theory-driven rationales for the delivery system for men's services. Almost everyone would agree that those questions, although difficult to answer, were very appropriate and necessary.

Only recently has research documented men's problems, and only in the past decade has it documented that gender roles are related to men's problems (see Chapters 6 and 7). Unfortunately, no theoretically based analysis has yet linked masculinity theories to student development concepts. In this chapter, I respond to the hypothetical vice president's questions by presenting theory, a conceptual model, and research on gender role conflict (GRC) that justify expanded psychoeducation services for boys and men in public schools and institutions of higher education. *Psychoeducation* is a pedagogical approach that uses psychological and learning principles to promote people's personal, emotional, and intellectual development in a classroom or group setting (O'Neil, 2001). It is an excellent way to educate men and women about gender roles and other areas of diversity.

INTEGRATING CHICKERING AND REISSER'S (1993) IDENTITY VECTORS WITH MASCULINITY IDEOLOGY AND GENDER ROLE CONFLICT

The critical issue at hand is how to theoretically link the psychology of men to various age groups that vary by race/ethnicity, class, and other diversity indexes. One theoretical perspective that has applicability across diverse groups involves *identity vector conceptualizations* in student development theory (Chickering & Reisser, 1993). The identity vector model is a seminal work in college student development, and it has clear relevance to GRC and the masculinity ideology constructs reviewed in earlier chapters and to any service delivery model for boys and men.

Chickering and Reisser (1993) indicated that the broad conceptual nature of the identity vector model allows practitioners "the option of putting their own understanding and interpretation into it and applying it within their own contexts" (p. 44). The contexts I use in this chapter are boys' and men's masculinity ideologies and GRC.

The seven identity vectors are (a) developing competence, (b) managing emotions, (c) moving through autonomy toward independence, (d) developing mature interpersonal relationships, (e) establishing identity, (f) developing purpose, and (g) developing integrity (Chickering & Reisser, 1993). Developing optimal student development outcomes with vectors a through d results in gains in the development of identity, purpose, and integrity, all of which are critical goals of any educational institution. These vectors, although well known, have not been fully operationalized in terms of how they are affected by restrictive gender roles and sexist attitudes that negatively affect growth and development. Therefore, any theoretical connections between the vectors and the psychology of men concepts can provide a useful framework for psychoeducational programing.

The identity development vectors are conceptually related to the psychology of men by two assumptions: first, that boys and men who endorse a restrictive masculinity ideology or experience GRC experience greater problems developing competence, managing emotions, moving from autonomy to interdependence, and developing mature relationships (vectors a–d), and, second, that boys and men who endorse a restrictive masculinity ideology or experience GRCs have greater problems establishing their identities and developing purpose and integrity (vectors e–g).

A Conceptual Model Integrating the Psychology of Men With Student Development Theory

A conceptual model that integrates theory and research reviewed in the earlier chapters with Chickering and Reisser's (1993) identity vectors in a single conceptual paradigm is illustrated in Figure 12.1. The model is similar to the more complex GRC model found in Chapters 3 and 6 of this volume, but it is less detailed and simpler to understand. The model shows GRC concepts that support programming; more detailed theory about the framework is found in Chapters 3, 5, and 6 and in earlier publications (O'Neil, 2008c; O'Neil & Crapser, 2011; O'Neil & Nadeau, 1999). This conceptual paradigm

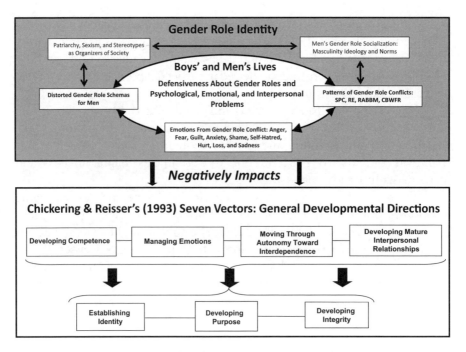

Figure 12.1. A conceptual paradigm explaining boys' and men's gender role conflict as it affects seven developmental vectors. SPC = Success, Power, and Competition; RE = Restrictive Emotionality; RABBM = Restrictive Affectionate Behavior Between Men; CBWFR = Conflict Between Work and Family Relations. From *Masculinities in Higher Education: Theoretical and Practical Considerations* (p. 35), J. A. Laker & T. Davis (Eds.), 2011, New York, NY: Routledge. Copyright 2011 by Routledge. Adapted with permission.

represents an additional way to justify any call to action for expanded services for boys and men.

Figure 12.1 shows six conceptual areas from the psychology of men that are theoretically related to male gender role identity. Chickering and Reisser's (1993) seven identity vectors are shown at the bottom of the figure. The directional and bidirectional arrows in the figure allude to the complexity of men's masculinity dynamics and require that one think outside of the educational status quo. Each boldface arrow implies possible educational programming possibilities as well as a direction for future empirical research.

Gender role identity, construed as a subset of Chickering and Reisser's (1993) overall notion of human identity, is shown as the dominant issue for boys and men during their gender role socialization. Gender role identity is continually shaped by the many interacting and socializing dynamics shown in the figure. All six conceptual areas affect men's gender role identity.

At the top left of Figure 12.1, the larger patriarchal society, sexism, and stereotypes are shown as organizers of society. In the top right corner of the figure, men's gender role socialization and, specifically, the masculinity ideology and norms, are shown.

On the right side of Figure 12.1, the four patterns of GRC—Success, Power, and Competition (SPC); Restrictive Emotionality (RE); Restrictive Affectionate Behavior Between Men (RABBM); and Conflict Between Work and Family Relations (CBWFR)—are shown. At the left of the figure are distorted gender role schemas that were fully defined in Table 5.1. Distorted gender role schemas develop from masculinity ideologies and norms learned in the United States' sexist society. At the bottom of the upper half of Figure 12.1 are listed the major emotions that result from GRC, including anger, fear, guilt, anxiety, shame, self-hatred, hurt, loss, and sadness. These negative emotions affect boys' and men's developmental growth and identity development. The oval in the top middle part of the figure represents men's defensiveness and relates conceptually to the many emotional, psychological, and interpersonal problems that ensue. Therefore, men's defensiveness is considered a critical issue.

All of the masculinity issues at the top of Figure 12.1 have negative effects on the seven identity vectors at the bottom. Patriarchy, sexism against men, gender role stereotypes, restrictive masculinity ideologies, distorted gender role schemas, GRC, and defensiveness all inhibit men from working on the identity vectors. The seven developmental issues in the vector model are more difficult to accomplish if one is sexist, experiencing GRC, or living out a restrictive masculinity ideology. Developing competence and managing emotions are difficult for a young man who experiences restrictive gender roles and GRC. Autonomy, interdependence, and developing mature relationships are compromised when restrictive gender roles shape attitudes and behaviors during, for example, the college experience. Identity development and finding purpose in one's life are difficult if one is distorting major gender role schemas and experiencing GRC. Likewise, integrity is difficult to define and embrace if one is a prisoner of one's own restrictive gender roles.

The model is another way to conceptualize men's problems and potentials as well as a coherent way to justify expanded programming for college men. In the following sections, I discuss the seven identity vectors in the context of masculinity ideology, masculine norms, and GRC. I integrate the vector model with the psychology of men in each subsequent section using the following three-step outline: (a) providing a definition of the identity vector, (b) explaining how masculine norms and GRC conceptually relate to the vector, and (c) reporting research from Chapters 6 and 7 that directly or indirectly links men's identity development with men's GRC. Theory and empirical evidence that connect GRC and masculinity ideology to Chickering and Reisser's (1993) identity vectors is critical if the field is to develop a full rationale for expanding men's services on U.S. campuses.

Developing Competence

Risk taking, self-trust, and facing fears about failure are all important in developing competence, and this sense of self-efficacy contributes to positive mental health. Developing competence requires that one manage feedback from others without defensiveness and is able to share power and personal control. Confidence in one's skills develops if the young man is open to growth and not defensive about it. Numerous masculinity norms and GRC can negatively affect the development of competence. Some of these include impaired cognitive performance, performance failure, physical inadequacy, intellectual inferiority, winning, pursuit of status, SPC, and the need for success and achievement. Many of these problem areas have been theoretically or empirically linked to men's GRC and restrictive masculinity ideology (O'Neil, 2008c, 2012b).

Competence is more difficult to develop if a young man experiences GRC and sees failure as the opposite of competence and feels shame and humiliation when failing to perform. A man who has rigid and restrictive masculinity ideology and believes that "real" men should never fail will struggle with developing competence and gaining confidence. Furthermore, everyone fails at something along the way to adult maturity and experiences strong emotions. Boys and men who believe that emotions are feminine are likely to avoid feelings related to failure. No one can develop competence without managing their emotions because fears of failure require the processing of emotions related to feeling emasculated or diminished.

Competence is also difficult to achieve if a young man is obsessed with proving his masculinity (Kimmel, 2011) through always winning, succeeding, and being in control. Competence also relates to how men feel about their intellectual abilities, physical strength, and body image. Distortions about any of these may cause a false sense of self by under- or overestimating one's physical and intellectual abilities. These kinds of GRC may contribute to a man's masculine façade, and defensiveness may occur to mediate any threats to competence or one's masculine identity. Psychosocial development is difficult for boys and men under these circumstances and therefore is a potential area for intervention by educators.

Research has demonstrated that masculinity ideology and GRC relate to issues of developing competence (O'Neil, 2008c; see also Chapter 7, this volume). Both GRC and restrictive male norms have been significantly correlated with lower self-esteem. GRC/stress research has also been significantly correlated with impaired cognitive performance, ineffective problem-solving attitudes, and negative attitudes toward help seeking. All of these have implications for developing competence or at least being open to increasing one's self-efficacy.

Managing Emotions

Managing emotions involves the ability to label, experience, and express feelings and respond to other people's feelings in effective ways. This may be difficult for men whose masculinity ideology includes devaluing feelings because affect is considered feminine. Restrictive Emotionality is a primary source of male anxiety, depression, stress, and substance abuse (see Chapter 7). Recognizing that emotions are human and necessary for effective functioning is one of the most important milestones on the way to male maturity. Constructs in the psychology of men related to managing emotions include emotional control, Restrictive Emotionality, emotional inexpressiveness, devaluation of emotions, and alexithymia.

Emotionally controlled and inexpressive men deprive themselves of feelings needed to discover personal truths that promote identity development. The ability to label, experience, and express emotions is critical to any growth processes but is particularly important during the adolescent years. Strong emotions such as anger, fear, hurt, longing, boredom, anxiety, anger, depression, guilt, and shame can disrupt a man's learning processes. No one can study or grow if he is experiencing these heavy emotions. When these feelings go unexpressed and accumulate over time, emotions can become overwhelming and disrupt sleep and daily problem solving. Boys and men who endorse a restrictive masculinity ideology by saying that "everything is okay" even if they are in pain and suffering are at high risk for emotional and interpersonal problems. Emotional intelligence is needed to process feelings that negatively affect the learning process or spoil important relationships. Men need to recognize that emotions are not masculine or feminine but *human* qualities that need to be courageously faced. Unfortunately, many men come to college with deficits in emotional intelligence at the very time when they need to face feelings that can help them with identity development, maturity, and academic achievement.

Empirical research indicates that GRC and restrictive masculinity ideologies correlate with significant emotional problems (see Chapters 6 and 7). In terms of managing emotions, GRC has been correlated with depression in 25 studies. Eight studies have shown that anxiety and stress are related to GRC. Gender role stress has been correlated with increases in systolic blood pressure; higher states of anger; verbal aggression; and increases in anxiety, negative affect, alexithymia, overt hostility, and aggression. Furthermore, masculinity ideology and norms have been correlated with difficulty in managing anger, psychological distress, and alexithymia. The gender role research on men's emotional problems reported in Chapters 6 and 7 provide convincing evidence that justifies special programs for boys and men.

Moving Through Autonomy Toward Interdependence

The word *autonomy* implies self-sufficiency, choosing one's goals responsibly, and being less dependent on others' opinions, by discerning one's own truths. Autonomy is the development of self-reliance and of being emotionally and behaviorally independent of others. *Interdependence* means that there is an awareness of the limits to self-reliance because we all depend on each other in important ways. Masculinity measures include self-reliance subscales that are theoretically related to the autonomy and interdependence identity vector (see Chapter 1). Young men, and women, need to work through approval from parents and other authority figures and affirm themselves as well as learn how to solve their own problems. Resolving past problems with parental attachment, detachment, or separation issues is important in developing autonomy. This process also includes recognizing interdependence as a necessary and important part of life.

When men's reliance on others is viewed as masculine weakness or failure, healthy autonomy and interdependence become difficult to develop. Furthermore, positive attitudes toward help seeking are difficult to develop when restrictive self-reliance limits a man's options. Men do not seek help as often as women because men often have unresolved issues regarding autonomy and interdependence. Furthermore, some men have stigmatized help seeking and believe that needing assistance with life's problems means one is not masculine. Macho self-reliance and denial about inevitable interdependence can be barriers to identity development and men's growth over the life span.

Masculinity ideology and GRC have not been directly correlated with autonomy and interdependence. They have been indirectly connected through negative attitudes toward help seeking, problems with attachment to parents, and negative problem-solving attitudes. For example, GRC has been correlated with negative attitudes toward help seeking in 16 studies (see Chapter 7). Ineffective problem-solving attitudes have been found to be correlated with GRC in two studies (see Chapter 7). Eleven studies have found that GRC is significantly correlated with problems with attachment to mothers and fathers in terms of separation, individualization, disidentification, and conflictual independence (see Chapter 7). Gender role stress has also been found to be correlated with fearful attachments and, finally, masculine norms have been found to be significantly correlated with negative attitudes toward help seeking and separation/individuation problems. Overall, the collective evidence suggests that GRC has been correlated with critical issues related to autonomy and interdependence and therefore these may be important areas to consider programming and intervention.

Developing Mature Interpersonal Relationships

Having mature interpersonal relationships implies that one appreciates individual differences and has the capacity for human intimacy with others. Numerous masculinity concepts negatively affect the development of mature relationships. These include antifemininity norms, power over women, dominance, being a playboy, disdain of homosexuals, avoidance of femininity, fear and hatred of homosexuals, nonrelational attitudes toward sex, subordination of women, SPC, RABBM, dominance, and aggression. Boys' and men's restrictive masculinity ideology can contribute to dysfunctional interpersonal relationships with other men as well as with women; gay, lesbian, bisexual, and transgendered people; and members of racial/ethnic minority groups.

Empathy, altruism, and acceptance of others are critical parts of developing mature relationships. Accepting people for who they are, free from stereotypes in both the interpersonal or intercultural realms, requires an emerging sense of self-identity. Furthermore, not accepting others who deviate from masculine and feminine norms because of their age, sexual orientation, or race/ethnicity can result in discriminatory attitudes that are devaluing and hostile toward others. Under these conditions, developing mature interpersonal relationships is nearly impossible and likely to produce sexist, racist, homophobic, and ethnocentric interpersonal interactions that can produce conflict, abuse, harassment, and even violence.

The capacity for intimacy in mature relationships implies making commitments based on honesty, responsiveness, and unconditional positive regard. Intimacy implies not dominance or dependency but the development of interdependence between two equals. It involves an acceptance of each other's flaws and personal assets and a commitment to long-term relationships that last through difficulties and separations. Masculinity ideology and norms that conform to rigid stereotypes of masculinity and femininity can inhibit the development of capacities for intimacy in relationships, whereas celebrating diversity means appreciating all kinds of human beings. When diversity is celebrated, mature relationships flourish and there is less chance for stereotypic biases, ethnocentric values, and racist attitudes that oppress people and human communities.

Many studies have indicated that GRC is correlated with difficulties in relationships, including poor interpersonal functioning, marital/relationship dissatisfaction, problems with intimacy, limited self-disclosure, spousal criticism, stereotypic thinking toward women, homophobic and antigay attitudes, and negative attitudes toward African Americans (O'Neil, 2008c; see also Chapter 7, this volume). Twenty-two studies have shown that GRC has been correlated with men's negative or violent attitudes toward women, including positive attitudes toward sexual harassment, rape myths, hostile sexism, and self-reported sexual and dating violence (see Chapter 7). In addition, gender role stress has been correlated with greater irritation with others, anger, jealousy, and controlling behaviors.

A similar pattern of research indicates how masculinity ideology and norms negatively affect relationships. Collectively, the studies are sobering and help explain how men's restrictive masculinity ideologies relate to interpersonal dysfunction between men and women and sexual minorities. Moreover, they provide evidence that masculinity conflicts are related to emotional abuse, sexual violence, and men's victimization of others. Any serious call to action should focus on helping men understand how their GRC is related to their potential to harm women and sexual minorities.

Establishing Identity, Developing Purpose, and Developing Integrity

The first four vectors for student development are critical in establishing purpose, integrity, and identity (see Figure 12.1). There is also a theoretical connection between these vectors and masculinity constructs. All of the masculinity ideology and GRC issues that affect the first four vectors significantly affect the three vectors of establishment of identity, development of purpose, and development of integrity. Developing purpose includes setting goals and being intentional with relationships, career plans, family, and one's community. Integrity is closely related to purpose in that, to develop it, one must internalize humanistic values and ethical standards. This means mediating rigid and uncompromising gender role beliefs about life and developing congruence between one's personal values and socially responsible behavior. Integrity involves principled thinking that mediates conflicts between one's personal self-interests and other people's needs as well as respecting other people's points of view. Establishing overall identity, according to Chickering and Reisser (1993), relates to many issues that have gender role implications, including comfort with one's own body and appearance, gender, and sexual orientation; self-concept; self-understanding; self-acceptance; self-esteem; and understanding one's sexuality, family of origin, ethnic heritage, and religious and cultural heritage. All of these issues can be directly tied to masculinity constructs in one way or another.

Summary of the Seven Identity Vectors and Developmental Directions

There is substantial theoretical overlap between Chickering and Reisser's (1993) identity vectors and the emerging concepts in the psychology of men. In this chapter, I have reviewed 25 different masculinity constructs that relate to Chickering and Reisser's first four identity vectors. Furthermore, the empirical research reviewed in this book supports the idea that masculinity ideology and GRC/stress are significantly correlated with the developmental issues involved in Chickering and Reisser's identity vectors. The masculinity constructs in the psychology of men are theoretically and empirically related to identity outcomes and strongly support any call for action for increased programming for boys and men.

IMPLICATIONS AND A PERSONAL INVITATION

In this chapter, I presented a conceptual paradigm, similar to the ones in previous chapters, that links the psychology of men with student development identity vectors (Chickering & Reisser, 1993). I cited direct and indirect empirical evidence indicating that masculinity problems negatively affect boys' and men's identity development. Middle school to high school transitions, high school to college transitions, losses of male power, defensiveness, and men's negative attitudes toward help seeking make programming challenging, but not impossible, for educators.

Theory and research indicate that young men are vulnerable to negative consequences of socialized gender roles. The lack of active programming for men is one of the most neglected areas in education. The lack of service delivery for men and boys perpetuates serious problems in schools and on U.S. campuses. The jury is still out on whether public school and higher education professionals will ever address boys' and men's problems. Telling the truth about boys and men requires a paradigm shift and higher levels of consciousness about the effects of sexism on men. The challenge is to fully accept that boys and men form a special group that needs help and support.

Whether the field of education can change its service delivery to help vulnerable boys and men who are negatively affected by socialized sexism is unclear. How many more school shootings, acts of campus violence, rapes, male suspensions and dropouts, and gay boys' suicides will it take to understand that masculinity ideologies and GRC are directly relevant to these serious problems? Is our inaction in this vital area part of a backlash against men and boys? When will we fully understand that sexism has negative consequences for everyone? Can we acknowledge this without creating a zero-sum game that pits men and women against each other?

More expansive discussions by educators about sexism are needed, because the cost of silence and inaction is great. Theory and research now exist to guide us, but we must generate greater empathy and compassion for boys and men to activate more direct services for them. The crisis of being a man in today's society is real and needs proactive attention by professional educators. I invite educators, scholars in the field of psychology, and readers of this book to get involved in this important work.

In the next chapter, I present a comprehensive service delivery model that can systematize services for men. The model recommends data gathering, resource development, program development, and the training of professionals to help implement expanded services for men. Also in the next chapter, I provide three examples of evaluated psychoeducational programs that have been implemented for college men, middle-school urban boys, and men and women in a coeducational workshop setting.

13

PREVENTION OF GENDER ROLE CONFLICT USING PSYCHOEDUCATION: THREE EVALUATED INTERVENTIONS

In Chapter 12, I established a theoretical and empirical rationale for psychoeducational programming with boys and men. As Robertson (2012) pointed out, psychoeducational programming for men is in reality teaching the psychology of men. In this chapter, I discuss a 10-step action-oriented preparation process and present a programming delivery model that pro motes the development of comprehensive preventive services for men at colleges and universities. Next, I describe three examples of psychoeducation programs that used gender role conflict (GRC) theory, and describe concepts of the psychology of men and present evaluation data. One preventive program is for college men and student affairs staff (Braverman, O'Neil, & Owen, 1992), another is for middle-school urban boys (O'Neil, Challenger, Renzulli, Crapser, & Webster, 2013) and the third intervention is for both men and women (O'Neil, 1996; O'Neil & Roberts Carroll, 1988).

http://dx.doi.org/10.1037/14501-014

A MEN'S SERVICE DELIVERY MODEL
FOR COLLEGES AND UNIVERSITIES

On the basis of the theory and research I have reviewed in this book, I recommend comprehensive services for boys and men that incorporate prevention concepts and psychoeducation (O'Neil, 2001). Preventive interventions can help men journey with their gender roles (O'Neil & Egan, 1992a) by exploring their sexist stereotypes. Specifically, my proposals include a systematic model that can serve as a template for developing ongoing, theoretically driven, empirically based programming and services for college men. A conceptual model for service delivery for a college or university setting is depicted in Figure 13.1. At the top of the figure is a three-step process that includes Step 1: Initial Development of the Delivery Model, Step 2: Levels of Delivery Interventions, and Step 3: Maintenance of the Delivery Model. I describe these three steps in more detail in the following sections.

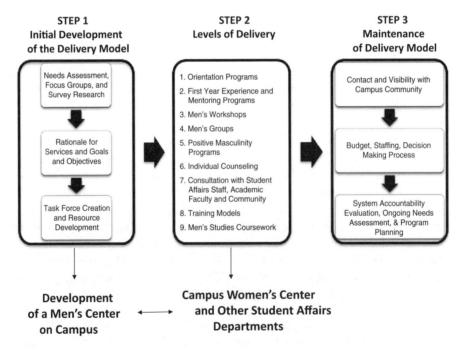

Figure 13.1. Programming delivery model for colleges and universities. From *Masculinities in Higher Education: Theoretical and Practical Considerations* (p. 39), J. A. Laker and T. Davis (Eds.), 2011, New York, NY: Routledge. Copyright 2011 by Routledge. Adapted with permission.

Step 1: Initial Development of the Delivery Model

Assessment of men's need for potential services is the first activity in developing any service delivery model. The purpose of needs assessment is to understand men as a target population in terms of attitudes, problems, potentials, and preferred modes of learning. The data could be gathered at freshmen orientation with questionnaires or focus groups. Data on upper-classmen could be gathered by resident assistants or through online surveys. Questions could ask about problem areas, needs, and the kind of programs that interest men. Data must be gathered on men from all races/ethnicities, nationalities, sexual orientations, and cultural backgrounds to ensure that programs are relevant to the multiple masculinity ideologies present on most campuses. Needs assessment data about men's issues could also be gathered from student affairs staff and faculty. In this way, the needs assessment could document the professional training needs of those who provide services for men.

After the needs assessment data are analyzed, a task force on men's services could be convened. Campus models ideally would be created by a task force or committee on men's services and programming. The task force would work together over a period of years and use the needs assessment data to develop measurable goals and objectives. Goals should be both short term and long term in nature.

Furthermore, men's resource development should be considered. The task force would decide the necessary personnel and educational resources needed to implement the delivery model. Programmers would write cogent rationales and data-based proposals that document men's programming needs using both the psychology of men and student development theory. In Chapter 12, I applied a synthesis of GRC theory and research to Chickering and Reisser's (1993) identity vectors to justify a call to action. Other theories and paradigms should be combined with findings and needs assessment data to bring a powerful legitimacy to men's programming.

Another important question is whether a men's center should be developed on campus (Davies, Shen-Miller, & Isacco, 2010). The justification for a men's center could be made using the needs assessment data as well as pertinent theory and research in the psychology of men. The men's center would be a central place to implement services for men described in Step 2 of the delivery model. The bidirectional arrow at the bottom of Figure 13.1 between the proposed men's center and the women's center and student affairs staff implies that the men's center would be directly connected to women's programming and other student affairs services. Alliances between men's center staff and those committed to women's issues are a critical part of any service delivery system that helps both genders.

Step 2: Levels of Delivery Interventions

The second step in the delivery model includes the possible interventions for men's services on campus (see O'Neil & Crapser, 2011, for full descriptions). The first five levels of service delivery are specific ways to do campus wide programming (see the middle section of Figure 13.1). Levels 6 through 9 include both direct and indirect services for men, including counseling, consultation, training, and academic coursework.

Men's Programming Levels and Emphasis on Positive, Healthy Masculinity

Programs offered during freshman orientation sessions could help students manage the transition from high school to college. This transition is considered to be one of the most difficult in a young man's life, with personal, social, familial, academic, and emotional issues interacting with leaving home for the first time. The freshman year is an ideal time to help young men reflect on their new status as independent adults in the context of their gender roles and college experience. In addition, organized mentoring programs could include information about being male and the specific problem areas that men experience during the college transition. Men's groups can be developed to critically engage and educate men on the complexities of growing up male. Numerous authors have provided ways to develop groups for men (Andronico, 1995); the challenge is to match men's documented needs to program content that is useful and effective.

Masculine gender roles are sensitive topics for young men, and therefore resistance to attending programs is to be expected. As I reported in Chapter 7, negative attitudes toward help seeking have been significantly correlated with GRC. One strategy to attract college men is offering programs on the positive aspects of being male. Ideas about affirming men and positive masculinity are emerging in the psychology of men (Kiselica, 2011; Kiselica & Englar-Carlson, 2010; O'Neil & Lujan, 2009b). Paradigms of positive masculinity that describe men's strengths when transcending sexist stereotypes are needed. Patterns of positive masculinity can help men learn alternatives to sexist attitudes and behaviors that cause GRC. Programming could emphasize what constitutes healthy masculinity. Men's strengths and potentialities could focus on themes such as responsibility, courage, altruism, resiliency, service, social justice, positive fathering, perseverance, generativity, protection of others, and nonviolent problem solving. Positive masculinity transcends what is wrong with men by identifying the qualities that empower males to improve themselves and provide service to other people and the larger society. Programs on healthy masculinity could change the overall perception that the psychology of men is about documenting what is "wrong" with boys and men.

Suggested Programming Areas

The extant empirical research and theory can help focus psycho-educational programming for men on campus (see Chapters 1, 3, 6, and 7, this volume). Given the likely resistance to men's programming on campus, content areas can be labeled something like "Men's Life Skills" rather than having a title that focuses exclusively on masculinity ideology or GRC. The life skills label should not stimulate as much resistance or controversy. The initial programming for freshmen and sophomores should emphasize needed life skills, ways to cope with college, help-seeking dilemmas for men, and criteria for positive masculinity, including affirmations of men's positive potential. With the initial success of these life skills programs, issues related to men's vulnerability in regard to GRC could be introduced in the context of male strengths and empowerment. Both process-oriented and outcome evaluations are critical to assess how and whether the programs have a positive impact over time.

Table 13.1 lists 30 thematic areas for educational programming for college men. These are ordered according to the degree to which they emphasize gender role issues. The programming areas include both life skills topics and information about gender roles. Areas 1 through 8 could be presented with limited emphasis on masculinity issues. Areas 9 through 17 cover topics where some masculinity issues could be introduced. Areas 18 through 30 are thematic areas where masculinity would be central to the programming. The 30 areas need to be assessed for their appropriateness for college men on the basis of cognitive complexity, affective ability, racial/ethnic backgrounds, nationality, and overall maturity. The way programs are titled matter because research indicates that program names can affect appeal to the targeted group and resistance to attending (Blazina & Marks, 2001; Robertson & Fitzgerald, 1992; Rochlen, McKelley, & Pituch, 2006). Titles like "Exploring Your Masculine Problems" may be immediately rejected, whereas titles such as "Maximizing Your Potential in Careers and Relationships" could engage a college man's curiosity and attention. Titles that directly challenge traditional stereotypes of the male gender role may be worrisome or activate resistance and masked fear. Programmers need to be aware of the stigmas and defensiveness that may be operating within men as they consider opportunities to learn about their masculine gender roles.

Counseling, Consultation, Training, and Teaching

Counseling services are critical resources for men who need help and a primary service for any college or university. Therapists in college and university counseling centers should be trained in the psychology of men. If they already are knowledgeable in this area, then they could also help train others on campus. Consultation with student affairs staff and academic faculty is

TABLE 13.1
Thematic Areas in Which to Implement
Psychoeducational Programs for College Men

Thematic area for programming	Description
1. Problem-solving skills	Knowledge about how to identify problems and the specific steps to resolve them in positive ways
2. Conflict management skills	Knowledge about how to work through disagreements using communication, negotiation, and compromise
3. Decision-making and goal-setting skills	Knowledge about the steps in decision-making and how to create and achieve goals that can be implemented
4. Career awareness and planning	Activities that foster increased career identity and that lead to career decision-making skills
5. Help-seeking dilemmas for men	Knowledge about the special problems men face seeking help for their problems because of masculine gender role socialization
6. Personal health care	Information about how to stay physically and psychologically healthy
7. Stress management	Knowledge about how to identify personal stressors and skills to mediate the thoughts and feelings that maintain the stress
8. Service learning, altruism, and helping others	Knowledge about the importance of service and altruism in terms of personal growth and development
9. Positive and healthy masculinity	Deriving a personal definition of positive and healthy masculinity
10. Assertiveness skills	Skills on how to use your personal power positively to protect your rights and roles
11. Self-control and centering	Skills on being able to control thoughts, feelings, and behaviors and the ability to develop an inner solidity
12. Empathy skills	Learning how to sensitively respond to others' feelings, thoughts, and experiences in caring ways
13. Listening skills	The ability to accurately hear and respond to another's person's thoughts and feelings
14. Competition	Knowledge about how to strive against a rival to win or gain something as well as the potential problems with this kind of interaction
15. Courage and resilience	How to learn to face your fears and bounce back from a failure, loss, or defeat
16. Developing integrity	How to develop a moral or ethical code of conduct to live your life
17. Sensitivity to social justice	Knowledge on how discrimination and oppression operate and how to be involved in eradicating social injustices
18. Emotional awareness and expression	Knowledge and experiences on how to label, experience, and express emotions appropriately

TABLE 13.1
Thematic Areas in Which to Implement
Psychoeducational Programs for College Men   *(Continued)*

Thematic area for programming	Description
19. Power in relationships	How to understand control, authority, influence, and coercion in relationships
20. Understanding psychological abuse	How power, control, and words are used to hurt others emotionally
21. Masculinity ideology	Knowledge about how men and boys learn assumptions about masculinity and sexist stereotypes that limit human potential
22. Patterns of gender role conflict	Knowledge about how restrictive gender roles can produce negative consequences for boys, men, and others
23. Relationships with girls and women	The critical issues with relationships with girls and women in terms of friendships, dating, coworkers, intimacy, and sexual relationships
24. Relationships with boys and men	The critical issues with relationships with other boys and men in terms of friendships, intimacy, teamwork, competition, and homophobia
25. Homophobia and heterosexism	Definitions of homophobia and heterosexism and how they relate to gender role identity and relationship with other men and oneself
26. Sexuality	The critical issues related to sexuality in terms of masculine identity and intimacy in human relationships
27. Understanding parents	Knowledge about how to manage the complex dynamics between sons and parents
28. Dealing with loss	How to deal with losing something or someone important to you in terms of experiencing grief and recovery
29. Fathers and becoming one	Exploring the relationship with one's father and thinking about this future role in terms of masculinity identity
30. Body image	How one feels about one's muscularity and overall perception of one's body

Note. From *Masculinities in Higher Education: Theoretical and Practical Considerations* (pp. 42–43), J. A. Laker and T. Davis (Eds.), 2011, New York, NY: Routledge. Copyright 2011 by Routledge. Adapted with permission.

critical to any service delivery system. Such consultation may be needed to determine what professional content in the psychology of men is essential for student affairs staff and faculty to know. Specific training programs and curricula need to be created and tested for effectiveness with faculty and student affairs staff. Consultation with academic faculty on developing courses that focus on men's studies could bring the delivery model into the classroom. Teaching the psychology of men has been gaining prominence over the past 10 years (O'Neil, 2001; O'Neil, Addis, Kilmartin, & Mahalik, 2004; O'Neil & Renzulli, 2013a, 2013b), but other disciplines, such as sociology, education, religion, and history, are also possible areas where courses on masculinity could be offered.

Step 3: Maintenance and Evaluation of the Delivery Model

This step includes important activities to keep any delivery model credible and moving forward. Community visibility on and off campus through disseminated research, brochures, radio interviews, and newspaper articles on men is essential to help explain the value of men's services. Furthermore, detailed budgets and requests for resources based on the needs assessment and program evaluation data are critical for any sustained effort to implement a service delivery model. Staffing the men's center and involving resident assistants and residence hall directors in program development may require yearly training. The inclusion of men's and women's programming could become part of the residence assistant and residence hall director job descriptions. Training upperclassmen peers to lead programming is another excellent strategy to involve students in service delivery for men.

This delivery model is just one way to conceptualize expanded services for men and, of course, it can be adapted to any educational setting. The presentation of a complete delivery model based on theory and research (see Chapter 12) may be more credible than implementing separate initiatives. In the next section, I discuss three examples of evaluated programs.

THREE EVALUATED PSYCHOEDUCATIONAL INTERVENTIONS TO PREVENT GENDER ROLE CONFLICT

Direct advocacy for increased services for boys and men is important, but administrators may want to review examples of programs that have worked and been evaluated. In this section, I report on three programs that have been evaluated for their usefulness and effectiveness. One was developed for college men and student affairs staff, and the second was implemented for middle-school boys in an urban setting. The third example is the 6-day gender role journey workshop that was offered to both men and women at the University of Connecticut from 1984 to 2006.

Intervention 1: Systematic Programming for College Men and Student Affairs Staff[1]

In this section, I provide details of 5 days of systematic programming designed to sensitize participants at the University of Richmond, in Virginia, to

---

[1] From "Systematic Programming on Men's Issues and Men's Studies on Campus," by D. G. Braverman, J. M. O'Neil, and S. Owen, 1992, *Journal of College Student Development, 33*, pp. 557–558. Copyright by American College Student Personnel Association. Adapted with permission.

the importance of men's issues. In 1991, I was invited by Dr. David Braverman (now at Springfield College) to provide consultation and direct programming to targeted groups of students, staff, and faculty. In the sections that follow, I describe the 5-day consultation as a systematic process.

Preassessment of Male Students

Campus men ($n = 148$) completed the Gender Role Conflict Scale (O'Neil, Helms, Gable, David, & Wrightsman, 1986) and the Gender Role Journey Measure (O'Neil, Egan, Owen, & Murry, 1993). These data then provided quantitative, baseline data on potential conflicts and attitudes of male students on campus. These data were used to develop the content and process of the campus programs.

Organization of Comprehensive Programming

Consultation was conducted with student affairs staff and academic faculty to target specific groups of men for the programs. A campus committee on men's issues was organized to help coordinate the different programs. The seven target populations for strategic programming were (a) student government leaders, (b) fraternity leaders and pledge educators, (c) and (d) students in two psychology classes, (e) student affairs professionals, (f) female students involved in a program called "Women Involved in Living and Learning," and (g) male freshmen involved in a program titled "Spinning Your Web." The latter two groups had regular and systematic programming on male and female roles throughout the semester. On the last night of the programming, a campus-wide multimedia presentation on John Lennon's gender role journey (O'Neil, 1988a) was presented. In addition, I had brief meetings with major student affairs administrators and the academic provost to advocate for more active programming on men's issues.

Structure and Content of the Intervention

Some variation in the programs existed, depending on the target group. The following content was included in most programs. First, an overview of major issues in men's studies was presented that clustered into the following five areas: (a) men's political issues related to sexism, (b) men's psychological–interpersonal issues, (c) men's gender role conflicts and problems, (d) multicultural aspects of masculinity, and (e) new directions for men journeying with gender roles. Second, a brief presentation was given on the "Masculine Mystique and Values System" (O'Neil, 1981a, 1981b). This information summarized how men are socialized to embrace restrictive gender roles that are potentially dysfunctional to them. Third, in the all-male student groups, participants responded to two items on a masculine GRC worksheet: (a) Indicate what you think men's conflicts are with their masculinity and gender roles and (b) Indicate your own personal concerns or problems with being a man. These questions were discussed in small groups, reported to the large group, and listed on newsprint for evaluation by the participants. Fourth, the six patterns of men's GRC (Restrictive Emotionality; Success, Power, and Competition; Restrictive Affectionate Behavior Between Men; Conflict Between Work and Family Relations; O'Neil, 1981b; O'Neil et al., 1986; see also Chapter 3, this volume) were presented and assessed using the Gender Role Conflict Scale. The results of this assessment were discussed in the large group. Fifth, the phases of the gender role journey (O'Neil & Egan, 1992a) were presented to help students assess their current views of sexism and gender role attitudes. Sixth, with student leaders and the student affairs staff, action plans were developed. The action plans asked respondents to list their personal, professional, and political plans of action related to men's issues over the next academic year. These action plans were shared with the large group. In all workshops, there was an emphasis on learning about men's issues; personalizing the concepts; and, when appropriate, projecting what participants can do to advance men's lives on campus. Last, a 12-item evaluation questionnaire administered to each targeted workshop group.

Evaluations of the Campus Programming on Men's Issues

All target groups, except the academic classes, systematically evaluated the program using a 12-item questionnaire that asked about the quality and importance of the workshops in their lives. In the five structured workshops, 150 participants attended, and 116 evaluations were received, for a 77% return rate. All the data cannot be reported here, but the following results reflect the participants' reactions to the workshops. A high number (92%) agreed that they had learned more about men's perspectives, and 76% indicated they had learned more about their own GRC. Three quarters of the participants reported a better understanding of their own gender role journey, and 92% agreed that the workshop was valuable to them. In terms of the future, 94% agreed that the workshops should be presented again, and 78% agreed that they could benefit from assistance in resolving their own GRC.

Implications for Future Programming for Men's Issues

The systematic campus programming and consultation just described is one approach to fostering more discussion about men's issues on campus. The programming was innovative in that it used preassessment data to guide program development, in involving staff through a campus committee on men's issues, in using established theory and research on men's GRC, and in translating baseline data and theory to steer experiential exercises for under-graduate students and staff.

Intervention 2: The Boy's Forum: A Gender Role Program for Urban Middle School Boys

The Boy's Forum was designed to empower seventh- and eighth-graders to understand their masculinity issues, psychosocial development, and gender role transitions (O'Neil et al., 2013). My colleagues and I used a psycho-educational group format whereby the boys learned from older male role models who believed that students can empower themselves. Our evaluation included a preassessment, an evaluation at the end of the program, and a 3-week follow-up that focused on how the program affected participants' thoughts, feelings, and behaviors. Using a nonexperimental design, our program evaluation spe-cifically assessed whether the Boy's Forum could affect boys immediately after the program and over a 3-week period.

Fifty-one boys, ages 13 and 14, participated in the 2-day Boy's Forum in an urban school in the Northeast. There were 29 seventh graders and 22 eighth graders. The sample included 32 Hispanic boys, 11 boys of mixed ethnic back-ground, six African American boys, one Caucasian boy, and one boy who did not identify his race.

Day 1: Description of the Boy's Forum Intervention

Few examples of gender role programs for middle-school boys exist, and even fewer exist for racial/ethnic minority boys. Our approach was simple and straightforward. The 2-day Boy's Forum encouraged the seventh- and eighth-grade boys to learn about the challenges of growing up male. The first day of the forum lasted for 100 minutes. This session began with an introduction explaining the purpose of the Boy's Forum and what the boys could learn. As reported earlier, a 14 item preassessment questionnaire was filled out by each boy. Next, information about growing up male in America was com-municated through the documentary "Boys Will Be Men: Growing Up Male in America" (Weidlinger & Moira Productions, 2001), which focuses on the challenges, expectations, and contradictions boys face. In the first 14 min-utes, evidence is presented that growing up male in America entails perils from infancy to the teenage years. One of the central questions of the film is whether boys grow up in a "culture of cruelty." The documentary draws from the work of many experts in the field of psychology of men, including Michael Thompson, coauthor of *Raising Cain: Protecting the Emotional Life of Boys* (Kindlon & Thompson, 2000), and William Pollack, author of *Real Boys: Rescuing Our Sons From the Myths of Boyhood* (1998b). The second part of the film shows constructive ways for boys to find themselves and develop a positive masculine self through an Outward Bound experience and the performing arts (i.e., poetry, storytelling, and self-expression). Overall, the documentary offers suggestions on how boys can successfully evolve into effective men.

After watching "Boys Will Be Men," the boys engaged in a question-and-answer session with several male teachers who discussed their adolescent experiences growing up and transitioning into high school. The programming approach was balanced by telling the truth about the problems of growing up male but also providing encouragement to work hard on self-empowerment and positive masculinity activities.

Day 2: Description of the Boy's Forum Intervention

The second day of the Boy's Forum lasted for about 50 minutes. I myself, a White university professor, gave a presentation titled "Things That Adults Didn't Tell Me When I Was 13 But I Wished That They Had."

My PowerPoint/personal disclosure presentation built on "Boys Will Be Men" but focused on my recollection of my boyhood problems when I was 13. Empowerment was the central message of the entire presentation. Several psychoeducational techniques were used in this presentation, including personal self-disclosure, showing personal and family pictures, personal vulnerability, and honesty. Using my own experiences, I shared my struggles with authority figures and my strained relationship with my father.

The PowerPoint lecture covered the following nine empowerment themes: (a) Everyone Has Problems; (b) Growing and Learning How to Learn Is Difficult; (c) Education Is Very Important; (d) Feeling Bad Ourselves Can be Changed; (e) How to Deal With Change and Transitions; (f) Finding Role Models, Mentors, and Positive People; (g) How to Deal With Emotions; (h) Dealing With Anger; and (i) How to Learn Problem-Solving Skills.

I discussed four problems areas I had experienced: being misunderstood by adults, struggling with math and reading, feeling sad and angry at my father, and having ongoing problems with authority figures. I also disclosed the following specific problems: finding learning to be difficult; being delayed in reading; having a limited vocabulary; expressing fears about failing; lacking confidence; having difficulties concentrating and staying focused; feeling at times indifferent to learning; believing that everybody was smarter than I; and feeling small, inferior, and inadequate. I disclosed that in seventh grade, I had been placed in a slow-learner group, which made me angry, sad, and hurt. The critical message to the boys was that I had fought back from these negative emotions and empowered myself by taking more responsibility for my learning, increasing my hope by believing that things could get better, trying harder and seeking help from counselors and teachers, and becoming more disciplined (more ordered and focused on a plan and personal dream). I also discussed the impact of two homeroom teachers who helped me mobilize my empowerment and potential.

My honest self-disclosure modeled and encouraged a process of emotional vulnerability for the boys as they explored their own lives.

Following this, I discussed empowerment themes. I made various recommendations that emphasized positive aspects of masculinity and personal empowerment. Table 13.2 enumerates 14 empowerment themes and lessons for the boys I discussed. These themes were the take-home messages to motivate students to face their gender role issues and solve their problems.

At the end of the presentation there was a brief question-and-answer session. Numerous male teachers spontaneously disclosed their own childhood trials and tribulations to the wide-eyed group of young boys. Finally, the program coordinator did a final wrap-up of the Boy's Forum, and the boys filled out a seven-item evaluation of the program. Three weeks later, each

TABLE 13.2
Boy Empowerment Themes and Lessons to Be Learned Presented
by the Guest Presenter

Empowerment themes	Lessons to be learned
1. Telling the truth, being real, and disclosing is healthy.	It is good to be honest with myself, self-disclose, and accept who I am.
2. Everyone has problems in living.	Knowing this makes it easier to face my problems.
3. Growing up and learning is difficult for everyone.	Knowing this takes some of the pressure off me.
4. Taking personal responsibility is required.	It is my life and I have to direct it.
5. Education predicts personal and career success.	This puts school in a different light.
6. Feeling bad about self and life can be changed.	My negative emotions and moods can be turned into positives.
7. Change and transitions are inevitable and challenging.	I can learn to adapt and change.
8. Seeking help is critical to success and not a failure.	I can get help without feeling bad about it.
9. Dealing with human emotions is critical.	Emotions can positively guide my thoughts and behavior.
10. Anger can guide us.	Anger can have positive outcomes.
11. Trying harder may be necessary.	I need to motivate myself.
12. Learning problem solving skills is possible.	I need to learn these skills to solve my life problems.
13. Discipline is required to achieve goals.	I need to organize my life to deliver on my contributions to life.
14. Having hope is always an option.	I can believe that things will get better.

Note. From "The Boy's Forum: An Evaluation of a Brief Intervention to Empower Middle School Urban Boys," by J. M. O'Neil, C. Challenger, S. Renzulli, B. Crapser, and E. Webster, 2013, *The Journal of Men's Studies, 21,* p. 198. Copyright 2013 by Men's Studies Press. Adapted with permission.

student was sent a 24-item follow-up questionnaire assessing how the forum had affected his thinking, feelings, and behaviors.

Analysis of the Evaluation Data

Because of the lack of documented programs for boys, we chose an exploratory, nonexperimental design that directly assessed whether the boys had found the Boy's Forum useful. Two self-report questionnaires were created to assess the boys' immediate reaction to the program and their reactions 3 weeks later. The follow-up questionnaire assessed the boys' thoughts, feelings, and behaviors. Twenty-four questions were prefaced by the following stem: "Because of the Boy's Forum . . . " (see Table 13.3). Therefore, the responses to each item were directly related to the boy's self-report on how the Boy's Forum had influenced him. All questions were answered using a Likert scale

TABLE 13.3
Three-Week Follow-up: Thoughts, Feelings,
and Behavior Agreement Percentages

"Because of the Boy's Forum . . . "	Percentage agreement
Thought more about my problems as a boy	72
Thought more about myself	75
Thought about my family problems	63
Thought about the video "Boys Will Be Men"	72
Thought more about my problems at school	78
Thought about how valuable education is to me	94
Thought about how useless education is	16
Thought more about my issues with authority	66
Thought more about the guest presentation	81
Thought more about the guest presenter's personal disclosures	65
Thought about how to deal with my next transition (high school, into eighth grade)	91
Thought about how to deal with my anger	59
Thought about reaching out for some help with my problems	41
Thought about finding a role model or mentor	66
Thought about how to develop my problem solving	65
Had positive feelings about the Boy's Forum	84
Had negative feelings about the Boy's Forum	6
Felt better about myself	66
Felt worse about myself	9
Talked with my parents about being a boy and my problems	38
Talked with another student about being a boy and my problems	38
Talked with a teacher or another adult about being a boy and my problems	25
Reached out for some help to someone with my problems	47
Wish the Boy's Forum would continue in the future	72

Note. From "The Boy's Forum: An Evaluation of a Brief Intervention to Empower Middle School Urban Boys," by J. M. O'Neil, C. Challenger, S. Renzulli, B. Crapser, and E. Webster, 2013, *The Journal of Men's Studies, 21,* p. 200. Copyright 2013 by Men's Studies Press. Adapted with permission.

that ranged from *strongly disagree* (1) to *strongly agree* (5). Percentage agreement for each item was calculated by adding the 4s (*agree*) and the 5s (*strongly agree*) together into a single percentage agreement score. Fifteen items asked the boys about how the Boy's Forum had affected their thinking processes over the 3-week period. Five items assessed how the Boy's Forum had affected their emotions, and four items assessed their actual behavior over the 3-week period.

Evaluation Immediately After the Boy's Forum

Immediate reactions to the 2-day Boy's Forum indicated that a majority of the boys evaluated the program positively and that the curriculum helped them. Over 60% of the boys indicated that because of the Boy's Forum they had a better sense of direction about being a boy, believed their feelings and worries about being a boy were normal, and had a better sense about being a boy. In addition, more than 60% of the boys indicated that the program had helped them and that my presentation had helped them with their feelings about growing up male. Eighty-six percent of the boys reported that it was a good idea to talk about male topics. Finally, only 29% of the boys reported that they had a better understanding of the issues boys face today. This suggests that the Boy's Forum did not fully address all aspects of being a boy.

Evaluation Three Weeks After the Boy's Forum:
Boys' Thinking, Feelings, and Behaviors

Thirty-two boys, or 63% of the participants, completed the 3-week follow-up questionnaire. Table 13.3 shows the percentages of students who agreed to the statement for each follow-up question. The boys reported considerable thinking over the 3-week period about the Boy's Forum. Because of the Boy's Forum, over 90% of the students thought about how to navigate the transition to eighth grade or high school and thought about how valuable education is for them. Only 16% reported that education was useless to them. More than 80% of the boys thought about my presentations about my boyhood problems over the 3-week period. More than 70% thought more about themselves, their problems as boys in school, and the "Boys Will Be Men" documentary. More than 60% of the boys reported that they thought more about their family problems, authority issues with adults, how to develop problem solving skills. The same percentage of boys reported thinking about my personal disclosures and finding a role model or mentor over the 3-week period. Finally, 59% reported that they had thought about how to deal with their anger, and 41% had thought about reaching out to someone for some help with their problems.

In terms of emotions over the 3 weeks, 84% said they had positive feelings toward the Boy's Forum. Sixty-six percent indicated feeling better about themselves because of the forum, but 9% of the boys said they felt worse. More than 70% of the boys wished the forum would continue in the future. Four questions assessed actual behaviors because of the Boy's Forum: 47% of the boys reached out for help from someone, 38% talked with their parents about their problems about being a boy, the same number discussed their problems with another student, and 25% talked with a teacher or another adult about their problems.

SUMMARY OF THE BOY'S FORUM

The Boy's Forum positively affected the boys immediately after the program and over the ensuing 3 weeks. The evaluation immediately after the program indicated that almost two thirds of the boys reported that the Boy's Forum helped them, and over 85% reported that talking about male topics was a good idea. At the 3-week follow-up, 84% of boys reported positive feelings toward the Boy's Forum, and 70% wanted it to continue.

These results indicate that gender role programming for urban adolescent boys can be successfully implemented. The data represent some of the first evidence demonstrating that boys can positively engage in masculinity issues at an early age. The follow-up evaluation specifically assessed whether the boys had cognitively internalized the program's messages over time.

The program also stimulated, in two thirds of the boys, thoughts about authority issues, anger, problem-solving skills, and role models/mentors. A majority of the boys also reported thinking over the 3-week period about my presentation and self-disclosures. This indicates that when boyhood stories are told to middle-school boys by an adult, the disclosure can have cognitive impact over at least a 3-week period.

Because of the Boy's Forum, a majority of the boys reported feeling better about themselves. Lower but still significant percentages of boys reported specific behaviors because of the forum. Almost half of the boys indicated that they reached out for some help with their problems. Almost 40% disclosed that they sought help from a parent or another student. These results suggest that a brief program like this can actually motivate students to seek help when they are encouraged to do so.

Intervention 3: The Gender Role Journey Workshop For Men and Women[2]

A 6-day, 36-hour gender role journey workshop designed to help adults analyze their gender role socialization and conflict was offered annually by me and my colleagues from 1984 to 2006, with more than 700 men and women

[2] From "A Gender Role Workshop Focused on Sexism, Gender Role Conflict, and the Gender Role Journey," by J. M. O'Neil and M. Roberts Carroll, 1998, *Journal of Counseling & Development, 67*, pp. 193–197. Copyright 1998 by John Wiley & Sons. Adapted with permission.

participating (O'Neil, 1996; O'Neil & Roberts Carroll, 1988). The workshop's conceptual base encouraged participants to examine their present and past experiences with gender roles. The four major concepts of the workshop were (a) sexism (Albee, 1981), (b) GRC, (c) gender role transitions, and (d) the gender role journey (O'Neil & Egan, 1992a).

Workshop Dimensions

The workshop design assumed that adults need to talk with each other about sexism and GRC as part of the healing process. It also assumed that alliances between men and women were possible and necessary for the growth and understanding of each sex and that discussions about gender roles and sexism can be difficult, dynamic, and emotional.

Six principles guided the preparation and implementation of the workshop. First, men and women struggle to integrate new definitions of gender roles as they face life events. Second, varying degrees of awareness about the negative outcomes of restrictive gender roles and sexism exist in people's lives. Third, an expanded "gender role vocabulary" is needed to express thoughts and feelings on changing gender roles. Fourth, conflicts and negative emotions occur as men and women become aware of sexism. Fifth, understanding and resolving GRC can occur using the phases of the gender role journey (see Chapters 3, 5, and 10, this volume). Finally, dialogue about gender roles and sexism can be constructive and nonviolent if there is a commitment to mutual support and understanding.

Workshop Participants

Separate workshops were offered over a 24-year period, but specific evaluation data were gathered in the 1985, 1986, and 1987 workshops, with a total of 84 participants enrolling from the fields of counseling, teaching, nursing, and other helping professions. Women outnumbered men three to one in each workshop; the average workshop size was 28 participants. The mean age of participants was 33, 38, and 36 for Workshops I, II, and III, respectively. The workshop leaders were one male PhD-level counseling psychologist (me) and one female master's-level counselor.

Workshop Curriculum, Process, Norms, and Media

Workshop Curriculum. The workshop's title was "Gender Role Conflict Issues for Helping Professionals," but over the years the unofficial title was the "Gender Role Journey Workshop." It was offered as a graduate summer school class in the counseling psychology program in the Educational Psychology Department at the University of Connecticut. The workshop curriculum is summarized in detail in Table 13.4. During each day, new themes were introduced

TABLE 13.4
Dimensions and Curriculum of the Gender Role Journey Workshop

Workshop dimension	Day 1	Day 2	Day 3	Day 4	Day 5	Day 6
Themes	• Workshop norms and expectations • Gender role journey phases • How to access the workshop • Stages of a group • Understanding the group process • Power and oppression • Men and women as victims of sexism • Metaphors for healing • Power and control issues in the workshop	• Research on sex differences, gender role socialization, and stereotyping • Patriarchy, sexism, oppression, and violence • Working with emotional pain • Working with defense mechanisms	• Patterns of men's and women's gender role conflict	• Adult life cycle and gender role transitions and themes	• Family socialization and mothers, fathers, sons, and daughters • Sexual orientation, race, class, ethnic background, and gender role socialization	• How to keep the gender role journey going • Action plans and goals • Summary of workshop • Community lunch closure and goodbye
Lecture topics	• Rationale and norms for workshop • Summary of need assessment data • Gender role vocabulary • Four kinds of violence • Sexism, racism, classism, homophobia, and ethnocentrism as violence • The gender role journey • Leader's disclosure on gender role journey	• Research on sex differences and gender role socialization • Gender role restrictions, devaluations, and violations • Pleck's (1981) sex role strain analysis • Gilligan's (1982) *In a Different Voice* • Jeanne Block's research • Matthew Fox's via negative	• Men's perceived losses of power • Men's patterns of gender role conflict (O'Neil, 1981a, 1981b) • Men's fears of femininity and masculine mystique • Women's patterns of gender role conflict • Research on men's gender role conflict • Leader's disclosure on patterns of gender role conflict	• Adult life cycle stages • Gender role transition and themes • John Lennon's gender role journey • Methods of transformation and gender role transitions	• Data on victimization and violence in the United States • Marvin Gaye's gender role journey • Leader disclosures: father–daughter relationships • Jane Fonda's or Marilyn Monroe's gender role journey • Healing the wounds • Definitions of racism and classism	• Working with pain over time • Developing action plans • How to use the workshop content • Reentry issues and problems • Purpose and function of action plans

Music and media used	**Music** • Concerto No. 1 in A Minor (Bach) • "Unity" (Holly Near) • Four Seasons (Vivaldi) • "Homecoming Queen's Got a Gun"; "I Like 'Em Big and Stupid" (Julie Brown) • "The Way We Were" (Barbra Streisand) **Music videos** • "That's What Friends Are For" (Dionne Warwick, Elton John, Stevie Wonder, and Gladys Knight) **Movie clips** • Nine to Five	**Music** • "Between Two Worlds and Forever the Optimist" (Patrick O'Hearn) • "Candle in the Wind" (Elton John) **Music videos** • "Cry" (Godley and Crème) • "Oh Father" (Madonna) **Movie clips** • Thelma and Louise	**Music** • "Free to Grow," "Feeling Better" (Holly Near) **Music videos** • "I Want to Know What Love Is" (Foreigner) **Movie clips** • Tootsie • Superman III • Kramer vs. Kramer	**Music** • "American Tune," "Bridge Over Troubled Water" (Simon and Garfunkel) • "Double Fantasy" (John Lennon and Yoko Ono) • "From the Goddess" (On the Wings of Song and Robert Gass) **Music videos** • "Woman is the Nigger of the World," "Mother," "Woman," "Imagine" (John Lennon) **Movie clips** • Kramer vs. Kramer	**Music** • "Child" (Holly Near) **Music videos** • "Motown Anniversary Video," "What's Going On," "Sexual Healing" (Marvin Gaye) • "Missing You" (Diana Ross) • "The River" (Bruce Springsteen) **Movie/TV clips** • On Golden Pond • Ordinary People • "The Honeymooners" (Jackie Gleason) • Mississippi Burning **Music** • Bach Concerto in D Minor for Two Violins (Isaac Stern) • "Comfort Zone" (Steven Halpern) • "Wrap the Sun Around You," "Voices" (Holly Near)
Structured exercises	• Guided imagery summary sheet • Psychological violence checklist	• Sex differences checklist • Identifying gender role stereotypes exercises	• Men's and women's gender role conflict inventions	• How to improve male–female relationships • Gender role themes checklist	• Gender role restrictions, devaluations, and violations questionnaire • Letting pain be pain and letting pain go exercise • Generating action plans and goals exercise • Overall workshop evaluations
Large- or small-group discussions	• Small-group processing of psychological violence checklist • Large- and small-group disclosures and discussion about guided-imagery experience	• Small-group exercise: identifying gender role stereotypes • Large-group discussion of identified stereotypes	• Large-group discussion of patterns of gender role conflict	• Small-group discussions: improving male-female relationships • Large-group discussion: improving male-female relationships	• Small-group discussion on family socialization • Large-group discussion on future plans and goals • Closing statements by workshop participants

Note. The curricula and media are updated annually, and therefore this table represents only the curriculum in the early years. From "A Gender Role Workshop Focused on Sexism, Gender Role Conflict, and the Gender Role Journey," by J. M. O'Neil and M. Roberts Carroll, 1988, *Journal of Counseling & Development, 67*, p. 195. Copyright 1988 by John Wiley & Sons. Adapted with permission.

using lectures, music and other media, structured-experiential exercises, and small- and large-group discussions. Mini-lectures, media presentations, and personal self-disclosures were the primary modes of teaching and learning.

The curriculum established specific definitions of gender role concepts through preassigned readings and lectures. This common terminology provided a concise understanding of the relationship between socialized gender roles and sexism. Furthermore, the workshop curriculum presumed that sexism is a form of violence between and among men and women and therefore a potentially volatile interpersonal issue. Consequently, the curriculum was defined as a vehicle for people to discuss, in a nonviolent way, the effects of sexism, using the gender role journey.

The curriculum was designed to elicit personal exploration in both the cognitive and affective domains of learning by using theory, research, and group activities. It was developed so that the ongoing group process would become part of the workshop content. Group leaders helped participants identify specific examples of sexism and GRC as they occurred within and between group members. Greater personalization of the curriculum was made possible by using music, movie clips, self-assessments, and group activities. Also, personal disclosures by the leaders and presentations of the gender role journeys of famous persons (e.g., John Lennon, Jane Fonda, Marvin Gaye) provided a basis for participants' own assessment of their journeys and conflicts.

Workshop Process. Before the workshop, participants read five articles that provided background on gender roles and sexism (see O'Neil, 1996; O'Neil & Roberts Carroll, 1988). These readings focused on men's sexism and gender role socialization, but equal time was given to women's issues in the lectures and the media used. A preworkshop needs assessment was administered through the mail to assess participants' expectancies, needs, and attitudes about gender roles. These data were gathered to better understand the participants and allow their direct input into the workshop design. Participants filled out daily evaluation forms assessing the day's activities and process. These provided feedback for preparing the next day's workshop content and process. On the last day of the workshop, participants prepared action plans, specifying in detail what they could do about sexism personally, professionally, and politically over the coming months.

Workshop Norms. Specific norms were established early in the workshop and guided the group process. The following workshop norms were established and monitored during the 6 days: personal comfort and safety; freedom of movement and self-expression; interpersonal respect; personal nonviolence; emotional and intellectual expressions; nonviolent expressions of anger; prohibition of victimization and interpersonal violence; mutual support; self-assessments, self-disclosures, and positive regard for individual differences; careful listening and tracking of the group process; monitoring personal talk time in the group; and developing friendships and alliances with others.

Media and Stimulus Diversity. Lectures and audio–video media were used continuously throughout the workshop as part of the stimulus diversity (see Table 13.4). *Stimulus diversity* was defined as using sequential teaching interventions to stimulate personal feelings, thoughts, and self-exploration. An example of how stimulus diversity worked in the workshop was the video presentations of the gender role journeys of many famous people from earlier and more recent years, including John Lennon, Jane Fonda, Marvin Gaye, Marilyn Monroe, Frank Sinatra, Elton John, Hillary Rodham Clinton, and Roger Maris. Their journeys were documented using various stimuli, including biographical profiles, music videos, and movie clips. Workshop participants could personalize their gender role issues by observing real-life dramas of sexism from famous people's lives.

Results of the Workshop Evaluations

The evaluation data came from self-report questionnaires that were descriptive and global in nature. Evaluations of all participants were conducted before and during the workshop, immediately after the workshop, at 1- and 3-month intervals after the workshop, and at 1 and 2 years after the workshop.

Likert scale items assessed personal learning form the workshop, emotional reactions to the workshop, and the degree to which the workshop had personally affected participants. In the following sentences, the percentages of agreement with each item for Workshops I, II, and III, respectively, are found within parentheses. In reference to personal learning, participants indicated learning more about themselves (100%, 100%, and 89%), having a better understanding of their socialization process (88%, 96%, and 92%), having a greater understanding of their relationships with their mother and father (84%, 76%, and 77%), and having increased sensitivity as to how stereotypes damage men and women (100%, 100%, and 96%). Regarding emotional reactions, participants indicated having felt emotional pain from issue(s) that emerged during the workshop (84%, 57%, and 52%) and having cried since the workshop because of pain experienced in the workshop (64%, 38%, and 19%). In reference to the degree of impact of the workshop on them, participants indicated that personal disclosures during the workshop continued to affect them (88%, 76%, and 78%), the workshop affected their relationships with the most intimate people in their lives (84%, 71%, and 59%), the workshop permanently altered their views of male–female relationships (68%, 86%, and 69%), and the workshop empowered them to effect change with GRC in people's lives (80%, 91%, and 74%).

Participants in Workshop 1 were sent a follow-up questionnaire 2 years after the workshop, and Workshop 2 participants received the same questionnaire 1 year later. These extended follow-ups assessed whether participants had taken action as planned on the last day of the workshop, as well as the overall impact of the workshop. More than 70% of the participants indicated they had carried out some of their personal and professional action plans, whereas 50% of Workshop 1 and 29% of Workshop 2 participants indicated that they had implemented some of their political action plans over both time periods. Finally, more than 87% of the participants indicated that the workshop continued to influence their lives either 1 or 2 years later.

Discussion

The workshop created an environment supporting dialogue about GRC and sexism using the gender role journey metaphor. The evaluation data indicated positive reactions to the workshop; participants reported personal learning, emotional experiences, and a continued impact of the workshop over time. When contacted 1 or 2 years later, a majority of the respondents indicated they had implemented some of their personal and professional action plans.

This workshop is one example of how research and theory on gender roles can be translated to therapeutic experiences for adults. Helping men and women build alliances within themselves and with each other is important in the ongoing gender role dialogue. Counselors and psychologists committed to more humane and nonviolent relationships between and among the sexes have much to offer adults by encouraging mutual alliances in the gender role journey and the prevention of sexism (Albee, 1981).

IMPLICATIONS FOR THE FUTURE

The delivery model and the three evaluated interventions described in this chapter provide examples of the nuts and bolts of operationalizing GRC in terms of preventive educational programs in a public school and in university settings with boys, men, and both men and women. The data indicate that these programs were received positively and made differences in the participants' lives.

The call to action in this book can be furthered by greater experimentation with ways to help both men and women journey with their gender roles (see Chapters 3 and 10, this volume). Moreover, the recent emphasis on teaching the psychology of men (Kilmartin, Addis, Mahalik, & O'Neil, 2013; Mahalik, Addis, Kilmartin, & O'Neil, 2013; O'Neil & Renzulli,

2013a, 2013b) is directly relevant to psychoeducational programming on GRC and masculinity ideology. Robertson (2013) made the critical point that teaching the psychology of men involves not just classroom pedagogy but also consciousness raising in the community about the perils of restrictive gender roles.

The call to action can take many forms, and everyone has something to offer the public whether one is a researcher, professor, high school teacher, clinician in private practice, or student affairs professional. Teams of professionals often work well in strategizing ways to infiltrate the status quo, because calls to action many times stimulate resistance and indifference.

V

A CALL TO ACTION: FUTURE DIRECTIONS IN ADDRESSING MEN'S GENDER ROLE CONFLICT

14

CALL TO ACTION REVISITED: PERSONAL REFLECTIONS, CONTEXTUAL SUMMARY, AND ACTION PLANS

> Let no one be discouraged by the belief that there is nothing one man or woman can do against the enormous array of the world's ills—against misery and ignorance, injustice, and violence. . . . Few will have the greatness to bend history itself; but each of us can work to change a small portion of events, and in the total of all those acts will be written the history of this generation. . . . It is from numberless diverse acts of courage and belief that history is shaped. Each time a man stands up for an ideal, or acts to improve the lot of others, or strikes out against injustice, he sends forth a tiny ripple of hope, and crossing each other from a million different centers of energy and daring, those ripples build a current which can sweep down the mightiest walls of oppression and resistance.
>
> —Robert F. Kennedy, speech given at the University of Cape Town, South Africa, 1966

I opened this book by discussing the current U.S. president, Barack Obama, and I close it by mentioning the man who was president when I grew up, John F. Kennedy (JFK), and his brother Robert F. Kennedy (RFK), my U.S. senator from 1966 to 1968. When I was 12, JFK became president of the United States, and his election was a significant event for me. His challenge to the nation to become more involved in improving society really excited me. JFK was my male role model: a young, articulate, energetic, strong, outspoken, and Irish Catholic man. These qualities were a perfect match for my religious and ethnic heritage, and I admired the human values he represented.

I always thought my attraction to JFK and RFK was based on their charisma and charm, and on their calls to take action against the problems in the world. I know now that it was deeper. They were men to emulate during

http://dx.doi.org/10.1037/14501-015
Men's Gender Role Conflict: Psychological Costs, Consequences, and an Agenda for Change, by J. M. O'Neil
Copyright © 2015 by the American Psychological Association. All rights reserved.

my gender role transition of puberty and the development of my masculinity ideology. As a young boy, I was not conscious of this masculine identification with the Kennedys, but now it is quite clear. The dark days of their respective deaths in November 1963 and June 1968 made me sad and angry, and they still haunt me when I dream of the good that could have occurred in our country had we not lost them.

These memories returned to me when I was searching the literature on masculinity ideology for this book, and they have crystallized the last context of gender role conflict (GRC) I will present here: domestic and foreign policy. In the course of my review, I found in the journal *Diplomatic History* an article titled "Masculinity as Ideology: John F. Kennedy and the Domestic Politics of Foreign Policy" (Dean, 1998). This article was an eye opener, convincingly arguing that the basis of JFK's presidency was the belief that American masculinity was in crisis and that men's problems were, in part, responsible for the decline in American power abroad. Dean made the following points:

- The cultural narratives of imperial manhood shaped the Kennedy Administration's foreign and domestic policies;
- JFK's masculine persona reflected not just style or personality but the influence of his gender roles on his policymaking;
- internalized ideals of masculinity influenced how JFK perceived threats posed by foreign powers;
- his domestic and foreign policies were based on the feared consequences of being judged as "unmanly"; and
- he believed the downward trend in the American economy was linked to threats to American masculinity, and he worried that feminized, luxury-loving, and declining "manhood" contributed to the waning of American hegemony over developing nations.

Dean wrote, "For Kennedy and his national security managers, self-conceptions of masculine toughness were inseparable from calculations concerning, for instance, the threat of Communism in Latin America or strategic dangers of appeasement in Viet Nam" (p. 30). Dean concluded that the ways in which powerful men view masculinity is a problem historians of politics and diplomacy should study.

This final context—how GRC affects domestic and foreign policy—may seem overreaching, but it is not, because it relates to critical decisions such as waging war or promoting peace. One might ask, for example, how JFK's GRC contributed to his decision to increase U.S. involvement in Vietnam in 1961 or his decision to invade Cuba (the Bay of Pigs fiasco) in 1962. What masculinity ideologies were operative in the deliberations during the Cuban Missile Crisis—the 13 days in 1962 when the verdict of global nuclear war or peace was being decided by a handful of men whose masculinity ideologies collided in intense conflict? Both JFK and RFK believed the Cuban Missile

Crisis and their own mishandling of the Bay of Pigs invasion could result in a takeover of the American presidency by the American military. The stakes were very high, and the gender role dynamics between the Kennedys and the military were intense and scary.

To put these masculinity conflicts into a more recent context, consider how masculinity ideologies played out after the terrorist attacks of September 11, 2001, with respect to the subsequent wars in Iraq and Afghanistan. The George W. Bush Administration justified the war in Iraq by presenting Congress with documented threats of nuclear and chemical weapons in Iraq that later proved to be unfounded. How was masculinity ideology used to influence Congress to endorse and fund these wars at a time when our vulnerable society was struggling to recover from the trauma of 9/11? Although the foreign relations contexts of GRC have not been discussed in this book, they are part of any macrosocietal analysis (see Chapters 3 and 6, this volume). How GRC influences domestic and foreign policy deserves more discussion by social scientists who want to discern how the United States participates in shaping the world order.

The gender roles that drove JFK's national and diplomatic policies were also evident on a personal level. Like most men, Kennedy was complex, with many positive attributes and personal limitations. My analysis of the documented history is that Kennedy experienced GRC in the form of Restrictive Emotionality (RE); Success, Power, and Competition; Restrictive Affectionate Behavior Between Men; Conflict Between Work and Family Relations; and other masculinity conflicts. The evidence from those who knew him well indicates he was introverted, had difficulty expressing emotion (RE) and giving and receiving affection (Restrictive Affectionate Behavior Between Men), was a compulsive womanizer, had difficulty with intimacy and self-disclosure, was at times a detached father during his children's infancy, was physically frail from numerous afflictions and chronic pain, and was sometimes a distant husband to his wife until after the Cuban Missile Crisis and the death of his infant son in August 1963. These gender-related problems were hidden behind a public persona (the masculine mask) of health, strength, vigor, and charm. As his father put it to him, "Can't you get it into your head that it's not important what you really are? The only important thing is what people think you are" (Clarke, 2013, p. 4).

Only recently have the many contexts of Kennedy's life been revealed so that the real man behind the myth can be seen (Clarke, 2013). My own contextual analysis of JFK's gender role journey was that he struggled with many of the same gender role issues that most men do: finding success and power, RE, proving your masculinity, closeness, intimacy, sexuality, spirituality, and physical health care. Restrictive gender roles and fears of femininity shaped his personality and affected his personal and political relationships. JFK was charming but introverted and unemotional and invulnerable even to those who knew him well. He suffered from chronic illness and physical fragilities much of his life and perhaps even posttraumatic stress disorder from his war experiences in the South Pacific (Clarke, 2013).

Of course, these limitations need to be weighed against JFK's positive attributes. He compartmentalized his complexities, revealing different parts of himself to different people. Like most men, he was constantly making and remaking himself, based on the situation. Although much of the analysis of JFK's GRC is based on historical evidence and others' perceptions of him, it is generally agreed that, like most men, he had masculinity problems (Dean, 1998).

A close examination of JFK's gender role journey suggests he experienced GRC most of his life but not the last 100 days (Clarke, 2013). His failed decision to invade Cuba (the Bay of Pigs fiasco), the intense fears during the Cuban Missile Crisis about a nuclear holocaust, and the death of his son, Patrick Kennedy altered JFK's GRC and masculinity ideology and brought out his full humanity. With the Cuban invasion he faced his policy failure and lack of judgment. With the missile crisis, he embraced the intense fears of thermonuclear war and the death of millions of people. The most emotional event was the death of his son, 2 days after his premature birth and Clarke (2013) concludes that this loss shaped the last 100 days of his life.

Considerable evidence indicates this overwhelming and shocking loss altered JFK's personality. Transcending his RE, he showed tears and anguish to almost everyone who helped during the medical emergency and funeral. Although it was hidden from the media, all of this sorrow resulted in his transformation, producing a gender role transition that changed his attitudes and behaviors in almost every aspect of his personal life. He opened up emotionally; began to be more intimate and affectionate with his wife, Jackie; embraced his role as father to his children in a new and more active way; and ended his long-time pattern of extramarital affairs. It may have changed his political perspectives as well. In short, after his son's death, something with JFK's gender role schemas shifted (see Chapter 5), probably allowing him to make gains in decreasing his GRC and altering his masculinity ideology and providing an example of how men change during critical life events and move past their sexist gender role socialization.

My purpose in writing this book was to expand contextual knowledge not only about men like JFK but also about the man living next door to you. In Chapter 1, I discussed a paradigm shift in how we define masculinity and noted that the pace of change has been dreadfully slow. This is because the deconstruction of masculine gender roles stimulates resistance from strong economic, political, and religious power bases that reinforce sexist masculinity. Beyond this political deconstruction process is the question of how to help men become full human beings. To do that, we need more theory, research, and ways to help men change.

In this final chapter, I ask readers to consider responding to my call to action by becoming involved in the psychology of men, women, and gender. The statistics on men's problems and the research I have reviewed on men's GRC should end any debate about whether boys and men have psychological problems because of restrictive gender roles. There is much to be done, and psychologists and other human services providers can lead the way.

To promote the expansion of the psychology of men, in this book I have presented new contexts, theoretical assumptions, and conceptual models related to GRC. When possible, I cited research evidence that supported the contexts and assumptions, and when research was lacking, I operationally defined contexts and cited other theories to support my position. As a consequence, not all of my ideas have direct empirical support, and some of the evidence is indirect or made by inference. In closing, I provide a synthesis of the many contexts and assumptions to promote more activism in the field of the psychology of men.

CONTEXTUALIZING THE CALL TO ACTION: WHAT SHOULD BE DONE NEXT

The seven contextual domains, the dozen conceptual models, the 40 theoretical assumptions, and the practical tools to help men I have described in this book represent an expanded view of the psychology of men. Future researchers and theoreticians can consider the conceptual models, the GRC research, and the practice implications and present their own data or reasoning to support, refute, correct, improve, and add to these initial ideas. What is important is to keep developing more knowledge, research, psychoeducational programs, and public policy changes that improve both men's and women's lives.

The contexts found in each chapter are summarized in Exhibit 14.1, which provides a snapshot of the major concepts in the book. Over 90 contexts are clustered into the following contextual domains: macrosocietal–sociopolitical; developmental–psychosocial; empirical and research; multicultural–diversity; gender role related; applied, therapeutic, and clinical; and applied, preventive, and psychoeducational. Twenty-three action plans are specified in the seven contextual domains and represent examples of what can be done in the future. My hope is that the seven contexts and the 23 action plans in Exhibit 14.1 can function as portals for consciousness raising and change at the personal, professional, and political levels.

The action plans are not exhaustive and are presented to stimulate your own thinking about how you can get involved. The old African proverb, best communicated by Eldridge Cleaver in the 1960s, is relevant here: "If

EXHIBIT 14.1
Synthesis of Contextual Domains and 23 Action Plans
to Promote the Psychology of Men

Examples of Macrosocietal and Sociopolitical Contexts

Patriarchy; hegemonic masculinity; societal sexism; stereotypes and biases against men; societal discrimination; personal and institutional oppression (e.g., racism, classism, ethnocentrism, heterosexism); social injustice; stereotyping about the socialization of boys and girls; differential socialization of boys and girls to sexist masculinity and femininity ideologies; and policies that support the status quo or promote positive psychological health, freedom and justice for all

Action Plans

1. Study and expose how the larger patriarchal society is structured to cause sexism, gender role conflict (GRC), oppression, and injustices for both men and women.
2. Study and expose how stereotypes, biases, and patriarchal masculinity ideologies promote discrimination and psychological problems for both men and women.
3. Advocate for policy changes at all levels of society that promote nonsexist and nondiscriminatory practices in education, family life, and work place environments.

Examples of Developmental and Psychosocial Contexts

Developmental tasks; psychosocial crises; demonstrating, resolving, reevaluating, and integrating masculinity; phases of the gender role journey; gender role schemas; distorted gender role schemas; gender role transformation processes and growth; healthy and positive masculinity

Action Plans

1. Study and document men's GRC and gender role transitions in the context of psychosocial development across the life cycle.
2. Study and document how the contextual, multicultural, and situational factors affect masculinity ideology, GRC, and psychosocial growth when mastering developmental tasks and resolving psychosocial crises.
3. Study and document the criteria for healthy positive masculinity ideologies and effective ways for boys and men to journey with gender roles that promote psychosocial growth and development.

Examples of Empirical and Research Contexts

GRC as a predictor of men's psychological problems; GRC as a moderator of men's psychological problems; GRC as a mediator of men's psychological problems; contextual and microcontextual factors as predictors of GRC; GRC as a mediator of contextual and microcontextual factors in predicting outcomes; descriptive contexts; microcontextual, functional, and situational contexts; positive and negative situations related to GRC; negative and positive behavior, outcomes and consequences of gender-related situations

Action Plans

1. Research the microcontextual, functional, and situational contexts of men's gender role socialization and GRC that result in positive and negative outcomes and consequences.
2. Develop theoretically based, empirically derived measures that assess the functional, microcontextual aspects of men's experiences with masculinity ideology and GRC.

EXHIBIT 14.1
Synthesis of Contextual Domains and 23 Action Plans
to Promote the Psychology of Men *(Continued)*

3. Institutionalize national research councils funded by private and public funds to systematize and report research on boys' and men's lives.
4. Standardize methods of dispersing research to the media and legislative bodies to promote public understanding and policy changes regarding boys and men.

Examples of Multicultural Diversity Contexts

Race/ethnicity; sex; class; socioeconomic status; biology; age; unconsciousness; stage of life; cultural values; nationality; religious orientation; physical disability; sexual orientation; sexual identity; acculturation; oppression from discrimination; internalized oppression; family interaction patterns; being a victim; being unemployed; being homeless; being violent

Action Plans

1. Study and document the situational, biological, unconscious, familial, multicultural, racial/ethnic, sexual orientation, and other situational indexes of diversity that shape men's gender role identity.
2. Study and document the psychological costs of the macrosocietal oppression (e.g., racism, classism, heterosexism) and personal discrimination that emanate from both restrictive masculinity ideologies and GRC.

Examples of Gender Role–Related Contexts

Gender role identity; fears of femininity; restrictive, sexist masculinity and femininity ideologies; patterns of gender role conflict; gender role devaluations, restrictions, and violations; defense mechanisms; male vulnerability; psychological and interpersonal problems; internalized oppression; violence from GRC

Action Plans

1. Study, document, and explain to the public how the macrosocietal and sociopolitical contexts of sexism and patriarchal values affect individual boys and men.
2. Study and document how, why, and when boys and men experience GRC using descriptive, functional, and microcontextual research approaches.
3. Study and document how men's gender role devaluations, restrictions, and violations occur in the context of societal discrimination, internalized oppression, psychological/emotional problems, defensiveness, violence, and male vulnerability.

Examples of Applied, Therapeutic, and Clinical Contexts

The gender role journey as therapy; readiness and motivation to change; evaluations of restrictive gender roles, sexism, and other oppressions; stages of change (precontemplation, contemplation, preparation, action, and maintenance); the client's presenting problem; masculine-specific conflicts; gender role devaluations, restrictions, and violations; deepening; the gender role journey as a portal; deconstruction of masculine and feminine roles; psychosocial assessment; gender role transitions; gender role schemas; distorted gender role schemas; macrosocietal contexts; internalized oppression; GRC as the wound; GRC concealing the wound; GRC as a vehicle to discovering the wound; assessing masculinity ideology; assessing patterns of gender role conflict; assessing distorted gender role schemas; assessing

(continues)

EXHIBIT 14.1
Synthesis of Contextual Domains and 23 Action Plans
to Promote the Psychology of Men   *(Continued)*

gender role devaluations, restrictions, and violations; transitions in gender role journey phases; Restrictive Emotionality; Success, Power, and Competition; Restrictive
Affectionate Behavior Between Men; Conflict Between Work and Family Relations;
Restrictive Emotionality; Success, Power, and Control; and homophobia as critical
issues during therapy

Action Plans

1. Study and document how to assess and remediate GRC and restrictive masculinity
   ideologies during men's therapy.
2. Study and document how men experience the stages and the processes of
   change during therapy in terms of deconstructing masculine and feminine gender
   roles, understanding their psychosocial development, embracing their human vulnerability and wounds, working through defenses, and understanding how macrosocietal and patriarchal structures contribute to men's psychological problems
   and internalized oppression.
3. Study and document how GRC is an interactive dynamic for clients, therapists,
   and the therapeutic interaction in terms of therapy processes and outcomes.
4. Document evidence-based ways to effectively intervene with men in therapy
   through cases studies and empirical research.

Examples of Applied, Preventive, and Psychoeducational Contexts

Teaching the psychology of men through psychoeducational programming; resistance
to programming; theoretical and empirical justification for programming; methods and
processes of programming; examples of evidence-based psychoeducational programming for boys, men, and women

Action Plans

1. Increase the development, experimentation, and evaluation of psychoeducational
   interventions with boys and men.
2. Institute a national clearinghouse of evaluated and effective interventions for boys
   and men that are available to psychoeducational programmers.
3. Increase the number of journal article submissions of evidence-based interventions
   with boys and men.
4. Developing more psychology of men courses in high schools, colleges, and
   universities throughout the United States and internationally.

---

you are not a part of the solution, you are a part of the problem" (http://www.
goodreads.com/author/quotes/42661.Eldridge_Cleaver).

In each domain in Exhibit 14.1 are examples of what can be done.
For example, more critical analyses are needed of the macrosocietal level
because without dramatic changes in how society is structured, most men
have no other option than the paradigms of masculinity endorsed by the
status quo. *Action* in this area means discussing the sociopolitical aspects of
sexism against men and women in the context of discrimination, oppression,
and human rights. All of these issues run counter to U.S. society's democratic

commitments to nondiscrimination, personal rights, and liberty and freedom for all.

In addition, further contextual analyses of how restrictive masculinity ideology and GRC interact in complex ways with psychosocial growth and mastery of developmental tasks are needed if healthy masculinity is to be understood and taught in families and schools. Parents and educators can become aware that their sons, daughters, and students face challenges in navigating the gender role dynamics of childhood and adolescence. The real challenge for educators that needs to be vigorously pursued is how to communicate the perils of restrictive gender roles to parents and the public.

The multicultural context needs further development to honor the many different kinds of masculinities and understand how GRC contributes to discrimination and oppression of men and women, resulting in social injustices and violence. Alliances and action plans with individuals who are committed to eradicating racism, homophobia, heterosexism, classism, and other forms of oppression need to be developed. These alliances require that psychologists from all racial/ethnic groups move past their own internalized oppression, guilt, and fear to form a common cause against the structures in society that condone patriarchal oppression. Frank discussions, trust building, and collaborative action plans can make a difference in developing allies and alliances.

In the research context, new empirical measures and research that better explains how, why, when, and where GRC is experienced are needed so that the resulting research is useful to clinicians and teachers of the psychology of men. Furthermore, research needs to examine the situational contexts of men's problems, men's real-life experiences, and the complexity of GRC so that there is less denial about men's problems. Teams of researchers and leaders in the Society for the Psychological Study of Men and Masculinity can set an empirical agenda for needed research over extended period of times based on the topics that are most likely to affect the larger society.

The advancement of the gender-related contexts requires more operationally defined concepts in the psychology of men that explain the complexity of gender roles in men's lives. Promising concepts such as precarious masculinity (Vandello & Bosson, 2013; Vandello, Bosson, Cohen, Burnaford, & Weaver, 2008) and gendered racism (Liang, Rivera, Nathwani, Dang, & Douroux, 2010) are excellent examples of the kind of theorizing that is needed for the discipline to move forward. Moreover, there are must-read publications that support the call to action I made in this book, including Wong and Wester's (in press) *Handbook of the Psychology of Men and Masculinities*; *A Counselor's Guide to Working With Men* (Englar-Carlson, Evans, & Duffey, 2014); the special issue on "Men in Counseling" in the *Journal of Counseling & Development* (Evans, Duffey, & Englar-Carlson, 2013); *Gender in the Therapy Hour: Voices of Female Clinicians Working With Men* (Sweet, 2012); *Tough*

Guys and True Believers: Managing Authoritarian Men in the Psychotherapy Room (Robertson, 2012); and other publications that disseminate knowledge about healthy positive masculinity (Kiselica, 2011; Kiselica & Englar-Carlson, 2010). In addition, I highly recommend two self-help books, *The Secret Lives of Men: What Men Want You to Know About Love, Sex, and Relationships* (Blazina, 2008) and *Invisible Men: Men's Inner Lives and Consequences of Silence* (Addis, 2011), for use with clients and men seeking renewal and transformation. I recommend these publications not only because they are written by the best and the brightest professionals in the field of the psychology of men but also because they move the discipline toward a more theoretically based, clinically aware, and empirically focused profession. All of these publications are evidence that activism is gaining momentum and that the paradigm shift mentioned in Chapter 1 is indeed occurring.

Activism in the therapeutic and clinical domains can be advanced by having the psychology of men integrated into counselor and psychology training programs given that Mellinger and Liu (2006) reported interest by faculty supervisors in the psychology of men but that few formalized training programs exist in educational and internship settings. Leaders in clinical training can advocate for the psychology of men to become a required content area in any accredited program in counseling, clinical, organizational, and school psychology.

The psychoeducational contexts are critical if evidence-based interventions that can help boys and men are to be developed. Teaching the psychology of men is one of the best ways to educate the public to the perils of restrictive gender roles. Examples of courses on the psychology of men and men's psychoeducational processes are now available to educators (Kilmartin, Addis, Mahalik, & O'Neil, 2013; Mahalik, Addis, Kilmartin, & O'Neil, 2013; O'Neil & Renzulli, 2013a, 2013b).

EMERGING TRUTHS AND CONCLUSIONS FROM THE GENDER ROLE CONFLICT RESEARCH PROGRAM

Thirty years of studying the contexts of men's GRC have made some truths obvious to me about men, masculinity, and GRC. At the risk of overgeneralizing, I can say that the following truths are self-evident to me.

First, human qualities are, without question, more healthy and functional than those assigned to men and women by stereotypes of masculinity and femininity that emanate from patriarchal values. Restrictive stereotypes have outlived their utility. They serve no function, nor do they offer any survival value they might have had (assuming they ever had any) over the centuries. Restrictive gender roles impede human development; dehumanize both men and women; and, under many circumstances, victimize men, women, and children. Unfortunately, there exist in the United States political, economic, and religious factions that want to control human behavior and set society's priorities according to repressive ideologies and endorse restrictive gender roles. Before feminism, no collective consciousness existed about the perils of sexist stereotypes that cause GRC. There has been some progress over the years, but even now public awareness of the peril of sexism appears to ebb and flow on the basis of economic realities in U.S. society. Only a persistent and critical deconstruction of these damaging stereotypes can reverse the negative effects of sexism, GRC, and restrictive gender roles in people's lives.

On the micropersonal level, the issues are complex and deeply embedded in our religious and family values and the educational institutions that teach our children. Conscious and unconscious endorsement of gender role stereotypes in childhood and adolescence sets a trajectory of self-restrictions, devaluations of, and violations for both sexes. Furthermore, stereotypes and GRC affect psychosocial development by negatively mediating developmental tasks and psychosocial crises. Gender role transitions necessary for healthy and positive masculinity and femininity are inhibited by GRC and the pursuit of highly sex-typed behaviors.

I agree that some gender role norms are needed for boys' and girls' gender role identities to develop, but standards based on sexist and distorted notions of manhood and womanhood are not. We need new gender role norms and a critical evaluation of the old ones that dehumanize people and cause GRC. Women feminists have developed concepts explaining the hazards of restrictive gender roles for women; now, scholars of the psychology of men need to accelerate their efforts to explain how sexism and other oppressions negatively affect both genders.

A second truth is that men's psychological problems are contextual, and addressing them requires complex thought on societal, situational, intrapersonal, and interpersonal levels simultaneously. The study of the contextual and situational contingencies of GRC is critical to explaining men's problems and potentials. Although evidence has shown that GRC relates to men's problems, the ways in which situational contingencies and third variables moderate and mediate their behaviors are largely unknown. It is my hope that the new models emphasizing contextual and situational contingencies that predict GRC as an outcome can advance research on gendered social learning (Addis, Mansfield, & Syzdek, 2010) and microcontexts (K. Jones & Heesacker, 2012). This is the future of research on GRC in the psychology of men.

One of the most important truths is that multicultural contexts of men's GRC help explain the diversity of male identities and how oppression produces discrimination and social injustices in men's lives. Furthermore, institutional and personal sexism, discrimination, and other oppressions contribute to men's GRC and emotional and psychological problems. The initial evidence I have reported indicates that GRC is correlated with men's internalized oppression and that discrimination against men is a mental health problem that deserves more attention, both theoretically and empirically.

Overall, the research supports using GRC constructs when conducting therapy with men. Correlational evidence exists that gender role devaluations, restrictions, and violations are related to men's problems and can be assessed in psychotherapy and used in psychoeducational programs. Evidence exists that journeying with GRC in therapy and other programs can be a meaningful metaphor for consciousness raising; healing; and the development of healthy, positive masculinity. Helping men resolve GRC in the context of stages and processes of change is the most effective way to help them help themselves (Brooks, 2010; Prochaska & DiClemente, 2005). GRC research and theory can justify the need for psychoeducational programs that raise consciousness about the perils of restrictive gender roles. Finally, with further refinement, the GRC construct has the potential to influence social and political policies that affect education, families, legislation, and even diplomatic processes.

FINAL THOUGHTS ON THE CALL TO ACTION

As I mentioned at the start of this book, the psychology of men has a long but inconsistent history, beginning with Freud and his followers. Adler's feminist concepts on gender and the psychology of men threatened the status quo and were disputed and then disregarded until the 1980s (Connell, 2005). Members of the status quo are still threatened by the addressing of masculinity issues because they are intensely personal and political and have significant implications for social change. Among the goals of the call to action in this book are to decrease the threat; explain what is at stake for mental health; and expose how patriarchal values destroy possibilities for becoming more human, whether one is male, female, or transgendered.

In Chapters 10 and 11, I discussed portals (openings or ways to break through) to men's inner lives as a critical dimension of engaging men in therapy. How to find the portals of men in therapy is usually an ambiguous, difficult process (Rabinowitz & Cochran, 2002). Likewise, on a national level, we need to look for "societal portals": opportunities to raise consciousness significantly about boys' and men's lives. The 9/11 attacks, the Boston Marathon bombings, the shootings in Columbine and Newtown, and other such terrible events have prompted examinations of the realities of men's experiences, but the serious questions we ask in the wake of these tragedies fade as the denial, difficulty, and complexity of the issues loom large in our violence-ridden psyches.

My call to action is designed to attract more psychologists and caring professionals to the cause of finding the portals of change needed to help both men and women who are negatively affected by the sexism and other oppressions that continue to pervade our outdated, unnecessary, and inhuman patriarchal society. As RFK said in the speech quoted at the beginning of this chapter, every ripple of activism can make a difference. The collective ripples of activism created by each of us can result in waves of change, exposing patriarchal abuse and oppression and restoring human values that enrich humanity and bring men and women closer, into alliances that strive for freedom and justice for all. I invite each reader to contribute to this idealistic but possible vision and cause.

REFERENCES

Abreu, J. M., Goodyear, R. K., Campos, A., & Newcomb, M. D. (2000). Ethnic belonging and traditional masculinity ideology among African American, European Americans, and Latinos. *Psychology of Men & Masculinity, 1,* 75–86.

Addelston, J. (1995). Gender role conflict in elite independent high schools. *Dissertation Abstracts International: Section B. The Sciences and Engineering, 57*(05), 3450.

Addis, M. (2011). *Invisible men: Men's inner lives and consequences of silence.* New York, NY: Time Books.

Addis, M. E., & Mahalik, J. R. (2003). Men, masculinity, and the context of help seeking. *American Psychologist, 58,* 5–14. doi:10.1037/0003-066X.58.1.5

Addis, M. E., Mansfield, A. K., & Syzdek, M. R. (2010). Is "masculinity" a problem? Framing the effect of gendered social learning in men. *Psychology of Men & Masculinity, 11,* 77–90. doi:10.1037/a0018602

Adler, A. (1927). *Understanding human nature.* Garden City, NY: Garden City.

Adler, A. (1936). *The practice and theory of individual psychology.* New York, NY: Harcourt. doi:10.1037/13512-000

Albee, G. W. (1981). The prevention of sexism. *Professional Psychology, 12,* 20–28. doi:10.1037/0735-7028.12.1.20

Alexander, P. E. (1997). The relationship between masculinity ideology and gender role conflict to parenting and marital issues. *Dissertation Abstracts International: Section B. The Sciences and Engineering, 59,* 3678.

Amato, F., & MacDonald, J. (2011). Examining risk factors for homeless men: Gender role conflict, help seeking, substance abuse, and violence. *The Journal of Men's Studies, 19,* 227–235. doi:10.3149/jms.1903.227

Amato, F. J. (2012). The relationship of violence to gender role conflict and conformity to masculine norms in a forensic sample. *The Journal of Men's Studies, 20,* 187–208. doi:10.3149/jms.2003.187

American Heart Association. (1994). *Heart and stroke facts: 1995.* Dallas, TX: Author.

American Psychological Association. (Producer). (2011). *Engaging men in psychotherapy* [DVD]. Available from http://www.apa.org/pubs/videos/

Andronico, M. (Ed.). (1995). *Men in groups: Insights, interventions, psychoeducational work.* Washington, DC: American Psychological Association.

Armed Forces Health Surveillance Center. (2012). Deaths by suicide while on active duty, active and reserve components, U.S. Armed Forces, 1998–2011. MSMR, 19(6), 7–10.

Arnold, W. J., & Chartier, B. M. (1984, May). *Identity, fear of femininity and intimacy in males.* Paper presented at the 45th annual convention of the Canadian Psychological Association, Ottawa, Ontario, Canada.

Baima, G. P. (2012). *Spiritual well-being as a mediator/moderator between male gender role conflict and psychological distress in a veteran sample* (Doctoral dissertation). Available from ProQuest Dissertation and Theses database. (UMI No. 3533193)

Baker, K. L., Robertson, N., & Connelly, D. (2010). Men caring for wives or partners with dementia: Masculinity, strain, and gain. *Aging & Mental Health, 14*, 319–327. doi:10.1080/13607860903228788

Baron, R. M., & Kenny, D. A. (1986). The moderator–mediator variable distinction in social psychological research: Conceptual, strategic, and statistical considerations. *Journal of Personality and Social Psychology, 51*, 1173–1182. doi:10.1037/0022-3514.51.6.1173

Beaglaoich, C., Sarma, K. M., & Morrison, T. G. (2013). New directions in gender role conflict research. In J. Gelfer (Ed.), *Masculinities in a global era* (pp. 17–52). New York, NY: Springer. doi:10.1007/978-1-4614-6931-5_2

Beaglaoich, C. O. (2013). *The development and validation of a measure assessing gender role conflict in male adolescents* (Unpublished doctoral dissertation). National University of Ireland, Galway, Ireland.

Beatty, A., Syzdek, M., & Bakkum, A. (2006). The Saint John's Experience Project: Challenging men's perceptions of normative gender role conflict. *The Journal of Men's Studies, 14*, 322–336. doi:10.3149/jms.1403.322

Bergen, D. J. (1997). Gender role conflict and coping: A preliminary investigation of college males. *Dissertation Abstracts International: Section A. Humanities and Social Sciences, 57*, 5059.

Berger, J. M., Levant, R. F., McMillan, K. K., Kelleher, W., & Sellers, A. (2005). Impact of gender role conflict, traditional masculinity ideology, alexithymia, and age on men's attitudes toward psychological help seeking. *Psychology of Men & Masculinity, 6*, 73–78. doi:10.1037/1524-9220.6.1.73

Berko, E. H. (1994). Shyness, gender-role orientation, physical self-esteem, and male gender role conflict. *Dissertation Abstracts International, 55*, 4100.

Betz, N. E., & Fitzgerald, L. (1993). Individuality and diversity: Theory and research in counseling psychology. *Annual Review of Psychology, 44*, 343–381. doi:10.1146/annurev.ps.44.020193.002015

Bevan, N. (2010). *Psychological help seeking: Understanding men's behavior* (Unpublished doctoral dissertation). University of Adelaide, Australia.

Biglan, A., & Hayes, S. C. (1996). Should the behavioral sciences become more pragmatic? The case for functional contextualism in research on human behavior. *Applied and Preventive Psychology, 5*, 47–57. doi:10.1016/S0962-1849(96)80026-6

Bingham, T. A., Harawa, N. T., & Williams, J. K. (2012). Gender role conflict among African American men who have sex with men and women: Association with mental health. *Journal of Public Health, 56*, 34–56.

Birthistle, I. (1999). *Male gender role conflict, coping skills, and hopelessness: Their relationship to the increasing male suicide rate* (Unpublished doctoral dissertation). Trinity College Dublin, Ireland.

Bjerke, A., & Skyllingstad, Y. E. (2002). *Gender Role Conflict Scale in Sweden* (Unpublished master's thesis). Institute of Psychology, Lund University, Lund, Sweden.

Blashill, A. J., & Hughes, H. H. (2009). Gender role and gender role conflict: Preliminary considerations for psychotherapy with gay men. *Journal of Gay & Lesbian Mental Health, 13,* 170–186. doi:10.1080/19359700902914300

Blashill, A. J., & Vander Wal, J. S. (2009). Mediation of gender role conflict and eating pathology in gay men. *Psychology of Men & Masculinity, 10,* 204–217. doi:10.1037/a0016000

Blazina, C. (1997). The fear of the feminine in the Western psyche and the masculine task of disidentification: Their effect on the development of masculine gender role conflict. *The Journal of Men's Studies, 6,* 55–68.

Blazina, C. (2001). Analytic psychology and gender role conflict: The development of the fragile masculine self. *Psychotherapy: Theory, Research, Practice, Training, 38,* 50–59. doi:10.1037/0033-3204.38.1.50

Blazina, C. (2003). *The cultural myth of masculinity.* New York, NY: Praeger.

Blazina, C. (2004). Gender role conflict and disidentification process: Two cases studies on fragile masculine self. *The Journal of Men's Studies, 12,* 151–161. doi:10.3149/jms.1202.151

Blazina, C. (2008). *The secret lives of men: What men want you to know about love, sex, and relationships.* New York, NY: HarperCollins.

Blazina, C., Eddins, R., Burridge, A., & Settle, A. G. (2007). The relationship between masculinity ideology, loneliness, and separation–individuation difficulties. *The Journal of Men's Studies, 15,* 101–109.

Blazina, C., & Jackson, S. (2009). Assessing for a pluralistic sense of masculinity: The Masculinity Across Role Scale (MARS), the Gender Role Conflict Scale—Adolescent (GRCS–A), and boys' scores of depression. In J. H. Urlich & B. T. Cosell (Eds.), *Handbook on gender roles: Conflicts, attitudes, and behaviors* (pp. 235–253). Orlando, FL: Nova Science.

Blazina, C., & Marks, I. (2001). College men's affective reactions to individual therapy, psychoeducation workshops, and men's support group brochures: The influence of gender role conflict and power dynamics upon help seeking attitudes. *Psychotherapy: Theory, Research, Practice, Training, 38,* 297–305. doi:10.1037/0033-3204.38.3.297

Blazina, C., Novotny, M. L., Stevens, D. N., & Hunter, M. (2008, August). Man's best friend: Pet companions, gender role conflict, attachment, and loss. In J. M. O'Neil & G. E. Good (Chairs), *Four studies assessing the contextual complexity of the gender role conflict construct.* Symposium conducted at the 116th Annual Convention of the American Psychological Association, Boston, MA.

Blazina, C., Pisecco, S., & O'Neil, J. M. (2005). An adaptation of the Gender Role Conflict Scale for adolescents: Psychometric issues and correlates with psychological distress. *Psychology of Men & Masculinity, 6,* 39–45. doi:10.1037/1524-9220.6.1.39

Blazina, C., Settle, A. G., & Eddins, R. (2008). Gender role conflict and separation individuation difficulties: Their impact on college men's loneliness. *The Journal of Men's Studies, 16*, 69–81. doi:10.3149/jms.1601.69

Blazina, C., & Shen-Miller, D. S. (2010). *An international psychology of men: Theoretical advances, case studies, and clinical innovations.* New York, NY: Routledge.

Blazina, C., & Watkins, C. E. (1996). Masculine gender role conflict: Effects on college men's psychological well-being, chemical substance usage, and attitudes toward help-seeking. *Journal of Counseling Psychology, 43*, 461–465. doi:10.1037/0022-0167.43.4.461

Blazina, C., & Watkins, C. E. (2000). Separation/individuation, parental attachment, and male gender conflict: Attitudes toward the feminine and the fragile masculine self. *Psychology of Men & Masculinity, 1*, 126–132. doi:10.1037/1524-9220.1.2.126

Block, J. H. (1984). *Sex role identity and ego development.* San Francisco, CA: Jossey-Bass.

Bloom, B., Cohen, R. A., & Freeman, G. (2012). Summary health statistics for U.S. children: National Health Interview Survey, 2011. *Vital and Health Statistics, 10*(254). Retrieved from http://www.cdc.gov/nchs/data/series/sr_10/sr10_254.pdf

Boehm, F. (1930). The femininity-complex in men. *The International Journal of Psycho-Analysis, 11*, 444–469.

Borthick, M. J. (1997). Gender role conflict and suicidal ideation in an adolescent and young adult population: Age 18–24 year old. *Dissertation Abstracts International, 58*, 4437.

Borthick, M. J., Knox, P. L., Taylor, J. R., & Dietrich, M. S. (1997, August). *Gender role conflict and suicide probability: Age 18–24 years.* Paper presented at the 105th Annual Convention of the American Psychological Association, Chicago, IL.

Brannon, R., & Juni, S. (1984). A scale for measuring attitudes toward masculinity. *JSAS Catalog of Selected Documents in Psychology, 14*(6).

Braverman, D. G., O'Neil, J. M., & Owen, S. (1992). Systematic programming on men's issues and men's studies on campus. *Journal of College Student Development, 33*, 557–558.

Breiding, M. J. (2004). Observed hostility and observed dominance as mediators of the relationship between husbands' gender role conflict and wives' outcomes. *Journal of Counseling Psychology, 51*, 429–436. doi:10.1037/0022-0167.51.4.429

Breiding, M. J., Windle, C. R., & Smith, D. A. (2008). Interspousal criticism: A behavioral mediator between husband's gender role conflict and wife's adjustment. *Sex Roles, 59*, 880–888. doi:10.1007/s11199-008-9491-6

Brewer, A. M. (1998). The relationships among gender role conflict, depression, hopelessness, and marital satisfaction in a sample of African-American men. *Dissertation Abstracts International: Section B. The Sciences and Engineering, 59*, 3049.

Brooks, G. (2010). *Beyond the crises of masculinity: A transtheoretical model for male-friendly therapy*. Washington, DC: American Psychological Association. doi:10.1037/12073-000

Brooks, G. R. (1998). *A new psychotherapy for traditional men*. San Francisco, CA: Jossey-Bass.

Brooks, G. R., & Silverstein, L. B. (1995). Understanding the dark side of masculinity. In R. Levant & W. Pollack (Eds.), *A new psychology of men* (pp. 280–333). New York, NY: Basic Books.

Brooks-Harris, J. E., Heesacker, M., & Mejia-Millan, C. (1996). Changing men's male gender-role attitudes by applying the elaboration likelihood model of attitude change. *Sex Roles, 35*, 563–580. doi:10.1007/BF01548253

Bruch, M. A. (2002). Shyness and toughness: Unique and moderated relations with men's emotional inexpressiveness. *Journal of Counseling Psychology, 49*, 28–34. doi:10.1037/0022-0167.49.1.28

Bruch, M. A., Berko, E. H., & Haase, R. F. (1998). Shyness, masculine ideology, physical attractiveness, and emotional inexpressiveness: Testing a mediational model of men's interpersonal competence. *Journal of Counseling Psychology, 45*, 84–97. doi:10.1037/0022-0167.45.1.84

Bryce, D. M. (2012). *Predicting men's relationship satisfaction with men through internalized homonegativity and restricted emotionality* (Doctoral dissertation). Available from ProQuest Dissertations and Theses database. (UMI No. 3535704)

Burke, K. (2000). *Gender role conflict and psychological well-being: An exploration in men enrolled to attend an initiatory weekend* (Unpublished master's thesis). University of Maryland, Baltimore.

Burns, S. M., & Mahalik, J. R. (2006). Physical health, self-reliance, and emotional control as moderators of the relationship between locus of control and mental health among men treated for prostate cancer. *Journal of Behavioral Medicine, 29*, 561–572.

Bursley, K. H. (1996). Gender role strain and help seeking attitudes and behaviors in college men. *Dissertation Abstracts International: Section A. Humanities and Social Sciences, 56*, 3884.

Cachia, P. (2001). *The interplay of gender role conflict and adult attachment* (Unpublished master's thesis). University of Malta, Malta.

Cadenhead, L., & Huzirec, C. (2002, August). Differences in clinical populations on gender role conflict. In C. Blazina & S. Pisecco (Chairs), *Gender Role Conflict Scale for Adolescents: Psychometric issues and applications*. Symposium conducted at the 110th Annual Convention of the American Psychological Association, Chicago, IL.

Campbell, J. (1988). *The power of myth*. New York, NY: Doubleday.

Campbell, J. L., & Snow, B. M. (1992). Gender role conflict and family environment as predictors of men's marital satisfaction. *Journal of Family Psychology, 6*, 84–87. doi:10.1037/0893-3200.6.1.84

Capraro, R. L. (2000). Why college men drink: Alcohol, adventure, and paradox of masculinity. *Journal of American College Health, 48,* 307–315. doi:10.1080/07448480009596272

Carson, E. A., & Sabol, W. J. (2012). *Prisoners in 2011.* Bureau of Justice Statistics. Retrieved from http://www.bjs.gov/content/pub/pdf/p11.pdf

Carter, R. T., Williams, B., Juby, H. L., & Buckley, T. R. (2005). Racial identity as mediator of the relationship between gender role conflict and severity of psychological symptoms in Black, Latino, and Asian men. *Sex Roles, 53,* 473–486. doi:10.1007/s11199-005-7135-7

Celentana, M. A. (2000). Men's gender role adherence, relational partner's psychological well-being, and constructivist measures of intimacy. *Dissertation Abstracts International: Section B. The Sciences and Engineering, 61,* 5555.

Centers for Disease Control and Prevention. (2005). Mental health in the United States: Prevalence of diagnosis and medication treatment for attention-deficit hyperactivity disorder—United States, 2003. *Morbidity and Mortality Weekly Report, 54,* 842–847.

Centers for Disease Control and Prevention. (2007). *Youth violence: Facts at a glance.* Retrieved from http://www.cdc.gov/violenceprevention/pdf/yv-datasheet-a.pdf

Centers for Disease Control and Prevention. (2009). *Leading causes of death in males United States, 2009* [Table]. Retrieved from http://www.cdc.gov/men/lcod/2009/index.htm

Centers for Disease Control and Prevention. (2012). *Trends in prevalence of alcohol use: National Youth Risk Behavior Survey 1991–2011* [Table]. Retrieved from http://www.cdc.gov/healthyyouth/yrbs/pdf/us_alcohol_trend_yrbs.pdf

Chamberlin, W. (1993). Gender role conflict as a predictor of problem solving, leadership style, authoritarian attributes, and conflict management attitudes. *Dissertation Abstracts International, 52,* 844.

Chamykarpour, M. A., Pourshahbaz, A., Dolatshahi, B., & Moshtagh, N. (2012a). *Gender role conflict and seven factor model of personality among Iranian college men.* Tehran, Iran: University of Social Welfare and Rehabilitation Sciences.

Chamykarpour, M. A., Pourshahbaz, A., Dolatshahi, B., & Moshtagh, N. (2012b). Psychometric properties of the Persian Version of the Gender Role Conflict Scale (GRCS). *Knowledge & Research in Applied Psychology, 13,* 1–12.

Chan, R. K., & Hayashi, K. (2010). Gender roles and help-seeking behavior and promoting help among Japanese men. *Journal of Social Work, 10,* 243–262. doi:10.1177/1468017310369274

Chartier, B. M., & Arnold, W. J. (1985, June). *Male socialization and the development of identity and intimacy in young college men.* Paper presented at the 46th annual meeting of the Canadian Psychological Association, Halifax, Nova Scotia.

Chartier, B. M., Graff, L. A., & Arnold, W. J. (1986, June). *Males' socialization and hostility toward women.* Paper presented at the 47th annual meeting of the Canadian Psychological Association, Toronto, Ontario, Canada.

Chase, L. (2000). Gender role conflict and the level of physical violence: A study of physically abusive men. *Dissertation Abstracts International: Section A. Humanities and Social Sciences, 61,* 2465.

Chickering, A. W., & Reisser, L. (1993). *Education and identity.* San Francisco, CA: Jossey-Bass.

Choi, H., Kim, J., Hwang, M., & Heppner, M. J. (2010). Self-esteem as a mediator between instrumentality, gender role conflict, and depression in male Korean high school students. *Sex Roles, 63,* 361–372. doi:10.1007/s11199-010-9801-7

Clarke, T. (2013). *JFK's last hundred days: The transformation of a man the emergence of a great president.* New York, NY: Penguin Press.

Cochran, S. V. (2005). Evidence-based assessment with men. *Journal of Clinical Psychology, 61,* 649–660.

Cochran, S. V., & Rabinowitz, F. (2000). *Men and depression: Clinical and empirical perspectives.* San Diego, CA: Academic Press. doi:10.1016/B978-012177540-7/50002-3

Cochran, S. V., & Rabinowitz, F. (2003). Gender-sensitive recommendations for assessment and treatment of depression in men. *Professional Psychology: Research and Practice, 34,* 132–140. doi:10.1037/0735-7028.34.2.132

Cohn, A. M., Jakupcak, M., Seibert, L. A., Hildebrandt, T. B., & Zeichner, A. (2010). The role of emotion dysregulation in the association between men's restrictive emotionality and use of physical aggression. *Psychology of Men & Masculinity, 11,* 53–64. doi:10.1037/a0018090

Cohn, A. M., Seibert, L. A., & Ziechner, A. (2009). The role of restrictive emotionality, trait anger, and masculinity threat in men's perpetration of physical aggression. *Psychology of Men & Masculinity, 10,* 218–224. doi:10.1037/a0015151

Cohn, A., & Zeichner, A. (2006). Effects of masculine identity and gender role stress on aggression in men. *Psychology of Men & Masculinity, 7,* 179–190. doi:10.1037/1524-9220.7.4.179

Cohn, A. M., Zeichner, A., & Seibert, L. A. (2008). Labile affect as a risk factor for aggressive behavior in men. *Psychology of Men & Masculinity, 9,* 29–39. doi:10.1037/1524-9220.9.1.29

Colby, K. M. (1951). On the disagreements between Freud and Adler. *American Imago, 8,* 229–238.

Columbo, J. R. (2008). *Personal dimensions of masculinity and psychological well-being of stay-at-home fathers* (Unpublished doctoral dissertation). Walden University, Minneapolis, MN.

Connell, R. W. (1994). Psychoanalysis on masculinity. In H. Brod & M. Kaufman (Eds.), *Theorizing masculinities* (pp. 12–39). Thousand Oaks, CA: Sage. doi:10.4135/9781452243627.n2

Connell, R. W. (1995). *Masculinities.* Cambridge, England: Polity Press.

Connell, R. W. (2005). *Masculinities* (2nd ed.). Berkeley: University of California Press.

Connell, R. W., & Messerschmidt, J. W. (2005). Hegemonic masculinity: Rethinking the concept. *Gender & Society, 19*, 829–859. doi:10.1177/0891243205278639

Coonerty-Femiano, A. M., Katzman, M. A., Femiano, S., Gemar, M., & Toner, B. (2001, August). *Gender role conflict in male survivors of childhood abuse.* Paper presented at the 109th Annual Convention of the American Psychological Association, San Francisco, CA.

Cortese, J. (2003). Gender role conflict, personality, and help seeking in adult men. *Dissertation Abstracts International: Section B. The Sciences and Engineering, 64,* 4609.

Cosenzo, K. A., Franchina, J. J., Eisler, R. M., & Krebs, D. (2004). Effects of masculine gender-relevant task instructions on men's cardiovascular reactivity and mental arithmetic performance. *Psychology of Men & Masculinity, 5,* 103–111.

Cournoyer, R. J. (1994). A developmental study of gender role conflict in men and its changing relationship to psychological well-being. *Dissertation Abstracts International: Section B. The Sciences and Engineering, 54,* 6476.

Cournoyer, R. J., & Mahalik, J. R. (1995). A cross-sectional study of gender role conflict examining college-aged and middle-aged men. *Journal of Counseling Psychology, 42,* 11–19. doi:10.1037/0022-0167.42.1.11

Courtenay, W. H. (2000a). Behavioral factors associated with disease, injury, and death among men: Evidence and implications for prevention. *The Journal of Men's Studies, 9,* 81–142. doi:10.3149/jms.0901.81

Courtenay, W. H. (2000b). Engendering health: A social constructionist examination of men's health beliefs and behaviors. *Psychology of Men & Masculinity, 1,* 4–15. doi:10.1037/1524-9220.1.1.4

Courtenay, W. H. (2000c). Teaming up for the new men's health movement. *The Journal of Men's Studies, 8,* 387–392. doi:10.3149/jms.0803.387

Courtenay, W. H. (Ed.). (2011). *Dying to be men: Psychosocial environmental and biobehavioral directions in promoting the health of men.* New York, NY: Routledge.

Courtenay, W. H., & McCreary, D. R. (2011). Masculinity and gender role conflict: How they influence the likelihood that men will engage in multiple high-risk behaviors. In W. H. Courtenay (Ed.), *Dying to be men: Psychosocial environmental and biobehavioral directions in promoting the health of men* (pp. 241–250). New York, NY: Routledge.

Covell, A. (1998). Characteristics of college males who are likely to sexually harass women: A test of a mediated model. *Dissertation Abstracts International: Section B. The Sciences and Engineering, 60,* 2400.

Cox, C. K. (2009). *Gender role conflict and acculturation as predictors of help-seeking attitudes in Mexican-American men* (Doctoral dissertation). Available from ProQuest Dissertations and Theses database. (UMI No. 3324382)

Crick, R. C., & Dodge, K. A. (1994). A review and reformulation of social information-processing mechanism in children's social adjustment. *Psychological Bulletin, 115,* 74–101. doi:10.1037/0033-2909.115.1.74

Cusack, J., Deane, F. P., Wilson, C. J., & Ciarrochi, J. (2006). Emotional expression, perception of therapy, and help seeking intentions in men attending therapy services. *Psychology of Men & Masculinity, 7*, 69–82. doi:10.1037/1524-9220.7.2.69

Daltry, R. (2009). *The impact of gender role conflict on the quality of life in female athletes* (Unpublished doctoral dissertation). LaSalle University, Philadelphia, PA.

Davenport, D. S., Hetzel, R. D., & Brooks, G. R. (1998, August). *Concurrent validity analysis of two measures of gender role strain.* Paper presented at the 106th Annual Convention of the American Psychological Association, San Francisco, CA.

David, D., & Brannon, R. (Eds.). (1976). *The forty-nine percent majority.* Reading, MA: Addison-Wesley.

Davies, J. A., Shen-Miller, D., & Isacco, A. (2010). The Men's Center approach to addressing the health crisis of college men. *Professional Psychology: Research and Practice, 41*, 347–354. doi:10.1037/a0020308

Davis, F. (1988). Antecedents and consequents of gender role conflict: An empirical test of sex-role strain analysis. *Dissertation Abstracts International, 48*(11), 3443.

Davis, J. M., & Liang, C. (2014). A test of mediating role of gender role conflict: Latino masculinities and help seeking. *Psychology of Men & Masculinity.* Advance online publication. doi:10.1037/a0035320

Davis, T. L. (1997). The effectiveness of a sex role socialization-focused date rape prevention program in reducing rape-supportive attitudes in college fraternity men. *Dissertation Abstracts International: Section A. Humanities and Social Sciences, 58*, 1599.

Davis, T. L. (2002). Voices of gender role conflict: The social construction of college men's identity. *Journal of College Student Development, 43*, 508–521.

Davis, T. L., & Liddell, D. L. (2002). Getting inside the house: The effectiveness of a rape prevention program for college fraternity men. *Journal of College Student Development, 43*, 35–50.

Dean, R. D. (1998). Masculinity as ideology: John F. Kennedy and the domestic politics of foreign policy. *Diplomatic History, 22*, 29–62. doi:10.1111/1467-7709.00100

Deaux, K., & Majors, B. (1987). Putting gender in context: An integrative model of gender-related behavior. *Psychological Review, 94*, 369–389. doi:10.1037/0033-295X.94.3.369

DeFranc, W., & Mahalik, J. R. (2002). Masculine gender role conflict and stress in relation to parental attachment and separation. *Psychology of Men & Masculinity, 3*, 51–60. doi:10.1037/1524-9220.3.1.51

Dodson, T., & Borders, D. (2006). Men in traditional and nontraditional careers: Gender role attitudes, gender role conflict, and job satisfaction. *The Career Development Quarterly, 54*, 283–296. doi:10.1002/j.2161-0045.2006.tb00194.x

Dolling, L. (2008). *Examining the relationship between marital status, masculinity, optimism, and men's professional and non-professional help seeking* (Unpublished thesis). Monash University, Churchill, Victoria, Australia.

Dukes, A. E. (2007). Adolescent males: Predicting attitudes towards guns and violence based on perceived gender stereotypes. *Dissertation Abstracts International, 67*(11), 3242900.

Eaton, D. K., Kann, L., Kinchen, S., Shanklin, S., Flint, K. H., Hawkins, J., . . . Wechsler, H. (2012). Youth risk behavior surveillance—United States, 2011. *Morbidity and Mortality Weekly Report, 61*(4). Retrieved from http://www.cdc.gov/mmwr/pdf/ss/ss6104.pdf

Eccles, J. S. (1987). Adolescence: Gateway to gender-role transcendence. In D. B. Carter (Ed.), *Current conceptions of sex roles and sex typing: Theory and research* (pp. 225–241). New York, NY: Praeger.

Eckes, T., & Trautner, H. M. (2000). *The developmental social psychology of gender.* Mahwah, NJ: Erlbaum.

Eicken, I. M. (2003). The relationship of emotional intelligence, alexithymia, and universal-diverse orientation, to gender role conflict. *Dissertation Abstracts International: Section B. The Sciences and Engineering, 66,* 4665.

Eimer, A., & Kidd, J. (2010). *Understanding men's underutilization of career counseling using gender role conflict theory* (Unpublished master's thesis). University of London/Birkbeck, London, England.

Eisler, R. M. (1995). The relationship between masculine gender role stress and men's health risk: The validation of a construct. In R. F. Levant & W. S. Pollack (Eds.), *The new psychology of men* (pp. 207–225) New York, NY: Basic Books.

Eisler, R. M., Franchina, J. J., Moore, T. M., Honeycutt, H. G., & Rhatigan, D. L. (2000). Masculine gender role stress and intimate abuse: Effects of gender relevance of the conflict situation on men's attributions and affective responses. *Psychology of Men & Masculinity, 1,* 30–36.

Eisler, R. M., Skidmore, J. R., & Ward, C. H. (1987). Masculine gender-role stress: Predictor of anger, anxiety, and health-risk behaviors. *Journal of Personality Assessment, 52,* 133–141.

Englar-Carlson, M. (2001). Two causal models of White male psychological help-seeking attitudes and preferences for psychotherapy. *Dissertation Abstracts International, 58,* 1599.

Englar-Carlson, M. (2006). Masculine norms and the therapy process. In M. Englar-Carlson & M. A. Stevens (Eds.), *In the room with men: A casebook of therapeutic change* (pp. 13–47). Washington, DC: American Psychological Association. doi:10.1037/11411-002

Englar-Carlson, M., Evans, M. P., & Duffey, T. (2014). *A counselor's guide to working with men.* Alexandria, VA: American Counseling Association.

Englar-Carlson, M., & Stevens, M. A. (Eds.). (2006). *In the room with men: A casebook of therapeutic change.* Washington, DC: American Psychological Association. doi:10.1037/11411-000

Englar-Carlson, M., & Vandiver, B. (2002, August). Comparing the dimensionality of the GRCS, MGRS, and SRES. In J. M. O'Neil & G. E. Good (Chairs),

Gender role conflict research: Empirical Studies and 20 year summary. Symposium conducted at the 110th Annual Convention of the American Psychological Association, Chicago, IL.

Enns, C. (2000). Gender issues in counseling. In S. Brown & R. Lent (Eds.), *Handbook of counseling psychology* (3rd ed., pp. 601–638). New York, NY: Wiley.

Enns, C. Z. (2004). *Feminist theories and feminist psychotherapies: Origins, themes and diversity.* Binghamton, NY: Haworth Press.

Enns, C. Z. (2008). Toward a complexity paradigm for understanding gender role conflict. *The Counseling Psychologist, 36,* 446–454. doi:10.1177/0011000007310974

Enns, C. Z., & Williams, E. N. (2013). *The Oxford handbook of feminist multicultural counseling psychology.* New York, NY: Oxford University Press.

Ervin, A. M. (2003). Male gender role conflict and internalized homonegativity: The impact of gay men's psychological well-being. *Dissertation Abstracts International: Section B. The Sciences and Engineering, 65,* 3704.

Evans, P. M., Duffey, T., & Englar-Carlson, M. (Eds.). (2013). Men in counseling [Special issue]. *Journal of Counseling & Development, 91*(4). doi:10.1002/j.1556-6676.2013.00108.x

Fahey, J. (2003). Male role issues among hospitalized alcohol abusers: Prediction of addiction severity, readiness to change, and intensity of drug-thinking style. *Dissertation Abstracts International: Section B. The Sciences and Engineering, 65,* 1544.

Faircloth, P. K. (2011). *Gender, identity, and career: An investigation of gender role conflict and job satisfaction with police officers* (Doctoral dissertation). Available from ProQuest Dissertations and Theses database. (UMI No. 3576684)

Faria, M. (2000). *Analysis of the components of gender role conflict* (Unpublished master's thesis). University Lusofona of Humanities and Technology, Lisbon, Portugal.

Fischer, A. R. (2007). Parental relationship quality and masculine gender role strain in young men: Mediating effects of personality. *The Counseling Psychologist, 35,* 328–358. doi:10.1177/0011000005283394

Fischer, A. R., & Good, G. E. (1997). Men and psychotherapy: An investigation of alexithymia, intimacy, and masculine gender roles. *Psychotherapy: Theory, Research, Practice, Training, 34,* 160–170. doi:10.1037/h0087646

Fischer, A. R., & Good, G. E. (1998). Perceptions of parent–child relationships and masculine role conflicts of college men. *Journal of Counseling Psychology, 45,* 346–352. doi:10.1037/0022-0167.45.3.346

Fitton, R. (2010). *The effects of instrumentality, expressiveness, and age on male gender role conflict* (Unpublished honors thesis). Leeds Metropolitan University, Leeds, England.

Fleming, M. L. (2012). *Help seeking attitudes toward mental health issues among military men who have served in combat* (Doctoral dissertation). Available from ProQuest Dissertations and Theses database. (UMI No. 3507990)

Ford, D. H., & Lerner, R. M. (1992). *Developmental systems theory: An integrative approach.* Thousand Oaks, CA: Sage.

Fox, M. (1988). *Original blessing: A primer on creation spirituality.* Santa Fe, NM: Bear and Company.

Fragoso, J. M., & Kashubeck, S. (2000). Machismo, gender role conflict, and mental health in Mexican American men. *Psychology of Men & Masculinity, 1,* 87–97. doi:10.1037/1524-9220.1.2.87

Franchina, J. J., Eisler, R. M., & Moore, T. M. (2001). Masculine gender role stress and intimate abuse: Effects of masculine gender relevance of dating situations and female threat on men's attributions and affective responses. *Psychology of Men & Masculinity, 2,* 34–41. doi:10.1037/1524-9220.2.1.34

Frazier, P. A., Tix, A. P., & Barron, K. E. (2004). Testing moderator and mediating effects in counseling psychology research. *Journal of Counseling Psychology, 51,* 115–134. doi:10.1037/0022-0167.51.1.115

Freud, S. (1937). Analysis terminable and interminable. In P. Rieff (Ed.), *Freud: Therapy and techniques* (pp. 233–271). New York, NY: Macmillan.

Friedman, A. (2011). *Bread losers: An investigation on the effects of employment status and socioeconomic status on male gender role conflict and depressive symptoms* (Unpublished doctoral dissertation). Texas Tech University, Lubbock. Retrieved from http://repositories.tdl.org/ttu-ir/handle/2346/58410?show=full

Garnets, L., & Pleck, J. (1979). Sex role identity, androgyny, and sex role transcendence: A sex role strain analysis. *Psychology of Women Quarterly, 3,* 270–283. doi:10.1111/j.1471-6402.1979.tb00545.x

Gertner, D. M. (1994). Learning men: Effects of a semester academic course in men's studies on gender role conflict and gender role journey of male participants. *Dissertation Abstracts International, 58,* 1599.

Gilbert, L. A., & Scher, M. (1999). *Gender and sex in counseling and psychotherapy.* Boston, MA: Allyn & Bacon.

Gilligan, C. (1982). *In a different voice: Psychological theory and women's development.* Cambridge, MA: Harvard University Press.

Glicken, M. D. (2005). *Working with troubled men: A contemporary practitioner's guide.* Mahwah, NJ: Erlbaum.

Glomb, S. M., & Espelage, D. L. (2005). The influence of restrictive emotionality in men's emotional appraisal of sexual harassment: A gender role interpretation. *Psychology of Men & Masculinity, 6,* 240–253. doi:10.1037/1524-9220.6.4.240

Goldberg, H. (1977). *The hazards of being male.* New York, NY: New American Library.

Good, G. E., Dell, D. M., & Mintz, L. B. (1989). Male role and gender role conflict: Relations to help seeking in men. *Journal of Counseling Psychology, 36,* 295–300. doi:10.1037/0022-0167.36.3.295

Good, G. E., Heppner, M. J., Hillenbrand-Gunn, T., & Wang, L. (1995). Sexual and psychological violence: An exploratory study of predictors in college men. *The Journal of Men's Studies, 4,* 59–71.

Good, G. E., Heppner, P. P., DeBord, K. A., & Fischer, A. R. (2004). Understanding men's contribution of problem solving appraisal and masculine role conflict. *Psychology of Men & Masculinity, 5*, 168–177. doi:10.1037/1524-9220.5.2.168

Good, G. E., & Mintz, L. B. (2001). Integrative therapy for men. In G. R. Brooks & G. E. Good (Eds.), *The new handbook of psychotherapy and counseling with men: A comprehensive guide to settings, problems, and treatment approaches* (Vol. 2, pp. 582–602). San Francisco, CA: Jossey-Bass.

Good, G. E., & Mintz, L. M. (1990). Gender role conflict and depression in college men: Evidence for compounded risk. *Journal of Counseling & Development, 69*, 17–21. doi:10.1002/j.1556-6676.1990.tb01447.x

Good, G. E., Robertson, J. M., Fitzgerald, L. F., Stevens, M., & Bartels, K. M. (1996). The relation between masculine role conflict and psychological distress in male university counseling center clients. *Journal of Counseling & Development, 75*, 44–49. doi:10.1002/j.1556-6676.1996.tb02313.x

Good, G. E., Robertson, J. M., O'Neil, J. M., Fitzgerald, L. F., Stevens, M., DeBord, K., . . . Braverman, D. G. (1995). Male gender role conflict: Psychometric issues and relations to psychological distress. *Journal of Counseling Psychology, 42*, 3–10. doi:10.1037/0022-0167.42.1.3

Good, G. E., Schopp, L. H., Thomson, D., Hathaway, S., Sanford-Martens, T., Mazurek, M., & Mintz, L. B. (2006). Masculine roles and rehabilitation outcomes among men recovering from serious injuries. *Psychology of Men & Masculinity, 7*, 165–176. doi:10.1037/1524-9220.7.3.165

Good, G. E., & Sherrod, N. B. (2001). Men's problems and effective treatments: Theory and empirical support. In G. Brooks & G. E. Good (Eds.), *The new handbook of psychotherapy and counseling with men: A comprehensive guide to settings, problems, and treatment approaches* (Vol. 1, pp. 22–40). San Francisco, CA: Jossey-Bass.

Good, G. E., & Wood, P. K. (1995). Male gender role conflict, depression, and help seeking: Do college men face double jeopardy? *Journal of Counseling & Development, 74*, 70–75. doi:10.1002/j.1556-6676.1995.tb01825.x

Goodwin, M. E. (2008). *Gender role conflict, depression, and personality's effects on help seeking behaviors, attitudes, and academic performance* (Doctoral dissertation). Available from ProQuest Dissertations and Theses database. (UMI No. 3342251)

Gough, F. (1999). *Masculinity and psychological health in Australian men: Metropolitan, regional, and age comparisons* (Unpublished postgraduate thesis). Victoria University of Technology, Melbourne, Australia.

Gould, R. L. (1978). *Transformation and change in adult life*. New York, NY: Simon & Schuster.

Gould, R. L. (1980). Transformation during early and middle adult years. In N. Smelser & E. Erikson (Eds.), *Themes of work and love in adulthood* (pp. 213–237). Cambridge, MA: Harvard University Press.

Graef, S. T., Tokar, D. M., & Kaut, K. P. (2010). Relations of masculinity ideology, conformity to masculine norms, and gender role conflict to men's attitudes toward and willingness to seek career counseling. *Psychology of Men & Masculinity, 11*, 319–333. doi:10.1037/a0019383

Graham, M. M., & Romans, J. C. (2003, August). Impact of gender role conflict on men's satisfaction with retirement. In J. M. O'Neil & G. E. Good (Co-Chairs), *Psychological and physical health correlates of gender role conflict: Five empirical studies.* Symposium conducted at the 111th Annual Convention of the American Psychological Association, Toronto, Ontario, Canada.

Gray, J. (1993). *Men are from Mars, women are from Venus.* New York, NY: HarperCollins.

Grethel, M. M. (2007). Childhood gender nonconformity, male gender role conflict, and body image concerns among female-to-male young adults. *Dissertation Abstracts International, 68*(03), 3253610.

Griffin, J. A. (2011). *Sexual compulsivity among sexual minorities: Relations to attachment orientations and gender role conflict* (Unpublished master's thesis). Loyola University Maryland, Baltimore.

Groeschel, B. L., Wester, S. R., & Sedivy, S. K. (2010). Gender role conflict, alcohol, and help seeking among college men. *Psychology of Men & Masculinity, 11*, 123–139. doi:10.1037/a0018365

Gulder, A. (1999). *Male gender role conflict: A German translation of the Gender Role Conflict Scale* (Unpublished thesis). Johann Wolfgang Goethe University, Frankfurt, Germany.

Gullickson, G. E. (1993). Gender role conflict in sex offenders. *Dissertation Abstracts International: Section B. The Sciences and Engineering, 55*, 2008.

Hammond, W. P., & Mattis, J. S. (2005). Being a man about it: Manhood meaning among African American men. *Psychology of Men & Masculinity, 6*, 114–126. doi:10.1037/1524-9220.6.2.114

Harnishfeger, B. R. (1998). The relationship of gender role conflict to male college students' receipt and use of violence in heterosexual dating relationships. *Dissertation Abstracts International: Section B. The Sciences and Engineering, 59*, 3108.

Harper, S. R., & Harris, F., III (2010). *College men and masculinities: Theory, research, and implications for practice.* San Diego, CA: Jossey-Bass.

Harway, M., & O'Neil, J. M. (Eds.). (1999). *What causes men's violence against women?* Thousand Oaks, CA: Sage.

Hayashi, S. (1999). Masculinity and mental health: The relationship between men's attitudes toward male gender roles and mental health indices: Anxiety, depression, affect regulation, and self-esteem. *JASS (the Japanese Assembly for the Study of Sex) Proceedings, 11*, 2–11.

Hayes, J. A., & Mahalik, J. R. (2000). Gender role conflict and psychological distress in male counseling center clients. *Psychology of Men & Masculinity, 1*, 116–125. doi:10.1037/1524-9220.1.2.116

Hayes, M. M. (1985). Counselor sex-role values and effects on attitudes toward, and treatment of non-traditional male clients. *Dissertation Abstracts International, 45,* 3072.

Hayes, S. C. (1993). Analytic goals and the variety of scientific contextualism. In S. C. Hayes, L. J. Hayes, H. W. Reese, & T. R. Sarbin (Eds.), *Variety of scientific contextualism* (pp. 11–22). Reno, NV: Context Press.

Hayes, S. C., Hayes, L. J., Reese, H. W., & Sarbin, T. R. (Eds.). (1993). *Variety of scientific contextualism.* Reno, NV: Context Press.

Heard, C. C. (2009). *Examining the relationship between religiosity and ethnic identity on gender role conflict among African-American men* (Unpublished master's thesis). Texas A&M University, Corpus Christi.

Heath, L. A., & Thomas, T. (2006). An intergenerational examination of male gender role conflict and psychological distress. In M. Katsikitis (Ed.), *Proceedings of the Joint Conference of the Australian Psychological Society and the New Zealand Psychological Society* (pp. 175–179). Auckland: Australian Psychological Society.

Heesacker, M., Wester, S. R., Vogel, D. C., Wentzel, J. T., Mejia-Millan, C. M., & Goodholm, C. R. (1999). Gender-based emotional stereotyping. *Journal of Counseling Psychology, 46,* 483–495. doi:10.1037/0022-0167.46.4.483

Heppner, P. P. (1995). On gender role conflict in men: Future directions and implications for counseling. *Journal of Counseling Psychology, 42,* 20–23. doi:10.1037/0022-0167.42.1.20

Heppner, P. P., & Heppner, M. J. (2008). The gender role conflict literature: Fruits of sustained commitment. *The Counseling Psychologist, 36,* 455–461. doi:10.1177/0011000007310865

Heppner, P. P., Witty, T. E., & Dixon, W. A. (2004). Problem-solving appraisal and human adjustment: A review of 20 years of research using the Problem Solving Inventory. *The Counseling Psychologist, 32,* 344–428. doi:10.1177/0011000003262793

Herdman, K. J., Choi, N., Fuqua, D. R., & Newman, J. L. (2012). Gender role conflict: Validation for a sample of gay men and lesbian women. *Psychological Reports, 110,* 227–232. doi:10.2466/02.07.PR0.110.1.227-232

Hernandez, A. M. (2006). *The effects of gender role conflict and self-esteem* (Unpublished senior thesis). University of La Verne, La Verne, CA.

Hernandez, J., Sánchez, F. J., & Liu, W. M. (2006, August). Factorial validity of the Gender Role Conflict Scale with gay men. In J. M. O'Neil & G. E. Good (Chairs), *Gender role conflict research and diversity: Sexual orientation, physical injuries, and nationality.* Symposium conducted at the 114th Annual Convention of the American Psychological Association, New Orleans, LA.

Hetzel, R. D. (1998). Gender role strain and perceived social support as correlates of psychological distress in males (men). *Dissertation Abstracts International, 58,* 1534.

Hill, M. S., & Fischer, A. R. (2001). Does entitlement mediate the link between masculinity and rape-related variables? *Journal of Counseling Psychology, 48,* 39–50. doi:10.1037/0022-0167.48.1.39

Hill, W. G., & Donatelle, R. J. (2004). The impact of gender role conflict on multi-dimensional social support in older men. *International Journal of Men's Health, 4*, 267–276. doi:10.3149/jmh.0403.267

Hobza, C. L., & Rochlen, A. B. (2009). Gender role conflict, drive for muscularity, and the impact of ideal media portrayals on men. *Psychology of Men & Masculinity, 10*, 120–130. doi:10.1037/a0015040

Hoff Sommer, C. (2000). *The war against boys: How feminism is harming our young men*. New York, NY: Simon & Schuster.

Holohan, S. (2008). *Gender role conflict and therapist orientation: A study of the male psychotherapist of Irish Council of Psychotherapy* (Unpublished master's thesis). Dublin City University, Dublin, Ireland.

Horhoruw, M. (1991). *Correlation between gender role conflict and male friendship behavior* (Unpublished master's thesis). University of Jakarta, Jakarta, Indonesia.

Horne, A. M., & Kiselica, M. S. (1999). *Handbook of counseling boys and adolescent males: A practitioner's guide*. Thousand Oaks, CA: Sage.

Horney, K. (1932). The dread of women. *The International Journal of Psycho-Analysis, 13*, 348–360.

Horney, K. (1967). *Feminine psychology*. New York, NY: Norton.

Houle, J., Mishara, B. L., & Chagnon, F. (2008). An empirical test of a mediational model of impact of the traditional male gender role on suicidal behavior in men. *Journal of Affective Disorders, 107*, 37–43. doi:10.1016/j.jad.2007.07.016

Howells, V. A. (2010). *Gender role conflict and drive for muscularity: Predictors of problematic drinking behaviors in college aged men* (Unpublished master's thesis). Washington State University, Pullman.

Hoyt, M. A. (2009). Gender role conflict and emotional approach coping in men with cancer. *Psychology & Health, 24*, 981–996. doi:10.1080/08870440802311330

Jackson, C. D. (2009). Exploration of factors associated with eating disorders in gay men. *Dissertation Abstracts International: Section B. The Sciences and Engineering, 69*, 7812.

Jacobs, J. R. (1996). Psychological and demographic correlates of men's perceptions of and attitudes toward sexual harassment. *Dissertation Abstracts International: Section A. Humanities and Social Sciences, 57*, 3826.

Jakupcak, M., Osborne, T. L., Michael, S., Cook, J. W., & McFall, M. (2006). Implications of masculine gender role stress in male veterans with posttraumatic stress disorder. *Psychology of Men & Masculinity, 7*, 203–211.

Jakupcak, M., Tull, M. T., & Roemer, L. (2005). Masculinity, shame, and fear of emotions as predictors of men's expression of anger and hostility. *Psychology of Men and Masculinity, 6*, 275–284.

James, S. D. (2005). Gender role conflict, attachment style, interpersonal problems, and help seeking in adult men. *Dissertation Abstracts International, 44*, 2006.

Jamison, D. F. (2006). The relationship between African self-consciousness, cultural misorientation, hypermasculinity and rap music preference. *Journal of African American Studies, 9,* 45–60. doi:10.1007/s12111-006-1018-z

Jana-Massri, A. (2011). *Gender role conflict and attitudes toward seeking professional help in Egypt* (Doctoral dissertation). Available from ProQuest Dissertations and Theses database. (UMI No. 3441979)

Jassim, A. (2012). *Gender role conflict in Iraq* (Unpublished master's thesis). Al-Mustansirya University, Bagdad, Iraq.

Jin, H. Z. (2012). *Getting men with high gender role conflict to seek counseling: The effects of the therapist's gender and type of outreach message* (Unpublished master's thesis). National University of Singapore.

Jo, E. (2000, August). Gender role conflict in Korean men. In J. M. O'Neil & G. Good (Chairs), *Gender role conflict research in the year 2000: Innovative directions.* Symposium conducted at the 108th Annual Convention of the American Psychological Association, Washington, D.C.

Johnson, R. (1986). *He: Understanding masculine psychology.* New York, NY: Harper & Row.

Johnston, C. A. B., & Morrison, T. G. (2007). The presentation of masculinity in everyday life: Contextualizations in the masculine behavior of young Irish men. *Sex Roles, 57,* 661–674.

Johnston, C. L. (2005). *An examination of gender role conflict among male forensic inpatients.* Unpublished manuscript, Argosy University, Phoenix, AZ.

Jome, L. M., & Tokar, D. M. (1998). Dimensions of masculinity and major choice traditionality. *Journal of Vocational Behavior, 52,* 120–134. doi:10.1006/jvbe.1996.1571

Jones, D. A. (1998). Gender role conflict, coping, and psychological distress in gay men. *Dissertation Abstracts International: Section B. The Sciences and Engineering, 59,* 4468.

Jones, E. (1958). *Sigmund Freud: Life and work* (Vol. 2). New York, NY: Hogarth Press.

Jones, K. (2010). *Afrocentricity, homosexual identity integration, and other factors affecting the mental and psychological well-being of gay Black men* (Doctoral dissertation). Available from ProQuest Dissertations and Theses database. (UMI No. 3404073)

Jones, K., & Heesacker, M. (2012). Addressing the situation: Some evidence for the significance of microcontexts with the gender role conflict construct. *Psychology of Men & Masculinity, 13,* 294–307. doi:10.1037/a0025797

Jun, D. C. (2009). *Male gender role strain: A pastoral assessment* (Unpublished doctoral dissertation). University of Stellenbosch, Stellenbosch, South Africa.

Jung, C. (1953). Animus and anima. In H. Read, M. Fordham, & G. Adler (Eds.), *The collected works of Carl C. Jung* (Vol. 7). New York, NY: Pantheon.

Jung, C. (1954). Concerning archetypes, with special reference to the anima concept. In H. Read, M. Fordham, & G. Adler (Eds.), *The collected works of Carl C. Jung* (Vol. 9). New York, NY: Pantheon.

Jurkovic, D., & Walker, G. A. (2006). Examining masculine gender-role conflict and stress in relation to religious orientation and spiritual well-being in Australian men. *The Journal of Men's Studies, 14,* 27–46. doi:10.3149/jms.1401.27

Kang, J. (2001). Relationship between masculine gender role conflict and psychological distress among Korean male college students. *Dissertation Abstracts International: Section B. The Sciences and Engineering, 62,* 4274.

Kaplan, R. (1992). Normative masculinity and sexual aggression among college males. *Dissertation Abstracts International, 53,* 3005.

Kaplan, R., O'Neil, J. M., & Owen, S. (1993, August). Sexist, normative, and progressive masculinity and sexual assault: Empirical research. In J. M. O'Neil (Chair), *Research on men's sexual assault and constructive gender role interventions.* Symposium conducted at the 101st Annual Convention of the American Psychological Association, Toronto, Ontario, Canada.

Karten, E. Y., & Wade, J. C. (2010). Sexual orientation change efforts in men: A client perspective. *The Journal of Men's Studies, 18,* 84–102. doi:10.3149/jms.1801.84

Kassing, L. R., Beesley, D., & Frey, L. I. (2005). Gender role conflict, homophobia, age, and education as predictors of male rape myth acceptance. *Journal of Mental Health Counseling, 27,* 311–328.

Kearney, L., King, E. B., & Rochlen, A. B. (2004). Male gender role conflict, sexual harassment tolerance, and efficacy of a psychoeducative training program. *Psychology of Men & Masculinity, 5,* 72–82. doi:10.1037/1524-9220.5.1.72

Kelly, J. J. (2000). Gender role conflict as a predictor of clinical depression in a sample of adult men. *Dissertation Abstracts International, 61,* 5568.

Kenrick, D. T. (1987). Gender, genes, and the social environment: A biosocial interactionist perspective. In P. S. Shaver & C. Hendrick (Eds.), *Sex and gender* (pp. 14–43). Newbury Park, CA: Sage.

Kierski, W., & Blazina, C. (2009). The male fear of femininity and its effect on counseling and psychotherapy. *The Journal of Men's Studies, 17,* 155–172. doi:10.3149/jms.1702.155

Kilianski, S. E. (2003). Explaining heterosexual men's attitudes toward women and gay men: The theory of exclusive masculine identity. *Psychology of Men & Masculinity, 4,* 37–56.

Kilmartin, C., Addis, M., Mahalik, J. R. M., & O'Neil, J. M. (2013). Teaching the psychology of men: Four experienced professors describe their courses. *Psychology of Men & Masculinity, 14,* 240–247. doi:10.1037/a0033254

Kilmartin, C. T. (2010). *The masculine self* (4th ed.). Cornwall on Hudson, NY: Sloan.

Kim, E. J. (1990). Asian-American men: Gender role conflict and acculturation. *Dissertation Abstracts International, 5*(11), 3635.

Kim, E. J., O'Neil, J. M., & Owen, S. V. (1996). Asian-American men's acculturation and gender role conflict. *Psychological Reports, 79,* 95–104. doi:10.2466/pr0.1996.79.1.95

Kim, J., Choi, H., Ha, C., & O'Neil, J. M. (2006, August). Self-esteem as a mediator between gender role, gender role conflict, and depression in university male students. In J. M. O'Neil & G. E. Good (Co-Chairs), *Gender role conflict research and diversity: Sexual orientation, physical injuries, and nationality.* Symposium conducted at the 114th Annual Convention of the American Psychological Association, New Orleans, LA.

Kim, J., Hwang, O., & Choi, H. (2005). Middle-aged gender role, gender role conflict, and marital satisfaction. *The Korean Journal of Counseling, 6,* 621–632.

Kim, J., Hwong, M., & Ryu, J. (2003). The cultural validation of Korean version of the GRCS (K-GRCS). *Asian Journal of Education, 4,* 25–41.

Kimmel, M. (2011). *The gendered society* (4th ed.). New York, NY: Oxford University Press.

Kimmel, M. S. (1994). Masculinity as homophobia: Fear shame, and silence in the construction of gender identity. In H. Brod & M. Kaufman (Eds.), *Theorizing masculinities* (pp. 119–142). Thousand Oaks, CA: Sage. doi:10.4135/9781452243627.n7

Kimmel, M. S. (2005). *Manhood in America: A contextual history.* New York, NY: Oxford University Press.

Kimmel, S. B., & Mahalik, J. R. (2005). Body image concerns of gay men: The roles of minority stress and conformity to masculine norms. *Journal of Consulting and Clinical Psychology, 73,* 1185–1190.

Kindlon, D., & Thompson, M. (2000). *Raising Cain: Protecting the emotional life of boys.* New York, NY: Ballantine.

Kiselica, M. S. (2011). Promoting positive masculinity while addressing gender role conflict: A balanced theoretical approach to clinical work with boys and men. In C. Blazina & D. S. Shen-Miller (Eds.), *An international psychology of men: Theoretical advances, case studies, and clinical innovations* (pp. 127–156). New York, NY: Routledge.

Kiselica, M. S., & Englar-Carlson, M. (2010). Identifying, affirming, and building upon male strengths: The positive psychology/positive masculinity model of psychotherapy with boys and men. *Psychotherapy: Theory, Research, Practice, Training, 47,* 276–287. doi:10.1037/a0021159

Klein, J. (2012). *The bully society: School shootings and the crises of bullying in America's schools.* New York, NY: New York University Press.

Korcuska, J. S., & Thombs, D. L. (2003). Gender role conflict and sex-specific drinking norms: Relationship to alcohol use in undergraduate women and men. *Journal of College Student Development, 44,* 204–216. doi:10.1353/csd.2003.0017

Kosmopoulos, A. D. (2008). *Male gender role conflict among gay fathers who are primary caregivers to their young children: An exploratory study* (Doctoral dissertation). Available from ProQuest Dissertations and Theses database. (UMI No. 3322256)

Kratzner, R. E. (2003). *Gender role conflict, instrumentality–expressiveness, personality, and psychological distress in college males* (Unpublished master's thesis). St. Louis University, St. Louis, MO.

Krugman, S. (1995). Male development and the transformation of shame. In R. F. Levant & W. S. Pollack (Eds.), *The new psychology of men* (pp. 91–126). New York, NY: Basic Books.

Laker, J. A., & Davis, T. (2011). *Masculinities in higher education: Theoretical and practical consideration.* New York, NY: Routledge.

Lammy, A. B. (2011). *Keeping control: Relations between men's gender role conflict, spirituality, and psychological well-being* (Doctoral dissertation). Available from ProQuest Dissertations and Theses database. (UMI No. 3488909)

Land, L. N., Rochlen, A. B., & Vaugh, B. K. (2011). Correlates of adult attachment avoidance: Men's avoidance of intimacy in romantic relationships. *Psychology of Men & Masculinity, 12,* 64–76. doi:10.1037/a0019928

Lane, J. M., & Addis, M. E. (2005). Male gender role conflicts and patterns of help seeking in Costa Rica and the United States. *Psychology of Men & Masculinity, 6,* 155–168. doi:10.1037/1524-9220.6.3.155

Larma, N. C. (2006). *Gender role conflict and depression as predictors of help-seeking in male veterans with erectile dysfunction* (Doctoral dissertation). Available from ProQuest Dissertations and Theses database. (UMI No. 3248028)

Lash, S. J., Eisler, R. M., & Schulman R. S. (1990). Cardiovascular reactivity to stress in men: Effects of masculine gender role stress appraisal and masculine performance challenge. *Behavior Modification, 14,* 3–20.

Laurent, M. G. (1997). Gender role conflict, cultural identity, and self-esteem among African-American men. *Dissertation Abstracts International: Section A. Humanities and Social Sciences, 59,* 1473.

Lease, S. H., Ciftci, A., Demir, A., & Boyraz, G. (2009). Structural validity of Turkish version of the Gender Role Conflict Scale and Male Role Norms Scale. *Psychology of Men & Masculinity, 10,* 273–287. doi:10.1037/a0017044

Leka, G. E. (1998). *Acculturation of Mexican American male population and gender role conflict.* Dissertation Abstracts International, 36, 1178.

Lerner, R. M. (1992). *Developmental systems theory: An integrative approach.* Newbury Park, CA: Sage.

Lerner, R. M. (2001). *Concepts and theories of human development.* Hoboken, NJ: Taylor & Francis.

Levant, R. F. (1995). Toward the reconstruction of masculinity. In R. F. Levant & W. S. Pollack (Eds.), *The new psychology of men* (pp. 229–251). New York, NY: Basic Books.

Levant, R. F. (1996). The new psychology of men. *Professional Psychology: Research and Practice, 27,* 259–265. doi:10.1037/0735-7028.27.3.259

Levant, R. F., Good, G. E., Cook, S. W., O'Neil, J. M., Smalley, K. B., Owen, K., & Richmond, K. (2006). The Normative Male Alexithymia Scale: Measurement of a gender-linked syndrome. *Psychology of Men & Masculinity, 7,* 212–224. doi:10.1037/1524-9220.7.4.212

Levant, R. F., Hirsch, L., Celentano, E., Cozza, T., Hill, S., MacEachern, M., . . . Schnedeker, J. (1992). The male role: An investigation of contemporary norms. *Journal of Mental Health Counseling, 14*, 325–337.

Levant, R. F., & Pollack, W. S. (1995). *A new psychology of men*. New York, NY: Basic Books.

Levant, R. F., & Richmond, K. (2007). A review of research on masculinity ideologies using the Male Role Norms Inventory. *The Journal of Men's Studies, 15*, 130–146. doi:10.3149/jms.1502.130

Levant, R. F., Richmond, K., Majors, R. G., Inclan, J. E., Rosello, J. M., Heesacker, M., . . . Sellers, A. (2003). A multicultural investigation of masculinity ideology and alexithymia. *Psychology of Men & Masculinity, 4*, 91–99.

Levinson, D. J., Darrow, C. N., Klein, E. B., Levinson, M. H., & McKee, B. (1978). *The seasons of a man's life*. New York, NY: Ballantine Books.

Liang, C. T. H., Molenaar, C., & Heard, S. (in press). Race, masculinity, and gendered racism: President Obama's influence on Black men. In L. Barker-Hackett (Ed.), *Obama on our minds: The impact of Obama on the psyche of America*. Lewiston, NY: Mellon Press.

Liang, C. T. H., Rivera., A. Nathwani, A., Dang, P., & Douroux, A. S. (2010). Dealing with gendered racism and racial identity among Asian American men. In W. Liu, D. Iwamoto, & M. Chae (Eds.), *Culturally responsive counseling with Asian American men* (pp. 63–82). New York, NY: Routledge.

Liang, C. T. H., Salcedo, J., & Miller, H. A. (2011). Perceived racism, masculinity ideologies, and gender role conflict among Latino men. *Psychology of Men & Masculinity, 12*, 201–215. doi:10.1037/a0020479

Lily, R. L. (1999). Gender role conflict among Black/African American college men: Individual differences and psychological outcomes. *Dissertation Abstracts International, 61*, 1088.

Lindley, L. D., & Schwartz, J. P. (2006, August). *Implications of gender role conflict: Religious fundamentalism, homophobia, and intimacy*. Paper presented at the 114th Annual Convention of the American Psychological Association, New Orleans, LA.

Liu, W. M. (2002a). Exploring the lives of Asian American men: Racial identity, male role norms, gender role conflict, and prejudicial attitudes. *Psychology of Men & Masculinity, 3*, 107–118. doi:10.1037/1524-9220.3.2.107

Liu, W. M. (2002b). The social class-related experiences of men: Integrating theory and practice. *Professional Psychology: Research and Practice, 33*, 355–360. doi:10.1037/0735-7028.33.4.355

Liu, W. M. (2005). The study of men and masculinity as an important multicultural competency consideration. *Journal of Clinical Psychology, 61*, 685–697. doi:10.1002/jclp.20103

Liu, W. M., Ali, S. B., Soleck, G., Hopps, J., Dunston, K., & Pickett, T. (2004). Using social class in counseling psychology research. *Journal of Counseling Psychology, 51*, 3–18. doi:10.1037/0022-0167.51.1.3

Liu, W. M., & Iwamoto, D. K. (2006). Asian American men's gender role conflict: The role of Asian values, self-esteem, and psychological stress. *Psychology of Men & Masculinity, 7*, 153–164. doi:10.1037/1524-9220.7.3.153

Liu, W. M., & Iwamoto, D. K. (2007). Conformity to masculinity norms, Asian values, coping strategies, peer group influences, and substance abuse among Asian American men. *Psychology of Men & Masculinity, 8*, 25–39.

Liu, W. M., Iwamoto, D. K., & Chae, M. H. (2010). (Eds.). *Culturally responsive counseling with Asian-American men.* New York, NY: Routledge.

Liu, W. M., Rochlen, A. B., & Mohr, J. (2005). Real and ideal gender role conflict: Exploring psychological distress among men. *Psychology of Men & Masculinity, 6*, 137–148. doi:10.1037/1524-9220.6.2.137

Liu, W. M., Soleck, G., Hopps, J., Dunston, K., & Pickett, T. (2004). A new framework to understand social class in counseling: The social class worldview model and modern classism theory. *Journal of Multicultural Counseling and Development, 32*, 95–122. doi:10.1002/j.2161-1912.2004.tb00364.x

Locke, T. F., Newcomb, M. D., & Goodyear, R. K. (2005). Childhood experiences and psychosocial influences on risky sexual behavior, condom use, and HIV attitudes/behaviors among Latino males. *Psychology of Men & Masculinity, 6*, 25–38.

Lontz, M. Q. (2000). The male gender and gender role conflict in relationship to well-being in retired adult men. *Dissertation Abstracts International, 61*, 2606.

Lynch, J., & Kilmartin, C. (1999). *The pain behind the mask: Overcoming masculine depression.* Binghamton, NY: Haworth Press.

Magovcevic, M., & Addis, M. E. (2005). Linking gender role conflict to nonnormative and self-stigmatizing perceptions of alcohol abuse and depression. *Psychology of Men & Masculinity, 6*, 127–136. doi:10.1037/1524-9220.6.2.127

Mahalik, J. R. (1999a). Incorporating a gender role strain perspective in assessing and treating men's cognitive distortions. *Professional Psychology: Research and Practice, 30*, 333–340. doi:10.1037/0735-7028.30.4.333

Mahalik, J. R. (1999b). Interpersonal psychotherapy with men who experience gender role conflict. *Professional Psychology: Research and Practice, 30*, 5–13. doi:10.1037/0735-7028.30.1.5

Mahalik, J. R. (2000). Gender role conflict in men as a predictor of self-ratings of behavior on the interpersonal circle. *Journal of Social and Clinical Psychology, 19*, 276–292. doi:10.1521/jscp.2000.19.2.276

Mahalik, J. R., Addis, M., Kilmartin, C., & O'Neil, J. M. (2013). Complexities and challenges when teaching the psychology of men: Four experienced professors discuss their pedagogical process. *Psychology of Men & Masculinity, 14*, 248–255. doi:10.1037/a0033257

Mahalik, J. R., Aldarondo, E., Gilberet-Gokhale, S., & Shore, E. (2005). The role of insecure and gender role stress in predicting controlling behaviors in men who batter. *Journal of Interpersonal Violence, 20*, 617–631.

Mahalik, J. M., Burns, S. M., & Syzdek, M. (2007). Masculinity and perceived normative health behaviors as predictors of men's health. *Social Science & Medicine, 64,* 2201–2209.

Mahalik, J. R., & Cournoyer, R. J. (2000). Identifying gender role conflict messages that distinguish mildly depressed from non-depressed men. *Psychology of Men & Masculinity, 1,* 109–115. doi:10.1037/1524-9220.1.2.109

Mahalik, J. R., Cournoyer, R., DeFranc, W., Cherry, M., & Napolitano, J. M. (1998). Men's gender role conflict and use of psychological defenses. *Journal of Counseling Psychology, 45,* 247–255. doi:10.1037/0022-0167.45.3.247

Mahalik, J. R., Good, G. E., & Englar-Carlson, M. (2003). Masculinity scripts, presenting concerns, and help seeking: Implications for practice and training. *Professional Psychology: Research and Practice, 34,* 123–131. doi:10.1037/0735-7028.34.2.123

Mahalik, J. R., & Lagan, H. (2001). Examining masculine gender role conflict and stress in relation to religious orientation and spiritual well-being. *Psychology of Men & Masculinity, 2,* 24–33. doi:10.1037/1524-9220.2.1.24

Mahalik, J. R., Lagan, H. D., & Morrison, J. A. (2006). Health behaviors and masculinity in Kenyan and U. S. male college students. *Psychology of Men & Masculinity, 7,* 191–202.

Mahalik, J. R., Levi-Minzi, M., & Walker, G. (2007). Masculinity and health behaviors in Australian men. *Psychology of Men & Masculinity, 8,* 240–249.

Mahalik, J. R., Locke, B. D., Ludlow, L. H., Diemer, M. A., Scott, R. P., Gottfried, M., & Freitas, G. (2003). Development of the Conformity to Masculine Norms Inventory. *Psychology of Men & Masculinity, 4,* 3–25. doi:10.1037/1524-9220.4.1.3

Mahalik, J. R., Locke, B. D., Theodore, H., Cournoyer, R. J., & Lloyd, B. F. (2001). A cross-national and cross-sectional comparison on men's gender role conflict and its relationship to social intimacy and self-esteem. *Sex Roles, 45,* 1–14. doi:10.1023/A:1013008800019

Mahalik, J. R., Pierre, M. R., & Wan, S. S. C. (2006). Examining racial identity and masculinity as correlates of self-esteem and psychological distress in Black men. *Journal of Multicultural Counseling and Development, 34,* 94–104.

Mahalik, J. R., & Rochlen, A. B. (2006). Men's likely coping responses to clinical depression: What are they and do masculinity norms predict them. *Sex Roles, 55,* 659–667.

Malebranche, D. J., Gvetadze, R., Millett, G. A., & Sutton, M. Y. (2012). The relationship between gender role conflict and condom use among Black MSM. *AIDS and Behavior, 16,* 2051–2061. doi:10.1007/s10461-011-0055-3

Manning, N. N. (2011). *Gender role conflict among formerly incarcerated and college Black males: The mediating effects of racial identity on psychological distress* (Doctoral dissertation). Available from ProQuest Dissertations and Theses database. (UMI No. 3472694)

Mansfield, A. K., Addis, M. E., & Courtenay, W. (2005). Measurement of men's help seeking: Development and evaluation of the Barriers to Help Seeking Scale. *Psychology of Men & Masculinity, 6,* 95–108. doi:10.1037/1524-9220.6.2.95

Marrocco, F. A. (2001). Gender role conflict in young males as a function of paternal/filial mutual identification and personal warmth and empathy. *Dissertation Abstracts International, 52,* 4226.

Maton, K. I., Anderson, C. W., Burke, C. K., Hoover, S. A., & Mankowski, E. (1998, August). Mankind Project's impact on men's goals, gender role conflict, well-being, and self-development. In E. Mankowski & K. Maton (Chairs), *Psychological impact and group characteristics of a mythopoetic men's organization.* Symposium conducted at the 106th Annual Convention of the American Psychological Association, San Francisco, CA.

McAnulty, S. W. (1996). *The effectiveness of a parenting program in reducing gender role conflict and changing male role norms on regional Australian fathers* (Unpublished master's thesis). Monash University, Churchill, Victoria, Australia.

McConville, G. (2004). *Gender role conflict, health and exercise behaviour in Australian males* (Unpublished master's thesis). Monash University, Churchill, Victoria, Australia.

McCreary, D. R., & Sadava, S. W. (1995). Mediating the relationship between masculine gender role stress and work satisfaction: The influence of coping strategies. *Journal of Men's Studies, 4,* 141–152.

McCreary, D. R., Saucier, D. M., & Courtenay, W. H. (2005). The drive for muscularity and masculinity: Testing the association among gender role traits, behaviors, attitudes, and conflict. *Psychology of Men & Masculinity, 6,* 83–94. doi:10.1037/1524-9220.6.2.83

McDermott, R. C., & Schwartz, J. (2013). Toward a better understanding of emerging adult men's gender role journeys: Differences in age, education, race, relationship status, and sexual orientation. *Psychology of Men & Masculinity, 14,* 202–210. doi:10.1037/a0028538

McDermott, R. C., Schwartz, J. P., Lindley, L. D., & Proietti, J. S. (2014). Exploring men's homophobia: Association with religious fundamentalism and gender role conflict domains. *Psychology of Men & Masculinity, 15,* 191–200 doi:10.1037/a0032788

McDermott, R. C., Schwartz, J. P., & Trevathan-Minnis, M. (2012). Predicting men's anger management: Relationship with gender role journey and entitlement. *Psychology of Men & Masculinity, 13,* 49–64. doi:10.1037/a0022689

McGill, O. D. (2011). *The influences of masculinity on restrictive emotionality among African American men* (Doctoral dissertation). Available from ProQuest Dissertations and Theses database. (UMI No. 3428416)

McGinness, C. (2011). *Twenty five years of change in men's gender role strain as measured by the Gender Role Conflict Scale* (Doctoral dissertation). Available from ProQuest Dissertations and Theses database. (UMI No. 3469159)

McMahon, J. (2009). *Gender role conflict in gay men living in Ireland.* Unpublished manuscript, Dublin Business School, Dublin, Ireland.

McMahon, T. J., Winkel, J. D., & Luthar, S. S. (2000, August). Gender role conflict, drug dependence, and fatherhood: A comparative analysis. In J. M. O'Neil & G. E. Good (Chairs), *Gender role conflict in the year 2000: Innovative directions.* Symposium conducted at the 108th Annual Convention of the American Psychological Association, Washington, D.C.

Media Education Foundation. (Producer). (1999). *Tough guise: Violence, media, & the crisis in masculinity* [DVD]. Retrieved from http://www.mediaed.org/cgi-bin/commerce.cgi?display=home

Mejias, J. C. (2010). *Male gender role conflict as seen through muscularity concerns of self-identified Latino men* (Doctoral dissertation). Available from ProQuest Dissertations and Theses database. (UMI No. 3378600)

Mellinger, T. N., & Liu, W. M. (2006). Men's issues in doctoral training: A survey of counseling psychology programs. *Professional Psychology: Research and Practice, 37,* 196–204. doi:10.1037/0735-7028.37.2.196

Mendelson, E. A. (1988). *An exploratory investigation of male gender-role development during early adulthood* (Unpublished doctoral dissertation). University of North Carolina, Chapel Hill.

Mendoza, J., & Cummings, A. L. (2001). Help-seeking and male gender role attitudes in male batterers. *Journal of Interpersonal Violence, 16,* 833–840. doi:10.1177/088626001016008006

Mertens, C. E. (2000). Male gender role conflict in depressed versus nondepressed medical populations (Doctoral dissertation). *Dissertation Abstracts International: Section A. Humanities and Social Sciences, 61,* 3068.

Mintz, L., & O'Neil, J. M. (1990). Sex, gender role, and the process of psychotherapy: Theory and research. *Journal of Counseling & Development, 68,* 381–387. doi:10.1002/j.1556-6676.1990.tb02515.x

Mintz, R., & Mahalik, J. R. (1996). Sex role ideology and gender role conflict as predictors of family roles for men. *Sex Roles, 34,* 805–821.

Mock, J. F. (1995). Influence of gender role journey and balance of power in the marital relationship, on the emotional and spiritual well-being of mid-life married women. *Dissertation Abstracts International, 56*(5), 9531244.

Monk, D., & Ricciardelli, L. A. (2003). Three dimensions of the male gender roles as correlates of alcohol and cannabis involvement in young Australian men. *Psychology of Men & Masculinity, 4,* 57–69. doi:10.1037/1524-9220.4.1.57

Moore, C. M. (1993). A study of male sex-role attitudes and self-concept differences between alcoholics and non-alcoholics and the effects of a psychoeducational group on these variables and the subsequent relapse rates. *Dissertation Abstracts International, 54,* 2215.

Moore, T. M., & Stuart, G. L. (2004). Effects of masculine gender role stress on men's cognitive, affective, physiological, and aggressive responses to intimate conflict situations. *Psychology of Men & Masculinity, 5,* 132–142.

Moradi, B., Tokar, D. M., Schaub, M., Jome, L. M., & Serna, G. S. (2000). Revisiting the structural validity of the Gender Role Conflict Scale. *Psychology of Men & Masculinity, 1,* 62–69. doi:10.1037/1524-9220.1.1.62

Moreland, J. R. (1980). Age and change in the adult male sex role. *Sex Roles, 6,* 807–818. doi:10.1007/BF00287236

Murphy, D. T. (2001). Mental health professionals gender-related stereotypes attributions regarding traditional men's experience of gender role conflict. *Dissertation Abstracts International, 65,* 2641.

Murray, T., & Lewis, V. (2014). Gender role conflict and men's body satisfaction: The moderating role of age. *Psychology of Men & Masculinity, 15,* 40–48. doi:10.1037/a0030959

Murtagh, A. (2012). *Male gender role conflict and its effects on the therapeutic relationship* (Unpublished master's thesis). Dublin Business Schools, Dublin, Ireland.

Nahon, D. (1992). *The effectiveness of masculinist group psychotherapy in the treatment of recently separated men* (Unpublished doctoral dissertation). University of Montreal, Montreal, Quebec, Canada.

Napolitano, J. M., Mahalik, J. R., & Kenny, M. E. (1999, August). *Relation of gender role strain and attachment to men's psychosocial development.* Paper presented at the 107th Annual Convention of the American Psychological Association, Boston, MA.

Naranjo, S. (2001). The self-destructive man: A study of gender role conflict. *Dissertation Abstracts International: Section B. The Sciences and Engineering, 62,* 1592.

Nauly, M. (2002). *Men's gender role conflict of Bataks, Minang (Kabaus) and Javanese* (Unpublished master's thesis). University of Indonesia, Depok, Indonesia.

Newman, B., & Newman, P. (2015). *Development through life: A psychosocial approach.* Belmont, CA: Wadsworth.

Newman, S. G. (1997). Self-silencing, depression, gender role, and gender role conflict in women and men. *Dissertation Abstracts International: Section B. The Sciences and Engineering, 58,* 6818.

Newport, F. (2011, June 3). *More than 9 in 10 Americans continue to believe in God.* Retrieved from http://www.gallup.com/poll/147887/americans-continue-believe-god.aspx

Nguyen, C. M., Liu, W. M., Hernandez, J. O., & Stinson, R. (2012). Problem solving appraisal, gender role conflict, help-seeking behavior, and psychological distress among men who are homeless. *Psychology of Men & Masculinity, 13,* 270–282. doi:10.1037/a0025523

Norton, J. (1997). Deconstructing the fear of femininity. *Feminism & Psychology, 7,* 441–447. doi:10.1177/0959353597073028

Norwalk, K. E., Vandiver, B. J., White, A. M., & Englar-Carlson, M. (2011). Factor structure of the Gender Role Conflict Scale in African American and European American men. *Psychology of Men & Masculinity, 12,* 128–143. doi:10.1037/a0022799

Noyes, B. B. (2004). *Gender role conflict as a predictor of therapy outcome* (Unpublished master's thesis). University of Utah.

Odes, E. (2008). Male perfectionists with close same-sex friends: Self-disclosure, gender role conflict, and relational interdependent self-construal. *Dissertation Abstracts International: Section B. The Sciences and Engineering, 69*, 7180.

Olsen, S. E. (2000). Gender role conflict and anxiety as predictors of anger in men. *Dissertation Abstracts International: Section B. The Sciences and Engineering, 61*, 1647.

O'Neil, J. M. (1979, March). *The male sex role and the negative consequences of the masculine socialization process: Implications for counselors and counseling psychologists.* Program presented at the annual meeting of the American College Personnel Association, Los Angeles, CA.

O'Neil, J. M. (1981a). Male sex-role conflict, sexism, and masculinity: Implications for men, women, and the counseling psychologist. *The Counseling Psychologist, 9*, 61–80. doi:10.1177/001100008100900213

O'Neil, J. M. (1981b). Patterns of gender role conflict and strain: Sexism and fear of femininity in men's lives. *The Personnel and Guidance Journal, 60*, 203–210. doi:10.1002/j.2164-4918.1981.tb00282.x

O'Neil, J. M. (1982). Gender role conflict and strain in men's lives: Implications for psychiatrists, psychologists, and other human service providers. In K. Solomon & N. B. Levy (Eds.), *Men in transition: Changing male roles, theory, and therapy* (pp. 5–44). New York: Plenum Press. doi:10.1007/978-1-4684-4211-3_2

O'Neil, J. M. (1988a, August). *Definition of gender role conflict: A study of John Lennon's life.* Paper presented at the 96th Annual Convention of the American Psychological Association, Atlanta, GA.

O'Neil, J. M. (1988b). *The Devaluations, Restrictions, and Violations Worksheet.* Unpublished manuscript, Department of Educational Psychology, University of Connecticut, Storrs.

O'Neil, J. M. (1988c). *The Gender Role Conflict Checklist.* Unpublished instrument, Department of Educational Psychology, University of Connecticut, Storrs.

O'Neil, J. M. (1990). Assessing men's gender role conflict. In D. Moore & F. Leafgren (Eds.), *Men in conflict: Problem solving strategies and interventions* (pp. 23–38). Alexandria, VA: American Association for Counseling and Development.

O'Neil, J. M. (1991, August). Men and women as victims of sexism. Metaphors for healing. In G. Brooks (Chair), *Practitioners' perspectives on male-female relations in the 90's.* Symposium conducted at the 99th Annual Convention of the American Psychological Association, San Francisco, CA.

O'Neil, J. M. (1993). A counseling psychologist in Russia as a Fulbright scholar: James in wonderland. *The Counseling Psychologist, 21*, 642–651.

O'Neil, J. M. (1996). The Gender Role Journey Workshop: Exploring sexism and gender role conflict in a coeducational setting. In M. A. Andronico (Ed.), *Men in groups: Insights, interventions, psychoeducational work* (pp. 193–213). Washington, DC: American Psychological Association. doi:10.1037/10284-013

O'Neil, J. M. (2001). Promoting men's growth and development: Teaching the new psychology of men using psychoeducational philosophy and interventions. In G. Brooks & G. E. Good (Eds.), *The new handbook of psychotherapy and counseling with men: A comprehensive guide to settings, problems, and treatment approaches* (Vol. 2, pp. 639–663). San Francisco, CA: Jossey-Bass.

O'Neil, J. M. (2006). Helping Jack heal his emotional wounds: The gender role conflict diagnostic schema. In M. Englar-Carlson & M. Stevens (Eds.), *In the therapy room with men: A casebook about psychotherapeutic process and change with male clients* (pp. 259–284). Washington, DC: American Psychological Association. doi:10.1037/11411-013

O'Neil, J. M. (2008a). Complexity, contextualism, and multiculturalism: Responses to the critiques and future directions for the gender role conflict research program. *The Counseling Psychologist, 36,* 469–476. doi:10.1177/0011000008314781

O'Neil, J. M. (Ed.). (2008b). Men's gender conflict: 25 year research summary [Special issue]. *The Counseling Psychologist, 36*(3).

O'Neil, J. M. (2008c). Summarizing twenty-five years of research on men's gender role conflict using the Gender Role Conflict Scale: New research paradigms and clinical implications. *The Counseling Psychologist, 36,* 358–445. doi:10.1177/0011000008317057

O'Neil, J. M. (2010). Is criticism of generic masculinity, essentialism, and positive-healthy-masculinity a problem for the psychology of men? *Psychology of Men & Masculinity, 11,* 98–106. doi:10.1037/a0018917

O'Neil, J. M. (2011). Exploring the psychology of Russian men with Russian psychologists during my Fulbright scholarship in the former Soviet Union. In C. Blazina & D. Shen-Miller (Eds.), *An international psychology of men: Theoretical advances, case studies, and clinical innovations* (pp. 361–383). New York, NY: Routledge.

O'Neil, J. M. (2012a, June). *Helping men with gender role conflict in psychotherapy.* Keynote address delivered at the 3rd National Psychotherapy With Men Conference, New York, NY.

O'Neil, J. M. (2012b). The psychology of men. In E. Altmaier & J. Hansen (Eds.), *Oxford handbook of counseling psychology* (pp. 95–127). New York, NY: Oxford University Press. doi:10.1093/oxfordhb/9780195342314.013.0014

O'Neil, J. M. (2013). Gender role conflict research 30 years later: An evidence-based diagnostic schema to assess boys and men in counseling. *Journal of Counseling & Development, 91,* 490–498.

O'Neil, J. M., Addis, M., Kilmartin, C., & Mahalik, J. (2004). Teaching the psychology of men: A potential growth area for psychology and Division 51: A report from the APA Honolulu convention. *SPSMM Bulletin, 10,* 36–47.

O'Neil, J. M., Challenger, C., Renzulli, S., Crapser, B., & Webster, E. (2013). The boy's forum: An evaluation of a brief intervention to empower middle school urban boys. *The Journal of Men's Studies, 21,* 191–205. doi:10.3149/jms.2102.191

O'Neil, J. M., & Crapser, B. (2011). Using the psychology of men and gender role conflict theory to promote comprehensive service delivery for college men:

A call to action. In J. A. Laker & T. Davis (Eds.), *Masculinities in higher education: Theoretical and practical considerations* (pp. 16–49). New York, NY: Routledge.

O'Neil, J. M., & Denke, R. (in press). An empirical review of gender role conflict research: New conceptual models and research paradigms. In Y. J. Wong & S. R. Wester (Eds.), *Handbook of the psychology of men and masculinities*. Washington, DC: American Psychological Association.

O'Neil, J. M., & Egan, J. (1992a). Men's and women's gender role journeys: Metaphor for healing, transition, and transformation. In B. Wainrib (Ed.), *Gender issues across the life cycle* (pp. 107–123). New York: Springer.

O'Neil, J. M., & Egan, J. (1992b). Men's gender role transitions over the life span: Transformations and fears of femininity. *Journal of Mental Health Counseling, 14*, 305–324.

O'Neil, J. M., & Egan, J. (1993). Abuses of power against women: Sexism, gender role conflict, and psychological violence. In E. Cook (Ed.), *Women, relationships, and power: Implications for counseling* (pp. 49–78). Alexandria, VA: American Counseling Association.

O'Neil, J. M., Egan, J., Owen, S. V., & Murry, V. (1993). The Gender Role Journey Measure (GRJM): Scale development and psychometric evaluations. *Sex Roles, 28*, 167–185. doi:10.1007/BF00299279

O'Neil, J. M., & Fishman, D. (1992). Adult men's career transitions and gender role themes. In H. D. Lee & Z. B. Leibowitz (Eds.), *Adult career development: Concepts, issues, and Practices* (2nd ed., pp. 132–162). Alexandria, VA: American Counseling Association.

O'Neil, J. M., Fishman, D. M., & Kinsella-Shaw, M. (1987). Dual-career couples' career transitions and normative dilemmas: A preliminary assessment model. *The Counseling Psychologist, 15*, 50–96. doi:10.1177/0011000087151003

O'Neil, J. M., Good, G. E., & Holmes, S. (1995). Fifteen years of theory and research on men's gender role conflict: New paradigms for empirical research. In R. F. Levant & W. S. Pollack (Eds.), *A new psychology of men* (pp. 164–206). New York, NY: Perseus.

O'Neil, J. M., Helms, B., Gable, R., David, L., & Wrightsman, L. (1986). Gender Role Conflict Scale (GRCS): College men's fears of femininity. *Sex Roles, 14*, 335–350.

O'Neil, J. M., & Lujan, M. L. (2009a). An assessment paradigm for fathers in therapy using gender role conflict theory. In C. Z. Oren & D. C. Oren (Eds.), *Counseling fathers* (pp. 49–71). New York, NY: Routledge.

O'Neil, J. M., & Lujan, M. L. (2009b). Preventing boys problems in schools through psychoeducation programming: A call to action. *Psychology in the Schools, 46*, 257–266. doi:10.1002/pits.20371

O'Neil, J. M., & Nadeau, R. A. (1999). Men's gender-role conflict, defense mechanism, and self-protective defensive strategies: Explaining men's violence against women from a gender-role socialization perspective. In M. Harway & J. M. O'Neil (Eds.), *What causes men's violence against women?* (pp. 89–116). Thousand Oaks, CA: Sage. doi:10.4135/9781452231921.n7

O'Neil, J. M., & Renzulli, S. (2013a). Introduction to teaching the psychology of men: A call to action. *Psychology of Men & Masculinity, 14,* 221–229. doi:10.1037/a0033258

O'Neil, J. M., & Renzulli, S. (2013b). Teaching the psychology of men: A national survey of professors' attitudes and content analysis of their courses. *Psychology of Men & Masculinity, 14,* 230–239. doi:10.1037/a0033255

O'Neil, J. M., & Roberts Carroll, M. (1988). A gender role workshop focused on sexism, gender role conflict, and the gender role journey. *Journal of Counseling & Development, 67,* 193–197. doi:10.1002/j.1556-6676.1988.tb02091.x

Osborne, T. L. (2004). Male gender role conflict and perceived social support: Predicting help seeking in men. *Dissertation Abstracts International: Section B. The Sciences and Engineering, 65,* 3175.

Paciej, A. (2010). *The relationship between the level of engagement and the development of masculinity identity among male college students* (Doctoral dissertation). Available from ProQuest Dissertations and Theses database. (UMI No. 3452821)

Park, J., & Seok Seo, Y. (2009). Gender role conflict and willingness to seek counseling in male university students: The mediating roles of social stigma and attitudes toward counseling. *The Korean Journal of Counseling and Psychotherapy, 21,* 25–48.

Pederson, E. L., & Vogel, D. L. (2007). Male gender role conflict and willingness to seek counseling: Testing a mediation model on college-aged men. *Journal of Counseling Psychology, 54,* 373–384. doi:10.1037/0022-0167.54.4.373

Perls, F. (1968). *Gestalt therapy verbatim.* Moab, UT: Real People Press.

Peterson, F. (1999, August). *Gender-role conflict as risk factor among male smokers.* Paper presented at the 107th Annual Convention of the American Psychological Association, Boston, MA.

Peterson, M. A. (1991). Male role identification, gender role conflict, and help seeking: Attitudes of male police officers. *Dissertation Abstracts International, 52*(09), 3186

Pierce, M. S. (2012). *Examining how men are supportive in close relationships: Attachment and gender role consideration* (Doctoral dissertation). Available from ProQuest Dissertation and Theses database. (UMI No. 3494741)

Pleck, J. (1981). *The myth of masculinity.* Cambridge, MA: MIT Press.

Pleck, J. H. (1995). The gender role strain paradigm: An update. In R. F. Levant & W. S. Pollack (Eds.), *A new psychology of men* (pp. 11–32). New York, NY: Basic Books.

Pleck, J. H. (2010). Foreword. In C. Z. Oren & D. C. Oren (Eds.), *Counseling fathers* (pp. xxiii–xv). New York, NY: Routledge.

Pleck, J. H., & Sawyer, J. (1974). *Men and masculinity.* Englewood Cliffs, NJ: Prentice Hall.

Pleck, J. H., Sonenstein, F. L., & Ku, L. C. (1993). Masculinity ideology and its correlates. In S. Oskamp & M. Costanzo (Eds.), *Gender issues in social psychology* (pp. 85–110). Newbury Park, CA: Sage.

Pollack, W. (1995). No man is an island: Toward a new psychoanalytic psychology of men. In R. Levant & W. Pollack (Eds.), *A new psychology of men* (pp. 33–67). New York, NY: Basic Books.

Pollack, W. (1998a). Mourning, melancholia, and masculinity: Recognizing and treating depression in men. In W. S. Pollack & R. F. Levant (Eds.), *New psychotherapy for men* (pp. 147–166). New York, NY: Wiley.

Pollack, W. (1998b). *Real boys: Rescuing our sons from the myths of boyhood.* New York, NY: Random House.

Pollack, W. S. (2001). "Masked men": New psychoanalytically oriented treatment models for adult and young men. In G. Brooks & G. E. Good (Eds.), *The new handbook of psychotherapy and counseling with men: A comprehensive guide to settings, problems, and treatment approaches* (pp. 525–543). San Francisco, CA: Jossey-Bass.

Potts, M. (2012, December 14). Obama, crying. *The American Prospect.* Retrieved from http://prospect.org/article/obama-crying

Preston, J. (2002). *Survivors: Stories and strategies to heal the hurt.* San Luis Obispo, CA: Impact.

Prochaska, J. O., & DiClemente, C. C. (2005). The transtheoretical approach. In J. C. Norcross & M. R. Goldfried (Eds.), *Handbook of psychotherapy integration* (pp. 300–334). New York, NY: Oxford University Press.

Prochaska, J. O., & Norcross, J. C. (2001). Stages of change. *Psychotherapy: Theory, Research, Practice, Training, 38,* 443–448. doi:10.1037/0033-3204.38.4.443

Pytluk, S. D., & Casas, J. M. (1998, August). *Male gender role conflict scales and diverse populations: A psychometric and exploratory study.* Paper presented at the 106th Annual Convention of the American Psychological Association, San Francisco, CA.

Rabinowitz, F. E., & Cochran, S. V. (2002). *Deepening psychotherapy with men.* Washington, DC: American Psychological Association. doi:10.1037/10418-000

Rainwater, S. (2011). *An examination of the dimensions of intimacy and male gender role conflict* (Doctoral dissertation). Available from ProQuest Dissertation and Theses database. (UMI No. 3433059)

Rando, R. A., Rogers, J. R., & Brittan-Powell, C. (1998). Gender role conflict in college men's sexually aggressive attitudes and behavior. *Journal of Mental Health Counseling, 20,* 359–369.

Rebecca, M., Hefner, R., & Olenshansky, B. A. (1976). A model of sex role transcendence. *Journal of Social Issues, 32,* 197–206.

Reiman, B. M. (1999). Religious orientation's prediction of gender role conflict in adult males. *Dissertation Abstracts International: Section B. The Sciences and Engineering, 60,* 3621.

Robertson, J. M. (2006). Finding Joshua's soul: Working with religious men. In M. Englar-Carlson & M. A. Stevens (Eds.), *In the room with men: A casebook of therapeutic change* (pp. 129–150). Washington, DC: American Psychological Association. doi:10.1037/11411-007

Robertson, J. M. (2012). *Tough guys and true believers: Managing authoritarian men in the psychotherapy room.* New York, NY: Routledge.

Robertson, J. M. (2013). Teaching the psychology of men: Not for classrooms only. *Psychology of Men & Masculinity, 14,* 268–270.

Robertson, J. M., & Fitzgerald, L. F. (1990). The (mis)treatment of men: Effects of client gender role and life-style on diagnosis and attribution of pathology. *Journal of Counseling Psychology, 37,* 3–9. doi:10.1037/0022-0167.37.1.3

Robertson, J. M., & Fitzgerald, L. F. (1992). Overcoming the masculine mystique: Preferences for alternative forms of assistance among men who avoid counseling. *Journal of Counseling Psychology, 39,* 240–246. doi:10.1037/0022-0167.39.2.240

Robin, L., & Reiger, D. (1991). *Psychiatric disorders in America.* New York, NY: Free Press.

Robinson, D. T., & Schwartz, J. P. (2004). Relationship between gender role conflict and attitudes toward women and African Americans. *Psychology of Men & Masculinity, 5,* 65–71. doi:10.1037/1524-9220.5.1.65

Robinson, M. A., & Brewster, M. E. (2014). Motivations for fatherhood: Examining internalized heterosexism and gender role conflict with childless gay and bisexual men. *Psychology of Men & Masculinity, 15,* 49–59. doi:10.1037/a0031142

Rochlen, A., & Mahalik, J. R. (2004). Women's perceptions of male partner's gender role conflict as predictors of psychological well-being and relationship satisfaction. *Psychology of Men & Masculinity, 5,* 147–157. doi:10.1037/1524-9220.5.2.147

Rochlen, A. B., Blazina, C., & Raghunathan, R. (2002). Gender role conflict, attitudes toward career counseling, career decision making, and perceptions of career advertising brochures. *Psychology of Men & Masculinity, 3,* 127–137. doi:10.1037/1524-9220.3.2.127

Rochlen, A. B., & Hoyer, W. D. (2005). Marketing mental health to men: Theoretical and practical considerations. *Journal of Clinical Psychology, 61,* 675–684. doi:10.1002/jclp.20102

Rochlen, A. B., McKelley, R. A., & Pituch, K. A. (2006). A preliminary examination of the "Real Men. Real Depression" campaign. *Psychology of Men & Masculinity, 7,* 1–13. doi:10.1037/1524-9220.7.1.1

Rochlen, A. B., & O'Brien, K. M. (2002). The relation of male gender role conflict and attitudes toward career counseling to interest in and preference for different career counseling styles. *Psychology of Men & Masculinity, 3,* 9–21. doi:10.1037/1524-9220.3.1.9

Rogers, J. R., Abbey-Hines, J., & Rando, R. A. (1997). Confirmatory factor analysis of the Gender Role Conflict Scale: A cross validation of Good et al., 1995. *Measurement and Evaluation in Counseling and Development, 30,* 137–145.

Rogers, T. E. (2009). *Using the theory of reasoned action to predict college men's intentions to seek psychological help* (Doctoral dissertation). Available from ProQuest Dissertations and Theses database. (UMI No. 3375680)

Rooney, L. (2011). *Police attitude toward individuals with intellectual disabilities: An investigation of age, education, contact, knowledge, and gender role conflict* (Unpublished doctoral dissertation). University Leicester, Leicester, England.

Rosenthal, P., Rosenthal, J. (Producers), & Ramis, H. (Director). (1999). *Analyze this* [Motion picture]. Australia: Village Roadhouse Pictures.

Ross, S. (2004). *Masculinity in crisis: An investigation into patterns of gender role conflict between age groups* (Unpublished master's thesis). University of London, England.

Rotter, J. B. (1966). Generalized expectancies for internal versus external control of reinforcement. *Psychological Monographs, 80*, 1–28.

Rye, M. S., Pargament, K. I., Ali, M. A., Beck, G. L., Dorff, E. N., Hallisey, C., . . . Williams, J. G. (2000). Religious perspectives on forgiveness. In M. E. McCullough, K. I. Pargament, & C. E. Thoresen (Eds.), *Forgiveness: Theory, research, and practice* (pp. 17–40). New York, NY: Guilford Press.

Sánchez, F. J. (2005). The relationship between masculine gender role conflict, negative identity, and being out. *Dissertation Abstracts International: Section A. Humanities and Social Sciences, 66*(08), 3118.

Sánchez, F. J., Bocklandt, S., & Vilain, E. (2009). Gender role conflict, interest in casual sex, and relationship satisfaction among gay men. *Psychology of Men & Masculinity, 10*, 237–243. doi:10.1037/a0016325

Sánchez, F. J., Westefeld, J. S., Liu, W. M., & Vilain, E. (2010). Masculine gender role conflict and negative feelings about being gay. *Professional Psychology: Research and Practice, 41*, 104–111. doi:10.1037/a0015805

Sbaratta, C. A. T. (2011). *Male psychology doctoral students: The influence of GRC on training* (Doctoral dissertation). Available from ProQuest Dissertations and Theses database. (UMI No. 3472702)

Schaub, M., & Williams, C. (2007). Examining the relations between masculine gender role conflict and men's expectations about counseling. *Psychology of Men & Masculinity, 8*, 40–52. doi:10.1037/1524-9220.8.1.40

Schenk, R. U., & Everingham, J. (Eds.). (1995). *Men healing shame: An anthology.* New York, NY: Springer.

Schiller, J. S., Lucas, J. W., & Peregoy, J. A. (2012). Summary health statistics for U.S. adults: National Health Interview Survey, 2011. *Vital and Health Statistics, 10*(256). Retrieved from http://www.cdc.gov/nchs/data/series/sr_10/sr10_256.pdf

Schopp, L. H., Good, G. E., Barker, K. B., Mazurek, M. O., & Hathaway, S. L. (2006). Masculine role adherence and outcomes among men with traumatic brain injury. *Brain Injury, 20*, 1155–1162.

Schwartz, J. P., Buboltz, W., Seeman, E. A., & Flye, A. (2004). Personality styles: Predictors of masculine gender role conflict in male prison inmates. *Psychology of Men & Masculinity, 5*, 59–64. doi:10.1037/1524-9220.5.1.59

Schwartz, J. P., Grammas, D. L., Sutherland, R. J., Siffert, K. G., & Bush-King, I. (2010). Masculine gender roles and differentiation on predictors of body image and self-objectification in men. *Psychology of Men & Masculinity, 11*, 208–224. doi:10.1037/a0018255

Schwartz, J. P., Higgins, A. J., & He, Y. H. (2003, August). Gender role conflict: Impact on body image of men. In J. M. O'Neil & G. E. Good (Co-Chairs), *Psychological and physical health correlates of gender role conflict: Five empirical studies*. Symposium conducted at the 111th Annual Convention of the American Psychological Association, Toronto, Ontario, Canada.

Schwartz, J. P., Magee, M. M., Griffin, L. D., & Dupuis, W. (2004). Effects of a group preventive intervention on risk and protective factors related to dating violence. *Group Dynamics: Theory, Research, and Practice, 8*, 221–231. doi:10.1037/1089-2699.8.3.221

Schwartz, J. P., & Tylka, T. L. (2008). Exploring entitlement as a moderator and mediator of relationship between masculine gender role conflict and men's body esteem. *Psychology of Men & Masculinity, 9*, 67–81. doi:10.1037/1524-9220.9.2.67

Schwartz, J., Tylka, T. L., & Hood, I. B. (2005, August). Gender role conflict and prejudice: The role of entitlement. In J. M. O'Neil & G. E. Good (Co-Chairs), *Gender role conflict research studies: Assessing contextual, therapeutic, and interpersonal variables*. Symposium conducted at the 113th Annual Convention American Psychological Association, Washington, D.C.

Schwartz, J. P., & Waldo, M. (2003). Reducing gender role conflict among men attending partner abuse prevention. *Journal for Specialists in Group Work, 20*, 1–15.

Schwartz, J., Waldo, M., Bloom-Langell, J., & Merta, R. (1998, August). Gender role conflict: Relationship to spouse abuse, self-esteem, acculturation, and intervention group outcome. In J. M. O'Neil & G. E. Good (Chairs), *Men's gender role conflict research advancing the new psychology of men*. Symposium conducted at the 106th Annual Convention American Psychological Association, Toronto, Ontario, Canada.

Schwartz, J. P., Waldo, M., & Higgins, A. J. (2004). Attachment styles: Relationship to masculine gender role conflict in college men. *Psychology of Men & Masculinity, 5*, 143–146. doi:10.1037/1524-9220.5.2.143

Scott, R. P. (2001). *The relationship between family structure and male gender role development* (Unpublished doctoral dissertation). University of Georgia.

Segalla, R. J. (1996). Shame proneness and its relationship to gender role conflict/stress and male expectations of and attitudes toward, professional psychological help. *Dissertation Abstracts International: Section B. The Sciences and Engineering, 56*, 6446.

Selby, B. W. (1999). The relation of attachment, adjustment, and narcissism to masculine gender role conflict. *Dissertation Abstracts International: Section B. The Sciences and Engineering, 61*, 5005.

Senn, C. Y., Desmarais, S., Verberg, N., & Wood, E. (2000). Predicating coercive sexual behavior across the lifespan in a random sample of Canadian men. *Journal of Social and Personal Relationships, 17*, 95–113. doi:10.1177/0265407500171005

Serna, G. S. (2004). The confounding role of personality in the relation to gender role conflict and substance abuse and sexual aggression against women. *Dissertation Abstracts International: Section B. The Sciences and Engineering, 65,* 1064.

Sharpe, M. J., & Heppner, P. P. (1991). Gender role, gender role conflict, and psychological well-being in men. *Journal of Counseling Psychology, 38,* 323–330. doi:10.1037/0022-0167.38.3.323

Sharpe, M. J., Heppner, P. P., & Dixon, W. A. (1995). Gender role conflict, instrumentality, expressiveness, and well-being in adult men. *Sex Roles, 33,* 1–18. doi:10.1007/BF01547932

Shek, Y. L. (2006). Asian American masculinity: A review of the literature. *The Journal of Men's Studies, 14,* 379–391. doi:10.3149/jms.1403.379

Shek, Y. L., & McEwen, M. K. (2012). The relationship of racial identity and gender role conflict to self-esteem of Asian American undergraduates. *Journal of College Student Development, 53,* 703–718. doi:10.1353/csd.2012.0065

Shepard, D. S. (2002). A negative state of mind: Patterns of depressive symptoms among men with high gender role conflict. *Psychology of Men & Masculinity, 3,* 3–8. doi:10.1037/1524-9220.3.1.3

Shepard, W. D. (2001). Masculine gender role conflict and psychological well-being: A comparative study of heterosexual and gay men. *Dissertation Abstracts International: Section B. The Sciences and Engineering, 63,* 4386.

Shepherd, C. B. (2009). *The relationship between male gender role conflict, drive for muscularity and help seeking: Using the theory of planned behavior to explain why men need help and don't seek help* (Unpublished master's thesis). Colorado State University, Fort Collins.

Shepherd, C. B., & Rickard, K. M. (2012). Drive for muscularity and help seeking: The role of gender role conflict, self-stigma, and attitudes. *Psychology of Men & Masculinity, 13,* 379–392. doi:10.1037/a0025923

Siffert, K. J. (2012). *A structural equation model investigating parental relationships and gendered-functioning among men: Links to Kohut's self psychology* (Unpublished doctoral dissertation). University of Houston, Houston, TX.

Sileo, F. J. (1996). Gender role conflict: Intimacy and closeness in male–male friendships. *Dissertation Abstracts International: Section B. The Sciences and Engineering, 56,* 4645.

Silva, D. D. (2002). A study of Latino and Latina university students' gender role conflict, acculturation, ethnic identity, and worldview. *Dissertation Abstracts International: Section B. The Sciences and Engineering, 63,* 2626.

Simonsen, G., Blazina, C., & Watkins, C. E. (2000). Gender role conflict and psychological well-being among gay men. *Journal of Counseling Psychology, 47,* 85–89. doi:10.1037/0022-0167.47.1.85

Sipes, M. L. (2005). A partial test of male gender role conflict theory: Current perceptions of gender role socialization, masculinity ideology, and gender role conflict; relations with personality and perceptions of interpersonal problems. *Dissertation Abstracts International: Section B. The Sciences and Engineering, 66,* 2840.

Smiler, A. P. (2004). Thirty years after the discovery of gender: Psychological concept and measures of masculinity. *Sex Roles, 50,* 15–26. doi:10.1023/B:SERS.0000011069.02279.4c

Smiler, A. P. (Ed.). (2006). Manifestations of masculinity [Special issue]. *Sex Roles,* 55(9–10). doi:10.1007/s11199-006-9114-z

Society for the Psychological Study of Men and Masculinity. (2012). *Mission statement.* Retrieved from http://www.division51.org/aboutus/mission.htm

Sosoka, G. J. (2001). *Male identity development over four years: Differences in college men's self-perceived gender roles.* Unpublished manuscript, University of Dayton, Dayton, Ohio.

Soublis, T. P. (2003). *Masculine gender role conflict and male ideology in adolescent males: Correlates with psychological distress.* Unpublished manuscript, University of Houston, Houston, Texas.

Spillman, J. (2007). *Gender role conflict and empathy with male counselors in training: An empirical investigations* (Unpublished doctoral dissertation). Idaho State University.

Stanzione, D. (2005). Male gender role strain, coping, and college adjustment. *Dissertation Abstracts International: Section B. The Sciences and Engineering,* 66, 2317.

Steinfeldt, J. A., & Steinfeldt, M. C. (2010). Gender role conflict, athletic identity, and help-seeking among high school football players. *Journal of Applied Sport Psychology, 22,* 262–273. doi:10.1080/10413201003691650

Steinfeldt, J. A., Steinfeldt, M. C., England, B., & Speight, Q. L. (2009). Gender role conflict and stigma toward help-seeking among college football players. *Psychology of Men & Masculinity, 10,* 261–272. doi:10.1037/a0017223

Stillson, R. W. (1988). Gender role conflict in adult men: A study of predictive variables. *Dissertation Abstracts International, 50,* 366.

Stillson, R. W., O'Neil, J. M., & Owen, S. V. (1991). Predictors of adult men's gender role conflict: Race, class, unemployment, age, instrumentality–expressiveness, and personal strain. *Journal of Counseling Psychology, 38,* 458–464. doi:10.1037/0022-0167.38.4.458

Strom, T. (2004, July). Gender role conflict and dispositional coping styles in college age men. In J. M. O'Neil & G. E. Good (Co-Chairs), *Gender role conflict research: Four empirical studies and new research paradigm.* Symposium conducted at the 112th Annual Convention of the American Psychological Association, Honolulu, HI.

Sue, D. W. (2005). Racism and the conspiracy of silence: Presidential Address. *The Counseling Psychologist, 33,* 100–114. doi:10.1177/0011000004270686

Sweet, H. B. (Ed.). (2012). *Gender in the therapy hour: Voices of female clinicians working with men.* New York, NY: Routledge.

Swenson, B. H. (1998). Men and self-disclosure about personal topics: The impact of gender role conflict, self-esteem, and early relationship with father. *Dissertation Abstracts International: Section B. The Sciences and Engineering, 59,* 4543.

Syzdek, M. Beatty, Kellom, G., & Farr, J. M. (2005, August). *Misperceiving other college men's gender role conflict.* Paper presented at the 113th Annual Convention of the American Psychological Association, Washington, D.C.

Szymanski, D. M., & Carr, E. R. (2008). The role of gender role conflict and internalized heterosexism in gay and bisexual men's psychological distress: Testing two mediational models. *Psychology of Men & Masculinity, 9,* 40–54. doi:10.1037/1524-9220.9.1.40

Szymanski, D. M., & Hilton, A. N. (2013). Feminist counseling psychology and lesbians, bisexual women, and transgendered persons. In C. Z. Enns & E. N. Williams (Eds.), *The Oxford handbook of feminist multicultural counseling psychology* (pp. 131–154). New York, NY: Oxford University Press.

Szymanski, D. M., & Ikizler, A. S. (2013). Internalized heterosexism as a mediator in the relationship between gender role conflict, heterosexist discrimination, and depression among sexual minority men. *Psychology of Men & Masculinity, 14,* 211–219. doi:10.1037/a0027787

Tate, N. S. (1998). *Social support and depression in male GP surgery attendees: An investigation of the link with gender role conflict.* Unpublished doctoral dissertation, University of Newcastle Upon Tyne, New Castle Upon Tyne, England.

Theodore, H. (1998). *The relationship between gender role conflict and psychological well being across the life span: A cross sectional study of Australian men* (Unpublished honors thesis). Charles Sturt University, Bathurst, Australia.

Theodore, H., & Lloyd, B. F. (2000). Age and gender role conflict: A cross-sectional study of Australian men. *Sex Roles, 42,* 1027–1042. doi:10.1023/A:1007088617819

Thomas, T. R. (2008). *Examining the relationship between gender role conflict and interpersonal guilt in men* (Doctoral dissertation). Available from the ProQuest Dissertation and Theses database. (UMI No. 3345518)

Thompkins, C. D., & Rando, R. A. (2003). Gender role conflict and shame in college men. *Psychology of Men & Masculinity, 4,* 79–81. doi:10.1037/1524-9220.4.1.79

Thompson, D. A. (2009). Impact of military experience, psychological distress, gender role conflict, self-concealment and perceived stigma on attitudes toward seeking professional help in veterans. *Dissertation Abstracts International: Section B. The Sciences and Engineering, 70,* 1960.

Thompson, E. H., & Pleck, J. H. (1986). The structure of the male norms. *American Behavioral Scientist, 29,* 531–543. doi:10.1177/000276486029005003

Thompson, E. H., & Pleck, J. H. (1995). Masculinity ideologies: A review of research instrumentation on men and masculinities. In R. Levant & W. Pollack (Eds.), *A new psychology of men* (pp. 129–163). New York, NY: Basic Books.

Thompson, E. H., Pleck, J. H., & Ferrera, D. L. (1992). Men and masculinity: Scales for masculinity ideology and masculinity-related constructs. *Sex Roles, 27,* 573–607. doi:10.1007/BF02651094

Thomson, D. (2005). Masculine role conflict, shame-proneness and psychological adjustment: Testing a mediational model. *Dissertation Abstracts International: Section B. The Sciences and Engineering, 65*(09), 4854.

Thomson, P. (1995). Men's sexual abuse: Object relations, gender role conflict, and guilt. *Dissertation Abstracts International: Section B. The Sciences and Engineering, 56*, 3467.

Todryk, L. W. (1999). Gender role conflict in sex offenders revisited: A follow-up study. *Dissertation Abstracts International: Section B. The Sciences and Engineering, 60*, 4256.

Tokar, D. M., Fischer, A. R., & Schaub, M. (1998, August). Men's personality, gender role traditionality, and gender role conflict. In J. M. O'Neil & G. E. Good (Co-Chairs), *Gender role conflict research: Expanding empirical research in men's studies*. Symposium conducted at the 106th Annual Convention of the American Psychological Association, San Francisco, CA.

Tokar, D. M., Fischer, A. R., Schaub, M., & Moradi, B. (2000). Masculine gender roles and counseling-related variables: Link with mediation by personality. *Journal of Counseling Psychology, 47*, 380–393. doi:10.1037/0022-0167.47.3.380

Tokar, D. M., & Jome, L. M. (1998). Masculinity, vocational interests, and career choice traditionality: Evidence for a fully mediated model. *Journal of Counseling Psychology, 45*, 424–435. doi:10.1037/0022-0167.45.4.424

Torres Rivera, E. (1995). Puerto Rican men, gender role conflict, and ethnic identity. *Dissertation Abstracts International: Section A. Humanities and Social Sciences, 56*, 4159.

Tracey, T. J. G. (Ed.). (1995). Masculine gender role conflict [Special section]. *Journal of Counseling Psychology, 42*(1), 3–23.

Trautner, H. M., & Eckes, T. (2000). Putting gender development into context: Problems and prospects. In T. Eckes & H. Trautner (Eds.), *The developmental social psychology of gender* (pp. 419–435). Mahwah, NJ: Erlbaum.

Tsai, Y. (2000). *The study of the relationship between gender role conflict and attitudes toward help seeking* (Unpublished master's thesis). National Changhua University of Education, Taiwan.

Tsan, J. Y., Day, S. X., Schwartz, J. P., & Kimbrel, N. A. (2011). Restrictive emotionality, BIS, BAS, and psychological help seeking. *Psychology of Men and Masculinity, 12*, 260–274.

Tsui, V. (2010). *Male victims of partner abuse: Barriers and facilitators to help seeking* (Doctoral dissertation). Available from ProQuest Dissertations and Theses database. (UMI No. 3424291)

Tyre, P. (2006, January 29). The trouble with boys. *Newsweek.* Retrieved from http://www.newsweek.com/education-boys-falling-behind-girls-many-areas-108593

U.S. Census Bureau. (2005). *School enrollment—Social and economic characteristics of students: October 2003.* Washington, DC: Author. Retrieved from http://www.census.gov/prod/2005pubs/p20-554.pdf

U.S. Department of Education. (2011). Percentage of high school dropouts among persons 16 through 24 years old (status dropout rate), by sex and race/ethnicity: Selected years, 1960 through 2010 [Table]. Retrieved from http://nces.ed.gov/programs/digest/d11/tables/dt11_116.asp

Uy, P. G., Massoth, N., & Gottdiener, W. H. (2013). Rethinking male drinking: Traditional ideologies, gender-role conflict, and drinking motives. *Psychology of Men & Masculinity*. Advance online publication. doi:10.1037/a0032239

Van Delft, C. W. (1998). *Gender role conflict and psychological distress in Army men* (Unpublished master's thesis). University of Maryland.

Vandello, J. A., & Bosson, J. K. (2013). Hard won and easily lost: A review and synthesis of theory and research on precarious manhood. *Psychology of Men & Masculinity, 14*, 101–113. doi:10.1037/a0029826

Vandello, J. A., Bosson, J. K., Cohen, D., Burnaford, R. M., & Weaver, J. R. (2008). Precarious manhood. *Journal of Personality and Social Psychology, 95*, 1325–1339. doi:10.1037/a0012453

Van Hyfte, G. J., & Rabinowitz, F. E. (2001, August). *Men's group affiliation and same-sex intimacy*. Paper presented at the 109th Annual Convention of the American Psychological Association, San Francisco, CA.

Varvel, S. J. (2008). *Gender role conflict, problem solving appraisal, and the psychological functioning of firefighters* (Doctoral dissertation). Available from ProQuest Dissertations and Theses database (UMI No. 3458963).

Vinson, C. A. (2011). *Influence of ethnic identity and perceived discrimination on male gender role conflicts' impact on well-being* (Doctoral dissertation). Available from ProQuest Dissertations and Theses database. (UMI No. 3430038)

Vogel, D. L., Wester, S. R., Hammer, J. H., & Downing-Matibag, T. (2014). Referring men to seek help: The influence of gender role conflict and stigma. *Psychology of Men & Masculinity, 15*, 60–67. doi:10.1037/a0031761

Von Drehle, D. (2007, July 26). The myth about boys. *Time*, 38–47.

Vu, P. H. (2000). Relations between acculturation and gender roles conflict, shame-proneness, and psychological well-being among Vietnamese-American men. *Dissertation Abstracts International, 61: Section B. The Sciences and Engineering*, 5011.

Wade, J. C. (1996). African American men's gender role conflicts: The significance of racial identity. *Sex Roles, 34*, 458–464.

Wade, J. C., & Brittan-Powell, C. S. (2001). Men's attitudes toward race and gender equity: The importance of masculinity ideology, gender-related traits, and reference group identity dependence. *Psychology of Men and Masculinity, 2*, 42–50.

Wade, J. C., & Gelso, C. J. (1998). Reference Group Identity Dependence Scale: A measure of male identity. *The Counseling Psychologist, 26*, 384–412. doi:10.1177/0011000098263002

Wade, J. C., & Rochlen, A. B. (2013). Masculinity, identity, and the health and well-being of African American men. *Psychology of Men & Masculinity, 14*, 1–6. doi:10.1037/a0029612

Wagner, M., Marder, C., & Blackorby, J. (with Cardosa, D.). (2002). *The children we serve: The demographic characteristics of elementary and middle school students with disabilities and their households*. Retrieved from http://www.seels.net/designdocs/SEELS_Children_We_Serve_Report.pdf

Walker, D. F., Tokar, D. M., & Fischer, A. R. (2000). What are eight popular masculinity-related instruments measuring? Underlying dimensions and their relations to sociosexuality. *Psychology of Men & Masculinity, 1*, 98–108. doi:10.1037/1524-9220.1.2.98

Walker, S. C. (2008). *An examination of the psychological impact of gender role conflict and the engagement in double-consciousness among African American men*. Available from ProQuest Dissertations and Theses database. (UMI No. 3320204)

Walls, R. S., & Walker, G. A. (2002). *The effects of gender strain and fear of femininity on men's predisposition to violence against women*. Unpublished manuscript, Monash University, Melbourne, Australia.

Watts, R. H., & Borders, L. D. (2005). Boys' perceptions of the male role: Understanding gender role conflict in adolescent males. *The Journal of Men's Studies, 13*, 267–280. doi:10.3149/jms.1302.267

Weidlinger, T. (Director), & Moira Productions (Producer). (2001). *Boys will be men: Growing up male in America* [DVD]. Oley, PA: Bullfrog Films.

West, C., & Zimmerman, D. H. (1998). Doing gender. In B. M. Clinchy & J. K. Norem (Eds.), *The gender and psychology reader* (pp. 104–124). New York: New York University Press.

Wester, S. R. (2008a). Male gender role conflict and multiculturalism: Implications for counseling psychology. *The Counseling Psychologist, 36*, 294–324. doi:10.1177/0011000006286341

Wester, S. R. (2008b). Thinking complexly about men, gender role conflict, and counseling psychology. *The Counseling Psychologist, 36*, 462–468. doi:10.1177/0011000007310971

Wester, S. R., Arndt, D., Sedivy, S. K., & Arndt, L. (2010). Male police officers and stigma associated with counseling: The role of anticipated risks, anticipated benefits and gender role conflict. *Psychology of Men & Masculinity, 11*, 286–302. doi:10.1037/a0019108

Wester, S. R., Christianson, H. F., Vogel, D. L., & Wei, M. (2007). Gender role conflict and psychological distress: The role of social support. *Psychology of Men & Masculinity, 8*, 215–224. doi:10.1037/1524-9220.8.4.215

Wester, S. R., Kuo, B. C., & Vogel, D. C. (2006). Multicultural coping: Chinese Canadian adolescents, male gender role conflict, and psychological distress. *Psychology of Men & Masculinity, 7*, 83–100. doi:10.1037/1524-9220.7.2.83

Wester, S. R., McDonough, T. A., White, M., Vogel, D., & Taylor, L. (2010). Using gender role conflict theory in counseling male-to-female transgendered individuals. *Journal of Counseling & Development, 88*, 214–219.

Wester, S. R., Pionke, D. R., & Vogel, D. L. (2005). Male gender role conflict, gay men, and same-sex romantic relationships. *Psychology of Men & Masculinity, 6,* 195–208. doi:10.1037/1524-9220.6.3.195

Wester, S. R., & Vogel, D. L. (2002). Working with the masculine mystique: Male gender role conflict, counseling self-efficacy, and the training of male psychologists. *Professional Psychology: Research and Practice, 33,* 370–376. doi:10.1037/0735-7028.33.4.370

Wester, S. R., Vogel, D. L., & Archer, J. (2004). Male restricted emotionality and counseling supervision. *Journal of Counseling & Development, 82,* 91–98. doi:10.1002/j.1556-6678.2004.tb00289.x

Wester, S. R., Vogel, D. L., O'Neil, J. M., & Danforth, L. (2012). Development and evaluation of the Gender Role Conflict Scale Short Form (GRCS–SF). *Psychology of Men & Masculinity, 13,* 199–210. doi:10.1037/a0025550

Wester, S. R., Vogel, D. L., Wei, M., & McLain, R. (2006). African American men, gender role conflict, and psychological stress: The role of racial identity. *Journal of Counseling & Development, 84,* 419–429. doi:10.1002/j.1556-6678.2006.tb00426.x

White, A. M. (2002). Gender role conflict and racial identity as indicators of Black men's help seeking attitudes. *Dissertation Abstracts International: Section B. The Sciences and Engineering, 63,* 2567.

White, A. M. (2006). Racial and gender attitudes as predictors of feminist activism among self-identified African American feminists. *The Journal of Black Psychology, 32,* 455–478. doi:10.1177/0095798406292469

Wilkinson, W. W. (2004). Authoritarian hegemony, dimensions of masculinity, and male antigay attitudes. *Psychology of Men & Masculinity, 5,* 121–131. doi:10.1037/1524-9220.5.2.121

Williams, E. N., & Enns, C. Z. (2013). Making the political personal. In C. Z. Enns & E. N. Williams (Eds.), *The Oxford handbook of feminist multicultural counseling psychology* (pp. 485–489). New York, NY: Oxford University Press.

Wimer, D. J., & Levant, R. F. (2013). Energy drink use and it relationship to masculinity, jock identity, and fraternity membership among men. *American Journal of Men's Health, 7,* 317–328. doi:10.1177/1557988312474034

Windle, C. R., & Smith, D. A. (2009). Withdrawal moderates the association between husband gender role conflict and wife marital adjustment. *Psychology of Men & Masculinity, 10,* 245–260. doi:10.1037/a0016757

Wisch, A., & Mahalik, J. R. (1999). Male therapists' clinical bias: Influence of client gender roles and therapist gender role conflict. *Journal of Counseling Psychology, 46,* 51–60. doi:10.1037/0022-0167.46.1.51

Wisch, A. F., Mahalik, J. R., Hayes, J. A., & Nutt, E. A. (1995). The impact of gender role conflict and counseling technique on psychological help seeking men. *Sex Roles, 33,* 77–89. doi:10.1007/BF01547936

Wolfram, H., Mohr, G., & Borchert, J. (2009). Gender role self-concept, gender role conflict, and well-being in male primary school teachers. *Sex Roles, 60,* 114–127. doi:10.1007/s11199-008-9493-4

Wong, Y. J., Pituch, K., & Rochlen, A. B. (2006). Men's restrictive emotionality: An investigation of associations with other emotion-related constructs, underlying dimensions, and anxiety. *Psychology of Men & Masculinity, 7,* 113–126.

Wong, Y. J., & Rochlen, A. B. (2005). Demystifying men's emotional behavior: New directions and implications for counseling and research. *Psychology of Men & Masculinity, 6,* 62–72. doi:10.1037/1524-9220.6.1.62

Wong, Y. J., & Wester, S. R. (in press). *Handbook of the psychology of men and masculinities.* Washington, DC: American Psychological Association.

Wood, J. M. (2004). An exploration into gender role conflict, attitudes toward females, and relationship beliefs (Doctoral dissertation). *Dissertation Abstracts International, 65,* 156.

Woodford, M. S. (2012). *Men, addiction, and intimacy: Strengthening recovery by fostering the emotional development of boys and men.* New York, NY: Routledge.

Zamarripa, M. X., Wampold, B. E., & Gregory, E. (2003). Male gender role conflict, depression, and anxiety: Clarification and generalizability to women. *Journal of Counseling Psychology, 50,* 333–338. doi:10.1037/0022-0167.50.3.333

Zhang, C. (2014). *Mediation of internalized homonegativity and moral emotions in Chinese gay men.* Unpublished manuscript, Department of Psychology, Southwest University, Chongquin, China.

Zhang, C., Blashill, A. J., Wester, S. R., O'Neil, J. M., Vogel, D. L., Wei, J., & Zhang, J. (2014). Factor structure of the Gender Role Conflict Scale Short Form (GRCS–SF) in Chinese heterosexual and gay samples. *Psychology of Men & Masculinity.* Advance online publication. doi:10.1037/a0036154

INDEX

Smith, D. A., 188
Snepp, Frank, 207
Social dynamics, 214, 215–216
Socialization, of boys and girls, 61–62
Social justice, 125–128
Social knowledge, 71
Social learning perspectives, 53–54,
    221–222
Social schemas, 71
Society for the Psychological Study of
    Men and Masculinity (SPSMM),
    15–16, 124, 126–127
Socioeconomic status (SES), 104, 142
Sociopolitical contexts, 344
Southeast Asian men, 144–145
Spillman, J., 198
Spirituality. *See* Religion and spirituality
Steinfeldt, J., 141
Steinfeldt, M. C., 141
Stereotypes
    assumptions about men based on, 10
    defined, 60
    in models of GRC, 56, 59–62
    multicultural considerations, 127
    research on, 189
Stigma, research on, 171, 195–196
Stimulus control, 258
Stinson, R., 147
Stress
    gender role, 307–310
    research overview, 170, 175–176
Student affairs staff, 320–323
Student development theory, 303–306
Substance abuse. *See* Alcohol and sub-
    stance abuse
Success, 34
Sue, Derald, 162
Suicidality, 146–147, 158, 179–180
Sutton, M. Y., 134
Syzdek, M. R., 112, 199
Szymanski, D. M., 138, 146, 177, 179

Taiwanese men, 144
Taylor, L., 138–139
Therapeutic adaptation of Gender Role
    Conflict Scale, 86
Therapeutic assessment of GRC, 227–248
    devaluations, restrictions, and valua-
        tions in, 230, 233–240
    diagnostic schema overview, 229,
        231–233, 236–237

diversity and multicultural consider-
    ations, 241
domains for, 228
implications for therapy practice,
    246–248
past approaches to, 230
using evidence-based diagnostic
    schema, 233, 237–246
Therapy
    action plans for, 345–346
    as contextual domain of men's GRC,
        215, 218–219
    research overview, 192–200
    sexist biases in, 16–17
    and therapeutic assessment of GRC,
        246–248
Thomas, T., 143
Thomas, T. R., 178
Thompson, E. H., 128
Tokar, D. M., 176, 196–197
*Tough Guys and True Believers:
    Managing Authoritarian Men
    in the Psychotherapy Room*
    (J. M. Robertson), 347
Transgendered men. *See* Gay and trans-
    gendered men
Transtheoretical approach to therapy,
    251, 254, 256–258, 279
Tsui, V., 147
Turkish men, 144
Tyre, Peg, 18

Unconscious gender role conflict, 43, 63
Understanding Human Nature (Alfred
    Adler), 11–12
Unemployment, 147, 174
Uy, P. G., 180

Vandello, J. A., 98, 112
Vander Wal, J. S., 138, 181
Veterans, 150, 174
Victimized men, 146–147, 218
Vietnamese American men, 136
Vilain, E., 179
Vinson, C. A., 134
Violations of others or self. *See* Gender
    role violations
Violence by men
    as epidemic, 16
    in gender role conflict models, 66–67
    prevention of, 204

Violence by men, *continued*
    research on, 148–149
    toward women, 190–191
Vogel, D., 138–139
Vogel, D. L., 134, 146, 194–196
Von Drehle, David, 18
Vu, P. H., 136
Vulnerability, masculine. *See* Masculine
    vulnerability

Waldo, M., 148, 190
Walker, S. C., 134
*The War Against Boys: How Feminism Is
    Harming Our Young Men* (Chris-
    tina Hoff Sommers), 18
Watkins, C. E., 186
West, C., 97
Westefeld, J. S., 179
Wester, S. R.
    on African Americans' GRC, 134, 146
    on college students' GRC, 175

on police officers' GRC, 149
on therapists' GRC, 198
on transgendered individuals,
    138–139, 194
White, M., 138–139
Wilkinson, W. W., 183
Windle, C. R., 188
Wolfram, H., 196
Women
    assessment of GRC in, 139–140
    attitudes toward, 171, 189–191
    Gender Role Conflict Scale for, 91
    as targets of gender role devaluation,
        44
Women's campus centers, 315
Work-family balance, 47, 263, 305
Working-with-pain paradigm, 296
Wrightsman, Lawrence, 35, 37

Zhang, C., 144
Zimmerman, D. H., 97

ABOUT THE AUTHOR

James M. O'Neil, PhD, is a professor of educational psychology and family studies in the Neag School of Education at the University of Connecticut as well as a licensed psychologist in private practice in South Windsor, Connecticut. In 1975, he received his doctorate from the Department of Counseling and Personnel Services at the University of Maryland. He is a Fellow of the American Psychological Association (APA) in Divisions 17, 35, 43, 51, 52, and 56. He is one of the founding members of the Society for the Psychological Study of Men and Masculinity (APA Division 51) and was named Researcher of the Year in 1997 for his 20-year research program on men's gender role conflict. Dr. O'Neil's research programs relate to men and masculinity, gender role conflict, the psychology of men and women, and violence and victimization. He has published more than 100 journal articles and book chapters, and his most recent book, coauthored with Michele Harway, *What Causes Men's Violence Against Women?* (1999), has been translated into Japanese and Korean. In 1991, he was awarded a Fulbright Teaching Scholarship by the Council for International Exchange of Scholars, to lecture in the former Soviet Union. In 1995, he was awarded Teaching Fellow status, the most prestigious distinction for a professor at the University of

Connecticut, for his outstanding excellence and dedication to the university teaching. In 2008, he received the Distinguished Professional Service Award from APA Division 51 for his 25-year research program on men's gender role conflict and his advocacy for teaching the psychology of men in the United States. He has advocated for professional activism with gender role and social justice issues throughout his 40 years as a counseling psychologist.